THE GEORGE GUND FOUNDATION
IMPRINT IN AFRICAN AMERICAN STUDIES

The George Gund Foundation has endowed
this imprint to advance understanding of
the history, culture, and current issues
of African Americans.

The publisher gratefully acknowledges the generous support of the African American Studies Endowment Fund of the University of California Press Foundation, which was established by a major gift from the George Gund Foundation.

Mainstreaming Black Power

Mainstreaming Black Power

Tom Adam Davies

UNIVERSITY OF CALIFORNIA PRESS

University of California Press, one of the most distinguished university presses in the United States, enriches lives around the world by advancing scholarship in the humanities, social sciences, and natural sciences. Its activities are supported by the UC Press Foundation and by philanthropic contributions from individuals and institutions. For more information, visit www.ucpress.edu.

University of California Press
Oakland, California

Library of Congress Cataloging-in-Publication Data

Names: Davies, Tom Adam, 1983– author.
Title: Mainstreaming black power / Tom Adam Davies.
Description: Oakland, California : University of California Press, [2017] | Includes bibliographical references and index.
Identifiers: LCCN 2016046168 (print) | LCCN 2016046784 (ebook) | ISBN 9780520292109 (cloth : alk. paper) | ISBN 9780520292116 (pbk. : alk. paper) | ISBN 9780520965645 (eBook)
Subjects: LCSH: Black power—United States—History—20th century. | African American political activists—History—20th century. | African Americans—Politics and government—20th century.
Classification: LCC E185.615 .D3854 2017 (print) | LCC E185.615 (ebook) | DDC 323.1196/0730904—dc23
LC record available at https://lccn.loc.gov/2016046168

Manufactured in the United States of America

25 24 23 22 21 20 19 18 17
10 9 8 7 6 5 4 3 2 1

For Shona

CONTENTS

ACKNOWLEDGMENTS

From the outset, this book project has been supported by a number of generous funding bodies, academic institutions, and professional organizations without which it simply would not have been possible. I am very grateful for scholarships from the Arts and Humanities Research Council; for research fellowships from the John F. Kennedy Presidential Library, the JFK Institute for North American Studies at the Freie Universität in Berlin, and the Institute of the Americas of University College London (UCL); and for research grants from the School of History at the University of Leeds, the British Association for American Studies, the Royal Historical Society, the Scouloudi Foundation in association with the Institute of Historical Research, and the School of History, Art History, and Philosophy at the University of Sussex. I am also grateful to Oxford University Press and the editors at the *Journal of American History*, who have very kindly allowed me to use portions of an article of mine in this book.

Thanks are also due to the many librarians and archivists who assisted me during this project. In particular, Traci Drummond at Georgia State University; Wesley Chenault and Cheryl Oestreicher at the Auburn Avenue Research Library; Archie Shabazz at the Atlanta University Center's Robert W. Woodruff Library; and everyone at the M. E. Grenander Department of Special Collections and Archives at State University of New York, Albany, and at the Schomburg Center for Research in Black Culture in Harlem were all of great assistance to me in various ways.

Researching and writing this book has been a remarkable experience. It began when I was a doctoral candidate at the University of Leeds, where I was supervised by Kate Dossett and Simon Hall. I could not have asked for two better advisors. Any merit this book has is in large part due to them. It was also a privilege to be a part of my graduate student cohort at Leeds. Doctoral work can be a lonely business, but thanks to a number of fantastic people—Peter Whitewood, Louise Seaward, Nicholas Grant, Vincent Hiribarren, Julio Decker, Say Burgin, Henry Irving, Rachael Johnson, Cathy Coombs, Andrew Hogan, Gina Denton, Mark Walmsley, Alex Lock, Ceara Weston, and Oliver Godsmark—it was anything but.

Research trips overseas introduced me to many other people who helped in so many different ways. A number of scholars—Devin Fergus, Alan Brinkley, Mark Brilliant, Scot Brown, Herbert Gans, and Frances Fox Piven—gave up their time to meet with me and discuss my research, and helped me work through my ideas. In the United States and Germany I was also fortunate to meet (or become reacquainted with) people who made sure that time not spent in the archives was unforgettable. In New York, Tom Wallace in effect made my entire first research trip fiscally possible by putting me up, rent-free, in Manhattan for six weeks, as well as showing me the sights. This is a debt I may never be able to repay in full. Joe Street was generous above and beyond the call of duty, and made afternoons at the Schomburg even more enjoyable. In Atlanta, GSU librarian Traci Drummond put me in touch with Sven Haynes—the best landlord (!) I could have hoped to meet. Through Sven I also got to meet some other great people (like Yolande—and Annika!). My stay in Los Angeles would not have been the same without Luis Domingo, David Weinstein, and the fantastic Matt and Mary Thialo. Similarly, Steve and Ji-Ea Capper (and all their crazy friends!), my house-mates Oliver and Dana, my landlady Rebecca Weinstein, and Anna Armentrout all helped to make my time in San Francisco and Berkeley so enjoyable. In Berlin my fellow Leeds student Julio Decker took it upon himself to show me all the best parts of the city, and at the JFK Institute at Freie Universität I met Damian Pargas, who has been a friend and valuable source of feedback and criticism ever since.

After finishing my studies at Leeds, I joined the faculty at the University of Sussex, where I completed revisions and finalized the monograph you are currently reading. Throughout that process, I was fortunate enough to work alongside an outstanding group of people across the History and American Studies Departments. I am very grateful for the friendship, wisdom, and support my colleagues have given me, in particular Adam Gilbert, Anne-Marie Angelo, Eric Schneider, Katharina Rietzler, Clive Webb, Claire Langhamer, Maria Roth-Lauret, Tim Hitchcock, Hester Barron, Daniel Kane, Sue Currell, Lucy Robinson, Chris Warne, Doug Haynes, Jacob

Norris, Gerardo Serra, Iain McDaniel, Claudia Siebrecht, Richard Follett, Hilary Kalmbach, Gerard Gunning, and Tom Wright. I owe an especially large debt of gratitude to Robert Cook, who gave generously of his time, read the manuscript in its entirety, and offered valuable criticism and advice throughout. The final book is all the stronger for his insight. I have also benefited enormously from the support of Stephen Tuck, who has championed my cause in numerous ways over the past three years.

I am also indebted to the UCL Institute of the Americas, where I enjoyed a visiting fellowship, from October 2015 to July 2016, that allowed me to focus on manuscript revisions. I am thankful to Jonathan Bell, Nick Witham, Ellen Wu, Tom Grisaffi, Juan Grigera, and Abi Espie for making me feel so at home and for making the institute such a great place to work.

I am also grateful to the readers for the University of California Press and to the efforts and support of my editor, Niels Hooper; his colleagues Bradley Depew and Kate Hoffman at the press; and copyeditor Steven Baker. Collectively they helped to make the whole process overwhelmingly positive and very straightforward throughout. Thanks must also go to Paul Hainsworth for lending his very considerable talent and very limited time to helping create this book's front cover design and for making something far better than I could have hoped for.

Closer to home, I owe a huge amount to my mother, father, and stepfather—and, indeed, my whole family—for all their love, encouragement, support, and advice. Without them I would not be where I am today. Special mention must also go to Aleks Kirkham, a true friend whose interest in the progress of this project has never wavered from the first minute. Last, but certainly not least, I owe the greatest amount to my wonderful wife, Shona, whose love and support sustain me, and without whom nothing would seem worthwhile.

ABBREVIATIONS

AATA	Afro-American Teachers Association
ACLU	American Civil Liberties Union
AFDC	Aid to Families with Dependent Children
ANVL	Atlanta Negro Voters' League
ASLC	Atlanta Summit Leadership Conference
AUC	Atlanta University Center
BPP	Black Panther Party for Self-Defense
BSRC	Bedford-Stuyvesant Restoration Corporation
CAA	community action agency
CAEHT	Community Association of the East Harlem Triangle
CAP	Community Action Program
CAPC	Community Antipoverty Committee
CAtP	Central Atlanta Progress
CATPL	Community Alert Patrol
CBC	Congressional Black Caucus
CBCC	Central Brooklyn Coordinating Council
CCC	Community Conservation Corps
CDBG	Community Development Block Grant
CDC	Community Development Corporation
CHIP	Community Home Improvement Program
CORE	Congress On Racial Equality
CUNY	City University of New York

D&S	Bedford-Stuyvesant Development and Services Corporation
EHBS	East Harlem Block Schools
EOA	Economic Opportunity Act
EOA Inc.	Economic Opportunity Atlanta, Incorporated
EOF	Economic Opportunity Federation
EYOA	Economic and Youth Opportunities Agency of Greater Los Angeles
FEPC	Fair Employment Practices Commission
FHA	Federal Housing Authority
HCC	Harlem Commonwealth Council
HOLC	Home Owners Loan Corporation
LAUSD	Los Angeles Unified School District
LCFO	Lowndes County Freedom Organization
LDF	Legal Defense Fund (NAACP)
MFDP	Mississippi Freedom Democratic Party
MFY	Mobilization For Youth
NAACP	National Association for the Advancement of Colored People
NAPP	Neighborhood Adult Participation Project
NOI	Nation Of Islam
NSC	neighborhood service center
NUL	National Urban League
NWRO	National Welfare Rights Organization
NYA	National Youth Administration
OB	Operation Bootstrap
OEO	Office of Economic Opportunity
OMBE	Office of Minority Business Enterprise
PPC	Poor Peoples' Campaign
R&R	Bedford-Stuyvesant Renewal and Rehabilitation Corporation
SCBM	Southern Conference of Black Mayors
SCLC	Southern Christian Leadership Conference
SIP	Special Impact Program

SNCC	Student Nonviolent Coordinating Committee
UCRC	United Civil Rights Committee
UFT	United Federation of Teachers
UPC	United Parents Council
UREC	Urban Residential Educational Center
WLCAC	Watts Labor Community Action Committee
WNIA	Westminster Neighborhood Improvement Association
WUCU	Watts United Credit Union
YTEP	Youth Training and Employment Program
YOB	Youth Opportunities Board of Greater Los Angeles

Introduction

In December 1967, Roger Wilkins finally submitted his long-awaited assessment of the Black Power movement to the United States attorney general.[1] Ever since the slogan "Black Power!" first emerged in mid-June 1966, controversy had raged over its meaning. Established civil rights leaders quickly branded Black Power a radical, separatist, and dangerous ideology. Roy Wilkins—the head of the National Association for the Advancement of Colored People (NAACP), America's oldest civil rights group and Roger's uncle—claimed that rejection of nonviolence and integrationism could "only mean black death." And America's most iconic civil rights leader, Reverend Dr. Martin Luther King Jr., argued that "to seek power exclusively for the Negro" meant "exchanging one form of tyranny for another. Black supremacy would be equally as evil as white supremacy." Leading national politicians, including President Lyndon Johnson and Vice-President Hubert Humphrey, and much of the nation's white media chorused this disapproval.[2]

Roger Wilkins, the African American head of the Department of Justice's Community Relations Service, delivered a very different verdict. Black Power, he insisted, was a hugely positive and necessary phenomenon, despite the fact that "black rage" animated much of its most sensationalist and declamatory rhetoric. It was best, he argued, to think primarily of Black Power as a "black consciousness movement," built on the "twin pillars of [racial] pride and unity," that sought to foster black self-respect and redefine blackness by reclaiming and venerating black history and culture. Furthermore, he argued, critics were wrong to stereotype Black Power as being innately radical or extremist. Still in the "ideology development phase," Wilkins explained, "the rhetorical range of [Black Power] positions is very wide, starting from militant middle-class system correctors on the right to people who say they are revolutionaries on the left." While issues such as violence and separatism clearly divided Black Power advocates across this spectrum, on other points they were united. On top of promoting racial pride and solidarity, they shared a desire for black economic empowerment. They had all, he contended, "turned to an economic analysis" of racial inequality. "They are tired of being objects of the American system and the objects of American institutions. In the American tradition, they want a piece of the action." No longer, Wilkins insisted, could the federal government continue "to ignore the black consciousness movement." Instead politicians had to try to "discriminate between the broad range" of Black Power supporters and to pick their way "through the rage and the rhetoric" in order ultimately to "work with people in the black consciousness movement on new ways to correct the system and to develop institutional solutions" that would meet their aspirations.[3] Wilkins's plea for legislators to engage with Black Power did not go unanswered.

This book offers a new perspective on the history of Black Power by examining how white politicians and officials and white-dominated institutions (both public and private) engaged with Black Power and sought to manage the demand for black political and economic empowerment that it amplified. It does this by exploring the nexus of public policies, black community organizations, white and black elected officials, liberal foundations, and Black Power activists in New York, Atlanta, and Los Angeles during the mid- to late 1960s through the 1970s. It breaks new historiographical ground by demonstrating how mainstream whites' efforts to engage and co-opt Black Power at the national and local level combined to help transform public policy making and cultivate a middle-class brand of Black Power politics, as well as to shape the development of African American politics and society in the longer term.[4]

The book traces how public policies intended to engage, modify, and sublimate the Black Power impulse—in particular, Democratic senator Robert F. Kennedy's Community Development Corporation (CDC) program and Republican president Richard Nixon's black capitalism policies—evolved as a response not only to the deepening urban crisis and growing black radicalism but also to the Johnson administration's troubled War on Poverty. Indeed it is not possible to understand such policies without understanding the antipoverty program and how it helped reconfigure the political landscape of America's white suburbs and black inner cities.

Kennedy's and Nixon's policies represented a calculated effort to negotiate the meaning of Black Power, and blunt its radical edge, that complicates traditional analyses of liberal and conservative policy making during the 1960s. Attuned to Black Power's more middle-class and philosophically conservative strands, these policies were also adapted to the increasingly conservative national political culture of the mid- to late 1960s and 1970s. Emerging during what historian Karen Ferguson calls a "key period of transition in twentieth century American history," when the "statist New Deal era began to move into postindustrial, trickle-down, and laissez faire neoliberalism," these policies mark an important stage in the federal government's retreat from welfare state liberalism—a retreat that gathered pace through the 1970s.[5]

Mainstreaming Black Power also assesses and compares how African Americans in New York, Atlanta, and Los Angeles challenged the constraints of public policies and used resources and programs in strategic and politically significant ways. It details how black activists in antipoverty groups, community and economic development organizations, and education reform movements interpreted Black Power innovatively, often appropriating those elements that fit best with their own agendas and forging alliances with fellow activists and groups from across the political spectrum in the process. By revealing how urban blacks fused programs of cultural enrichment and institution building as they used public policies to empower and revitalize their communities, this book illuminates both the mainstreaming of Black Power and its development at the grassroots level.

Finally, in assessing the longer-term consequences of mainstream white engagement with Black Power, this book demonstrates how policies aimed at reforming Black Power and subverting radical black politics played an important and understudied role in exacerbating inequality among African Americans from the late 1960s onward. As these policies became entrenched in national and local politics—especially during the 1970s in cities under black political control, such as Atlanta and Los Angeles—they succeeded in expanding opportunity for upwardly mobile, middle-class and elite blacks, just as the interests of poor and working-class blacks (and poor black women in particular) were being delegitimized in public policy and broader political discourse.

This story of black middle-class success and growing disadvantage for poor and working-class African Americans is one that reveals the power of white interests—acting in concert with elements of the black community and in response to the pressures of black activism more generally—to define the limits and nature of racial progress. Opportunities for black advancement, strongly shaped by both class and gender biases, were made available—

often through public policy—when they promised to be most compatible with, and beneficial to, dominant white political and economic interests. More radical political solutions favored by militant black grassroots activists and movements sought a fundamental transformation of U.S. society and politics that directly threatened entrenched white interests. Such efforts were strongly and successfully resisted—in part through the brutal state-sponsored repression of black radicals, but also through the policies and political maneuvering detailed in this book. Put simply, the most productive paths toward economic and political empowerment made available to African Americans during the Black Power era were those that overlapped and bolstered white interests and demands.

Ultimately, therefore, this book is to a large extent about how mainstream white politicians, institutions, organizations, and power structures responded to and used the emergence of Black Power as a way to defend, maintain, and reinforce white privilege in the face of the challenge it posed. Indeed, in the final analysis, the enduring and definitive power of whites to dictate the pace and direction of racial progress and change may be the most important—though perhaps the least recognized—story of the Black Power era.

The arguments made in this book rest on a particular understanding and view of Black Power. As historian Peniel Joseph has suggested, despite its breadth and flexibility as an ideology, Black Power was nevertheless characterized by certain fixed core values and goals. These included pursuing self-determination through black political and economic empowerment, the redefinition of black identity, greater racial pride and solidarity, and emphasis on a shared African heritage and history of racial oppression.[6]

However, this book—and its analysis of Black Power's significance and impact—is grounded in the principle that it was an imprecise ideology open to interpretation.[7] As Black Power theoretician Julius Lester explained, while "Black Power" as a slogan was "a clarion call, [. . .] a psychological weapon, giving strength to those who yelled [it] and fear to those who heard [it]," as a concept "it was more ambiguous." "Literally, it meant power for black people, and everyone had his own definition of what that power was to consist [of] and how it was to be obtained."[8] There was, therefore, no one fixed way to achieve the core goals that Joseph outlines (principally, political, economic, and cultural empowerment). Black Power activists might broadly agree on ends, but not necessarily on the means.

The inherent ambiguity and malleability of Black Power as an ideology constitute an essential theme of this book. These qualities made possible the spectrum of Black Power advocates that Roger Wilkins identified in his report. At times, Black Power ideology helped bring together a broad and diverse range of people striving for greater self-determination on picket lines, in meeting halls, and in the work of community development and institution building. But Black Power's malleability also made it susceptible to the efforts of white power brokers seeking to co-opt the Black Power impulse and to shape the character and define the limits of African American progress more broadly. The flexibility of Black Power as a concept became clearer over time, as both white officials and urban blacks articulated—through rhetoric, policies, and activism—their own, often contrasting visions of Black Power.

Overall, therefore, this book is less concerned with trying to produce a comprehensive definition of what Black Power stood for (beyond the accepted general core values) than with considering three key concepts: (1) how the ideas, tactics, and language readily associated with Black Power permeated the community activism, and everyday lives, of ordinary African Americans at the local level; (2) how and why mainstream politicians and institutions exploited Black Power's flexibility as an ideology and organizing tool in their efforts to guide the course of black advancement; and (3) the subsequent impact and meaning of those efforts.

As Black Power crystallized in the mid-1960s, mainstream white politicians and institutions engaged with Black Power, largely through public policy, in an effort to contest its very meaning and to draw African Americans away from protest, radical and redistributive politics, and violent extremism. At the same time, white power structures at the local level worked assiduously to manage the grassroots demand for black self-determination, economic empowerment, and urban improvement that Black Power magnified, while preserving the racial and socioeconomic status quo.

The idea of mainstream politicians seeking to influence the course of black activism, politics, and progress was, of course, nothing new. For the preceding two decades Cold War liberals had sought to constrain dissent, legitimize moderate civil rights activism, and shape the course of racial progress by channeling protest through the courts and the ballot box and trying to increase black integration into the economic mainstream through support (albeit limited) for fair employment practices and school desegregation.[9] However, the panpartisan negotiation of Black Power considered here differed from this approach in two significant ways. First, it moved away from integrationist goals and existing approaches to mitigating economic inequality, acknowledging both the shifting ideological currents within the black freedom struggle (driven by Black Power's emergence) and the declining support for integration and Great Society welfare state liberalism among the nation's so-called silent majority of middle-class white voters. Second, it sought not only to channel black energy and progress through the nation's political and legal institutions and its workplaces and schools, but also to bind African Americans to, and physically and emotionally invest them in, the economic practices and political and social principles of America's private economy and capitalist society.

The policies intended to co-opt and nurture the Black Power impulse that this book examines—such as Robert Kennedy's CDC program and Richard Nixon's black capitalism policies—were part of a broader battle over the scope and direction of domestic politics. As the urban crisis deepened in the mid-1960s, growing numbers of African Americans argued that realizing the goal of racial equality required a state-sponsored redistribution of power, wealth, and resources from the top down. This kind of leftist, progressive politics characterized the message of leading radical Black Power groups such as the Black Panther Party (BPP) and antipoverty and welfare rights activists and, in the final few years of his life, it also dominated the political vision of Martin Luther King Jr.[10]

Grassroots enthusiasm for a more equal society and politics was reflected in the popularity of the Johnson administration's War on Poverty among poor communities nationwide, which helped to spark, expand, and embolden movements for social and economic justice. In the process, the antipoverty program became an incubator of nationalist organizing and racial identity politics in cities such as New York and Los Angeles, forming an important part of the soil from which Black Power grew.[11]

At the same time, however, by giving rise to a well-organized, highly vocal, and coordinated national welfare rights movement and generating urban political conflict more generally, the War on Poverty set in motion developments and reinvigorated existing debates over the racial and moral politics of welfare state liberalism that had a lasting influence on race relations and politics at both the local and national levels. This book expands our understanding of the War on Poverty by revealing more fully its impact on the development of Black Power, on future landscapes of reform, and on mainstream politics more broadly.

In the face of growing urban black radicalism, and concerned about the War on Poverty's apparent limitations, Robert Kennedy set out an alternative political vision, much of which Richard Nixon would later echo. The two politicians offered policies that identified free-market capitalism as the solution to African Americans' problems. Prioritizing the development of businesses in black communities, they were guided by the belief that the private sector—not the federal government—had the major role to play in remedying racial and urban inequality. These policies aimed not only to expand the black middle class and get unemployed African American men back to work but also to reinforce existing class and gender hierarchies. What poor inner-city blacks needed, they argued, was not more government welfare handouts or antipoverty programs, but assistance in economically and physically rehabilitating their own communities. This rhetoric was designed to appeal to the more conservative strands of Black Nationalist ideology that emphasized black self-reliance and championed black ownership and economic empowerment, as well as to growing white animosity toward "big government" and integration. Crucially, these policies were also intended to woo the millions of ordinary African Americans—what Nixon adviser Daniel Patrick Moynihan called the "black silent majority"—who were far more interested in enjoying the material comforts of American consumer culture than they were in pursuing radical politics or revolution.[12]

Long committed to fighting for equal access to the rewards of public policy, African Americans were not passive subjects of the machinations of mainstream institutions and policy makers. Indeed, spurred on by Black Power's emergence, black community activists often used War on Poverty programs and community development schemes as a way to challenge traditional urban power arrangements and advance their own visions for political and economic empowerment and urban improvement. As historian Rhonda Williams has suggested, the "self-determination politics" of many Black Power and community activists entailed demanding more—not less—of government officials and making the most of the funds and resources that public policies and institutions offered.[13]

Comparing and contrasting black community activism in New York, Los Angeles, and Atlanta—three regionally distinct cities with long traditions of black political organizing and protest—further nuances our increasingly sophisticated picture of the black freedom struggle. This book uncovers the complex, often close, and sometimes distinctive relationships that existed between civil rights and Black Power organizations and other grassroots activists and groups at the local level, many of which are either absent or peripheral in the existing scholarship.[14] Probing the history and the enduring legacies of community-built institutions at the local level—many of which operated well beyond the 1970s, and in some cases still are—this book also challenges traditional, truncated narratives of the civil rights–Black Power–era fight for racial equality.[15]

Analyzing developments in all three cities also highlights the importance of local political conditions in shaping both community activism and socioeconomic change at the local level. In New York, Mayor John V. Lindsay supported black and other minority group engagement with public policy, emboldening grassroots activism in the process. In Los Angeles, by contrast, Mayor Sam Yorty often opposed African American community organizations, setting the tone for local officials' efforts to limit minority influence over public policy. In Atlanta, where white and black elites worked together to guide local racial progress, the situation was different again. This postwar biracial power arrangement had helped make the city a haven for the middle classes and business interests, and marginalized working-class and poor blacks both from the benefits of public policy and from political power more generally. National political developments and the evolution and negotiation of Black Power all unfolded in different ways within these three contrasting political landscapes. However, when it comes to the pace and direction of racial progress and change, a broadly similar pattern emerges in all three cities.

Ultimately, public policy at both the national and local levels tended to deliver the greatest gains to upwardly mobile, middle-class and elite blacks. This book argues that, as much as the progress of middle-class and elite blacks from the mid-1960s through the 1970s resulted from a number of factors (not least of which was their own talent and industry), many of the opportunities they enjoyed (and capitalized on) were created as part of the broader political project that aimed to co-opt and nurture the Black Power impulse that this book charts in the nation's inner cities. As early as 1969, Julius Lester recognized that "the principle beneficiaries of Black Power have been the black middle-class." Those who had "benefited the least from Black Power," he explained, were "those whose needs are the most acute—the black poor. They have gained pride and self-respect, but unlike the black intelligentsia, there has been no opportunity to parlay this new pride and self-respect into something more concrete."[16]

In many ways, that middle-class African Americans profited during the mid- to late 1960s and the 1970s is not surprising. It was, after all, a period of ongoing political realignment during which white public support for the moral, racial, and economic principles of welfarist Great Society liberalism declined precipitously and was superseded by a homeowner interest–focused, anti-tax, suburban conservative politics. Despite the highly racialized nature of this realignment, it would not be unreasonable to assume that, in an environment where public policy was shifting further toward the interests of the middle class and economic elites—and where the civil rights movement had paved the way for the black middle class and helped bring down major legal obstacles to racial progress—upwardly mobile African Americans would also benefit from (and, indeed, favor) such policies.[17]

While the deepening of intraracial inequality—in particular under black city leadership—from the 1970s onward cannot be attributed solely to the public policies at the center of this book, they nevertheless played an important part in the process. As such, they represent a largely untold story of Black Power's impact and offer a new perspective on how Black Power changed America.[18] Perhaps the most significant aim of this book, therefore, is to retrieve, and incorporate into the history of Black Power, the story of black middle-class success, which, to borrow a phrase from historian Alan Brinkley, is "somewhat of an orphan" in the historiography of the period.[19] This aspect of the era's history is divorced from studies of Black Power, largely because such a narrative is at odds with the dominant radical grassroots-oriented image of that movement. The struggle for social and economic justice, and against racism, state repression, and the broader evils of U.S. imperialism, is a far more romantic, heroic, and seductive story than one of middle-class progress, which might seem prosaic by comparison.[20]

Mainstreaming Black Power combines the view from the national level with three urban case studies of New York, Atlanta, and Los Angeles as it maps how the fascinating and understudied relationship between Black Power, American politicians and institutions, and grassroots black activists developed. In doing so, it draws throughout on a rich, broad base of scholarship and a wealth of different primary sources. The interaction between the national and local, between the powerful and those seeking self-determination, and between the ideas of policy makers and grassroots activists and their implementation and impact on the everyday is gleaned from federal, state, and local government records; political party collections and administrative records; the papers of antipoverty activists and agencies and of civil rights and Black Power organizations; private foundation collections; the personal papers of activists and local elected officials; oral histories; and reports and material drawn from a range of different African American and white media sources.

The narrative unfolds across four broadly chronological chapters and starts with the War on Poverty, the significance of which stretches across the whole book. Chapter 1 explores the War on Poverty's genealogy by tracing its roots in New Deal and Cold War liberal policy making and 1950s social science research, and by revealing the gendered social and economic assumptions that both underpinned the Johnson administration's antipoverty program and limited its effectiveness. It then maps how the War on Poverty unfolded in New York, Los Angeles, and Atlanta and at the federal level, explaining how it became intertwined with the black freedom struggle and the ideological shift toward Black Power, before detailing the multiple and contrasting ways in which elected officials responded to the challenge the program posed to their political authority. The chapter concludes by addressing the War on Poverty's impact on the American political landscape as it mobilized the urban poor and stirred grassroots protest and political controversy, fueling white welfare backlash politics and making support for redistributive social spending increasingly untenable for politicians nationwide.

Chapter 2 explains how Kennedy's CDC program and Nixon's black capitalism initiatives evolved out of the apparent failures and limitations of the War on Poverty and looked to confront the deepening urban crisis, the growth of black radicalism, and increasing white hostility to the racial politics of Great Society liberalism. After examining the rationale and assumptions that guided this shift in policy, the chapter explores how inner-city African Americans engaged with the opportunities it presented. Focusing first on the Bedford-Stuyvesant Restoration Corporation (BSRC), the nation's first CDC, established with Kennedy's help in Central Brooklyn in early 1967, and then on a number of similar black-controlled organizations in New York and Los Angeles, it shows how Black Power ideology shaped the institution-building and community development efforts of those organizations, as they used programs to foster racial pride and unity, celebrate black history and culture, and promote greater community self-determination. In the process, these African American–run organizations, dedicated to urban rehabilitation and building local black economic power, helped to institutionalize important aspects of the Black Power mission as part of the mainstream of American life.

Chapter 3 maintains the focus on Black Power's impact at the local level by examining what were often multiracial battles over public education. In New York and Los Angeles, education reform movements evolved from existing school desegregation protest and antipoverty organizing and were shaped by the emergence of Black Power. Demanding "community control" of public schools, movement participants insisted upon the transfer of decision-making power away from white city officials to locally elected community school boards, as well as the need for black principals, teachers, and more culturally relevant curricula. In Atlanta, grassroots organizers had a different vision for improving local public education. Focused on the need for busing to integrate the city's schools, education activism in Atlanta's poor and working-class black neighborhoods grew out of Black Power–inflected welfare and tenants' rights activism that privileged social and economic justice over racial identity politics. Tracing the trajectory of education reform in each city from the mid-1950s forward, this chapter explores the different ways white politicians, institutions, and organizations supported, facilitated, absorbed, subverted, and defeated grassroots-led challenges to established white educational authority.

A number of the major themes of this book converge in the fourth and final chapter, which assesses how African Americans fared under black political leadership during the 1970s. After first exploring the upsurge in the number of black elected officials from the mid-1960s onward, the chapter turns to developments in Los Angeles and Atlanta, cities that in 1973 both elected their first black mayor (Tom Bradley and Maynard Jackson, respectively). An in-depth analysis of Bradley and Jackson's campaigns and first two terms in office focuses on the various factors that shaped their respective political philosophies and mayoralties. Confronted by broader national economic problems, and with limited city resources at their disposal, both Bradley and Jackson deferred to white downtown business interests and pursued pro-growth policies that ultimately reinforced the disadvantages facing their poor and working-class black constituents. For the black middle class and elite in both cities, however, African American city leadership proved to be a wellspring of opportunity, thanks in part to the development, and deeper entrenchment in federal policy, of Kennedy and Nixon's middle-class interest–focused policies, policies that came to constitute the most viable avenues for advancing black interests available to both mayors.

Through these four chapters, this book charts how mainstream white politicians and institutions worked, often through public policies, to meet the challenge that Black Power's emergence presented and to manage the black demand for political and economic empowerment that it amplified. In this way, public policies that were intended to reform Black Power—and that consciously privileged the interests of the black and white middle classes and economic elite—can be thought of as having constituted one front of a broader two-front battle that in places overlapped and worked to constrain and shape the course of black progress and socioeconomic change. On one front, various mainstream organizations and institutions (including local and national law enforcement agencies) moved to stifle the challenge of black radicals and community activists advocating the fundamental transformation of American politics and society. On the second front, others—such as Robert Kennedy and the Ford Foundation—strove through public policies to redirect and channel African American progress in directions that endorsed the principle structures and values of mainstream American society.

The three urban case studies that this book combines collectively underscore the powerful influence that mainstream white policy makers and organizations had on the character of racial progress and empowerment. They reveal how the effort to mainstream Black Power—an effort in which whites and blacks were both involved—ultimately served to preserve and reinforce the very principles, hierarchies, institutions, and racial geographies that underpinned white political and economic supremacy.

ONE

"A Mouthful of Civil Rights and an Empty Belly"

THE WAR ON POVERTY AND THE FIGHT FOR RACIAL EQUALITY

In early June 1967, War on Poverty officials in Washington approved a $238,429 award to the Community Alert Patrol (CATPL), a black community group in South Central Los Angeles. Established in the aftermath of the infamous Watts rebellion in mid-August 1965, CATPL's fifteen-member team monitored the conduct of local law enforcement in an effort to combat police brutality, an issue that concerned local people and that had sparked the Watts riots. Unarmed, group members—many of whom were local youths with criminal records—were explicitly forbidden to intervene in police affairs directly. The group aimed to improve community-police relations, they explained, by acting as a "buffer" between the two.[1] CATPL hoped to use War on Poverty funds to expand its operations by purchasing a garage and relevant equipment. This, in turn, would allow the group to provide local black youths with the chance to learn automobile repair trade skills, acquire valuable on-the-job experience, and earn an income servicing CATPL's patrol vehicles.[2]

Once news of the award broke, surprised local officials and politicians were quick to criticize the decision. Republican senator George Murphy expressed disbelief that neither Mayor Sam Yorty nor the Los Angeles Police Department (LAPD) had been notified of the application's approval.[3] State governor and leading conservative Ronald Reagan implored Sargent Shriver, head of the Office of Economic Opportunity (OEO)—the federal agency responsible for the War on Poverty—to block CATPL funding. Outraged at the lack of OEO consultation, Mayor Yorty complained directly to President Lyndon Johnson, lamenting the prospect of federal tax funds being used "to finance direct interference with the vital operations of our nationally heralded police force"—an objection echoed by LAPD chief Thomas Reddin.[4]

Many city voters agreed, and some saw CATPL as a dangerous experiment that undermined established authority. As one local citizen explained in a letter to Governor Reagan: "In order to keep peace with the Negro community the police officer will be forced to abide by the Community Alert Patrol—and the Community Alert Patrol will demand more and more power! Our whole system begins to crumble because of a few." [5]

The furor over the OEO's decision had the desired effect. Washington officials suspended award of the grant, advising CATPL they would support the group only on condition that it stop its police-monitoring activities. The grant was rubberstamped after CATPL reluctantly agreed.[6] This episode highlights a number of this book's key themes. First, it reveals black communities' commitment to using the War on Poverty and other public policies to combat racial discrimination and urban inequality. Second, it exemplifies the kind of political controversy generated by the War on Poverty. In Los Angeles, and in cities nationwide, conservative opponents identified the antipoverty program as another ill-considered liberal social policy devised by distant, interventionist Washington bureaucrats that wasted taxpayers' money. Last, the episode demonstrated the strength and success of white mainstream opposition to black activism and to the scope of public policy where it threatened established power arrangements or white privilege and authority. In this case, it was the authority of the LAPD—a vital organ and symbol of local white political control—that seemed at risk. Allowing CATPL members—some of whom were urban black youths with police records—to continue monitoring the police's conduct at the taxpayers' expense threatened an intolerable subversion of local power relations.

As this chapter demonstrates, the War on Poverty enabled challenges to established urban power arrangements that met this pattern of decisive white mainstream political resistance time and again. Ultimately, white mainstream politicians and groups, and the pressures they created, played the definitive role in dictating the boundaries of public policy and the potential for change.

The debates and controversy generated by the War on Poverty have done much to shape its reputation. At the time, opponents typically portrayed the War on Poverty as a costly failure that embodied the excesses of big government and paternalistic welfare state liberalism. In the decades since, ascendant conservatives have reinforced and popularized this powerful and persuasive critique of the antipoverty program as a misguided attempt to mitigate economic inequality. Only during the past decade have historians begun to undermine this dominant conservative narrative and its core assumptions by reassessing the War on Poverty's impact on inequality and on American society more broadly.

Scholars such as Peter Edelman have argued that, far from being a failure, the War on Poverty was remarkably successful given its meager funding. Indeed, by 1974, after ten years of antipoverty operations, the number of Americans estimated to be living below the poverty line had been halved. Moreover, the Johnson administration's Great Society program—of which the War on Poverty was a vital part—helped better the lives of millions of Americans by providing improved education, housing, food, and medical care to communities where they were desperately lacking. Despite conservatives' best efforts to roll back the antipoverty program, Edelman explains, it has in fact proved highly resilient. Many War on Poverty programs and subagencies (albeit in different guises) remain in operation today, and they "continue to make a substantial difference in the quality of life of millions of Americans."[7]

The significance of the War on Poverty, however, extends far beyond the question of its success or failure.[8] As Edelman suggests, "the War on Poverty energized thousands upon thousands of people across the country and served as a stepping stone into politics, continuing activism, civic participation, and economic success."[9] This chapter establishes how the War on Poverty made a vital and lasting impression on black community activism, mainstream engagement with Black Power, white voters' support for redistributive liberalism, and future landscapes of reform. In doing so, it sets out and explores a number of important ideas and themes that stretch across the book.

First, it outlines black enthusiasm for the War on Poverty and explores its relationship to historical shifts in conceptions of American citizenship shaped first by the New Deal welfare state and then by the apotheosis of a Cold War domestic consumer culture. Promising to help break the shackles of poverty, African Americans responded energetically to President Johnson's antipoverty legislation. Where the New Deal and postwar public policy had served white (and especially white male) interests primarily, African Americans claimed ownership of the War on Poverty. By engaging with the political question of how to meet African Americans' desire for economic citizenship, the War on Poverty established the political framework that the alternative policies discussed in chapter 2 challenged.

Second, the chapter identifies the War on Poverty's roots in urban minority social problems, shedding light on both how and why the antipoverty program became so thoroughly entwined with the black freedom struggle in ghetto communities across the nation. It helps to explain the War on Poverty's limitations by exploring the sometimes conflicting core assumptions of Cold War liberalism that guided War on Poverty planners and other administration policy makers—assumptions and limitations that, as chapter 2 reveals, vitally shaped alternative public policies put forward to meet African American aspirations for economic empowerment and urban improvement.

Attention is then turned to how the War on Poverty helped transform the American political landscape. While President Johnson hoped the antipoverty program could improve the lives of millions of Americans, it engendered challenges to the nation's political equilibrium that he neither expected nor desired. These challenges were often bound up with poor black and other minority communities' battles for racial and economic justice. As one of the bill's supporters on Capitol Hill, Democratic representative Sam Gibbons from Florida, warned: "If you're scared what poor people will do when they get motivated and interested in their government then you ought to be against this legislation because it is going to bring them into the mainstream." [10] By bringing the poor into the realm of politics, the War on Poverty precipitated a clash between established city power brokers and poor people that reverberated from local politics to the corridors of Congress. Conflict over the War on Poverty not only highlighted the desire for greater self-determination among inner-city blacks but also fueled racial identity politics among minority groups, illuminating the growing vitality of nationalism in the nation's ghettos. As later chapters demonstrate, the War on Poverty attracted and channeled nationalist organizing at the local level, making it a key site of Black Power's development in communities nationwide.

Finally, while the War on Poverty created a vibrant, diverse, and multiracial coalition of antipoverty supporters—including a wide range of religious, labor, civil rights, Black Power, and liberal interest groups—it also widened the fissures between conservatives and liberals, and eroded white working and lower-middle-class support for the Democratic Party. The War on Poverty fueled important debates about government, race and public policy, and economic justice, taxes, and the welfare state that played a vital role in the development of Black Power and in the late-1960s' rightward shift in, and subsequent realignment of, American democracy. As later chapters also demonstrate, these debates helped constrain political possibilities under black mayors such as Tom Bradley in Los Angeles and Maynard Jackson in Atlanta through the 1970s and beyond.

PUBLIC POLICY, ECONOMIC CITIZENSHIP, AND
THE BLACK FREEDOM STRUGGLE

To understand how the War on Poverty became so entwined with the urban black freedom struggle, and the influential role it played in driving divisive political debate and shaping future policy reforms, it is necessary to (1) explore its roots in both contemporary crises and the New Deal liberal tradition on which it built; (2) outline the longer history of African American demands for economic citizenship and the ways those demands were shaped by previous public policy; and finally—where we now begin—(3) trace the unusual trajectory of the War on Poverty's emergence onto the nation's political agenda.

Whereas President Franklin Roosevelt's New Deal three decades earlier had been a response to the Great Depression and the economic crisis and mass poverty it produced, the War on Poverty instead emerged during a period of unparalleled national abundance. The postwar economic boom produced an American society in the 1950s and early 1960s characterized by increasing domestic affluence, the inexorable rise of mass consumerism, and suburbanization. However, this increasing material comfort was not shared by all. By 1960 over forty million Americans—22 percent of the population—lived a very different life, below the poverty line.[11] They remained largely on the margins of the nation's economy, political landscape, and wider public consciousness, until the publication of two books—economist John Kenneth Galbraith's *The Affluent Society* in 1958 and sociologist Michael Harrington's *The Other America* in 1962—helped to scandalize the extent of America's "poverty amidst plenty." [12]

Harrington's work, in particular, proved highly influential in Washington, impressing President John F. Kennedy and helping to establish poverty as a target for federal action.[13] In late 1963, with the presidential election nearly a year away, Kennedy's advisers began to draw up possible domestic programs for the president's reelection campaign and took the first steps in planning what later became the War on Poverty. Kennedy's assassination on November 22, 1963, however, saw the embryonic proposal pass on to the enthusiastic stewardship of his successor, Lyndon B. Johnson, who ordered the program's swift development. Soon after, on January 8, 1964, President Johnson used his first State of the Union address to tell the nation that his administration was declaring "unconditional war on poverty." [14]

The War on Poverty's rapid rise was, generally speaking, most unusual. Unlike most social legislation, it was not the result of organized or public

FIGURE 1. "President Lyndon B. Johnson delivers his State of the Union address to a joint session of Congress on Jan. 8, 1964." © Associated Press.

pressure. Rather, it resulted primarily from a convergence of concerned professional academic elites and the activist inclinations of federal government liberals.[15] In light of its relatively unheralded arrival, some conservative opponents saw the War on Poverty as proof positive of the creeping socialism of interventionist and interfering liberal policy makers intent on subverting the traditional values and foundations of American society. As the decade progressed, this kind of sentiment resonated with increasing numbers of white American voters who began to question the moral and political dimensions of liberal social spending.

For many African Americans, however, the arrival of antipoverty legislation was especially welcome. Statistical analysis confirmed the unmistakable intersection between race and poverty. Over 50 percent of all African American families lived below the government-defined poverty line ($3,000 or less annual income for a family of four) compared to just 20 percent of white families. In 1962 the average black family income was $3,023—barely above the poverty line—whereas the average white family's was nearly double at $5,642.[16]

In the early 1960s, from a total black population of just under 19 million, 3.6 million black men were unemployed, and 40 percent of those with jobs worked in low-skilled and low-paid industrial labor or service positions, effectively trapped there by insufficient education and the prejudice of employers and unions.[17] Attending underfunded and underperforming schools, the vast majority of black youths were denied the necessary standard of education required to compete for skilled jobs in an economy witnessing rapid technological advancement. Worse still, those who found employment would more than likely be paid less than their white counterparts for doing the same job. African Americans who did attain four years of college education still faced earning less over their lifetimes than a white person with far less schooling. When President Johnson declared that the War on Poverty would produce better education and more job training and employment opportunities, then, his words understandably resonated among African Americans.[18]

When first debated on Capitol Hill at the same time as the Civil Rights Bill, antipoverty legislation struck many black leaders as a much needed answer to the racial and economic problems besetting the nation's urban centers. Speaking at congressional hearings in April 1964, Whitney Young, head of the National Urban League (America's largest racial progress and urban interest advocacy group) made it clear that civil rights legislation would not "solve the problem of poverty." "We're afraid," he continued, "that we'll end up with a mouthful of civil rights and an empty belly." Failure to enact antipoverty legislation, he explained, could have dire consequences. "The alternatives are very clear—either help Negroes to become constructive, useful citizens or they will become destructive, disgruntled dependents."[19] In agreement was Dr. Martin Luther King Jr., who celebrated the War on Poverty and civil rights legislation as "twins" and as complementary parts of the nation's attack on racial discrimination.[20]

President Johnson did much to encourage African Americans' strong identification with the War on Poverty. In announcing the impending antipoverty bill, he explicitly identified the need to tackle black poverty. Shortly after a meeting between Johnson and civil rights establishment leaders, James Farmer, executive director of the Congress of Racial Equality (CORE), told reporters that the president had "made it very clear that he feels the fight on poverty and illiteracy is a vital part of the fight against discrimination."[21] African Americans across the nation shared Johnson's vision and seized upon the War on Poverty as a way to advance their struggle for greater self-determination, economic empowerment, and a better standard of living.

Although the War on Poverty was a specific, somewhat unheralded response to the period's myriad socioeconomic issues, it was also another chapter in a domestic liberal tradition that, since the New Deal, had forged a highly contradictory and problematic relationship between the black freedom struggle, public policy, and the federal government, and had encountered persistent white political resistance. On the one hand, New Deal liberalism had done much to invigorate African Americans' battle against discrimination. As historian Anthony Badger has argued, although the New Deal failed to deliver substantial material gains to black Americans, it did help establish civil rights as a genuine political issue. It also reconfigured labor relations and enabled the expansion and empowerment of unions, some of which offered important support in the struggle for racial and economic justice. Moreover, it had explicitly attempted to deal with economic inequality. By seeking to reshape the U.S. economy in a bid to create employment opportunities for the working poor, the New Deal gave the federal government an unprecedented stake in the economic well-being of African Americans, convincing many of the value of interventionist federal support in the struggle against poverty and racism. By bringing blacks into the Democratic fold, the New Deal transformed the Democratic Party, and inspired a political realignment that produced the broad liberal consensus responsible for the legislative civil rights revolution of the mid- to late 1960s.[22]

At the same time, however, the two-tier New Deal welfare state heavily disadvantaged and marginalized African Americans by helping to reify the nation's white supremacist, male-dominated socioeconomic order. As historian Alice Kessler-Harris has explained, the top-tier legislation—which consisted primarily of policies tied to employment (in particular the Social Security Act and unemployment insurance)—targeted white middle-class men and their families. These "entitlements" protected the interests of households headed by male breadwinners earning a "family wage" that supported a housewife and dependent children, enshrining this social paradigm as a cultural ideal. Southern congressmen worked to ensure that the vast majority of employed African Americans were initially excluded from top-tier programs. Second-tier policies were largely means-tested direct aid "relief" or "welfare" programs—in particular, Aid to Families with Dependent Children (AFDC)—which became increasingly associated with poor and unmarried or single female–headed families in minority communities. Employment and family structure thus became hardwired into the celebrated normative model of American life. As Kessler-Harris argues, when the federal government tied "wage work to tangible, publicly provided rewards, employment emerged as a boundary line demarcating different kinds of citizenship. Casual laborers, the unskilled and untrained, housewives, farm workers, mothers and domestic servants all found themselves on one side of a barrier not of their own making."[23] African Americans (especially women) remained tethered to the bottom of the nation's socioeconomic and racial order. This gendered view of economic citizenship persisted in both the War on Poverty and the alternative public policies discussed in chapter 2.

The Roosevelt administration proved a reluctant ally of blacks in their growing aspiration to secure access to "family wage" jobs and the New Deal state largesse and citizenship status they conferred. The black demand for fair employment practices and greater economic opportunity was a fundamental part of the broader fight to secure the vision of first-class citizenship that the New Deal welfare state had simultaneously pedestaled and denied most African Americans. It was, as labor historian Nancy MacLean has suggested, a view of citizenship shaped profoundly by the intrinsic place of the "work ethic and success myth" at the heart of American culture, which privileged employment and economic empowerment, alongside political and civil rights, as necessary and fundamental parts of full inclusion in national life.[24]

The Fair Employment Practices Commission (FEPC), created by Roosevelt in June 1941 in response to black agitation against discrimination in the nation's expanding war industries, promised an unprecedented extension of the federal government's protective legal and moral authority over blacks' economic rights. Across the nation, African Americans—millions of whom had left the South for cities in search of jobs in defense industries— committed themselves to using the FEPC as a tool for racial change and their advancement in the workplace. However, high hopes among African Americans for a strong FEPC were sorely disappointed. With weak powers of enforcement, and in the face of considerable political resistance (especially in the South), the FEPC did virtually nothing to challenge the persistence of endemic discrimination in the workplace.[25]

Despite the FEPC's inadequacies, President Roosevelt again appeared to lend support to black demands for a greater share in national abundance when, during his January 1944 State of the Union address, he outlined an "Economic Bill of Rights." In a resurgent post-Depression United States, Roosevelt identified economic security as a new, fundamental right of all American citizens—"regardless of station, race, or creed"—which included, among other things, the right to remunerative employment, decent housing, medical care, and a good education.[26] Institutional racial discrimination, however, remained a critical roadblock after the war, as public policy continued to enable ever increasing numbers of white men and their families to enjoy these "rights" while deliberately inhibiting their extension to blacks and other minorities.

At the same time, poverty became increasingly out of step with a changing national identity. As Lizabeth Cohen has explained, the exigencies of the Cold War and the goal of postwar prosperity saw American "policymakers, business and labor leaders, and civic groups" join together to reshape the nation's image. What they helped create was a national "economy, culture, and politics built around the promises of mass consumption, both in terms of material life and the more idealistic goals of freedom, democracy, and equality." Under this changing conception of Americanism, then, truly "full" citizenship required the economic means necessary to access the material comfort and personal freedoms that this consumer lifestyle seemed to hold.[27]

African American hopes for a share in increasing national prosperity were undermined by the onset of the Cold War, which transformed domestic politics and constrained debate over racial and economic justice. As anticommunist crusaders attacked the New Deal liberal-labor–civil rights coalition in the late 1940s and 1950s, black leaders increasingly turned away from questions of poverty and economic disadvantage and instead prioritized less controversial targets and methods, such as legally challenging segregation and disfranchisement and securing formal legal equality. The result, historian Adam Fairclough has explained, was that as "the economic radicalism of the New Deal order faded away, the scope of racial equality narrowed. Few questioned the established economic order in the 1950s, and as a result, existing structural inequalities persisted and became in some respects even more pronounced."[28]

As calls for fundamental reform of America's political and economic institutions were effectively suppressed during the early Cold War, national debate on racial inequality shifted toward an alternative analysis of American racism that centered on the influential work of Swedish economist Gunnar Myrdal. In *An American Dilemma,* his celebrated 1944 study of southern race relations, Myrdal presented racism in the United States as both a sectional, southern issue and a problem of moral conscience. As such, eradicating racial injustice required only appeals to the better nature of white Americans and the inherently egalitarian "American Creed."[29] This analysis became central—at least on the surface—to the nonviolent direct action phase of the civil rights movement during the mid- to late 1950s and early 1960s.

However, while the movement's efforts to desegregate the nation's hotels, restaurants, cinemas, and stores promised to open the doors of consumerism and commercial choice for middle-class and elite blacks, they did little to improve the economic status of the majority of African Americans mired in poverty. Access to remunerative jobs and better-quality education and housing remained their best hope for greater prosperity and "full" citizenship. In the early 1960s, as the constrained political atmosphere of the early Cold War was slowly lifting, the focus of black activism—especially beyond the South—began to revive an economic analysis of racial inequality in the United States. This was demonstrated by the "March on Washington for Jobs and Freedom," which brought nearly 250,000 people (the vast majority of whom were black) to the National Mall to protest racial discrimination and economic inequality on August 28, 1963.[30] It was a powerful restatement of African Americans' demand for full citizenship and desire for economic independence, and of the need for structural reform in the name of racial and economic justice.

The War on Poverty further undermined the Myrdalian model by stimulating ferment in black urban communities nationwide that made plain the national reach and structural nature of racial inequality. In the process, the antipoverty program played a vital part in an ongoing shift within the black freedom struggle: the drawing of focus away from the rural South to the problems of the urban North that led to the crystallization of the Black Power movement. Furthermore, as Roger Wilkins explained in the memo discussed at the outset of this book, an economic analysis of racial inequality—which the War on Poverty helped to vivify—was consistent across the political and philosophical spectrum of Black Power ideology. In America's ghettos, an emergent Black Power movement offered a critique of racial discrimination in the United States that emphasized its economic and institutional roots, rejecting the Myrdalian framework and the faith that many civil rights advocates had in the value of moral appeals to white America.[31]

Announced just four months after the March on Washington, then, the War on Poverty was nothing if not timely. Two decades on, President Johnson's antipoverty legislation seemed to extend Roosevelt's "Economic Bill of Rights" to African Americans. As the War on Poverty unfolded, it inspired and shaped both black activism and white conservative political resistance, developments that helped transform domestic national politics. As this chapter ultimately reveals, by energizing the black freedom struggle, the antipoverty program engendered challenges to established power arrangements and national political culture that undermined the liberal consensus—a legacy shaped by the peculiar circumstances and underlying principles that guided its development.

MAINTAINING THE URBAN CRISIS? INTERNAL CONFLICTS AND COMPETING VISIONS IN THE WAR ON POVERTY

When announcing his intention to wage "war on poverty," Lyndon Johnson declared that it was a war that "must be won in the field, in every private home, in every public office, from the courthouse to the White House." Fighting the battle to "help more Americans [...] escape from squalor and misery and unemployment rolls," he continued, would require "better schools, and better health, and better homes, and better training, and better job opportunities" for the disadvantaged.[32] This broad-based vision for tackling poverty emerged from the interconnected work of social scientists and domestic liberal policy makers during the 1950s. Much of the controversy generated by the antipoverty program resulted from the conflicting and sometimes contradictory ways these two groups understood the War on Poverty's purpose. Nowhere was this clearer than in the program's capacity for politicizing and mobilizing the urban poor, the roots of which lay in postwar New York City and the social science research that came to underpin the War on Poverty.

In the late 1950s, a team of Columbia University academics led by Richard Cloward and Lloyd Ohlin conducted a study of the warring black and Puerto Rican youth gangs of Manhattan's Lower East Side. Their research grew out of policy makers' concerns over the increasing incidence of juvenile delinquency among male urban minority youth since the end of World War II.[33] Gang violence not only raised the fear of racial violence and crime but also seemed to relate to a number of other concerns connected to the inner cities, including the social impact of mass black urban in-migration, widespread unemployment and deprivation, social disaffection, and urban decay. Social scientists' focus on young black men reflected a gendered approach to urban problems, inherited in part from the New Deal, that would later characterize the War on Poverty and subsequent public policies aimed at remedying inner-city racial inequality.

Ohlin and Cloward's research fitted into a broader shift within 1950s public policy making, one in which the Ford Foundation—their primary nongovernmental backer—played a leading role. As historian Alice

O'Conner has explained, the Ford Foundation, one of the nation's largest philanthropic institutions, supported the burgeoning social sciences throughout the decade and became a proactive intermediary for Washington officials, providing funding, technical assistance, and academic expertise for research projects. In the process, the foundation "helped to mediate an intellectual and policy shift away from the bricks and mortar concern of early urban renewal and toward the human face of the urban crisis."[34]

In 1960, after nearly four years of in-depth study, Cloward and Ohlin published their findings, which set out their so-called opportunity theory. Put simply, they contended that juvenile delinquency resulted from a lack of opportunity for young minority males to achieve conventional societal goals—principally, gainful paid employment, self-sufficiency, and economic independence. Frustrated in their bid to meet these expectations, they instead found their manhood, and a sense of self-worth, through a life of crime and violence. This was a self-perpetuating vicious circle that eroded traditional moral behavior and promised an even bleaker—and potentially more violent—future for minority groups in urban America. The lack of opportunity, however, was seen as both a symptom and a cause of the myriad inequities of inner-city life that many youngsters had to endure: grinding poverty, urban squalor, broken families, crime, inadequate health care, and a substandard education.[35] A lasting solution to these problems, the authors argued, required a program to improve local social services and create opportunities for social mobility through job training and education in which the whole community was engaged. As later conflicts over the War on Poverty proved, this idea had radical potential as it rested on the premise that the poor had to control their own organizations and lobby local power structures to improve the state of their communities.

In 1961 an organization called Mobilization For Youth (MFY) was set up on the Lower East Side to put the "opportunity" theory to the test by organizing the local community and offering neighborhood-based jobs training, as well as education and family services programs.[36] Strongly committed to tackling the urban crisis, the Ford Foundation broadened the application of Ohlin and Cloward's ideas by placing the "opportunity" theory at the heart of their experimental "Gray Areas" programs of the early 1960s, which targeted deprived minority communities in cities such as Oakland, New Haven, and Boston.[37]

Cloward and Ohlin's pioneering work soon attracted the attention of policy makers in Washington, D.C. In May 1961 President Kennedy established a legislative task force on juvenile delinquency headed by Richard Boone (a Ford Foundation employee) and David Hackett (a close personal friend of Robert Kennedy). Highly impressed by MFY, Hackett and Boone took up the "opportunity" theory as the intellectual basis for what proved to be the War on Poverty's most controversial element: the Community Action Program (CAP).[38] Cloward and Ohlin's influence did not end there, however. As the title of the War on Poverty's legislative centerpiece—the Economic Opportunity Act (EOA)—suggested, their work profoundly shaped the character of the entire antipoverty program.

Signed into law by the president on August 20, 1964, the EOA created the Office of Economic Opportunity (OEO), a new governmental body charged with coordinating the nation's antipoverty effort and administering a wide range of programs. In addition to the CAP, these included Headstart, which aimed at improving elementary-level education; Job Corps, to provide job training for unemployed young adults and school dropouts; Neighborhood Youth Corps, to prolong the education of disadvantaged children and teenagers; Legal Aid, which offered legal services and advice to the poor; and Volunteers In Service To America (VISTA), a domestic version of the Peace Corps that delivered services to poor communities.[39]

Federal officials' eager acceptance of the social science theory behind the MFY and the Ford Foundation's work betrayed several important and interlocking assumptions that guided domestic liberal social policy making during the early Cold War. As O'Connor has explained, policy makers in Washington broadly accepted "culture of poverty" theories that implied the need for the reforming of attitudes and behavior rather than more substantial change. They therefore saw urban problems not as the result of institutional racial discrimination or capitalism but of natural and unstoppable socioeconomic forces that could be successfully managed, if not solved, by the state-sponsored application of technocratic and scientific expertise. This premise fit perfectly with Cold War liberalism's antipathy toward structural economic reform (like the Myrdalian analysis of American race relations). As a result, O'Connor argues, MFY's "strategy of reorienting services and empowering poor constituencies," which so vitally shaped the War on Poverty, "was at best a partial response to a problem that required more fundamental structural change to address the roots of inequality."[40] From the outset, then, an important contradiction lay at the heart of the War on Poverty: it possessed the radical potential for mobilizing the poor, but its fundamentally conservative economic and philosophical foundations would tightly circumscribe its ability to substantially reduce poverty. As chapter 2 demonstrates, this contradiction would help inspire alternative approaches to dealing with racial inequality in America's cities.

The announcement of the War on Poverty quickly revealed the lack of broader consensus over how best to deal with economic inequality and revived a long-standing and wider debate about the nature and limits of government responsibility. For some, the government was overstepping the mark. Conservatives and business interests across the country criticized the War on Poverty as an extension of the "big government" New Deal liberalism that they had always opposed. Economist Henry Hazlitt voiced this sentiment when, drawing on conservatives' anti–New Deal rhetoric of the 1930s, he outlined the Right's vision for combating deprivation: "The way to cure poverty is not [. . .] 'share the wealth' schemes, and socialism but by precisely the opposite policies [. . .] a system of private property, free markets, and free enterprise [. . .] to keep this system, to reduce government intervention instead of increasing it; [and] to reduce government taxation." [41] Others welcomed Johnson's announcement. The AFL-CIO executive committee, leaders of America's largest labor union, applauded the Johnson administration's intentions and argued (as many black leaders did) that "success in winning civil rights for Negroes and other minority groups is inseparably linked to effectively waging war on want." Though strongly supportive, the committee members worried that the proposed legislation did not go far enough, and insisted that federal public works employment programs would be required if millions were to be lifted out of poverty. Failing to commit enough resources to the antipoverty program, they warned, could have lasting consequences. "If we now engage in merely a token effort—a mere skirmish instead of a war—we will be deluding the millions of impoverished and frustrating the expectations of the nation and of the world." [42]

President Johnson, however, had his own view of the War on Poverty. Johnson endorsed Cold War liberals' assumption that the American economy did not require structural change, and thus dismissed the idea of federal job creation programs. Johnson possessed an unshakeable faith in the nation's free enterprise system and believed that the $11 billion tax cut his administration passed in February 1964 would stimulate economic growth, in turn creating more private-sector jobs. The War on Poverty would complement the tax cut by preparing the poor, through skills training, to take up those jobs. [43] As such, the antipoverty program's underlying fiscal philosophy was far from radical. As leading Democratic congressman Wilbur Mills later suggested, aiming to "convert those willing to learn and willing to work from tax recipients—through the welfare program and similar efforts—to taxpayers" meant that, at its core, "the structure and strategy of the program" was "entirely conservative." [44]

The Johnson administration's view of the War on Poverty was also predicated on its commitment to what historian Robert Self has called "breadwinner liberalism"—the New Deal welfare state's highly gendered social and cultural mission, which privileged and idealized the "Citizen-Worker" male earning a "family wage" and providing for his wife and children in an environment of middle-class domesticity. During the postwar economic boom, the GI Bill further bolstered the white wage-earning male privilege encoded in the New Deal by making home ownership, credit, and education more affordable and accessible to returning white soldiers and their families while systematically denying those benefits to black veterans. [45]

Increasing the number of male breadwinner–headed black households became a key concern of New Frontier and Great Society policy makers during the 1960s because they identified the chronic levels of unemployment among African American men as the root cause of both black poverty and wider social breakdown. In this logic, the psychologically crippling and emasculating effects of being unable to fulfill their expected role as breadwinners led black men to abandon their families and, in their despair, turn to alcoholism, drug abuse, and crime in increasing numbers.

This in turn resulted in both deeper poverty and rising levels of welfare dependency, as the number of AFDC-supported single female–headed black families in the nation's inner cities increased markedly—developments then blamed for the spread of juvenile delinquency among the hundreds of thousands of young African Americans growing up without a traditional male authority figure at home. These interlocking suppositions ensured that liberals' solutions to urban poverty, the breakdown of the black family, and the deepening social problems of the ghetto rested on two main aims: increasing the employment of black men, and better educating and preparing black male youth for jobs and for constructive civic duty in the short and longer term. [46]

From the outset, Washington officials made it very clear that the antipoverty legislation was chiefly designed to put men back to work and on the way to restoring them to traditional and idealized social, economic, and familial roles—a goal the president wholly endorsed. Johnson's view of the War on Poverty was forged by his past experience as head of the Texas arm of the National Youth Administration (NYA), a New Deal agency dedicated to providing education and work to impoverished teenage and young adult (especially male) Americans in the mid-1930s. Consequently, Johnson saw greatest value in the Job Corp and Neighborhood Youth Corps, the War on Poverty programs that most closely resembled the NYA. Johnson's leadership of the NYA kindled both his desire to help the poor and disadvantaged and his strong commitment to the gendered politics of breadwinner liberalism, two traits that defined his vision for the antipoverty program.[47] However, Johnson did not fully appreciate that the social science theory behind parts of the War on Poverty aimed at politically mobilizing the nation's poor.

As the War on Poverty was rolled out nationwide in late 1964, it began what proved to be a highly controversial journey. Nowhere was this more evident than in the nation's inner-city ghettos, where the War on Poverty enabled the urban poor to challenge city halls across the nation for control of antipoverty programs, bringing political turmoil to cities across the country.

MAKING WAVES: COMMUNITY ACTION BEGINS

The political impact of the War on Poverty was felt across the country. While some rural southern blacks used the antipoverty program to challenge Jim Crow, the War on Poverty was fought most fiercely in America's inner-city ghettos.[48] As the *Los Angeles Times* suggested, "Nationwide the birth pangs of the new effort are indelible from the White House to the human warrens of Harlem, the kindling wood hovels of Atlanta's Buttermilk Bottom, the red brick tenements of Philadelphia's Brewerytown, and the sun-baked shacks of Los Angeles' Willowbrook district."[49] Offering the poor the chance to control antipoverty programs for themselves, the Community Action Program (CAP) swiftly became the primary site of conflict in the War on Poverty in New York and Los Angeles. In the process, the CAP highlights two major concerns of this book: first, the close relationship between public policies and community activists who strove to capitalize on, and maximize, the opportunities they presented; second, the enduring commitment of mainstream and entrenched white class interests to dictating the pace and direction of socioeconomic and political change (and their success in doing so).

Under the CAP, each targeted poor area was required to set up (with federal money) a community action agency (CAA) to act as a clearinghouse to administer and coordinate social service, education, job training, and legal services programs. Whereas the New Deal had channeled money through local political elites, recognizing and reinforcing existing power structures, the CAP made it possible for CAAs to receive federal money directly, in theory allowing local politicians to be bypassed altogether. War on Poverty planners had also written into CAP guidelines the need for "maximum feasible participation" of the poor themselves in the planning and delivery of those programs. While this reflected Ohlin and Cloward's desire to mobilize and empower poor communities in the fight against poverty, the specific phrase "maximum feasible participation" was born of policy makers' desire to ensure that white southern politicians would not be able to exclude blacks from local programs.[50]

But "maximum feasible participation" was an imprecise and flexible term, and the degree of control over CAP operations it allowed the poor was hotly contested. The CAP soon became a lightning rod for political controversy. Many of the country's poor citizens understood "maximum feasible participation" to mean they—not local politicians—should control antipoverty programs. However, most city executives—fearful of seeing their power eroded—argued that the guidelines sanctioned only the limited involvement of the poor in program and service design. The legislation's indefinite language, however, meant neither interpretation could be definitively declared "wrong."

Wherever the poor did fight to win control over antipoverty programs, the struggle brought political disruption for urban politicians (many of them big-city Democratic power brokers) that threatened to undermine completely the pursuit of consensus so central to President Johnson's vision of liberal politics.[51] The War on Poverty's success in politically mobilizing the poor—especially the minority poor—was reflected in the myriad struggles for control over antipoverty programs in cities and communities nationwide. These struggles produced a fundamental clash of political cultures and precipitated a fierce backlash against the poor's incursion into established urban power arrangements.

Few cities exemplified the conflict over the CAP better than New York, where the antipoverty apparatus set up by Democratic mayor Robert Wagner Jr. and his deputy Paul Screvane failed to include the poor. Wagner had been elected in 1954 with a majority of black votes, but progress for African Americans under his leadership was slow. While the city claimed some victories, including the nation's first (albeit very weak) antidiscrimination housing bill in 1957, in other areas, such as school integration, virtually nothing was achieved.[52] Mayor Wagner had been a vocal supporter of civil rights throughout his time in office, but concrete gains for the city's black population under his leadership had been few and far between.

The Wagner administration's handling of the War on Poverty was another disappointment for black New Yorkers. Democratic Harlem congressman Adam Clayton Powell criticized city hall for excluding the poor, accusing municipal leaders of running antipoverty programs as "giant fiestas of political patronage."[53] Richard Cloward, MFY's research director, argued that "City Hall doesn't want powerful organizations built in the ghetto by Negroes and Puerto Ricans. It doesn't want any ghetto in City Hall; it wants more City Hall in the ghetto."[54] Paul Screvane, head of the city's official antipoverty body, the New York City Council Against Poverty (NYCCAP), mirrored the response of municipal politicians nationwide when he declared: "We are not about to turn this thing over to private organizations to administer. We have to have at least some say in the way the money is spent." Wagner agreed with Screvane that "such decisions should be made by City officials who are all trained professionals in their fields."[55]

Poor communities across the country recognized the opportunities offered by the new legislation and began preparing to take advantage of them. In New York, for example, the Central Brooklyn Coordinating Council (CBCC), a coalition group representing over one hundred membership organizations from the local black community, held a "War on Poverty Conference" shortly after its launch attended by more than five hundred local residents.[56] After years of antipoverty experimentation in the city, New York's poor black communities understandably assumed the War on Poverty was intended for them. In a city where poor whites outnumbered poor blacks two to one, the pilot antipoverty agency, MFY, had been established in an area with a largely black and Puerto Rican population, and the next two set up in the years before 1964—HARYOU-ACT and Youth-In-Action (YIA)—were located, respectively, in Harlem and Bedford Stuyvesant, the city's two largest black ghettoes.[57]

Screvane and Wagner's unwillingness to relinquish full control of the city's antipoverty programs seriously delayed New York's War on Poverty. The city's first plan called for the establishment of a policy board with sixty-two members, including just six representatives from poor communities, a plan rejected by both the OEO and state governor Nelson Rockefeller for so badly underrepresenting the poor. When New York finally had a plan accepted, it was one of the last cities in the country to do so.[58] Wrangling over inclusion of the poor had seriously undermined the city's antipoverty efforts during its first year. As one local newspaper argued, "The poverty program was created to help the impoverished citizens, but in New York City, red tape, indecision, politics and mismanagement have hamstrung the program and kept it from reaching the vast majority of the people it was designed to help." [59]

On the West Coast, the first year of Los Angeles's War on Poverty also proved acrimonious. Like New York, Los Angeles had been home to early-1960s experimental antipoverty programs. In April 1962, following an earlier meeting with David Hackett and Richard Boone of President Kennedy's juvenile delinquency task force, local officials established the Youth Opportunities Board of Greater Los Angeles (YOB). However, while the YOB was created to improve the delivery of services to poor neighborhoods, it was dominated by city bureaucrats and saw the poor only as clients of its services. [60] In early September 1964 Mayor Sam Yorty made clear his vision for the city's War on Poverty, telling reporters it would offer "work training for unemployed men and women through participation in community and public works programs." Control of the effort, he implied, would rest with city agencies. [61]

Concerned about Yorty's intentions, local African American community groups, led by the Welfare Planning Council, joined together to form the Economic Opportunity Federation (EOF) in order to challenge the YOB for designation as the city's official antipoverty body. The EOF demanded full inclusion of the poor in running the War on Poverty and was backed by several local liberal Democrats, including Congressman Augustus Hawkins, who opposed the mayor. [62] City officials instantly dismissed the EOF, with YOB head (and Yorty ally) Robert Goe declaring that the "makeup and experience" of the YOB made it "the best possible agency to coordinate the antipoverty program here." [63]

In January 1965, after three months of dispute, the OEO proposed a merger between the YOB and EOF in order to end the stalemate. The resultant organization, OEO leaders argued, would keep the YOB at the heart of the city's antipoverty operations, while the EOF's involvement would bring the substantial community representation that they and much of the local black poor desired and upon which the release of OEO funds was contingent. However, Mayor Yorty rejected the OEO's solution because it placed more community and private-agency representatives on the new organization's board than city officials (twelve to ten). While Yorty's position reflected his genuine belief that public funds had to remain under the authority of public officials, it was also intensely political. Elected with strong black support in

1961, Yorty had failed to make good on his campaign promise to stop police brutality and had instead become a strong supporter of the LAPD and a close ally of the city's openly racist police chief, William Parker. This bolstered Yorty's image among white voters but deepened black disillusionment with his leadership. Having abandoned black voters, the mayor strove to prevent them from making any inroads into his political power.[64]

In February 1965 the YOB and EOF agreed on the proposed merger, which would produce the Economic and Youth Opportunities Agency of Greater Los Angeles (EYOA). However, Yorty again refused to accept the plan, demanding that city officials alone direct antipoverty programs. In late May frustrated black Angelenos gathered in Congressman Hawkins's South Central office and formed the Community Antipoverty Committee (CAPC), an umbrella organization committed to challenging Yorty that comprised all the area's leading civil rights groups and their leaders, as well as a number of community groups. Norman O. Houston of the NAACP, Dr. Thomas Kilgore of CORE, Reverend H. H. Brookins of the United Civil Rights Committee (UCRC) and Archie Hardwick of the Westminster Neighborhood Improvement Association (WNIA), among others, were all prominently involved. Though predominantly black, the CAPC also included some Mexican American and Japanese American groups, highlighting broader minority interest in the War on Poverty. At the same time, anger over the mayor's position spawned new community organizations, such as the Watts Action Committee and the Southeast Citizens Improvement Association, which demanded control over local antipoverty programs. As the president of one of the groups announced: "We've decided that there is no group or person outside this community who will do the job for us [. . .] we are going to do it for ourselves."[65]

The CAPC and other local minority groups continued to battle the recalcitrant mayor until, in August of that year, Watts, a black ghetto neighborhood in South Central Los Angeles, erupted in six days of rioting, breaking the deadlock.[66] In the aftermath, national attention focused on Los Angeles, and President Johnson sent LeRoy Collins, director of the federal government's Community Relations Service, to bring an end to the EYOA debacle. The subsequent negotiated settlement created an organization in which poor community representatives were narrowly outnumbered by public officials. Although an improvement on Yorty's terms, many black and Latino Angelenos resented the settlement for failing to better represent them, and anger over the protracted saga remained in the minority community for some time. Nevertheless, the EYOA's confirmation as the city's official lead antipoverty agency did mean that, just over a year after the War on Poverty had been signed into law, the city's antipoverty effort could finally begin.[67]

A "BLACK" WAR ON POVERTY? RACIAL IDENTITY POLITICS AND INTERRACIAL CONFLICT IN THE WAR ON POVERTY

By introducing resources, jobs, and power into poor minority communities, where they had traditionally been absent, the War on Poverty was always likely to result in a clamor for control over its rewards. What was, perhaps, less inevitable was the regularity with which local struggles were drawn along racial lines. Across the country, the War on Poverty inspired racially nationalist organizing, becoming a catalyst and conduit for the subsequent emergence of Black Power and various other racial liberation movements in America's ghettos. African Americans in New York and Los Angeles swiftly identified the War on Poverty as prime territory for black advancement. However, this led to repeated clashes with other minority groups. Interracial conflict, rather than cooperation, came to characterize the War on Poverty in both cities.

Throughout the 1965 New York mayoral election, candidates appealed to the aspirations of urban minority communities. Liberal Republican candidate John V. Lindsay reached out to those groups traditionally marginalized, or excluded from city government altogether, telling voters that a Lindsay administration War on Poverty would empower the poor. It was clear, he concluded, that the poor were no longer content with being "merely a delegation to City Hall. They want to be a part of City Hall." Victorious at the polls later that year, Lindsay soon set about making good on his campaign promises.[68]

Throughout his two terms in office, Mayor Lindsay strove, in his own words, "to bring democracy to the streets of New York." Nowhere was this more apparent than in the city's War on Poverty, which he expanded significantly soon after taking office by designating an additional ten official "poverty areas" (bringing the total up to twenty-six) in the city and establishing an official CAA—or "community corporation," as they were known—in each. Every community corporation was required to have two-thirds of its board made up of representatives drawn from the local poor community. It was an approach, he later explained, designed to meet the expectations of "the disadvantaged of our city streets who [. . .] want, and sometimes fiercely demand, participation in the decisions affecting their lives."[69] As historian Vincent Cannato has suggested, Lindsay was truly committed to making the city "a laboratory for Great Society social policy" and proved adept at attracting federal funds for the city's antipoverty fight.[70]

Lindsay believed that combatting New York's socioeconomic problems required significant reform of city government, and in mid-August 1966, eight months into his first term as mayor, he signed an executive order creating the Human Resources Administration (HRA). The HRA was the city's new, all-encompassing apparatus for coordinating employment, social service, antipoverty, and public assistance programs. It consisted of five departments, each with different responsibilities, including the Community Development Agency, which was given oversight of the city's War on Poverty.[71]

Lindsay's reorganization of city government was also intended to serve an important political purpose. Entering office as a Republican mayor in a city with an overwhelming majority of Democratic voters—the first elected in in two decades—Lindsay encountered a hostile Democratic political machine and uncooperative city bureaucracy. In the face of their resistance, Lindsay looked to unite the city's sizable minority groups and white liberals and progressives in a new political coalition of his own and, toward that goal, began opening up city government—in particular its expanded official antipoverty apparatus—to the city's poor black and Puerto Rican communities.

In mixed neighborhoods, this approach fueled significant and sustained interracial conflict over War on Poverty jobs and resources. Peaking in late 1969–early 1970, clashes over the antipoverty program were ongoing in nearly every mixed black and Puerto Rican neighborhood in the city. In South Bronx, local blacks were outraged when Frank Lugano, the Puerto Rican board chairman of the South Bronx Community Corporation, fired Frank Wright, its African American executive director. The incident was just one in a number, a local reporter noted, that reflected "a struggle for power in the South Bronx poverty agency which has jobs and political patronage to bestow." The situation was replicated elsewhere, as another report explained: "In East Harlem, Shirle Brown the black executive director of the district's community corporation, MEND, is under fire from Puerto Rican board members who are trying to dismiss him. In Coney Island, delegate agencies occupied the community corporation offices for a week in August in a dispute over Black–Puerto Rican appointments. Minor conflicts, even acts of violence, between the two groups have broken out in East New York, Williamsburg, and Brooklyn."[72] Leading local Puerto Rican politician

Herman Badillo argued that conflict resulted from making the two groups fight over "one small piece of the pie." "The best way to solve the problem," Badillo continued, "is for Mayor Lindsay to appoint blacks and Puerto Ricans to important positions in other areas besides the Council [Against Poverty] and Human Resources, such as Finance, Public Works or Parks and Culture."[73] Badillo's words reflected not only the strength and pervasive nature of racial identity politics within the city's War on Poverty, but also the extent to which, under Lindsay, minority groups claimed ownership of the antipoverty program and, increasingly, city government jobs too.

The racial dynamics of Los Angeles's War on Poverty differed significantly from those in New York. As only the second-largest minority group in the city, black Angelenos found themselves increasingly in conflict with the largest—Mexican Americans—over the spoils of the local antipoverty program. As historian Robert Bauman has revealed, interracial conflict was especially pronounced between EYOA, the city's official antipoverty body, and the Neighborhood Adult Participation Project (NAPP), the first and only community action organization established by the EYOA. Few local blacks or Chicanos supported EYOA, believing it to be a political tool of Mayor Yorty. NAPP, on the other hand, was headed by Opal Jones, a black female civil rights activist strongly committed to empowering local poor communities and defending community action. While EYOA concentrated on social service delivery, NAPP instead focused primarily on community organizing through its thirteen "outpost" offices in poor communities across the city. Each NAPP office employed up to thirty neighborhood aides, the vast majority of whom were members of the local poor and, more often than not, were female. At least half of these aides were usually deployed as liaisons between parents and various local institutions (such as schools and welfare offices). The remaining NAPP neighborhood aides spent their time organizing people around issues of local importance.[74]

During its first year, NAPP mobilized local groups to lobby for improved city services such as garbage collection, better street lighting, and child-care facilities. Irritated by their activity, and perceiving NAPP as a threat to his power (in particular because of Jones's close ties to Congressman Hawkins and Councilman Tom Bradley), Mayor Yorty soon moved against NAPP. First, Joe Maldonado, the Mexican American head of EYOA and a Yorty ally, fired Jones for refusing to abandon NAPP's community organization–focused approach. However, after Jones appealed, OEO intervened and not only reinstated her but also stripped EYOA of authority over NAPP.

FIGURE 2. Protesters march down a downtown Los Angeles sidewalk, with one sign reading "NAPP For Community Action," in 1966. Los Angeles Times Photographic Archive, Library Special Collections, Charles E. Young Research Library, University of California, Los Angeles. Used under a Creative Commons Attribution 4.0 International License.

However, the newly independent organization soon became mired in growing interracial conflict stemming from anger among its Latino employees, who felt Hispanics were seriously underrepresented within NAPP and the antipoverty program more broadly. Although Mexican Americans constituted the largest minority poor group in the city, only three of NAPP's thirteen outposts were in areas with majority Chicano populations: Boyle Heights, East Los Angeles, and Pacoima. Those centers were also the only ones with Mexican American directors. Arguing that the city's War on Poverty was favoring blacks (just as Puerto Rican groups in New York had), Chicano NAPP staff members demanded that Jones give Mexican Americans a greater share of organizational jobs and power. Despite increasing Latino representation as a result, interracial tensions in NAPP continued to simmer. In 1969 the OEO (now under directives from the Nixon White House) stepped in to restructure the organization. The result was a shift in NAPP's focus toward job training and firmly away from community organization.[75] Interracial antagonism also fatally undermined EYOA as opposition from the city's Chicano groups—again over the issue of underrepresentation— eventually increased to such an extent that the organization was shut down in 1972 and its powers transferred elsewhere.[76]

Speaking at a "Save Our War on Poverty" conference in May 1972, Opal Jones reflected that the scarcity of antipoverty resources had done much to inspire interracial conflict in the city's program:

> For seven long years we have struggled to work in these [antipoverty] programs in Los Angeles. Our funds have been steadily reduced year after year and as the poverty and problems increased, the money decreased. In spite of the attacks against the community based programs we continued to try and work with many odds, blocks and many obstacles which were forever put in our way. Year after year we have had to go and beg for more funds. We have been placed in a pitiful and dreadful situation where we have been pitted in battle against each other: Blacks against Browns and Browns against Blacks; Blacks against Blacks and Browns against Browns. [...] We must unite against the forces that make us fight over the crumbs of the War on Poverty.[77]

Regional NAACP director Leonard Carter regarded the "increased competition and polarization developing between black and brown communities" in the city with trepidation. In a letter to Congressman Augustus Hawkins in mid-1972, Carter lamented that after having "carried the brunt of the civil rights movement," African Americans now saw the gains they had made in employment and education under threat from the region's Latino community: "Today, the pressure is on from our Spanish-speaking citizens and they are rightfully demanding a greater share of jobs." The problem was, Carter complained, that "it is becoming increasingly clear that many brown representatives are attempting to remove blacks from jobs and then to replace them with browns."[78]

Panracial class solidarity, then, was an exception, rather than the rule, in both New York and Los Angeles. The clear trend of racial identity politics in both cities' antipoverty programs reflected the growing strength of nationalist ideologies in black and other minority communities. It also underlined the War on Poverty's capacity for nurturing racial nationalism, something most clearly visible in the organizations examined in the following chapter. Lastly, racial conflict between minority groups over antipoverty jobs and resources further discredited the War on Poverty and lent weight to white criticism that it was a liberal, pro-minority program that put taxpayers' money in the hands of fractious, militant inner-city communities that brought unwelcome disruption to public life.

CALMER WATERS? ATLANTA'S WAR ON POVERTY

Whereas in New York and Los Angeles the War on Poverty engendered challenges to established local power structures, in Atlanta it seemed largely to strengthen them. This can be explained, at least partially, by the way in which Atlanta's political elites managed local blacks' efforts for inclusion. Just as the Watts riots began amid the turmoil swamping LA's antipoverty program, the *Los Angeles Times* lauded the apparently smooth running of the War on Poverty in Atlanta, calling it "a beacon which burns through the miasma of cynicism engulfing the efforts in some big northern cities."[79] A year later, local liberal newspaper the *Atlanta Journal* celebrated Atlanta's place just below Pittsburgh at the top of the OEO's funding rankings, commending the "alertness [. . .] of city and county officials" in "taking advantage of what was available for a most important kind of work."[80] Atlanta's success was also due in part to the virtual absence from the city's antipoverty program of serious conflict and delays of the kind that had beset efforts in New York and Los Angeles. Key to this was the city's established pattern of top-down biracial political cooperation.

As soon as the War on Poverty was announced, Mayor Ivan Allen ensured that the city's biracial leadership elite was well represented within the city's official antipoverty agency, Economic Opportunity Atlanta, Incorporated (EOA Inc.). The organization's board included some of the city's leading black power brokers, including Martin Luther King Sr., insurance executive and publisher Jesse Hill Jr., and real estate mogul W. L. Calloway. Dr. Tillman Cothran, former professor of sociology at Atlanta University and the cochair of the Atlanta Summit Leadership Conference (ASLC)—the preeminent contemporary black leadership organization—was appointed associate director of EOA Inc.[81] Other local black elites who expected to be included pushed to ensure they were. One such leader was local NAACP head John Calhoun, who leveraged his relationship with Dan Sweat, EOA

Inc.'s white associate director, to secure an appointment in the organization. As Sweat explains: "John showed up the first day on the job and said—my first day in the job—and says 'I'm here to go to work.' And I said 'what are you talking about?' He said, 'Well,' he said, 'This is the greatest opportunity of my lifetime for blacks. It has so much potential, and I'm not going to get left out. I've got to be involved.'"[82]

As whites continued to leave the city en masse for the suburbs and blacks' numerical strength grew, Atlanta's black establishment pressed to increase its political power at every opportunity, an effort in which its members were generally quite successful.[83] As local historian Harold H. Martin has suggested: "The dialogue between the Black Summit Conference leaders and the EOA [Inc.] board set a pattern that would be followed for many years to come: the blacks asking for more and more recognition, more and more participation in government at all levels, and the white leaders agreeing."[84]

Lacking the influence of well-connected African Americans like Calhoun, Atlanta's poor black citizens found their opportunities within the city's antipoverty effort much more limited. The "citizens advisory councils"—the vehicles for community participation in antipoverty affairs—had no say in policy or decision making. In late November 1965, grassroots leaders from across the city came together to discuss their concerns over the citizens advisory councils' lack of power and the absence of poor representatives on the EOA Inc. board. Their subsequent request to discuss these issues with EOA Inc. officials in person, however, was rejected. In the words of Reverend Cadamus Samples, the board's refusal to meet with them was "a slap in the face. We were made to feel like floor mats. These people are supposed to be our representatives and we can't even speak to them." Although Otelus Shelman, the groups' other leading spokesman, wrote to Sargent Shriver insisting on the need for poor people to be represented at the "upper administration levels" of the city's War on Poverty, little changed as a result. The poor would never acquire any meaningful degree of decision-making power in the city's antipoverty program.[85]

While the poor lacked influence over Atlanta's War on Poverty, they were not excluded from the program altogether. What limited opportunities for involvement they did have resulted from the antipoverty organizational model that developed in the city. Atlanta's official antipoverty agency, EOA Inc., had grown out of the West End Project, a neighborhood service center set up in a poor mixed neighborhood in 1962 in order to relocate services from the downtown business area to the point of delivery—that is, into the poor community itself. The West End center, a contemporary assessment explained, was "run by local indigent personnel and supervised and guided by social service type organizational employees." Because city officials perceived the West End Project as a great success, EOA Inc. used it as a template in creating "neighborhood service centers" (NSCs) in a number of designated poor communities, black and white, across the city. These NSCs focused overwhelmingly on the delivery of services to the city's poor residents, so much so in fact that, according to one report, after two years of operation less than half of 1 percent of EOA Inc.'s budget was allocated for Jobs Corp, the War on Poverty's main job training element.[86] Under this paradigm, the poor were identified primarily as clients and the role of service planning and delivery reserved mainly for professional social workers. Candidates for the handful of center management roles were drawn habitually from the ranks of Atlanta's well-educated black middle class. As the city's War on Poverty developed, NSC activities became dominated by programs like Headstart, homemaking, drug and alcohol rehabilitation, and child care. In September 1965 the city received $6.3 million in additional antipoverty funding that was used to add a further eight of these multipurpose service centers to the four originally created, nearly all of them built in poor African American neighborhoods. This social service–oriented model was seen by some critics to exemplify the shortcomings and limitations of the War on Poverty insofar as it did little to undermine the structural causes of poverty.[87]

Like the West End Project, the city's NSCs did provide some opportunities for the direct involvement of the poor through employment as "neighborhood aides." However, the organizational status of neighborhood aides raised questions about the EOA Inc.'s disposition toward involvement of the poor in the antipoverty program. As Otis Cochran of local community group the Vine City Improvement Association complained, "The only staff positions involving the poor are the aide positions, and the valuable pension program does not include them." Denied the full benefits enjoyed by their more senior colleagues, neighborhood aides were effectively given second-tier status within EOA Inc.[88] Regardless, competition over the limited number of these jobs available was strong. In a statement to a local newspaper, one anonymous group of neighborhood aides charged that, contrary to the spirit of the War on Poverty, the positions were not going to the genuinely poor: "There are some people working with the EOA [centers] who are paid a good salary. These people have husbands working at Lockheed, the Post Office, Conley, teaching school, and other high paying jobs. In the first place these women were not in poverty. The women without husbands who needed the jobs, and could have done the job, were left out [and] their applications overlooked."[89]

Implicit in the aides' criticism was their expectation that the War on Poverty should provide poor single black women (and their children) a route to the family wage they lacked, as well as the status it conferred. In their estimation, women with employed husbands already enjoyed the fruits of economic citizenship and thus were less deserving of these jobs. While the War on Poverty was seen as a prime opportunity for extending economic citizenship to those historically denied it, it revealed a complex contest over female empowerment that was itself (somewhat paradoxically) shaped by the existing male-breadwinner social paradigm. Concerns over who exactly should enjoy the benefits of the antipoverty program were not exclusive to women. In a letter to EOA Inc., Edward Moody, a prominent spokesman for the poor of the Summerhill-Mechanicsville area, complained that the board of a recently created local child care association (sponsored by the local NSC) was remarkably unrepresentative of the area's poor residents: "The present [board] members are 'what's in it for me?' members. The community is resentful of the employees driving expensive autos to and from work. The applicants['] applications are tampered with. Certain people are employed. Always a family tie. A board member or a friend. Employees are allowed to work two jobs. Employees['] mates are already doing good."[90]

The apparent anti-poor bias in EOA Inc. was manifested in other organizational arrangements. W. H. Montague, president of the Georgia AFL-CIO, spoke out against EOA Inc. after it declared its policy on the garnishment of employee wages. In late November 1967, at a meeting presided over by Martin Luther King Sr., the organization stated that it did not consider indebted individuals "desirable employees" and warned that any employee receiving a garnishment would be sacked.[91] As indebtedness was an issue that disproportionately affected the poor, EOA Inc.'s rules seemed one more way to inhibit their involvement. Montague lambasted EOA Inc.'s position as "worse than the most recalcitrant, unenlightened, and backward Georgia employer" and "contrary to the entire conception of the poverty program."[92]

The poor would find themselves on the fringes of Atlanta's War on Poverty from its first day till its last. A consistent critic of the city's efforts, local newspaper editor J. Lowell Ware suggested in late 1971: "We tire of saying it but the efforts of government and private business to provide work for those who need it, housing for those who must have it, and a way up and out of the pit of poverty is, and has been, a rotten little game in which career bureaucrats and hardened social work hacks grow fat while a generation of children linger, wither and die before they reach age ten."[93]

Although restricted involvement of the poor was an issue in all three cities, the War on Poverty in Atlanta proved to be far less of an organizational platform for mobilizing the city's poor black community than it did in New York and Los Angeles. While the limits of the NSC model ensured that community organizing and mobilization were rarely practiced within Atlanta's antipoverty program, the fact remains that there appears to have been a much more vocal and sustained resistance to the exclusion of the poor in New York and Los Angeles. In Atlanta, although the War on Poverty did provide improved services to the poor, it was more a source of administrative positions for local middle-class and elite blacks than it was an engine of local community activism as it proved to be in New York and Los Angeles.[94] The community organizations (discussed in chapter 2) that emerged in the mid- to late 1960s from the intersection of Black Power, antipoverty organizing, and alternative public policies never materialized in Atlanta during this period. Their absence can be explained, at least in part, by the way in which the War on Poverty unfolded, the entrenched model of biracial cooperation between black and white elites, and the relatively less intense grassroots activism in Atlanta compared to New York and Los Angeles.

The War on Poverty in Atlanta also highlighted two other significant facts. First, it revealed that the War on Poverty—and especially its poor-as-clients social service–delivery model—was seriously limited, struggling as it did to effectively reduce poverty levels. Second, it showed that class, as much as race, dictated the terms and conditions of black engagement in the War on Poverty. Opportunities were available to middle-class and elite black Atlantans, but not for their less fortunate counterparts. Increasing middle-class opportunity would also become a defining characteristic of the alternative public policies discussed in the following chapter, as it would remain in local racial politics in Atlanta. Class bias also lay at the heart of mainstream political reaction to the War on Poverty's impact where it energized and mobilized the inner-city minority poor.

THE POOR IN POLITICS: AN UNWELCOME CHALLENGE

The resistance of local authorities and urban power brokers to the transformative political change threatened by the War on Poverty soon found voice at the national level too. Speaking before the U.S. House of Representatives in August 1965 as an extension to the antipoverty bill was being debated, OEO chief Sargent Shriver found himself under attack from congressional leaders angry at the widespread political ferment the antipoverty program appeared to be encouraging in poor urban communities nationwide. As Alphonso Bell, a member of the House ad hoc subcommittee of the War on Poverty and Republican representative from Los Angeles, complained to Shriver: "We're all in favor of fighting poverty, but you're opening the gunwales to loads of political activity." [95]

The following month, the director of the Bureau of the Budget, Charles Schultz, explained to President Johnson that "many mayors assert that the CAP is setting up a competing political organization in their own backyards." Underlining the importance of mayoral support, Schultz advised that "we ought not to be in the business of organizing the poor politically." He recommended that OEO be ordered to stop sponsoring elections to poverty planning boards, to tone down its conflicts with city politicians over representation of the poor (which, he acknowledged, "may cause some friction with civil rights groups"), and step up its efforts to involve the poor at the working, rather than the planning, level of the antipoverty program. [96]

In late November 1965, the United States Conference of Mayors (USCM) submitted a special report to OEO based on consultations with representatives of ninety-three local governments. The report revealed widespread concern with community action and the relationship between public and private agencies, and also blamed CAP inefficiencies on the lack of technical expertise among many of the poor communities involved. There was, the report argued, too much focus on the form of organization rather than on substantive program building. Local CAAs, the report insisted, "should operate as service centers." In many ways, Atlanta's War on Poverty exemplified the USCM's ideal formula. Decision-making power and oversight of antipoverty programs, the mayors believed, had to rest with public officials and qualified professionals. [97]

President Johnson shared municipal politicians' concerns over the CAP. As Guian McKee explains, Johnson's past experience as head of the Texas arm of the New Deal's National Youth Administration (NYA) played a critical role in shaping his own view on this matter. As Texas NYA chief, Johnson had had programmatic and financial control, reflecting the federal government's implicit trust in his expertise and suitability for that role. As such, Johnson agreed that control of CAPs should rest with city officials, and had assumed that it would. Moreover, Johnson's gendered political vision of the War on Poverty meant he valued programs that trained and employed men most highly. The president had therefore paid little regard to the CAP when War on Poverty legislation was drawn up. Here, Johnson's view clashed with those of the antipoverty program's authors most significantly. While he subscribed completely to the principles of New Deal breadwinner liberalism, advocates of community action sought instead to mobilize and empower the very groups that had been most marginalized by the New Deal welfare state. As historian Thomas F. Jackson has argued, although many African Americans perceived the antipoverty program as a tool for widening and accelerating the battle for equality, Johnson "had no idea that his War on Poverty would become so thoroughly entangled with the black quest for independent political power." Johnson's far more limited vision did not include politically mobilizing the nation's poorest citizens, and he swiftly turned against it when faced with the political strife it created.[98]

Politicians' concerns over the CAP were, in some respects, well founded. Poor communities' general lack of administrative and managerial experience did threaten to undermine the efficiency and quality of War on Poverty programs. In New York, Mayor Lindsay's aide Jim Carberry gave voice to this problem. Advising Lindsay on how best to explain to angry community groups the city's delayed application for OEO funds, Carberry suggested being honest. The truth, he argued, was that

> this administration tried too diligently to engage the poor in preparation of the applications for funding. The poor, inescapably, do not have typewriters. They don't spell very well. They are not precise in language and they are unfamiliar with the requirements of preparing project proposals. They don't have adding machines and their figures don't balance. Consequently, an effort to truly give poor people a rightful and effective voice in determining the use of poverty money creates an additional workload on those who are formally charged with preparing the bureaucratically correct applications to OEO. Moreover, it requires one hell of a lot of time to translate the often conflicting requests of the poor into proper, accurate applications.[99]

The emphasis on community participation regularly resulted in delays to antipoverty programs nationwide. CAAs with significant and diverse community representation often found themselves bogged down in long debates over how best to organize, something generally avoided by top-down, tightly controlled, city hall–led CAAs, which often established and implemented programs swiftly. Moreover, as some feared, the introduction of money and resources into poor neighborhoods led in some cases to corruption and mis-use of funds. As later head of New York's antipoverty program Major Owens explained, "Once you introduce money into the situation poor people behave like anyone else—the greed factor takes over and you have problems." [100] Ultimately, as historian Thomas Sugrue has suggested, "it is unclear whether maximum feasible participation actually improved services to the poor." [101]

Beneath these issues of suitability and practicality lay a broader clash of cultures and expectations, as a letter to Los Angeles congressman Augustus Hawkins from his South Central district office aide Charles Knox reveals. Reporting back on a meeting he had attended in the Compton-Willowbrook area, Knox complained, "I could summarize the meeting by calling it a big 'mess.' However, intrinsic in the interaction is the raw and often time unin-telligible approach to the board's problems." The underlying and inescapable issue, he asserted, was that the poor were ill-equipped for such positions of authority, leadership, and management. "Unfortunately, inherent in a board of thirteen low-income representatives, who display all of the common disa-bilities of the poor, is resentment, conflict, destruction, etc." To overcome this problem, he suggested that "the board needs the direction of a very firm and emotionally secure chairman who will ride herd and nip a lot of the internal jealousy and conflict in the bud." The board members were, he con-cluded, "guilty in maintaining internal struggles that limit good planning in all areas. I certainly don't want to be overly critical or subjective in evaluat-ing the meeting. However, I feel just and objective in surmising from what seems to be occurring on the board, another demonstration of N-[igger] business." [102]

An African American himself, Knox's intraracial criticism reveals that class tensions, and a clash of political cultures, could just as easily occur between established black middle-class and professional political elites and black poor citizens as it could between the black community and white offi-cials. It was a conflict that encompassed issues of education, class, cultural orientation, and the expected standards of behavior that prevailed within mainstream political life. Moreover, it raised broader questions about the place of the poor within national politics, the class bias of mainstream U.S. politics and society, and the limits of inclusive democracy. Importantly, these questions were later amplified by the growth of a vibrant welfare rights move-ment that placed increasingly militant poor black women on the front line of a national debate about the moral and political dimensions of the taxpayer-funded American welfare state and the pursuit of economic justice.

If politicians were unhappy with the results of the War on Poverty, so were many poor communities. Aside from frustrated ambitions to control antipoverty programs, many inner-city minority communities were angered by the underfunding of the War on Poverty. As New York senator James H. Scheuer explained to a House subcommittee on poverty, the program's first-year appropriations of $800 million dollars amounted to "less than $30 an impoverished person." [103] Sargent Shriver made plain the insufficiency of War on Poverty appropriations and the underutilization of its programs when he testified before a Senate subcommittee on the OEO's first two years of operations. Headstart, he explained, had reached more than 700,000 poor children and their families each year, but this represented less than one-third of the total number of children aged three to five targeted by the program. Of the nation's 8 million children aged six to fifteen, he estimated that OEO operations were reaching only about 300,000. Out of 3 million impoverished sixteen- to twenty-one-year-olds, only 20 percent of those attending school and 40 percent of dropouts were involved with antipoverty efforts. Success in getting job training and placements to adults was even more limited, with just 6 percent of the 9.5 million poor people aged between twenty-two and fifty-four receiving jobs or vocational training in 1966. Worse still, antipoverty programs were consistently meeting the needs of only around 5 percent of the 5.4 million elderly Americans living below the poverty line.[104] In a June 1967 message to Congress, President Johnson admitted that although 8 million poor Americans had been reached by the War on Poverty during its first two and a half years, another 24 million remained unaffected by the program.[105]

Greater financial commitment to fighting poverty at home, however, was precluded by the cost of fighting communism abroad. As a *Atlanta Journal* editor suggested:

> The declaration of the War on Poverty [. . .] accompanied by exuberant White House promises of relief for the country's 34 million people below the poverty line, amounted to a national promise and an official underwriting of hope. Yet the program had funding which, from the start, was judged by authorities on the subject to be grossly inadequate for the promises being made. Then, six months after the act [EOA] was passed, the escalation of the war in Vietnam and the beginning of full American involvement there threw a major obstacle in front of the program.[106]

Black disillusionment was only deepened by the apparent willingness of the federal government to sacrifice the pursuit of social and economic justice in favor of an increasingly controversial war overseas. According to Martin Luther King Jr., it was a symptom of a society that had habitually and chronically failed African Americans, and another injustice that fed the groundswell of black disappointment from which the Black Power movement grew.[107]

In October 1966, presidential aide Robert Kintner acknowledged in a memo to Johnson that the funding of the War on Poverty had become "a real political issue, as you know better than I, in every large city in this country." [108] The following month, in a detailed message to the president entitled "Great expectations vs. Disappointments," Bureau of the Budget director Schultz suggested that the administration's lofty rhetoric concerning the elimination of poverty at home was quickly becoming a political liability for the White House. "States, cities, depressed areas, and individuals," Schultz wrote, "have been led to expect immediate delivery of Great Society programs to a degree that is not realistic." With the deepening military conflict in Southeast Asia now diverting increasing levels of federal funds away from domestic programs, the "frustration, loss of credibility, and even deterioration of state and local services" he expected to result would, he predicted, prove "very troublesome in the 1968 campaign." [109]

At the same time that the War on Poverty was disappointing social and economic justice advocates, the political turmoil it caused had helped turn the political tide decisively in favor of conservative opponents of redistributive liberal social policy. As a confidential White House report explained, "The outcome of the 1966 midterm elections, in terms of Congressional support for the War on Poverty, is very grim. In the House, the program has fallen from a position of relative strength to one of desperate jeopardy." The Democrats, and liberals in particular, suffered heavy reversals. Of the seventy-one politicians unseated in the elections, fifty-five had been behind the War on Poverty. Of their replacements, only eight could be counted as supporters, with a further six considered "doubtful" and the rest understood to be hostile to the antipoverty program. American voters, conservatives argued, had delivered a resounding verdict on the Johnson administration's policies and its handling of the urban crisis. In the 90th Congress the War on Poverty would, in all likelihood, face a clear and sizable majority opposition. Its future seemed bleak at best. As the White House report concluded, "The War on Poverty is in great peril in the House. On paper it looks as though the conservative coalition can work its will against our legislation, at least to the point of drastically restructuring and reorganizing the program." [110]

With the stage set for the War on Poverty's retrenchment, the report's dire predictions were soon realized. Antipoverty program opponents oversaw a number of sizable cuts to OEO funding in 1966–67. On the ground, the impact was considerable. In Los Angeles, Mayor Yorty wrote to Sargent Shriver to warn him that the planned cuts (an expected loss of $10 million in OEO funds for the city) "shall severely handicap the functioning of the local CAP agency [. . .] this could mean the loss of about 500 jobs for poverty area residents and the disappearance of programs serving approximately 135,000 people." [111] In Atlanta, EOA Inc. head Charles Emmerich wrote to Richard Boone, then head of the Citizens Crusade Against Poverty (CCAP), to explain that

> EOA Inc. is struggling to reduce its opportunity programs in line with the reductions outlined by Sargent Shriver. The reductions represent approximately 50% of our anticipated budget for 1967. When you consider that EOA Inc.'s program has been escalating over a two year period and during this same period it has become very close to the community, it is easy to understand our frustration. Our local committees are cooperating beautifully, but it is heartbreaking when they are required to reduce programs which are efficiently and effectively serving their communities. Frankly we find the reduction extremely difficult to accept and it is also most difficult to maintain a reasonable degree of high morale among our disadvantaged. Again they began to build up real hope and enthusiasm and now, as always, they are told this seems to be another broken promise. [112]

With President Johnson backing away from the War on Poverty from late 1965, growing political opposition eventually led to the passage of two congressional amendments in 1967 that diluted the CAP's potential for politically engaging the poor. The Quie and Green Amendments assured local officials of the authority to decide which community groups were eligible for OEO funds and also required that one-third of antipoverty board seats go to elected officials, with another third to consist of local social service and welfare professionals, as well as representatives from private-sector organizations. [113] City politicians across the country had exerted their influence to restrict the antipoverty legislation's capacity to challenge established authority, pushing back against poor communities' attempts to interlope in existing urban power arrangements. However, while politicians succeeded in winning control over the War on Poverty, they proved less able to control the increasing fiscal burden of public assistance programs that it generated. The growing cost of liberal social spending produced a backlash that had far-reaching consequences for American politics.

BROADENING THE INSURGENCY: WELFARE RIGHTS AND THE WAR ON POVERTY

One of the War on Poverty's most important political legacies was its helping to amplify, mobilize, and expand urban movements for social and economic justice. By offering a platform for disadvantaged communities to assert and defend their rights, the War on Poverty became intertwined with other important movements within the broader antipoverty coalition. The most significant of these was the welfare rights movement. As the War on Poverty intensified the focus on economic rights and urban organizing within the black freedom struggle, it provided extra impetus and support for a nascent welfare rights movement that grew rapidly in the mid- to late 1960s. Led primarily by inner-city black (and other minority) mothers, the blossoming of a national welfare rights movement brought vigorous challenges to local and federal government for comprehensive reform of the existing, much maligned welfare system and for a fuller extension of benefits.[114]

Welfare rights activism centered on Aid to Families with Dependent Children (AFDC), the program created by the 1935 Social Security Act. AFDC became an important support system for many inner-city blacks as millions left the rural South for the urban North in the decades following the Great Depression. Unlike the top-tier New Deal welfare programs (such as Social Security, workmen's compensation insurance, and unemployment insurance), which aimed to protect and valorize the male breadwinner–headed family paradigm, AFDC actively undermined it. By providing assistance only to female-headed households, the program effectively incentivized the father to leave the home, thereby destabilizing the traditional two-parent family structure in poor black communities nationwide, stigmatizing single mother–led black families and further dislocating AFDC recipients from the idealized vision of American citizenship and social organization.[115]

Worse still, payments were usually low, sometimes barely enough to cover food, rent, and other bills, leaving little, if anything, for other expenses. Welfare rights protesters often demanded more money for essential items for their children such as school uniforms and shoes and for extra winter clothing. A strained relationship existed between AFDC clients and their (often hostile) welfare caseworkers. Many welfare recipients especially resented home eligibility checks that investigated for evidence of a "man in the house," arguing they were inhumane and demeaning. As one black AFDC mother from Los Angeles explained to Sargent Shriver when he visited the city in August 1966:

> How much do you think the human mind and body can stand? [...] You think there is something nice about being on welfare and having a social worker come snooping under your bed, to see if you got a man there? It don't leave no dignity. You know it would be real nice if some of you people could change yourselves and be poor for a while. You see what the poor people have to go through. Who wants welfare? Who wants to have someone look down their nose at you all the time to give you a piece of bread? That's enough to make you want to blow your own brains out.[116]

The recent wealth of scholarship on the welfare rights movement has revealed its roots in earlier civil rights protest and its place within the broader tradition of African American consumer and economic rights activism.[117] The War on Poverty played a central role in transforming relatively isolated, disparate protest groups into a national, coordinated movement. As poor inner-city residents, welfare recipients naturally formed a vital War on Poverty constituency and were a primary target for organizing by advocates of the poor. In a May 1966 article, New York sociologists (and Mobilization For Youth staff members) Richard Cloward and Frances Fox Piven outlined a plan for forcing reform of the welfare system as a precursor to building a fairer society. Although opponents of the welfare state often criticized the cost of the nation's welfare system, it was in fact, they argued, both inadequately provisioned and seriously undersubscribed:

> A vast discrepancy exists between the benefits to which people are entitled under public welfare programs and the sums which they actually receive. [...] It is widely known, for example, that nearly 8 million persons (half of them white) now subsist on welfare, but it is not generally known that for every person on the rolls at least one more probably meets existing criteria of eligibility but is not obtaining assistance. The discrepancy is not an accident stemming from bureaucratic inefficiency; rather, it is an integral feature of the welfare system which, if challenged, would precipitate a profound financial and political crisis. The force for that challenge, and the strategy we propose, is a massive drive to recruit the poor onto the welfare rolls.[118]

In 1967, growing welfare enrollment and activism led to the founding of the National Welfare Rights Organization (NWRO). The group's chief architect was George Wiley, a former chemistry professor and CORE leader. In late August 1967, more than 250 groups from eighty cities in thirty states convened in Washington, D.C., to establish a national organization. As Wiley explained, "From deep in the ghettos and barrios of American cities welfare recipients and other poor people have been banding together to seek a better life for them and their families." [119] Efforts to expand the numbers on welfare rolls proved highly successful. In 1960 there were 3.1 million AFDC clients. By 1965 that figure climbed to 4.3 million. Five years later it had rocketed to nearly 8.5 million. As historian Marisa Chappell has explained, over a quarter of all new recipients were added in just two states: New York and California. [120]

As more and more local groups formed across the country, welfare rights organizations became fundamentally intertwined with the War on Poverty and minority women's struggle for liberation, not just from poverty but from racial and gender discrimination too. While the Johnson administration had intended the War on Poverty to decrease welfare enrollment (a natural corollary to the training and employment of African American men in the nation's ghettos), it was far more successful in vaulting a highly vocal, militant, female-led welfare rights movement to national prominence.

Welfare rights activism reached its climax in a national discussion, stretching from 1969 through 1972, over welfare reform and a guaranteed minimum income, a discussion that centered on the Nixon administration's proposed Family Assistance Plan (FAP). [121] The apotheosis of welfare rights activism, and the fiscal burden brought by growing welfare enrollment, played an important part in the increasing polarization of American politics, in shaping future public policy reform, and, later, in limiting the scope of black political power.

RESHAPING AMERICAN POLITICS: THE BROADER CONSEQUENCES OF THE WAR ON POVERTY

A memo to President Johnson in late December 1963 revealed that the Kennedy administration's choice between instituting a federal program that sought to attack poverty and forming one that addressed the problems faced by America's middle-income citizens had been a close call. While Kennedy was keen to help the nation's poorest citizens, he and his economic advisors also feared alienating the "American in the middle"—in the $3,000–$10,000 income bracket—who they saw as "the key to our economy, society, and political stability." Perfectly capturing the gendered perspective of breadwinner liberalism, their assessment explained: "He pays most of the taxes, carries most of the credit, makes or breaks the consumer goods market, is the home-buyer, car-buyer, etc. He is also the man in the gunsights of the future: automation is his job threat, high costs of education are his worry as a parent, high costs of elderly medical care fall heaviest on him as son. His consent is vital—his dissent is fatal—to our social progress vis-à-vis Negro rights, etc." [122] As the decade wore on, millions of white voters in this constituency, later characterized by Richard Nixon as the "Silent Majority," abandoned the Democratic Party and liberalism, forming the first shoots of what contemporary political commentator Kevin Phillips famously termed the "emerging Republican majority." [123] The War on Poverty, and the welfare rights movement it helped to expand, played an important part in this developing political realignment. As antipoverty efforts and welfare rights protest became inextricably bound up with movements for racial and economic equality, many "middle Americans" increasingly resented liberal social policies that they believed privileged the interests of poor black and other minority groups. Writing in 1970, Mayor John Lindsay recognized this growing sentiment among white New Yorkers:

> In the last few years, governments at all levels have mounted a wide range of programs to aid the deprived. They have, in the main, been meager programs; they have in no sense represented the commitment of resources and energy we need—but they have been visible. Many governments, New York City's included, have attempted to break through the decades of neglect and demonstrate to our most deprived citizens that government cares about them and it can respond to their grievances. And seeing this—seeing at least the effort and concern among one part of the citizenry—the mainstream New Yorker may well ask: "Where is an effort being made to answer *my* grievances? Is the black man to be bettered at my expense?" [124]

The sense of injustice over redistributive liberal social policy was a powerful emotion among many white American voters across the country and became a vital axis of conservative political resurgence from the mid-1960s onward. Spiraling welfare enrollment was especially troubling for many who saw the growing fiscal burden it placed on the taxpayer as a violation of the sanctity of property rights and as undermining the cultural meaning and value of work and self-reliance. As a white voter in Los Angeles explained eloquently in a letter to African American congresswoman Yvonne Braithwaite:

> I believe that our government, in the years passed and at present, is drifting into a welfare program which places the recipients in a position of expecting welfare, believing it is their right to have welfare, and that being on welfare is an honorable profession. On the other hand, many of the donors, including myself, feel that being forced through taxation, or having the results of our labors appropriated in the guise of taxation, and redistributed to others, is not good for our country. In other words an undercurrent develops in the mind of the donor, which leaves the donor with a sense of frustration, a feeling of "What's the use?" and, "Why be a fool? Why should I work to take care of those who are able to work but who prefer to be recipients?"[125]

It was not just the moral and economic dimensions of redistributive liberalism that upset American voters. The apparent link between liberal social policy and a broader protest culture among dissenting minorities and the white Left also deepened the disenchantment among the nation's "Silent Majority." Some blamed the antipoverty program for stoking the fires of urban discontent, rewarding agitators, and encouraging challenges to authority, established institutions, and traditional values. The sight of antipoverty warriors and welfare rights activists—sometimes with Black Power militants alongside them—agitating against the very government that was funding them offended many people. Labor writer Victor Riesel captured this view when he accused the OEO of funding people to "spend their time confronting, frequently battling, the police, picketing city halls and boards of education, closing down schools, struggling with union workers, and [. . .] discrediting the U.S." It was clear in Riesel's mind that antipoverty officials were on a mission to "go out and 'revolutionize' the nation's ghettos."[126]

In July 1964, just two months after Whitney Young had warned Congress of the possibility of unrest during War on Poverty hearings, Harlem and Bedford-Stuyvesant, New York's two largest black ghettos, were rocked by six days of rioting. Precipitated by the shooting of a black youth by a white police officer, it started a pattern that developed a familiar rhythm over the following four summers in black ghettos nationwide.[127] Reaching a new scale in Watts in August 1965, by the time the last wave of rioting ended in 1968, it had claimed many dozens of lives and caused billions of dollars' worth of damage to property and businesses across the nation.[128] Some opponents saw the hand of the War on Poverty in the devastation of America's urban centers. As segregationist Atlanta businessman and Georgia governor Lester Maddox complained in a letter to the president: "Hundreds of millions of federal dollars are being expended by [. . .] the War on Poverty programs to encourage, train, and finance the bums, criminals, beatniks and misfits who have brought near chaos to our Country as they burn, kill, and wreck much of America." [129]

Seeking to defend the OEO against what he called "unfounded and irresponsible charges," Shriver sent President Johnson a report following the 1967 riots extolling the positive role played by War on Poverty summer programs in both preventing and minimizing racial disturbances in cities across the nation.[130] Atlanta and Los Angeles were singled out for special praise. Shriver quoted a telegram he had received from Mayor Ivan Allen that read: "OEO's assistance is proof positive of the value of federal-local cooperation. Recreation funds and EOA CAP Centers have contributed greatly to cooling off summer problems. CAP Center and personnel provided quick communications facility for easing explosive situation in Dixie Hills disturbance. Continued OEO help to urban cities is a must. Thanks for the helping hand." In Los Angeles, police chief Thomas Reddin (Parker's successor) commended NAPP for distributing tens of thousands of leaflets that emphasized the damage riots did to the black community and urged locals to "Keep Cool This Summer." Another city official identified OEO programs in ghetto communities as an important factor in the declining number of juvenile arrests.[131] The following year, there was outcry in New York over the impact that cuts to OEO funds would have on the city's summer jobs programs. The loss of twenty thousand summer jobs for ghetto youth, Mayor Lindsay argued, would undoubtedly increase the chance of "violence and bloodshed" in the streets. "If violence again occurs in our cities," he concluded, "those in Washington who have ignored our pleas for help will have to assume their share of responsibility." [132]

While these cases all demonstrated the War on Poverty's role as a positive force in the nation's cities, they also gave weight to criticism that the antipoverty program was little more than "riot insurance" designed to prevent urban unrest by buying off militants and preoccupying inner-city youths in summer work programs. Even if, as mayors like Lindsay intimated, some antipoverty programs were, to a degree, riot prevention measures, opponents argued that they had failed. As California Republican Assembly chairman Dick Darling suggested: "The more money that has been appropriated for all these programs (federal cities programs including the War on Poverty, welfare, urban renewal, housing) the more violence we have had. Therefore it would seem that congressional spending alone will not end city riots." [133]

The increasingly vociferous agitation, protest, and in many cases open rebellion and rioting of urban minority groups against their condition during the mid-1960s, political scientist Ira Katznelson has explained, "came to undermine the security of the dominant and middle-classes." [134] As historian Dan Carter has argued, although most northern whites ostensibly eschewed overtly segregationist politics, many nevertheless shared southerners' "deep and visceral apprehensions" concerning African Americans, and rioting brought these fears to the surface. Urban rioting shattered the civil rights movement's carefully sculpted media image of blacks as peaceful and nonviolent, stoking fear and feeding prejudice among whites everywhere.[135] When added to the maelstrom of campus unrest, antiwar demonstrations, countercultural protest, rising crime, and growing welfare dependency, the riots helped deepen a growing sense of resentment and anger among many whites. In the process, the broader national consensus over existing liberal prescriptions for managing social, racial, and economic change disintegrated. White ethnic working- and middle-class voters began to question and abandon their support for integration, civil rights legislation, the liberal welfare state, and economically redistributive government spending, all of which, many believed, privileged racial minorities and the poor (especially African Americans) at their expense, and, worse still, encouraged urban disorder, welfare chiseling, and declining respect for authority, the established social order, and traditional American values.[136] Not only had liberals' policies failed to provide answers to the nation's problems, but increasing numbers of voters blamed them for making them worse.

This growing white racial resentment and disillusionment with liberal policies had already found its voice in national politics in efforts to roll back or narrow the scope of domestic reforms. For example, in May 1967, southern and northern conservatives in Congress combined to pass an amendment (by a vote of 232 to 171) discontinuing the Rent Supplement Program. Established in the Housing Act of 1965, this program specifically targeted tenants in public housing and new and rehabilitated Federal Housing Authority–financed accommodations (but not privately owned slum housing). The program had been described by one black poor advocacy group as "one of the very few which offer decent housing to the poor at rents more or less in keeping with their incomes." Some critics had used the rising cost of war overseas to justify their position; others, led by Bronx Republican congressman Paul Fino, made clear the racial and socioeconomic dimensions of their opposition. Accusing the federal government of conspiring to "spread rent supplement into middle-income suburbs and neighborhoods," Fino dismissed the program as a "racial and economic balance sheet" that "rewards rioters and subsidizes spongers." For Fino (who also strongly opposed the antipoverty program and busing), rent supplements were another example of liberals' attempts to socially engineer the nation toward integration and redistribute whites' hard-earned wealth to the undeserving inner-city minority poor. In the process, he believed, big-government, welfare state liberalism not only trampled the personal and economic freedoms of the white majority but also violated core traditional American values associated with self-reliance, hard work, and private initiative and responsibility.[137] This kind of conservative message resonated with increasing numbers of American voters from the mid- to the late 1960s and vitally shaped the political environment in which alternative public policies for dealing with racial and economic inequality developed.

As the following chapter illustrates, leading national politicians such as Richard Nixon and Robert F. Kennedy put forward different solutions for dealing with economic inequality that were deliberately sensitive to the changing political landscape. Rather than advancing the existing liberal–civil rights coalition's government-focused, integrationist, and economically redistributive politics, they instead offered alternatives designed not only to appeal to, or appease, white conservatives but also as a way to meet and sublimate the growing demand for black empowerment in the nation's ghettos. In the process, they encouraged the pursuit of a more middle-class, capitalist enterprise–oriented vision of Black Power intended to draw African Americans away from the transformative political solutions championed by social and economic justice movements and by some of Black Power's most radical adherents.

TWO

Community Development Corporations, Black Capitalism, and the Mainstreaming of Black Power

On a cold, icy February morning in New York City in 1966 local black residents Elsie Richardson and Donald Benjamin led Senator Robert F. Kennedy around Bedford-Stuyvesant, their struggling neighborhood in the center of Brooklyn. They trudged through ankle-deep snow to show Kennedy some of the problems blighting the area: run-down housing, piles of refuse, abandoned buildings, and filthy streets. It was a bleak picture. For Benjamin and Richardson, however, the tour was a pivotal moment. Both had spent many years working with the Central Brooklyn Coordinating Council (CBCC), a group that represented more than one hundred membership organizations from the local black community, struggling to convince the city government to commit resources to the area in a bid to arrest its seemingly interminable decline. Having met with little success until then, with Kennedy's tour they finally captured the interest of an influential and concerned politician. Ever since the nation had been rocked by the Watts riots in August 1965, Kennedy had dedicated his efforts to seeking a solution to black inner-city poverty and urban decay. For Kennedy there was no greater single problem facing the nation. As he told a group of New York community leaders in late January 1966, "What is at stake is not just the fate of the Negro in America but the fate of all Americans, of the legacy of our past and the promise of our future." Bedford-Stuyvesant, the junior senator feared, was another Watts waiting to happen. The tour of "Bed-Stuy" made a lasting impression on Kennedy, and he resolved to pilot his new strategy for tackling the ghetto there. Ten months later the first steps were taken on the way to the establishment of the Bedford-Stuyvesant Restoration Corporation (BSRC).[1]

Restoration, as it came to be known, was the first incarnation of Kennedy's community development corporation (CDC) blueprint, which he developed and articulated as the urban crisis deepened after Watts. Set against the Johnson administration's faltering War on Poverty, Kennedy's plans represent an alternative and competing liberal vision for maintaining the fight against growing wealth inequality, at a time when such measures were losing support among white voters. Although Kennedy strongly endorsed the War on Poverty's mission, he became increasingly convinced that it was incapable of bringing the positive, long-term, and structural economic change to the nation's ghettos that they so badly needed. By failing to create jobs or tackle urban blight, the War on Poverty, Kennedy argued, left two important root causes of urban disorder, past and future, virtually untouched. The CDC was a nonprofit, tax-exempt organizational model intended to address these limitations and help channel the creative energy of urban black communities into the revitalization of the nation's ghettos. Kennedy's vision for remedying urban poverty rested on the expansion of private enterprise in ghetto communities by inducing external businesses to relocate to the inner cities and by supporting entrepreneurship among local blacks. Capitalism (as an engine of urban regeneration and as a source of jobs, investment capital, and local taxes) was fundamental to Kennedy's schema for inner-city economic development.

Senator Kennedy's CDC strategy was also intended to shape black activism in the nation's turbulent urban centers in a number of important and overlapping ways. Programs for the physical and economic rehabilitation of black ghetto communities were intended to swell the black middle class and develop a conformist and conciliatory urban black leadership from its expanded ranks. Spreading prosperity and core American values, Kennedy believed, would also inhibit the growth of anti-American radicalism, helping ease racial tensions in the longer term. Furthermore, Kennedy's plans also sought to co-opt and nurture the inchoate and growing black radicalism in the nation's cities by involving militants in the CDC's efforts to bring positive change to ghetto communities. This process, he hoped, would bring black militants—and the disaffected black urban youth who might follow them—closer to the mainstream society and institutions with which so many of them were disillusioned. As such, Kennedy's efforts ultimately offer an excellent example of what Devin Fergus has called the "interplay" between liberalism and Black Power.[2]

Kennedy's ideas soon received backing from other significant sources. Just as the Watts riots had spurred Kennedy into action, they also convinced the Ford Foundation that new approaches and greater effort were needed to

FIGURE 3. Senator Robert Kennedy discusses school with young Ricky Taggart of 733 Gates Avenue in Bedford-Stuyvesant, February 4, 1966. Photograph by Dick DeMarsico. Courtesy Library of Congress, Prints and Photographs Division, New York World-Telegram and the Sun Newspaper Photograph Collection (LC-USZ62–133361).

eradicate inner-city deprivation and blight. Kennedy's CDC blueprint for urban reform was eagerly taken up by the foundation, which, realizing the limitations of War on Poverty organizational models (which the foundation itself had played such an important role in producing), agreed that "efforts to deal with depressed areas must be comprehensive and long-term; social, physical, environmental, and economic redevelopment efforts are all required." CDCs were an especially promising development, the foundation explained, because they united the principles of local control and self-determination with a more comprehensive program for urban redevelopment that promised to "increase jobs and income, to improve housing and secure better services from local government, business and utilities, and foster a sense of hope in communities that have been stagnant or deteriorating." The foundation would ultimately become the biggest nongovernmental backer of CDCs in the nation.[3]

Kennedy's emphasis on economic development was seized upon by other leading national figures. During his campaign for the White House in 1968, Republican presidential nominee Richard Nixon offered a program for "black capitalism" that would direct federal support and contracts to existing black businesses as well as fostering the creation of new ones. On March 5, 1969, shortly after assuming his position in the White House, Nixon broadened its scope to include all minority groups by issuing an executive order establishing the Office of Minority Business Enterprise (OMBE). It would soon become his administration's flagship policy for black Americans. "Encouraging increased minority-group business activity," Nixon announced, "is one of the primary aims of this administration."[4]

These solutions arrived at a vital moment in the ongoing national political realignment, a shift in mainstream public opinion to which they were consciously tailored. Declining public and political support for existing antipoverty interest group politics and protest was highlighted perfectly by the reception given to the Poor People's Campaign (PPC), run by the Southern Christian Leadership Conference (SCLC) in 1968. Intended as an interracial nonviolent direct action campaign of sustained and massive civil disobedience—larger than anything SCLC had ever attempted—the PPC planned to bring more than fifteen hundred demonstrators from across the country to Washington, D.C., to pressure the government into renewing its commitment to and expanding antipoverty and public assistance measures.[5] The campaign's primary focus was the creation of jobs for the poor. However, whereas the solutions put forward by Kennedy and Nixon rested on increasing the role of the private sector, the PPC demanded interventionist federal action. As SCLC's Reverend Ralph Abernathy wrote to Secretary of Labor Willard Wirtz, "We say the system must change and adjust to the needs of millions who are unemployed and under-employed. Government must lead the way as the employer of first resort." The PPC also urged greater federal spending to improve housing, health care, and education, as well as giving the poor greater control over manpower training, antipoverty, and urban renewal programs. With the ranks of PPC supporters and demonstrators packed with welfare mothers and NWRO activists, another key demand was that the freeze on AFDC payments passed by Congress in 1967 (itself a sign of the political tide turning against liberal welfare politics) be immediately lifted.[6]

On May 12, 1968, in the wake of SCLC leader Martin Luther King Jr.'s murder the previous month, PPC demonstrators arrived in Washington and set up an encampment, known as "Resurrection City," on the National Mall to reassert their commitment to the fight for racial and economic justice. Local demonstrations in twenty major cities nationwide were coordinated to coincide with those in Washington. The reception they received was telling. Not only was the media broadly critical of the PPC, but, as Gerald McKnight has explained, the FBI conducted a "sleeves-rolled up campaign" with "extra firepower" against the PPC at the behest of "Capitol Hill lawmakers and responsible government officials."[7] In championing the cause of redistributive politics in the pursuit of economic justice, SCLC and the PPC found themselves preaching to an increasingly hostile political mainstream. Kennedy's and Nixon's prescriptions for black advancement—focused instead on the capitalist development and improvement of ghetto communities—were far more in step with the nation's changing political landscape.

This turn in public policy also came at a pivotal moment in the black freedom struggle and presented African Americans with new opportunities to articulate their own visions of political and economic empowerment and urban rehabilitation. Black enthusiasm for new approaches emerged from the failure of public policy, civil and voting rights legislation, and existing activism to meet these aspirations, aspirations that had underpinned long-standing battles for access to better jobs, housing, and education, and for political empowerment, in black urban communities across the nation. These battles, which overlapped and intertwined with civil rights activism, had been further illuminated by African American communities' clamor for control of antipoverty programs, and found a new voice in the emergence of the "Black Power" slogan in mid-June 1966.[8]

Although historians were slow to address the relevance of these alternative public policies to African American communities' struggles against racial and economic inequality (and the trajectory of U.S. politics), recent years have seen the publication of some important work.[9] CDCs have received relatively little attention from historians, but this is beginning to change. Recent scholarship has addressed the ways in which African American–run CDCs in Rochester, Cleveland, Newark, and Chicago challenged local economic underdevelopment, powerlessness, and urban decay.[10] This chapter builds on that work by exploring a number of black organizations (many of them CDCs) that engaged with the economic development and capitalist venture theories put forward during the mid- to late 1960s. These organizations often moved beyond narrow definitions of community and economic development by also using their programs to foster racial pride and unity, celebrate black history and culture, and promote greater community self-determination. In the process, these African American–run and –controlled organizations, dedicated to urban rehabilitation and building local black economic power, helped to institutionalize important aspects of the Black Power mission within the mainstream of American life. Collectively, they help illuminate the different ways in which the negotiation of Black Power ideology, through these community organizations, translated into the everyday lives of urban blacks.

This chapter begins by exploring the challenges faced in attempts to revive the nation's ghettos, then it assesses the trajectory of Kennedy's CDC program emerging from the failures of the War on Poverty, and outlines the CDC strategy's broader socioeconomic and political mission. An in-depth and extended case-study follows of the nation's first CDC, the Bedford-Stuyvesant Restoration Corporation (BSRC). This narrative is punctuated by a discussion of Nixon's theory of black capitalism and its reception, along with Kennedy's designs, among the Black Power community. After exploring the history of Restoration, attention is then turned to similar organizations in New York and Los Angeles that, like BSRC, helped to shape a mainstream vision of Black Power as they operated at the intersection of community activism, the Black Power movement, the private sector, liberal foundations, elected officials, and the War on Poverty.

REIMAGINING THE WAR ON POVERTY: RFK AND THE COMMUNITY DEVELOPMENT CORPORATION

Mainstream political engagement with Black Power owed a great deal to the supposed shortcomings of existing efforts to tackle inequality. Kennedy's CDC strategy was consciously directed toward addressing the economic underdevelopment and physical decline of the inner cities, two interrelated problems that he believed the War on Poverty failed to address. Indeed, neither issue came under the purview of those primarily responsible for the antipoverty legislation—social scientists and Cold War liberal policy makers of the 1950s and early 1960s. As discussed in chapter 1, academic research into urban problems focused on the human side of the growing urban crisis, while policy makers broadly accepted "culture of poverty" theories that explained urban decline as the natural result of socioeconomic and demographic changes wrought by white flight. As a result, both groups tended to overlook the deep-rooted and structural nature of urban decay and inequality in America's ghettos and their relationship to public policy.

The pioneering work of historian Kenneth T. Jackson uncovered the role played by New Deal housing policies of the early 1930s in reshaping the nation's racial and economic landscape. The Great Depression decimated the mortgage market, resulting in multiple bank failures and widespread foreclosures. In a bid to return stability and, above all, profit to the housing market, the Roosevelt administration created the Home Owners Loan Corporation (HOLC) in 1933. Across the United States, HOLC agents, in league with local property and financial interests, instituted an ostensibly qualitative assessment practice that subdivided cities into numerous communities. This process, called zoning, made the racial homogeneity of a community a primary factor in its grading, critically linking a neighborhood's racial composition and its property values. Communities with relatively new buildings and a white middle-class population were usually designated as "A"-grade neighborhoods, identifying them as highly desirable and secure investment environments. Areas with aging property or a significant nonwhite population received the lowest two grades, "C" and "D," which labeled them areas of bad financial risk. Dilapidated, poor white neighborhoods often, therefore, received low ratings (in particular immigrant ethnic communities, especially those with majority southern and eastern European populations). Any area with a concentrated black population, however, was invariably classed as "D" grade and was colored red on HOLC maps, giving rise to the term "redlining." [11]

Zoning had a dramatic impact on the demographic make-up and socioeconomic geography of the nation's cities for two main reasons. First, it actively incentivized white flight to the suburbs. In cases where racial prejudice was not the primary inspiration for whites' migration from racially mixed inner-city neighborhoods to white suburbs, the threat that racial integration posed to the value of their homes often proved sufficient. Likewise, racially restrictive housing covenants and the fierce resistance of many white communities to residential integration grew from both racial prejudice and fear of financial loss. Moving to a newly built home in a racially exclusive white suburban community was made all the more enticing—and afforda-ble—by the long-term, low-interest, federally subsidized mortgages that the government made available to millions of white home buyers. The endemic and aggressive discriminatory practices of real estate agents who preyed on fears at the prospect of integration helped to accelerate and sustain the white exodus, delivering handsome profits for vested financial and property inter-ests in cities across the nation. Second, these same circumstances were the catalyst to selective deindustrialization, as vast numbers of business owners across the country followed in the footsteps of white home owners and aban-doned the cities for the suburbs.[12] As David Freund has explained, New Deal federal housing policies created a "state-regulated and state-funded system of home finance" that not only encouraged but, in fact, "explicitly required appraisers and lenders to maintain and further promote residential segrega-tion." In the process, HOLC institutionally enshrined and fueled the dis-criminatory racial politics of housing that would prevail for the following half century and beyond.[13]

If one corollary of zoning was the suburban aggregation of wealth, high-quality schools, leisure facilities, commercial outlets, and expanding employ-ment opportunities, then it had the direct opposite effect on the nation's ghettos. As Craig Wilder has explained, for African Americans everywhere, the redlining of their communities had a number of pernicious consequences: it decreased neighborhood property values, made it virtually impossible for blacks to obtain affordable home finance, and effectively restricted their scope for residential mobility to other redlined neighborhoods. Furthermore, zoning spurred disinvestment from redlined areas as businesses, jobs, capi-tal—and even municipal services—abandoned the inner cities, turning the nation's ghettos into virtual economic wastelands.[14]

Zoning produced numerous other disadvantages for ghetto communities. First, inadequate local education and the general absence of local jobs paying decent wages formed the root of vicious cyclical poverty in the nation's ghet-tos. Second, ghetto areas became an unappealing environment for main-stream retail firms. As a result, businesses in ghetto areas tended to be small-scale, owner-run operations, and few in number. They were often in the hands of nonlocal (usually white) merchants who took advantage of local residents. The net effect, as a 1967 government report explained, was that "many low-income community consumers pay higher prices for and receive lower quality housing, food, clothing, furniture, appliances, medicine, and other goods and services than their neighbors in more advantaged communities." Furthermore, the report concluded, redlining (which branded ghettos "high risk" investment areas) converged with exploitative commercial practices to ensure that "the low-income consumer is often forced to rely for credit and loans on loan sharks or unscrupulous merchants whose credit charges are often considerably higher than the legitimate financial institutions to which he is denied access." [15] These businesses were a source of considerable resentment in many ghettos and became primary targets of looting and destruction during the widespread urban rioting of the mid- to late 1960s.[16]

Urban decay was also inextricably bound up with the federal government's housing policies. Lacking capital resources and cut off from affordable home finance and credit options, most ghetto residents could view home ownership only as a distant dream. The vast majority of residential property in most ghettos (aside from public housing) was owned by nonresident private landlords, many of whom were discouraged from properly maintaining their properties by redlining's deleterious impact on local property values. Many let their buildings go to ruin with tenants in them; others abandoned their properties altogether, with many becoming firetraps and centers of gang activity and drug use.[17] Seeking to maximize profits, ghetto landlords habitually overcrowded their properties, often severely. For example, Atlanta's black ghettos occupied only 20 percent of the city's residential land but housed nearly 45 percent of its population.[18] These commonplace practices accelerated the decline of America's urban centers.

Despite acute awareness of the problem, city governments generally committed little energy to enforcing housing codes in either privately owned slums or their own public housing stock. The apparent collusion between unresponsive municipal officials and so-called slumlords led many ghetto residents to one inescapable conclusion. As a CORE report from early 1965 suggested, "A government such as New York's, which provides only enough [housing] inspectors to examine every structure in its jurisdiction once every nine years, has implicitly joined the landlords." [19]

As far as Robert Kennedy was concerned, dealing with urban communities' economic underdevelopment and degeneration—two of the biggest concerns of their residents—required specific programs that targeted them. The War on Poverty, he believed, promised to solve neither problem because, as a product of the social science–grounded approach of liberal policy makers during the 1950s and early 1960s, it aimed at improving services and reforming people rather than transforming the economic structures that underpinned and reinforced inequality.[20] Many community organizations created under or funded by the War on Poverty reflected this mission. Few did so better than the Westminster Neighborhood Improvement Association (WNIA) in Watts.

Established in November 1960, Westminster began life as a quasi–social service agency aimed at helping local families. Mirroring the growing national concern with juvenile delinquency, the organization's formative years were spent working with local parents and youth—particularly those in the Hacienda Village, Jordan Downs, and Nickerson Gardens public housing projects—toward "the solution of neighborhood conditions and problems such as school dropouts, youth and adult unemployment and community services." These goals were pursued through a range of programs and services, including intensive counseling, home visitation, social group work, and "opportunities for informal education and experiences to improve personal skills, family relations and parent functioning." Their overall aim was to help "strengthen families and encourage hope for the future."[21]

Efforts to improve the educational attainment of local children came through a one-on-one tutorial program set up in 1964 that united talented young volunteer college students with local parent groups and thousands of local children in elementary and high schools in Watts.[22] In the aftermath of the riots, Westminster was awarded federal funding and quickly began to grow. Starting with just two staff members, within six years WNIA had eighty-two employees working at greatly expanded facilities.[23] WNIA used a $1 million OEO grant to initiate the Youth Training and Employment Program (YTEP), designed to place 650 young people from Watts into "meaningful employment" annually. According to WNIA chief Archie Hardwick, the program targeted high school dropouts and graduates who "lacked the basic educational skills required to achieve financial independence and personal growth." It also involved "attitudinal education" meant to prepare enrollees for specialized manpower development training, job placement, or a return to school.[24] Community organizing efforts were directed by Westminster's "community aides," who advised local families about available programs and services and, as one aide explained, encouraged locals to "form neighborhood councils and discuss problems they would like to help do something about."[25]

In the scope of its programs, Westminster was broadly typical of many War on Poverty community organizations, such as the neighborhood service centers (discussed in chapter 1) that formed the backbone of Atlanta's antipoverty program. In New York, HARYOU-ACT and MFY also operated on the same premise (hardly surprisingly given that HARYOU-ACT officials traveled to Los Angeles in late 1964 to oversee WNIA's program development, staff training, and OEO grant proposals).[26]

Westminster did stretch beyond the War on Poverty's narrow vision of social service, education, and job training delivery, and became an important part of the changing (and increasingly Black Power–oriented) post-riots local cultural scene. Prominent black cultural nationalist Ron Karenga gave lessons on African history and taught Swahili to local children in Westminster's community center. Furthermore, Westminster helped establish the Watts Writers Workshop, a program inspired by the New Deal's Federal Writers Project and run by Hollywood screenwriter Budd Schulberg. The project gave local youth the chance to develop and demonstrate their artistic and literary skills, thereby undermining the prevailing "culture of poverty" theory that informed policy makers' analysis of rioting and of the ghetto itself. The Watts Writers Workshop, historian Daniel Widener has argued, reflected local commitment to a cultural liberalism that "linked politics and aesthetics as clearly as subsequent Black Arts Movement and Black Power activists did."[27] Furthermore, in mid-April 1966, WNIA set up the Watts United Credit Union (WUCU), the first California credit union to be organized under a grant from the OEO. Serving more than seventy thousand locals from a twenty-five-block area, WUCU helped many Watts residents attain low-interest loans otherwise unavailable to them.[28] In doing so, Westminster demonstrated the eagerness among urban blacks to use the War on Poverty to pursue their own programmatic vision for cultural enrichment and economic empowerment—a feature characteristic of the CDC-type organizations examined later in this chapter.

Westminster's efforts certainly proved popular with local people and its programs had a transformative and empowering effect on some in the community. As WUCU employee Carl Rucker explained: "Westminster has really changed my life. I'm starting to see Watts as a community with hope. [...] Given the opportunity I've seen a lot of people change through these antipoverty programs."[29] By helping to improve local social services, widen access to credit, and increase local opportunities for employment training, remedial education, and cultural enrichment, Westminster made itself an important institution in the eyes of many Watts residents.

Despite these positive contributions, however, organizations like Westminster nevertheless encapsulated the War on Poverty's shortcomings. While job training might find jobs for thousands of unemployed black inner-city youths, it would fail to reach tens of thousands of others. Moreover, such programs did nothing to address the virtual absence of jobs in ghetto areas, a quandary that did not go unnoticed in the black community. As Watts NAACP leader Edward Warren asked, "You take and train them, and then where are they going to go, what are they going to do, where are they going to find a place to fit in?" [30] Credit unions like the WUCU could help reduce local people's exposure to predatory lending practices, but alone they offered very limited potential for broader local economic change. Without proper enforcement of housing codes and the construction of affordable new housing, the iniquitous slumlord-tenant relationship would continue to predominate. The problems that social welfare programs targeted would persist if the structural disadvantages that helped produce those problems remained unchallenged. Similarly, community organizers battling those problems were fighting an unwinnable war. The War on Poverty had demonstrated and invigorated African Americans' fervent desire for urban improvement, greater self-determination, and economic empowerment, but had failed to provide them with tools that could bring substantial progress toward achieving those goals. As prominent Black Power advocate and Westminster YTEP recruiter Tommy Jacquette argued in mid-1967, "With all the talk and meetings, and the expensive antipoverty machinery, we're right where we were two years ago. What the white people call improvement is nothing but tokenism. It's like the patient is in danger of bleeding to death but all the Man can think of is to apply a Band-aid." [31]

With anger and disillusionment turning to unrest, Senator Kennedy was keen to find a more comprehensive solution to the problems of black inner-city poverty, economic underdevelopment, and urban blight that would meet the demands and engage the energy of increasingly restive ghetto communities. In the six months following the Watts riots, Kennedy's ideas crystallized into a coherent plan of action. The senator detailed his vision in a series of three speeches in January 1966. "Wiping out the ghetto," he declared, was "essential to the future of the Negro and of the city itself." It was a task, he argued, that the federal government could not accomplish alone. He called for "a total effort at regeneration" that mobilized "the skills and resources of the entire society, including all the latent skills and resources of the people of the ghetto themselves, in the solution of our urban dilemma." The answer, he believed, was the community development corporation (CDC), a tax-exempt, not-for-profit body able to receive and spend federal antipoverty funds, an entity that would be set up in urban poverty areas to give overall direction to specific programs for their physical and economic regeneration.[32] If pioneered successfully, Kennedy hoped, his CDC strategy would help reorient national policy away from the seemingly ineffective and politically divisive approaches of the War on Poverty.

Kennedy also harbored grander political ambitions, as growing domestic discontent with Lyndon Johnson's presidency emboldened potential challengers to his renomination in 1968. Although Kennedy had become a senator only in 1964, the presidency, as Johnson feared, was his long-term goal. Long-standing rivalry and animosity between the two men worsened as Kennedy's criticism of the Vietnam War and its impact on domestic affairs grew. As historian and Kennedy confidante Arthur Schlesinger Jr. has suggested, once conflict in Southeast Asia started to envelop the Great Society, Kennedy decided to strike out on his own, hoping to boost his political profile in the process. However, as much as Kennedy's developing political platform was a calculated effort to enhance his prospects for the presidency by expanding his support base among poor, minority, and white liberal voters, it also reflected a deep, genuine, and growing personal concern with the social and economic impact of poverty and racism in the United States.[33]

The federal government's role in the fight against poverty, Kennedy believed, needed to be reassessed. Convinced that the long-term salvation of the inner cities could not (and should not) be achieved with government funds alone, Kennedy challenged American industry and business to bring their "ingenuity" to the task at hand and "become a generator of social change and improvement" in the nation's slums. The process of urban rehabilitation, Kennedy argued, could itself be an immediate and sizable source of jobs for ghetto residents, especially for young unemployed black men—the very group that had been so prominently involved in the destruction of Watts. Sponsorship of the construction and rehabilitation of housing, when paired with the extension of affordable home finance credit options to local families, was designed to increase local levels of property ownership and also reduce absentee landlordism. Finally, physical regeneration of the ghetto was also intended to make it a more conducive and appealing environment for business, and this objective dovetailed with a more direct program for boosting inner-city economic development. External businesses would be offered inducements to relocate to the ghetto, and local private enterprise was to be facilitated and supported, financially and otherwise. Together these programs and initiatives would be critical to developing the commercial vitality of the ghetto and expanding employment opportunities for its residents—

things the War on Poverty had failed completely to do.[34] Assigning the private sector a major role would also allow government to share costs and workload while ensuring a smaller role for inefficient federal and local government bureaucracies. This, in turn, would help protect Kennedy's plans from the "guerilla skirmishes of local politics," which he felt had undermined the War on Poverty so seriously. Moreover, this approach promised to mitigate the disapproval of conservatives vehemently opposed to an activist federal state and public spending, and of a white public increasingly disinclined toward the redistributive politics of welfare liberalism.[35]

Working closely with liberal Republican and fellow New York senator Jacob Javits, Kennedy helped produce an amendment to the Economic Opportunity Act that installed his CDC blueprint in the War on Poverty's legal framework. Called the Special Impact Program (SIP), it was designed to allow for CDCs to receive additional government funding for economic development programs that created local jobs and provided vocational training to prepare long-term unemployed residents for those jobs. For example, a medical health care facility to be constructed in a poor community not only would provide employment for locals in the process of construction but, through the provision of appropriate training and educational opportunities, would also, upon completion, be staffed by local residents.[36] The Kennedy-Javits amendment, as it was known, provided significant funding for CDCs across the country in the following years and codified Kennedy's efforts to reorient the War on Poverty toward job creation and urban regeneration.[37]

Kennedy also envisaged important political consequences as flowing from the rehabilitation of urban slums and their economies. The desperate conditions of ghetto life threatened to alienate legions of urban blacks from mainstream U.S. society and make the inner cities a breeding ground for extremism. As Kennedy warned shortly after the Watts riots, "The army of the resentful and desperate is larger in the North than the South, but it is an army without generals—without captains—almost without sergeants." Kennedy criticized southern civil rights leaders and the black middle class for not reaching out to the growing black urban underclass. Their failure to do so, he argued, meant that demagogues had "often usurped the positions of leadership" in ghettos across the country. Kennedy's CDC blueprint, therefore, was intended to encourage the development of moderate black leaders as a counterbalance to the appeal of violence or political radicalism among the desperate and disadvantaged. Cultivating a new urban black leadership, Kennedy reasoned, could be achieved only by giving black communities a greater degree of control in shaping their own destiny. "We will be tempted to run these programs for their [the poor's] benefit," he argued, but "it is only by inviting their active participation [. . .] that we can help them develop leaders who make the difference between political force—with which we can deal—and a headless mob." [38]

The middle class, Kennedy believed, represented the best hope for developing responsible, moderate ghetto leadership, and the preexisting core of middle-class blacks in Bed-Stuy (reflected in its relatively high level of residential owner occupancy of 15 percent, compared to only 2 percent in Harlem) made the neighborhood particularly suitable for his strategy of embourgeoisement. Accordingly, Restoration's focus on developing Bed-Stuy's economy, physically rehabilitating the neighborhood, and making affordable financing available to local residents was intended to stabilize the existing middle class and expand it by lifting other residents up from poverty. Restoration was clear in its belief that the black middle class was "the foundation on which growth and opportunity for the entire community depend." The wider emphasis on private enterprise and economic opportunity would also foster local entrepreneurship and help nurture American middle-class and reformist values, drawing urban black society as a whole more fully into the existing American capitalist system and ethos. [39]

Just like the liberal policy makers behind the War on Poverty, Kennedy subscribed to a vision of breadwinner liberalism that identified the employment of black men as the key to black economic and social progress, as well as a vital step toward reducing levels of welfare enrollment. As Kennedy wrote to McGeorge Bundy, head of the Ford Foundation, in early 1966: "No-one—as far as I know—is presently thinking of using their housing or jobs programs as a lever for fundamental social change—for the building of the community, for the reintegration of the Negro family, for the integration of the slum Negro into the ethos of private property, of self-government, of doing what is necessary instead of asking the government to do it." [40]

Molding a more conciliatory and middle-class-oriented black urban society and politics would also require engaging with the growing threat of black radicalism that greatly concerned the young senator. His CDC plans sought to do this in two ways. First, they intended to channel militants' passion and drive for black advancement away from radicalism in what Kennedy saw as a more positive direction, by directly involving them in the endeavor to revitalize their communities. By emphasizing the need for greater black self-determination and for the creation of jobs, economic opportunity, and black business ownership, Kennedy's CDC blueprint was expressly intended to appeal to the demands of urban black communities and militant radicals. Second, Kennedy wanted to reach out to the vast numbers of young, disaffected, undereducated, and unemployed black males in the nation's ghettos. This demographic—long a primary concern of social scientists and liberal policy makers—was also the group to which the empowering and masculinist rhetoric of militants like Malcolm X was most appealing. Indeed, these black males were the key target audience of many Black Power radicals. As Black Panther Party founder Huey Newton later explained, the organization grew from the desire to politicize, and engage the potential of, the "lowerclass brother" in the nation's ghettos—the "brother on the block," as cofounder Bobby Seale would say—in the service of remaking their communities and resisting white domination and oppression.[41] Kennedy's approach to black radicals and ghetto youth was driven by both his own palpable concern with their cause and a firm conviction that, if properly harnessed, their creative potential would be a powerful tool in the task of improving the nation's ghettos.[42] As he told a Senate subcommittee in August 1966, his CDC program was designed to "meet the increasing alienation of Negro youth." "We must," Kennedy asserted, "work to try to understand, to speak and touch across the gap, and not leave their voices of protest to echo unheard in the ghetto of our ignorance." Their alienation, he warned, came from "a frustration so terrible, an energy and determination so great, that it must find constructive outlet or result in unknowable danger to us all." Kennedy believed that including black male militants in his ghetto regeneration plans offered the best hope of connecting with black urban youth and of drawing both groups toward mainstream American society, and away from the despair and frustration that might breed violence, crime, and urban disorder.[43]

In this respect, Kennedy's intentions seem to accord with Devin Fergus's reassessment of the relationship between liberals and black radicals. Challenging the notion that Black Power led to the disintegration of the liberal consensus, Fergus argues that liberalism actually helped to "bring a radical civic ideology back from the brink of political violence and social nihilism," demonstrating its capacity to "reform revolution."[44] Between January 1966, when Kennedy first outlined his CDC plans, and December of that year, which witnessed the first stages of their implementation, Black Power became a fixture in America's urban political landscape, ensuring that Kennedy's approach to black radicalism would certainly be put to the test in

Bed-Stuy. Kennedy's CDC blueprint proved effective in engaging local Black Power militants, in the process revealing that his vision for tackling urban and racial inequality was underpinned by the same gendered assumptions and biases that guided the War on Poverty.

BEGINNING THE EXPERIMENT IN BED-STUY

Occupying a 653-city-block area, and with close to 450,000 inhabitants, by the mid-1960s Bed-Stuy was America's second-largest ghetto behind Chicago's South Side. If Bed-Stuy had been a city by itself, it would, in population alone, have been the twenty-ninth largest in the country. Although conditions in Bed-Stuy compared to those in the nation's more notorious inner-city slums, they had not always been that way. Less than two decades earlier, in 1950, the relatively salubrious Bed-Stuy had a population over 50 percent white and was home to a large number of upper- and middle-income white families, many of which lived in the large and impressive homes lining its streets. The familiar story of white exodus from the central cities, repeated in so many of the nation's urban centers, also played out in Bed-Stuy, and by the mid-1960s whites constituted less than 10 percent of the area's residents. By then, African Americans were the new majority, representing over 80 percent of the local population, with the remainder consisting almost entirely of recent Puerto Rican immigrants.[45]

Like most of the nation's ghettos in the mid-1960s, Bedford-Stuyvesant exhibited all the classic indicators of extreme social and economic deprivation. It had no hospital and an infant mortality rate nearly twice the national figure. Local schools performed badly, doing what they could with meager resource allocations, and dropout rates in the area were high. Young people who did finish school found decent employment opportunities scarce. The local unemployment rate was nearly 50 percent higher than the city average, and over 42 percent of all men who were employed were in unskilled jobs. The area's median income was $1,500 below the citywide figure, and 70 percent of local families earned less than the $5,400 basic "subsistence" level set by the U.S. Department of Labor, with 36 percent earning less than $3,000 annually.[46] Despite its sizable middle-class core, then, poverty was deeply entrenched in Bed-Stuy and presented a formidable challenge.

To give his Bed-Stuy experiment the best chance of success, Kennedy sought the backing of other important groups. The support of the Ford

Foundation and other philanthropic organizations reinforced the project's liberal identity and widened its financial base. Key New York Republicans and fellow liberals Senator Javits and Mayor Lindsay were invited on board in the belief that with city hall's blessing and bipartisan political support (which several of the foundations involved had stipulated) the project would be insured against political attack. Despite promising to be of little political benefit to either, both Javits and Lindsay threw their weight behind the plans, and their links to New York's Republican-dominated business community were vital in Kennedy's attempts to bring yet more powerful whites into the equation. Assisted by Javits, Kennedy assembled a stellar cast. Prominent business leaders, lawyers, and financiers from the upper echelons of New York society, including investment banking guru Andre Meyer and former secretary of the treasury C. Douglas Dillon, pledged themselves to the cause. Beyond the extra gravitas, expertise, and business acumen they would bring to the project, Kennedy hoped their involvement would set an example for the wider American business community.[47]

With all the pieces seemingly in place, Senator Kennedy finally announced the creation of the Bedford-Stuyvesant Renewal and Rehabilitation Corporation (R&R) and its sister organization, the Bedford-Stuyvesant Development and Services Corporation (D&S), at a CBCC convention on December 9, 1966, just over ten months after his first tour of Bed-Stuy. While R&R's board was composed almost entirely of local blacks, the D&S board was made up of the high-profile whites Kennedy had recruited. This all-white corporation was charged with attracting and securing the levels of funding that would allow R&R to pursue plans ambitious and large-scale enough to effect real change in Bed-Stuy. Beyond this, as key Kennedy staff member Thomas Johnston suggested, the D&S board's greatest value would lie in "the perspective of its collective experience" and its ability to "assist in anticipating and dealing with problems as they arise." R&R was the vehicle for developing local leaders and ensuring community participation in the planning and prioritizing of regeneration programs. As Kennedy and his staff described the co-venture to the Ford Foundation, it would be a novel attempt to "produce a new blend of planning action in the nation's second largest ghetto by linking the powerful with those thirsting for power in a unique pattern of working relationships." Having two different boards, clearly separated on racial lines, brought important benefits. Not only did it allow for the "powerful" to guide and influence those "thirsting for power," but a separate corporation for the white businessmen would give them a more clearly defined role and set of responsibilities, helping to sustain their interest in the longer term.[48] R&R was made separate for other reasons. First, Kennedy hoped that the experience of controlling R&R would help set local black politics on a moderate, responsible, and constructive trajectory. Second, it would satisfy CBCC's demand for community participation. Kennedy was keen that R&R should be strongly and unmistakably identified as the community's organization run for, and by, local blacks who were independent of the white corporation but worked alongside it.[49]

Unfortunately, R&R quickly ran into serious problems and was dissolved just four months after its creation, to be replaced in late March 1967 by the newly formed Bedford-Stuyvesant Restoration Corporation. A 1969 Ford Foundation report on Restoration's performance during its first two years shed light on the tumultuous events that led to its birth. The breakdown of R&R, though due to many factors, largely stemmed from a fundamental miscalculation on the part of Kennedy and his staff concerning the prevailing local politics. Negotiating these proved far more difficult than they had imagined.

The first seeds of trouble were sown when Kennedy tasked R&R's chairman, Judge Thomas Russell Jones, with appointing an executive director. Jones, who had been a prominent figure in the local Democratic Party for many years, a state assembly representative, and now a civil court judge, enjoyed a close relationship with Kennedy. In choosing a chief executive for R&R, Jones clashed with a group of CBCC leaders on the R&R board who were determined to play a key role in Kennedy's plans. Five women constituted the core of this leadership group: Elsie Richardson, Lucille Rose, Louise Bolling, Almira Coursey, and Constance McQueen. Friction between this group and Jones, Kennedy, and the senator's staff intensified as it became increasingly clear that the group were going to be denied the central role in the organization they believed they deserved. Tensions reached a climax at a meeting on March 30, 1967, when Jones attempted to expand R&R's board membership to both increase its representativeness and dilute the power of the CBCC female leadership. According to reports, when the group refused to support him, Jones "lost his cool" and castigated the women for being a "matriarchy" that was trying to "emasculate" him. In doing so, Judge Jones echoed sentiments shared by others in Bed-Stuy. Local militants, including Brooklyn CORE leader and Black Power firebrand Sonny Carson also resented CBCC's female leaders, believing they exerted undue influence over the organization, denied black men the chance for leadership, and skewed the

CBCC's priorities and activism toward middle-class concerns rather than those facing Bed-Stuy's majority of poor and working-class residents.[50]

The animosity toward the CBCC female leaders expressed by Judge Jones and Carson was informed, at least in part, by a broader debate over the place of African American women in contemporary black society that had been amplified less than two years earlier by the release of a controversial government report entitled *The Negro Family: The Case for National Action*. As black feminist activist and intellectual Angela Davis has argued, the Moynihan Report, as it was known, "directly linked the contemporary social and economic problems of the Black community to a putatively matriarchal family structure." Ultimately, as Davis has asserted, the report placed the "absence of male authority among Black people" at the heart of a "tangle of pathology" in America's ghettos. The report's solution, Davis continues, was the reintroduction "of male authority [. . .] into the black family and the community at large." In the process, Moynihan voiced the gendered assumptions underlying liberal policy makers' view of the War on Poverty and breadwinner liberalism. Furthermore, as historian Steve Estes has suggested, because the report was released in the immediate aftermath of the destruction of Watts in August 1965, it came to be seen as the White House's official analysis of the urban disorders that shook the nation during the mid- to late 1960s. As a consequence, rioting—an activity in which young black urban males were primarily implicated—came to be explained in part by the lack of male leadership in the nation's black urban communities. This discourse of stigmatized black female dominance and emasculated black manhood, bearing the federal government's imprimatur, was an important backdrop to the discord between Kennedy, Judge Jones, Carson, and the CBCC women. As an anonymous, presumably male Restoration source quoted in the *New York Times* said of the boardroom struggle: "The situation really confirms all that's been written about the power of the matriarchy in Negro communities, and the resentment many men feel about it."[51]

Ultimately, CBCC and their female leaders, though widely representative of the local community, did not have the respect of local black militants, whose support Kennedy had prioritized for a number of reasons. First, he envisaged that the involvement of male black radicals would help tie them and their supporters to moderate community leaders, the growing black middle class, and mainstream society. Second, Kennedy believed that men like Carson would be far more useful than CBCC's female leaders in helping the organization connect with the area's black male youth. Finally, getting the "most vocal and dissident elements in the community" on board, and keeping "a tight rein over" the part they played, would, at the very least, help constrain their potential to criticize the effort. Attempting to justify their exclusion, Thomas Johnston later advised the CBCC leadership that their organization was simply not "sufficiently representative of the community as a whole to serve as a focus for the development effort."[52]

The solution was the creation of Restoration—with Judge Jones retained as chairman, a wider cross-section of community representatives, and the supposedly "safe members" of R&R brought on board too. Outraged at having been pushed out of Kennedy's plans, the CBCC leaders, along with their supporters in the community, organized a protest rally in support of R&R against the new corporation, an event that drew close to one thousand people. Those who attended heard fierce denunciations of Kennedy and Jones, among others, but the rally was most significant for the manner in which it ended. In bringing Sonny Carson, head of Brooklyn CORE, on to Restoration's board, Jones had sought and been assured of Carson's assistance in shoring up community support for the new corporation. True to his word, Carson and other CORE members turned the rally on its head when they seized the microphone and, declaring Restoration the best possible outcome for the whole community, lambasted the female leadership of CBCC, and R&R, for "emasculating the community and denying us our models of black manhood." The split between R&R and the new corporation was left beyond repair, and as Restoration took its first steps, R&R began to recede into the background.[53]

D&S's executive director at the time, the young investment banker Eli Jacobs, wrote to the Ford Foundation to express his regret that R&R had "proved unworkable due to a small number of women unrepresentative of the community and uninterested in effecting positive change," and assured the Foundation that, with Restoration now taking R&R's place, the whole project was back on track. Jacobs also happily reported that Restoration had appointed an executive director of whom they had high expectations. The man chosen to lead BSRC, Franklin Thomas (Judge Jones's preferred candidate), arrived with impressive credentials. A lifetime Bed-Stuy resident, Thomas had been an assistant U.S. attorney before becoming New York City's deputy commissioner of police, the position he left to join Restoration. Thomas certainly fitted the model of strong black male leadership that some in Bed-Stuy had been calling out for, and his appointment, along with the exclusion of the female leadership group, raised a number of interesting questions about the gender dynamics within Restoration.[54]

Local male opposition to female leadership not only provided a useful common ground for Kennedy and his staff to occupy in their efforts to sideline CBCC's female leaders and cement a working relationship with local black militants, but was also entirely compatible with Kennedy's paternalistic brand of liberalism. Kennedy's own relationship with some of the women in question was strained, as he confessed to Judge Jones: "I have never been dealt with as rudely and abruptly, by anybody—even my worst adversaries—than I have been by some of the women of Bed-Stuy. They take particular delight in accusing me, in harassing me. [. . .] I don't know what to do but I just can't stand it." Kennedy gave Jones the green light to start a new corporation without them: "Whatever way you want to do it," he told the judge, "you do it." Jones later justified his actions by explaining that, although the social pressures on African American men "had led to a larger and larger role being played by black women," the "white society—the dominant society—doesn't have that kind of orientation; it operates on the basis of the leadership of men." [55]

It was a bitter pill for the CBCC leaders to swallow as their years of hard work in relative obscurity appeared to be diminished as Kennedy's project stole the headlines in Bed-Stuy. Clearly the CBCC female leaders' prominent community activism and strong leadership abilities violated the era's gender stereotypes and posed an unwelcome challenge to some local male leaders. For most of the group their deep commitment to the struggle for racial justice and a better city for their families and communities continued well beyond R&R's defeat. While Almira Coursey joined the Restoration board, the others continued their work with CBCC (with Elsie Richardson and Lucille Rose later progressing to high-ranking and influential roles in city government) and persisted in redefining the contemporary societal boundaries of female agency and authority. Restoration, however, was being fashioned in the image of the typical American business, an entity that exuded the national capitalist culture and where male dominance was still the norm. In early 1969, after just less than two years of operation, the D&S board included just one woman alongside ten men, while Restoration could count three female board members out of a total of twenty-six. More than a decade later, in 1981, this gender disparity remained virtually unchanged with five women now included on a twenty-five-strong Restoration board, while a reduced D&S board of five retained its sole female representative. Kennedy's efforts to reshape urban black communities therefore rested upon reinforcing gender hierarchies and stereotypes in the local black community that dominated, and were instated in, the mainstream white society and its political and economic structures.[56]

RICHARD NIXON, BLACK CAPITALISM, AND BLACK POWER

The assassination of Robert Kennedy on June 6, 1968, in Los Angeles sent shockwaves across the nation. Although Restoration and much of the nation mourned Kennedy's death, his vision for black advancement did not die with him. Restoration pushed ahead with expanding its economic and community development programs, while Republican presidential hopeful Richard Nixon appropriated and repackaged Kennedy's ideas. While on the campaign trail, Nixon began touting "black capitalism," a theory founded on increasing financial support (including the allocation of federal contracts) to black-owned businesses, which were few in number. As a 1969 government report revealed, just over 163,000 of the nation's 22,500,000, African Americans owned businesses. These businesses, however, employed an average of only 1.9 people, reflecting their predominantly small scale. This was also true of most nonwhite businesses, which meant that the nation's minorities—17 percent of the population—owned only about 4 percent of its businesses, and these accounted for just 0.7 percent of total sales in the national economy. The development of black businesses had been badly suppressed, discouraged, and limited by the cumulative effect of numerous discriminatory economic patterns, but especially those structuralized by zoning.[57]

The Nixon administration's Office of Minority Business Enterprise (OMBE), therefore, was designed not only to foster new minority businesses but also to help existing ones seeking to overcome difficulties, achieve stability, and expand. In this sense, the OMBE was building on the work of an existing federal agency, the Small Business Administration (SBA), which, following a 1967 congressional EOA amendment, already earmarked half its $2.65 billion loan budget for businesses in ghetto areas. The OMBE did move beyond the SBA's remit, however, by expanding federal procurement from minority-owned firms and creating affirmative action–inspired minority contract set-asides.[58] Whereas Kennedy sought to induce businesses to relocate in ghetto areas, the Nixon administration operated in the hope that boosting the amount of federal contracts going to black and other minority businesses in ghetto areas would naturally result in urban regeneration as more capital flowed into those businesses and communities. As chapter 4 demonstrates, these programs—along with affirmative action, with which they were fused—would become the primary avenue for black economic progress in Atlanta and Los Angeles, both under black political control, during the mid-1970s.

In pinning its "long term hope for the inner-city," as OMBE head Maurice Stans explained, on its success in creating "a viable economic environment in which minorities can achieve economic power through the business mechanism," the Nixon administration's mission overlapped with Kennedy's CDC strategy.[59] As Nixon's lead aide on civil rights matters, Len Garment, later asserted, "The key concept in the President's approach to minorities is "mobility." [. . .] The ability of minorities to choose freely involves economic considerations, which means jobs, ownership of businesses, community economic development, etc." [60] As a result, CDCs received considerable federal support during Nixon's presidency. However, the president's theory of black capitalism and minority business enterprise was far less comprehensive a scheme for inner-city regeneration than that outlined by Kennedy and endorsed by the Ford Foundation. While black capitalism operated in the hope that the growth of black business would result in the amelioration of ghetto communities, Kennedy's CDC strategy specifically directed business toward, and stimulated, urban rehabilitation. As the Ford Foundation suggested, the SBA and OMBE's focus on "the individual or small corporate entrepreneur" was too narrow in scope. Such "frequently marginal and dispersed enterprises," the foundation reasoned, "cannot [. . .] carry the burden of redevelopment." [61]

Nixon's championing of black capitalism went hand in hand with his strong identification with the politics of "law and order." Inspired by the tactics Ronald Reagan used to capture the governor's mansion in California in 1966, Nixon consciously crafted a conservative self-image and rhetoric to appeal to the nation's white "Silent Majority," constantly pitting so-called law-abiding, patriotic, taxpaying voters—the American mainstream— against liberal politicians, racial agitators and militants, countercultural ideals and lifestyles, and antiwar demonstrators. The strategy proved highly effective, as it had for Reagan.[62] "At a popular level," historian Michael Flamm explains, "'law and order' resonated both as a social ideal and a political slogan because it combined an understandable concern over the rising number of traditional crimes—robberies and rapes, muggings and murders—with an implicit and explicit unease about civil rights, civil liberties, urban riots, antiwar protests, moral values and drug use." Conservatives identified the activist, paternalistic liberalism of the Democratic Party as the root cause of these problems and argued that in attempting to cure the apparent ills of society, liberals had succeeded only in making them worse. The answer, Nixon argued, was not funding more liberal social programs, but putting an end to protest and unrest by ensuring respect for the nation's laws and institutions. The Nixon campaign's "law and order" rhetoric tacitly promised voters that his election would see "troublemakers" put behind bars and an advocate of hardworking "middle Americans" installed in the White House.[63] Although an implicitly racialized distinction between the "Silent Majority" and black and other minority groups was embedded in Nixon's rhetoric, his program for black capitalism, as a corollary to his "law and order" message, represented a chance for African Americans to join the "Silent Majority" by eschewing protest and instead focusing on working constructively within the system.

Aside from Nixon's narrower conception of black capitalist development and the divisive political vision that undergirded it, significant parallels existed between Nixon's black capitalist initiatives and Kennedy's CDC strategy. First, both were intended to appeal to urban black communities clamoring for greater self-determination, economic empowerment, and urban improvement. Promoting constructive rehabilitation of the inner cities and integration into the nation's economic mainstream was designed to swell the ranks of the black middle class and win over black organizations and voters, drawing them away from the supposed extremism of groups like the Black Panthers.[64] Second, they were also expressly intended to appeal to urban Black Power radicals who identified with a rich, long-standing, and quasi-conservative strand of black political thought and activism that venerated economic nationalism.

As historians Laura Hill Warren and Julia Rabig explain, the promotion and practice of black business enterprise had deep and broad roots in the twentieth-century African American experience. Booker T. Washington's advocacy of black entrepreneurship, economic cooperation, and self-reliance helped position him as the preeminent race leader at the turn of the century. His closest rival, W. E. B. Du Bois, was similarly supportive of black economic nationalism, a position championed most powerfully by the period's leading black nationalist, Marcus Garvey. The decades prior to the Great Depression in 1929 were a golden age for black businesses when, largely shut out of the mainstream national economy, many flourished by catering specifically to African Americans' social and cultural needs and tastes. As businesses struggled during the 1930s, economic nationalist practices persisted and evolved elsewhere. Cooperative societies and consumer boycott campaigns in northern cities, and the leveraging of New Deal programs to create cooperative farming and land ownership schemes in the South, demonstrated the enduring importance of economic questions to the black freedom struggle.[65]

Over the following two decades, as domestic Cold War politics inhibited much black economic activism, the Nation Of Islam (NOI) worked, as it had since the 1930s, to build collective black economic power and self-reliance through the ownership and operation of community-based black businesses in cities across the country.[66] During the early 1960s, the NOI's vision of economic and racial empowerment was given its most powerful reiteration by NOI minister and leading Black Power ideologue Malcolm X:

> The economic philosophy of Black Nationalism means that in every church, in every civic organization, in every fraternal order, it's time for our people to become conscious of the importance of controlling the economy of our community. If we own the stores, if we operate the businesses, if we try and establish some industry in our own community, then we're developing to the position where we are creating employment for our own kind. Once you gain control of your own economy, then you don't have to picket and boycott and beg some cracker downtown for a job in his business.[67]

Fundamentally conservative in many ways, this kind of vision was underpinned by an insistence on self-reliance, racial solidarity, and mutual support. Black self-determination was predicated on personal responsibility and initiative—and the economic independence promised by business ownership and employment were vital parts of that. It also often involved a firm rejection of government assistance and welfare dependency.[68] This quintessentially masculinist vision was a powerful sentiment within the broader black freedom struggle, as the example of Restoration's founding demonstrated. It was also given voice by black cultural icon and singer James Brown in songs such as "I Don't Want Nobody to Give Me Nothing (Open the Door I'll Get It Myself)," as well as by Malcolm X, who regularly told young, poor urban black men to "get off welfare. Get out of that compensation line. Be a man. Earn what you need for your own family. Then your family respects you. [...] So husband means you are taking care of your wife. Father means you are taking care of your children. You are accepting the responsibilities of manhood."[69]

Reinvigorated during the Black Power era, this masculinist strand of black politics—which bore striking similarities to the business-oriented and socially conservative politics of mainstream white conservatives—fit with both Kennedy and Nixon's strategies, which sought to reify, not challenge, existing gender hierarchies. Indeed, while campaigning for the Democratic nomination in May 1968, Kennedy delivered a pronouncement on the growing welfare crisis that could have come straight from Malcolm X himself. As Kennedy argued:

> The answer to the welfare crisis is jobs, self-sufficiency, and family integrity; not a massive new extension of welfare; not a great new outpouring of guidance counselors to give the poor more advice. We need jobs, dignified employment at decent pay; the kind of employment that lets a man say to his community, to his family, to the country, and most important, to himself— "I helped to build this country I am a participant in its great public ventures. I am a man." [...] The first domestic task of any administration must be [...] to create jobs and put men to work.[70]

While electioneering, Nixon had similarly endorsed the need for "black ownership [...] black pride, black jobs, black opportunity and yes, Black Power in the best, most constructive sense of that often misapplied term."[71] Nixon's appeals did not go unheeded. The most notable success the president-elect found here was in securing the support of Floyd McKissick, the recent head of CORE and one of the nation's leading spokesmen for Black Power. As the work of Devin Fergus, Tim Minchin, and other historians has revealed, McKissick became Nixon's champion for black capitalism in late 1968. McKissick's vision led to the creation in 1973 of "Soul City" in majority-black, rural, poverty-stricken Warren County, North Carolina: the first American town ever planned and constructed by a minority-owned developer. Bringing together state and federal funds, it was an effort to attract private industry and jobs, stem black outmigration, and deliver economic growth to a depressed area, while simultaneously building black economic and political strength (though not at the exclusion of whites). Although Soul City ultimately failed to achieve what McKissick had hoped, it nevertheless demonstrated the appetite among leading Black Power advocates for the state-sponsored development of black communities and the scope that it offered for greater self-determination and economic empowerment.[72]

Programs for remedying racial and economic inequality that rested on community development and the expansion of black business, therefore, shared the gendered assumptions of both liberal policy makers (as the War on Poverty and the Moynihan Report had emphasized) and many in the broader

Black Power movement. They played to a vision of black progress grounded in the renewal and empowerment of black manhood through the responsibilities of business, family, and community leadership. In so doing, they reinforced negative ideas about black female agency by primarily recognizing and consciously privileging the needs of black men. In the process, these policies made an implicit distinction, and judgment, regarding the value of public policy for the cause of black advancement, valorizing programs dedicated (first and foremost) to employing and empowering black men, and echoing conservative opposition to existing welfare state policies intrinsically associated (though not exclusively) with the political and economic rights of poor single black mothers in America's ghettos. This basic dichotomy and narrative heavily inflected debates over domestic public policy and racial inequality throughout the 1960s and beyond. As the final chapter demonstrates, the limits of black political action on poverty in cities such as Atlanta and Los Angeles throughout the 1970s were also fundamentally shaped by this discourse.

Many African Americans, however, rejected solutions that rested on capitalist development, just as contemporary critics of Washington and Garvey and the black Left had consistently done earlier in the twentieth century. Black political journalist Earl Ofari expressed this opposition in late 1968: "The long term effect of a concentrated drive to put more individual black faces in business, will only result in a change in color of the exploiter." The cause of black liberation and empowerment, he insisted, required the replacement of capitalism "with a socialistic system based on humanitarian principles. This would have as its goal the complete equalitarian distribution of the U.S.'s land, wealth, and power among all the people who, after all, have contributed the most toward the building of the U.S. financial empire." All black capitalism offered, Ofari continued, was "a deadend form of a reactionary form of nationalism rather than a real solution to the problems of black people."[73]

For those Black Power groups operating at the most radical and leftist end of the spectrum—most notably the Black Panther Party—black capitalism was completely antithetical to their political worldview, and party leaders recognized the potential for black business development programs to advance a middle-class vision of Black Power, just as Kennedy and Nixon intended. As Eldridge Cleaver wrote in a letter to Stokely Carmichael, former Student Nonviolent Coordinating Committee (SNCC) chairman, in July 1969:

Pigs have seized upon [Black Power] and turned it into a rationale for Black Capitalism. With James Farmer [former head of CORE before becoming an assistant secretary in the Health, Education and Welfare Department] in the Nixon Administration to preside over the implementation of Black Capitalism under the slogan of "Black Power," what value does that slogan now have to our people's struggle for liberation? [. . .] Even though you were right when you said that LBJ would never stand up and call for Black Power, Nixon has done so and he's bankrolling it with millions of dollars. Now [. . .] in effect your cry for Black Power has become the grease to ease the black bourgeoisie into the power structure.[74]

For the BPP, programs promoting black business development promised primarily to bolster a system in need of radical change, while pushing the struggle for Black Power away from revolutionary and redistributive politics and into the nation's political mainstream. Ultimately, however, the Panthers' revolutionary socialist outlook was simply not typical of the wider African American community. As Jeffrey Ogbar has argued, "Among the nation's major black organizations [the Black Panther Party] alone glorified what it called lumpen proletariat culture, seeking to give voice to the voiceless masses of poor urban black people by adopting lumpen speech, culture and politics."[75] Despite their large footprint in the historiography of the Black Power movement, the Panthers were always on the fringe of black political opinion during the late 1960s and early 1970s, and their political philosophy was a key reason for that. Their marginal position was illuminated by an encounter between Cheryl Foster, the housing coordinator of the Harlem branch of the BPP, and a young "street hustler" in May 1970. Recounting the incident, Foster wrote: "He said that most young people in Harlem don't think revolutionary, but capitalist because they love to have money in their pockets and an El Dorado parked out front. He said he liked the BPP but felt that it was just wasting its time."[76]

In a bid to close the ideological gap between themselves and the majority-black community, the Panthers began to soften their dogmatic stance and in June 1971 revised their analysis of black capitalism. Admitting that the party's initial "blanket condemnation" was a mistake, national leader Huey P. Newton explained that he had come to see that "since the people see Black Capitalism in the community as black control of local institutions, this is a positive characteristic because the people can bring more direction and focus to the activities of the capitalist."[77] In doing so, Newton was acknowledging the broad appeal in the black community of mainstream, business-focused approaches to combatting inequality that politicians like Kennedy and Nixon had promoted.

Finally, economic enterprise and community development programs were deliberately sensitive to the shifting terrain of white political opinion during the mid- to late 1960s. By focusing on improving and strengthening black communities and by endorsing black control of their own separate institutions, these policies moved away from the liberal civil rights establishment's emphasis on integrationist goals and strategies, support for which among white voters nationwide was rapidly diminishing.[78] Just as important, although both schemes involved government spending on black ghetto communities (another key source of discontent on the Right), they represented an alternative to the public assistance and welfare state spending on African Americans that was so inimical to conservatives. Government backing of CDCs and minority businesses not only offered the potential for financial return but also promised to encourage and foster the traditional American values of hard work, individual initiative, and self-reliance that, in turn, would undermine the culture of poverty and welfare dependency that many whites imagined as prevailing in ghetto communities. Furthermore, Kennedy's CDC strategy and programs for minority economic development offered the chance to channel the creative energy of ghetto communities away from demonstrations and rioting (another major source of white anger and fear) and into the business of urban revival and black integration into the economic mainstream.

Highly disturbed by the spread of urban unrest, the nation's corporate business community also offered its support for Kennedy's and Nixon's policies. For example, at a White House meeting in March 1969, representatives of the Life Insurance Association of America told Nixon and his advisors that the organization "desired to be a catalyst, bringing private resources back into the ghetto to rebuild," and to help channel the same resources "that developed the suburbs after the war" into improving the nation's inner cities.[79] In May of the following year, the American Bankers Association announced a program that would provide $1 billion in financing for minority businesses by 1975.[80] Greater reliance on the private sector in the solution of poverty offered American businesses potential tax incentives, the prospect of profit and positive public relations exposure, and, most important, a chance to help ease hard socioeconomic conditions in the ghetto, which threatened the domestic peace and urban stability so vital to smooth business operations.[81]

Appealing to middle-class sensibilities and to conservative socioeconomic strands of political opinion among both blacks and whites, these strategies were adapted to survive in a nation shifting to the right and increasingly opposed to integration, welfare state liberalism, and the sustained protest culture of movements for social and economic justice. As Nixon's director of the Office of Management and Budget, Charles Schultz, later explained, the White House's emphasis on minority business enterprise development was designed to "help the administration with minorities, particularly Blacks, without carrying a severe negative impact on the majority community as is often the case with other civil rights issues." [82]

Along with Kennedy's CDC vision, these turns in public policy making presented urban black communities with new opportunities to build on, diversify, and advance their pursuit of racial equality. The following section explores Restoration's programmatic outlook as it developed and extended beyond narrow theories of economic development and came to embody the type of Black Power—more centrist and moderate than radical—that became integrated into mainstream American life. Organizations similar to Restoration—such as the Community Association of the East Harlem Triangle (CAEHT) and the Harlem Commonwealth Council (HCC) in New York, and the Watts Labor Community Action Committee (WLCAC) and Operation Bootstrap (OB) in Los Angeles—are then examined. Run by blacks, and working toward the physical, economic, and psychological uplift of their local communities and environments, these organizations mani-fested racial pride and identity. This affirmation often involved the promo-tion and celebration of African American history and heritage and the crea-tion of forums for the development and expression of the black arts and culture, as well as efforts to erect new, more responsive institutions in black communities. In the process, these organizations illuminated the ways in which black urban communities articulated visions for greater self-determi-nation, economic empowerment, urban improvement, and cultural enrich-ment—visions often shaped by the existing economic and political institu-tions and philosophies that guided their development.

BLACK POWER IN ACTION: THE BEDFORD-STUYVESANT RESTORATION CORPORATION

Perhaps the most significant issue confronting BSRC executive director Franklin Thomas during the organization's early days was coming to grips with the corporation's unusual twin organizational structure. The relation-

ship between the black and white boards was complicated and took time to settle down. Thomas had warned of the dangers of having two separate boards. In a letter to the D&S board in January 1967, shortly after he had first been contacted about the possibility of joining the project, Thomas suggested that "with dual leadership a cynic might well say that the Negro community has a Negro board with a Negro executive director and no money, while the actual work, power and authority reside outside the community." Thomas's fears were certainly realized during the twin corporations' first year of coexistence, during which D&S executive director Eli Jacobs clearly perceived Restoration as the junior partner in the project.[83]

Having D&S dominate proceedings was arguably beneficial for Restoration during its early months while it found its feet, hired a full staff, and built up a list of programmatic priorities. In late 1967, understanding that a dominant D&S would stymie Restoration's long-term growth and development, Kennedy convinced John Doar, former assistant attorney general for civil rights in the U.S. Justice Department, to take over from Jacobs in January 1968. A popular choice in the eyes of the local media, Doar quickly struck up a good partnership with Franklin Thomas, though Thomas still chafed at the dual board structure. Doar's arrival heralded a number of important changes that put the twin corporations on an even footing. Franklin Thomas's salary was increased to match Doar's. Control over disbursement of funds—which effectively entailed programmatic control—had been closely guarded by Jacobs, but became a responsibility shared by Thomas and Doar in April 1968. In addition, all funds were placed into a joint account shared by the twin corporations. Doar also moved D&S into the same offices as Restoration, ensuring that for the first time, both corporations and their staff worked in the same building. While this had always been the plan once construction work on their ambitious headquarters was completed, the interim period had seen the two corporations based in different offices, further underlining their separation. Under Thomas and Doar the two organizations developed an amicable, effective, and productive working relationship that gave Restoration the power and space it needed to grow and overtake D&S as the prime mover of the twin corporations—as Kennedy had intended and as Thomas desired. While Restoration was becoming an increasingly powerful black organization at the boardroom level, its programs in the community were beginning to shape its development into a model of institutional Black Power.[84]

Had Robert Kennedy not been assassinated in June 1968, he would have lived to see his original ideas pursued faithfully by Restoration. Kennedy knew that a great deal of the despair in the nation's ghettos was due to the appalling conditions their residents had to endure. Likened by D&S board member J. M. Kaplan to "a decaying cemetery," Bed-Stuy was a case in point. Revitalizing the ghetto was central to Restoration's mission, and, as Franklin Thomas suggested, the organization adhered to the principle that urban redevelopment was itself "a big industry and the people who ought to benefit from that process are the people who live in that area." True to Kennedy's CDC blueprint, Restoration ensured that as many local residents as possible were employed in its regeneration efforts. Ultimately, Restoration's construction and rehabilitation programs made it one of the neighborhood's largest housing sponsors and landlords.[85]

Beyond the construction of new properties, another integral part of Restoration's plan to rehabilitate Bed-Stuy was the Community Home Improvement Program (CHIP), a popular initiative that reflected the organization's ethos perfectly. Run annually, the scheme offered participating blocks the chance to have the exterior of their buildings completely renovated. All those employed in the process of renovation were local residents receiving on-the-job training. Each block wishing to participate had to meet certain criteria. First, residents had to have formed their own block association. Second, each home owner had to pay a certain fee, regardless of the amount of work being done on his or her property, and a minimum of 60 percent of the home owners on each block had to sign up. Finally, all participants had to pledge to maintain their properties' exteriors and, if necessary, make interior changes, using only local labor. The CHIP demonstrates the ways in which Restoration tied together the area's rehabilitation with the creation of employment opportunities for local residents while working to forge a stronger sense of community and civic pride. Furthermore, as Edward Schmitt has suggested, it was not only the home owners who benefited from the scheme, as the "CHIP workers even began wearing their hard hats as a badge of pride."[86]

Restoration's motto was to make the neighborhood "a place to live, not to leave," and an important corollary to Restoration's housing programs was the help it offered local residents in becoming property owners. A legacy of redlining, the area's reputation among mortgage lenders was so bad that it was almost impossible for anyone, let alone impoverished black citizens, to obtain home finance there. Restoration and D&S endeavored to change the pattern of lending by working with banks and the Federal Housing Authority (FHA) to create a mortgage pool available to owners or occupiers of one- to four-bedroom family dwellings in Bed-Stuy. Under the guidance of D&S board member George Moore, eighty-five banks agreed to participate and collectively provide $100 million in funding. The FHA also agreed to act as guarantor for approved loans. The mortgage pool, described by the Ford Foundation as "potentially the most significant housing program being carried out by the twin corporations," helped make home ownership possible for hundreds of local families. Restoration also bought local residential properties (foreclosures acquired via the FHA) and sold them through a low-income home ownership scheme. Under this initiative, priority was given to applicants who lived on the same block where the property for sale was located. At the very center of Restoration's housing program lay the desire both to regenerate Bed-Stuy and to facilitate property ownership among local black residents, itself a critical step on the way up the economic ladder for many poor African Americans.[87]

Although Bed-Stuy was, as Eli Jacobs suggested, "a marketplace of 400,000—perhaps the most densely concentrated market you will find on this planet," the area's physical rehabilitation and its potential for private enterprise alone would not be enough to attract new residents and businesses. Kennedy's plans, therefore, outlined two other major approaches for developing the local economy. One of these was encouraging large businesses to locate premises in Bed-Stuy and employ local residents. To this end D&S used its influence and connections to help bring a number of sizable businesses into the area. The most notable success story came when IBM, one of America's largest companies, located a new plant in Bed-Stuy in 1968. Of the initial 155 local residents that IBM employed, nearly 40 percent had no high school diploma. It was hoped that, if IBM's venture into the ghetto was a success, other large businesses would follow. As with the mortgage pool, the twin corporations were dedicated to changing attitudes in the private sector: vital, if deep-seated, patterns of discrimination that existed in virtually every aspect of commercial life were to be overturned. Although the number of companies that followed IBM's lead was not as high as the twin corporations would have liked, Bed-Stuy residents at the time nevertheless identified IBM's arrival as a symbol of the positive changes taking place in their neighborhood. The plant went on to grow in size and in 1994 was eventually sold by IBM to Advanced Technological Solutions Inc. (AST), a company set up by a group of the plant's black and Puerto Rican employees, who, with the help of "the city, the local community and IBM," completed a $6.5 million leveraged buyout of the plant. In doing so, AST instantly became "one of the nation's largest minority employee-owned businesses."[88]

The other main thrust of Restoration's economic development program involved promoting and financially assisting business ownership among local residents. Finance was always arranged in cooperation with an external bank, a deliberate tactic designed to start breaking down the reputation of black businesses as credit risks. Technical and managerial expertise was also made available in order to instill good business practices and help new ventures grow sustainably and securely. By late 1972, Restoration had helped provide nearly $9 million to more than one hundred local, black-owned businesses, which had resulted in a number of firsts for Bed-Stuy, including the first black-owned car dealership in the whole of New York State. Restoration also worked to extend opportunities for opening national chain business franchises to Bed-Stuy residents, and in October 1971, much local fanfare accompanied the start of construction on what became the first black-owned and -run McDonalds restaurant. Fostering private enterprise among local residents, as a Ford Foundation report noted, also brought "intangible benefits that flow from the emergence of new black-owned businesses [. . .] the sense of satisfaction that the community derives from such developments is not measurable in economic terms." [89]

While Restoration's efforts to increase levels of black property ownership, to support and finance black businesses, and to improve local employment opportunities were all intended, as their director of economic development, George Glee, declared, to "make the rhetoric of Black Power a Black reality," they are not enough in themselves to consider placing Restoration within a framework of Black Power. As historian Peniel Joseph has suggested, although Black Power encompassed many activities and aspirations, it was characterized by certain fixed core values and goals. These included pursuing self-determination through black political and economic empowerment, the redefinition of black identity, greater racial pride and solidarity, and a critical emphasis on a shared African heritage and history of racial oppression. To develop a fuller understanding of Restoration as an institutional expression of Black Power, therefore, we must now turn our attention to the aspects of Restoration's work that explicitly sought to foster greater racial pride and celebrate African American history and culture, build community solidarity and empower Bed-Stuy residents, and help local blacks shape the development of new institutions in their community. [90]

An example of Restoration's support for the promotion and celebration of black culture and heritage can be found in the Design Works of Bedford-Stuyvesant, which, with a $180,000 loan from Restoration, began life in 1969 as a small silk screen studio with three employees. The company produced textiles, clothing, and jewelry inspired by or based on African designs. Five years later the company had over one hundred staff and an annual turnover in excess of $600,000 and sold its products worldwide. By assisting Design Works, Restoration helped to put local blacks at the forefront of a cultural industry that grew rapidly through the 1970s.[91]

Other aspects of Restoration's work further demonstrated its commitment to advancing and protecting black history and heritage. Between 1827 and 1875 a free black community called Weeksville had existed in Brooklyn, encompassing part of what later became Bed-Stuy. As the area's history increasingly came to light during the late 1960s, Restoration became involved in efforts to preserve the site and, in mid-1973, purchased a number of historic properties on Old Hunterfly Road. Restoration not only saved the site from demolition but, in collaboration with the Weeksville Society, also helped to secure it "New York City Landmark" status. The same buildings on Old Hunterfly Road are now home to the Weeksville Heritage Center, which helps to keep a unique part of Brooklyn's black history alive to this day.[92]

Beyond its emphasis on black history and culture in the wider sense, Restoration was also committed to promoting racial solidarity and positive, constructive relations at the community level. Annual "Soul Sunday" festivals, sponsored by Restoration and other local groups, combined a celebration of black music with the opportunity for local residents to relax and socialize together. A number of "neighborhood restoration centers" established in late 1967 fostered and supervised the creation of new block associations, worked with existing ones to determine and prioritize the community's needs, and encouraged organization around issues of importance. These centers, a vital link between Restoration and Bed-Stuy's residents, helped to empower the local community by giving them the tools they needed to effect change in their own lives. For example, in 1968 a number of the block associations Restoration helped form joined forces with other local groups (including CORE and CBCC) and negotiated with the city to secure a dramatic improvement in their neighborhood's sanitation services—a service that most took for granted but that Bed-Stuy residents had been long denied.[93]

The neighborhood centers also helped conduct voter registration drives, encouraging the growth of African Americans' collective voting strength in Bed-Stuy. Free tax clinics were made available to local residents, and a Tenant Aid program was run that not only educated tenants about their legal rights and responsibilities but also met their emergency needs, including making repairs, restoring essential services, and, if necessary, dealing directly with intransigent landlords on the tenant's behalf. Beyond this, the centers ran summer schools for local children where they were taught practical life skills, performed community service, and enjoyed classes in African culture and languages. The entire thrust of such activities was to help educate Bed-Stuy residents and move them toward greater independence, self-reliance, and responsibility and instill in them the belief that they could begin to deal with their problems and assert their rights, both as individuals and collectively, through the existing structures of American society.[94]

Perhaps the best example showing Restoration as an expression of Black Power can be found in the organization's impressive headquarters, situated on Fulton Street, right at the heart of Bed-Stuy. Restoration's original plans had always intended to give Bed-Stuy the centerpiece it lacked by creating offices that would serve as the community's focal point. The organization hired black architects, construction superintendents, and administrators to carry out the ambitious plans it had for converting a former milk-bottling plant known as Sheffield Farms that the twin corporations had purchased in early 1967. Restoration's commitment to using local residents in all its building schemes resulted in delays, and construction on the site was not finished until 1972; in 1975 it was expanded, taking over adjacent buildings. Restoration Plaza, as it was called, was worth the wait. Once completed, it swiftly became the commercial heart of Bedford-Stuyvesant. More important, though, the Billie Holiday Theater and large art gallery that Restoration Plaza also included made a highly significant contribution to local cultural life. The platform these facilities provided for black artists, writers, musicians, poets, and actors, of all ages, was unrivaled in Brooklyn. Controversial and challenging plays by black playwrights dealing with the experience of poverty and racism in America dominated the theater's program. The art gallery was dedicated to showcasing the work of black artists from Bed-Stuy and around the world. Together their ethos represented a celebration of black art and culture and promotion of its black producers past, present, and future.[95]

Restoration Plaza also included a large auditorium and meeting rooms that served as a physical space for local community groups to conduct their affairs. There is no better example of how Restoration helped the local black community to fashion new opportunities for itself than the events that led to the creation of Medgar Evers College. The creation of an innovative educational affiliate in the area had been an early goal of the twin corporations, and in April 1967 William Birenbaum, formerly of Long Island University, was hired and assembled a team of educators (many of whom were black) to assist in the planning and creation of the new facility. The final plan, for a four-year college to be administered by a community board with significant student representation, had strong community support. D&S board member William Paley played a critical role in persuading the City University of New York (CUNY) to pledge $30 million toward the college's creation. However, fearing that critics would label an all-black campus "segregated," CUNY demanded changes to the plans that Birenbaum was unwilling to accept. In response to this impasse a group of community members formed the Bedford-Stuyvesant Coalition on Educational Needs and Services Negotiating Team and, with the support of Restoration, took over the planning from Birenbaum and continued discussions with CUNY, ultimately securing acceptance of the original plans for the college. Restoration was the community group's base throughout the entire process, and the group benefited from the close involvement of board members Judge Jones and, in particular, Albert Vann, the head of the Afro-American Teachers Association (AATA). The result was the creation of Medgar Evers College, today one of the most respected black educational facilities in New York City.[96]

By working to facilitate the creation of Medgar Evers College, Restoration helped the local community to physically build black institutional power: a place where black teachers taught black children and where direct input into college governance gave parents a greater level of influence over their children's educations, and indeed futures, than ever before. In addition, Vann's AATA held its meetings in the Restoration offices, ran talent schools to help discover and recruit local teachers, and held the first New York City Black Teachers Convention there in May 1972, further underscoring the vital contribution Restoration made to the educational opportunities available to local blacks.[97]

Restoration also came to stand at the center of developments that shaped new political institutions and reconfigured local black political power. In early 1975 around seven hundred local residents gathered in the main "community room" at Restoration Plaza to witness the creation of a new local political organization and to honor Carl L. Butler, a recent addition to Restoration's board, for his election as district leader for Bed-Stuy's 56th Assembly District (AD), a powerful position in local and county Democratic politics. Alongside Butler was Restoration's own Albert Vann, who had just been elected by local residents to the New York state legislature as assemblyman for the 56th AD. Together they launched the Crispus Attucks Regular

Democratic Club, which marked a significant power shift within local black politics (both Butler and Vann has displaced long-standing incumbents). Congresswomen Shirley Chisholm characterized these developments as "part of the wind of change bringing the infusion of new blood in the political system from the national down to the local level." It seemed fitting, then, that such an occasion should take place in Restoration Plaza, perhaps the biggest and most vital symbol of the change under way in Bed-Stuy.[98]

As Restoration's impact on the local community grew over time, its organizational self-image and projected personality changed too. Although D&S may have overshadowed Restoration at the very beginning, this effect proved momentary. Indeed, as Schmitt has suggested, the "balance of power" between the two corporations began to shift in Restoration's favor from as early as mid-1967. With Restoration conducting the overwhelming majority of the twin corporations' business, some Restoration staff began to question the continued need for D&S. As one employee explained in early 1969, he sometimes felt that D&S still existed only to make sure Restoration "don't steal the money." This kind of self-assurance is, arguably, exactly what one might expect from employees of an organization that embodied and exercised literal black power and that meant to keep on doing so. Although the twin organizational structure remained until 2000 (when D&S was subsumed into the Restoration board), it came to play an important part in forging Restoration's image as a black organization. This was evident in the wake of John Doar's departure from D&S in December 1973, when a Restoration source was quick to reassure people that Doar's resignation would "not alter the racial division between the two groups." Whereas in the early days the racially split twin corporation structure had concerned many in Restoration, not least Franklin Thomas, by the time of Doar's exit it had become an integral part of the organization's identity.[99]

Restoration's continued association with controversial individuals such as Sonny Carson reflected its growth as an organization that celebrated its blackness, made no apology for its methods, and unswervingly dedicated itself to the Bed-Stuy community. In late 1968 Carson (already a contentious figure when he joined Restoration at its inception) was prominently involved in the Ocean Hill–Brownsville School controversy along with fellow Restoration board member Albert Vann. As the following chapter shows, this fierce clash between black activists and the white, predominantly Jewish United Federation of Teachers (UFT) over decentralization and community control of public schools was mired in charges of white racism and black anti-Semitism, leaving a bitter legacy for the city. Restoration continued to support Sonny Carson publicly even when, in 1973, he was arrested, tried, and convicted on charges of kidnapping and attempted murder.[100]

Popular with neighborhood youth, and projecting a powerful local image of strong black masculinity, Carson remained a militant, and a part of Restoration, for the rest of his life. As a local journalist wrote following Carson's death in late 2002:

> One would only have to spend a day at his basement office at Restoration Plaza to grasp the pivotal role that Carson played in the socio-political economy of Bedford-Stuyvesant and, by extension, the black community at large. Carson was the elder statesman, the tribal counselor, and the warrior king adorned, staff in hand, in regal Afrocentric garments as he held court and weighed in on matters from the most trivial of domestic affairs to issues of great import to the black diaspora.[101]

In its continued support of and identification with Carson, Restoration's projection of itself was clear and uncompromising: it was concerned, first and foremost, with conforming to the standards and norms of the black community that it represented. In this way, while Restoration had been shaped by the influence of Robert Kennedy and his CDC blueprint, and continued to embody the conventions of the male-dominated national political and economic culture, it was able to move beyond those influences and define its own distinctly black image. For Restoration, conforming to white mainstream society was not absolute and did not mean renouncing the promotion of racial pride and solidarity.

Restoration's history can contribute to our understanding of Black Power as it adapted to mainstream America. Almost everything about the organization was wholly dedicated to empowering local black citizens and improving their living standards. Restoration sought to increase local black property ownership and expand economic and employment opportunities for Bed-Stuy residents by rehabilitating and improving their community, attracting outside investment, and fostering local black entrepreneurship. By the beginning of 1981 Restoration and its affiliates and subsidiaries had directly generated over $250 million for the benefit of Bed-Stuy.[102] On top of this, Restoration's headquarters (whose commercial space has contributed so vitally to the resuscitated Bed-Stuy economy we see today) provided a vital platform for black artists, musicians, playwrights, and actors to work and develop their skills, helping to promote and support the teaching and practice of black art and culture. The critical role Restoration played in saving an important local black historical site for future generations reflected the organization's commitment to the preservation and celebration of African American history and heritage. Neighborhood restoration centers worked to encourage constructive and positive community relations and helped mobilize, educate, and empower local residents to deal more effectively with the challenges of daily life, both individually and collectively. In facilitating the establishment of Medgar Evers College, Restoration helped local blacks create an educational institution that would be more responsive to their needs than any that had preceded it. By the mid-1970s, Restoration Plaza also witnessed important changes in local black politics. The organization, along with some of its most prominent members, sat right at the heart of those changes. Though fundamentally shaped and influenced by the prevailing, male-dominated, corporate capitalist culture, Restoration was still able to pursue its own agendas and associations and forge its own identity, one that celebrated and venerated its blackness. In this way, Restoration can be seen as part of another side of the Black Power movement—beyond the dominant imagery and controversial rhetoric of its most militant exponents—that was at first shaped by, and then began to refashion, the political, social, and economic fabric of mainstream urban America.

BUILDING BLACK POWER:
BEYOND BEDFORD-STUYVESANT

Although Restoration's developmental path cannot be considered typical, it was by no means the only African American organization committed to the regeneration of inner-city communities, the growth of local black political and economic power, the creation of new, locally controlled institutions, and the fostering of greater racial pride and unity. This section looks at four other organizations (some of them CDCs) that flourished during the same period (roughly 1965–1975) and whose missions overlapped with Restoration's to varying degrees.

Across the East River from Brooklyn lies Manhattan, the site of Harlem—New York's most famous black ghetto—the eastern portion of which is home to the Community Association of the East Harlem Triangle (CAEHT). Members of the Chambers Memorial Baptist Church of New York established CAEHT in 1961 to oppose the city's plans to turn a significant section of the East Harlem Triangle into an industrial park, a proposal that threatened to displace more than ten thousand local black and Puerto Rican families. Foremost among the founders was Alice Wragg Kornegay. In 1942, at the age of ten, she relocated to East Harlem from Georgetown, South Carolina, to live with cousins after both her parents had died. Supporting herself through college (where she attained a degree in social work), Kornegay became a pillar of the East Harlem community and one of its most forthright advocates for social and economic justice and local improvement. As CAEHT's first president, Kornegay seized on the opportunity presented by the arrival of antipoverty funds to broaden the scope of the organization's activities. In February 1966, with the help of OEO funding, the group moved to new, larger headquarters. At the opening ceremony, before an audience including many local government and antipoverty officials, Kornegay made clear the organization's intentions: "Let the city be on notice. We intend to press for action on the renewal of our community and along the lines we want, not what they want for us. The time is past where we are willing to let others make our decisions for us. We intend to help ourselves." [103]

In 1967, using OEO funds acquired through the Kennedy-Javits SIP amendment, CAEHT helped spawn the Harlem Commonwealth Council (HCC), a CDC dedicated to the economic development of the local black community. Kornegay joined with a number of prominent local black male leaders to plan and set up HCC, including Columbia University sociologist Preston Wilcox, Isaiah E. Robinson Jr. of the Harlem Parent's Association, Arthur B. Hill (then New York's second highest–ranking black police officer), and Roy Innis, the director of Harlem CORE, who would become CORE's national director the following year. Focused on building up a local black economic base, HCC was intended to complement CAEHT's housing, education, and social service programs. [104]

Similar organizations emerged in South Central Los Angeles in response to the difficult conditions facing local blacks. Foremost among these was the Watts Labor Community Action Committee (WLCAC). As historian Robert Bauman has shown, over time, WLCAC also grew into an organization that evinced many of the core aspects of the Black Power mission, just as Restoration had. [105] Predating Restoration, WLCAC began life under the War on Poverty's Community Action Program. On May 24, 1965, a group of trade union leaders representing more than sixty thousand members in the local area came together with concerned local academics and students to establish an organization that would address the area's worst problems, in particular housing, education, health care, the lack of recreational facilities, and most important, the parlous state of the local economy and severe lack of jobs. The chief architect was Ted Watkins, an international representative for the United Auto Workers (UAW) local who coordinated the involvement of other union leaders, as well as researchers from the University of California's Institute of Labor Relations and local black students from Jordan High School.[106] Watkins would remain at the organization's helm until his death in 1992, during which time WLCAC developed into one of the most important black institutions in South Central Los Angeles. Just as Westminster had, WLCAC grew rapidly, benefiting from the huge influx of federal antipoverty funds into Watts following the August 1965 riots (from an initial $1.3 million in 1964, the figure jumped to $19.5 million in the months after the riots, and peaked at $46.5 million in 1967).[107]

Finally, Operation Bootstrap (OB) provides another example of the urban improvement and black empowerment ethos that permeated many urban community organizations from the mid-1960s onward. Former CORE leader Lou Smith and Korean War veteran Robert Hall set up OB in the aftermath of the Watts riots as a self-help organization focused primarily on providing education and vocational job training and guidance for ghetto youth. OB's philosophy was neatly captured by its motto, "Learn Baby Learn"—a conscious, affirmative reappropriation of the infamous "Burn Baby Burn" slogan that had echoed through Watts during the riots. Unlike other local organizations, such as Westminster and WLCAC, OB saw itself as an alternative to the War on Poverty and was completely opposed to the idea of government funding. Indeed, as Smith later wrote to *Black Enterprise* magazine to correct an error in its previous issue: "You listed our corporation, Operation Bootstrap, as being funded by the OEO. That just ain't so. We never have, and never intend, to accept government funding. That principle is the cornerstone of Bootstrap philosophy." [108]

OB, Smith argued, was dedicated to showing "what determined, hardworking, young people can do for themselves—by themselves." [109] Instead, the organization attracted all its funding from private donations (many from white liberal Angelenos) and from its associations with mainstream businesses including such major corporations as IBM, Shell Oil, Singer, Litton Industries, and Scientific Data Systems. Working out of six buildings in the Watts ghetto, OB offered classes in computer programming and operation, as well as a range of skilled industrial job–related classes using training equipment provided by its business backers.[110] Unlike War on Poverty job training programs, the arrangement between OB and its partner businesses ensured trainees who successfully completed their practical training were guaranteed to graduate to a position with the relevant company afterward.[111] OB's message of self-reliance and its emphasis on private over public funding won strong approval from leading conservative Ronald Reagan, who visited the organization's workshops during the 1966 gubernatorial campaign. Condemning the War on Poverty as liberal Democrats' "'Big Brother' form of assistance government," Reagan affirmed that OB's interest in "helping people help themselves. [. . .] fits in with what I have believed all along." [112]

Like Restoration, all four of these organizations, in one way or another, were dedicated to the physical improvement of their neighborhoods and the creation of new local institutions. In 1968 CAEHT, or the Triangle Association, as it was known, worked with other local groups to produce an urban renewal plan for East Harlem of their own. Submitted to Mayor Lindsay's office, their plan, though not implemented in full, nevertheless prevented the wholesale transformation of the community threatened by the city's existing, 1961 scheme. In their plan's preamble CAEHT described its existence—in language evocative of the rhetoric of radical Black Power groups like the Panthers—as the "the story of a dogged fight of a deprived community for the right to survive." [113] Under Kornegay's leadership CAEHT made a substantial and lasting contribution to socioeconomic life in East Harlem. The association built badly needed local, affordable low-income housing, ran a preschool education program and a Planned Parenthood center, organized local tenants, and trained local people to become welfare inspectors (an effort designed not only to increase employment opportunities but also to mitigate the unpleasantness of existing welfare inspections).[114] In 1974, in collaboration with the community and local black architects and contractors, CAEHT built the East Harlem Center, a $4 million multi-social-service complex that included a child day-care center, a senior citizens care center, and city welfare agency offices.[115] Furthermore, HCC later purchased land for the expansion of a neighborhood hospital and helped construct Harlem's first residential mental health treatment center for teenagers.[116]

In Los Angeles, heavily influenced by his own experiences in New Deal youth programs, WLCAC's Ted Watkins set up the Community Conservation Corps (CCC) following the August 1965 uprising. The CCC provided community service work for those implicated most strongly in the rioting: unemployed young adults and teenage school dropouts. Overseen by local union members and other adult "role models," the CCC aimed to instill a greater sense of discipline and civic pride among its young participants and encourage their personal and social development. The intention was clear: Watts's youth would be engaged in the business of repairing and beautifying their neighborhood rather than tearing it down. Perhaps more significant, as Bauman has explained, the CCC became a vehicle for building racial pride among local youth who explicitly appropriated the symbols and language of Black Power in their work. Through programs like the CCC, WLCAC's dedication to redeveloping and revamping South Central Los Angeles resulted in the creation of eleven urban parks (converted from vacant lots), numerous playgrounds, senior citizens and neighborhood centers, and the renovation of local properties, as well as the planting of more than twenty-two thousand trees in the local area.[117] Much as with Restoration's CHIP scheme, local people (in particular, local youth) were actively engaged in the rehabilitation and improvement of their neighborhoods.

As WLCAC grew, its impressive track record attracted funding from both the Ford and Rockefeller Foundations, allowing further expansion. The organization's youth-focused job training and education program led to the creation of the $2.5 million Urban Residential Educational Center (UREC) in the nearby town of Saugus, forty miles from downtown Los Angeles, with Department of Labor, union, and private foundation funds. Accredited by the Los Angeles City Schools system, UREC was a vocational training and education center that offered courses in "business, automobile mechanics and body repair, culinary arts, horticulture, and stationary engineering." These programs were intended, organizers explained, to "give enrollees the chance to see what being part of the American structure is like, and to begin to lift their sights beyond their narrow lives in the ghetto into new lifestyles and opportunities."[118]

In 1971 WLCAC was designated as a CDC by the state OEO and broadened its program to include housing and local business development. An assembly bill, authored by local black politician Leon Ralph and passed in 1968, enabled WLCAC's housing construction arm, the Greater Watts Development Corporation (GWDC), to initiate a "housing replacement project" designed to help relocate low-income residents displaced from their homes by state highway construction projects. As work on the new "Century Freeway" commenced in 1971–72, GWDC began to build replacement low-income homes for the affected residents.[119] Their first steps in housing were supported by a state grant to build thirty new homes in 1971, while a low-interest $2 million loan from Chrysler Corporation–UAW in 1972 allowed the organization to expand its construction program.[120]

Elsewhere in South Central, Operation Bootstrap built the Honeycomb Child Development Center, which, as sociologist Russell Ellis explains, was created as "a place where the children of the ghetto [. . .] could be cared for, find strong black identities, and get an educational head start on the public school system."[121] OB also offered a number of educational courses for local school children that focused on the improvement of all aspects of literacy and public speaking, mathematics and computational skills, social dynamics, civics, and black history and culture. Classes in Swahili were also offered.[122] Indeed, as the following chapter demonstrates, OB lent strong support to local students' demands for educational reform, by both running black history courses (which local students wanted and which were absent from local school curricula) and providing the physical space for students to meet, plan their protests, and parley with school officials. Furthermore, Smith and Hall later funded the creation of a Black Studies department at local Irvine College from the proceeds of one of OB's most successful business ventures, Shindana Toys.[123]

Economic nationalism—as a route to creating jobs, building a local black economic base, and improving local conditions—was another major underlying principle and concern of all these organizations. In New York, the Harlem Commonwealth Council's focus on developing the local economy stemmed from the economic nationalism of CORE leader Roy Innis, whose influence within HCC grew during the late 1960s. Economic development, Innis argued, should not be narrowly defined as purely "black capitalism" but, rather, was "the creation and acquisition of capital instruments by means of which we can maximize our economic interest." The development of black business was, therefore, fundamentally tied to greater self-determination and economic power for the community as a whole, not just for the individual.[124]

Following the path set down by Innis, HCC strove to develop a local black economic base by gaining control of businesses and the jobs they held, as well as increasing black property ownership in Harlem, a community long dominated by outside interests. By the early 1960s, 96 percent of Harlem's residential properties and 80 percent of its commercial properties were owned by nonlocal people or companies. No African American owned a commercial property on 125th Street, Harlem's main business artery, until 1964. The economic underdevelopment of Harlem was also predicated on the widespread poverty among its residents (one-third were on the city's welfare rolls) and the fact that most Harlem residents who did have a job worked outside the area. As a consequence, money constantly flowed out of Harlem, while little flowed in. Intended to reverse that trend, by the late 1970s, HCC was the largest owner of real estate on 125th Street. The council also committed itself to developing relationships with banks in order to attract greater capital investment to the area. Both HCC and CAEHT explicitly supported Freedom National Bank—Harlem's only black-owned bank—by holding a majority (or, in the case of CAEHT, all) of their accounts with the bank. Throughout the 1970s, greater access to finance allowed HCC to acquire a number of profitable, multi-million-dollar-turnover local businesses, increase their profitability and expand their operations, and thereby create more employment opportunities for local people. After eleven years of operation, HCC's assets had grown from less than $50,000 in 1967 to over $28 million by 1978, by which point it managed fifteen different businesses.[125] In a faltering national economy, and while American manufacturing in particular declined, HCC's business portfolio helped keep jobs in Harlem that might otherwise have been lost.

WLCAC's outlook was founded on the principle that "economic power is the first step on the long road to community stability and personal opportunity," and it was committed to creating a more productive and positive financial climate in South Central Los Angeles. For example, in 1967 WLCAC set up a credit union and consumer advice center that, like Westminster's, brought affordable credit options to local people who had historically been denied them. In mid-1968, at the same time that the Los Angeles BPP was meeting with the Oakland-based national party leaders Newton, Cleaver, Hilliard, and Seale and discussing plans to set up various black-owned and -run "cooperative 'service' businesses, laundries, and grocery stores," WLCAC was already in the process of doing exactly that. Sharing the Panthers' vision of cooperative black business ventures, WLCAC had by the early 1970s created a number of community-owned businesses employing local people. These included "two service stations, two restaurants, a farm, seven supermarkets, a landscaping company, [and] a construction company." As a nonprofit enterprise, WLCAC invested all monies earned from its commercial operations back into its community programs.[126]

Not only did WLCAC's business ventures create local employment opportunities, but many also aimed at making Watts as self-sufficient as possible. In 1967 WLCAC bought a defunct egg ranch and turned it into a poultry farm business. In 1969 the committee expanded operations at its Saugus base (home of the UREC) to include a two-hundred-acre farm and a

FIGURE 4. Service station training at a Watts Labor Community Action Committee–run station at 103rd Street and Central Avenue in Watts, December 14, 1967. Courtesy Los Angeles Public Library Photo Collection, Los Angeles Public Library.

cattle ranch. By selling its produce in WLCAC supermarkets and restaurants in the black community, the organization was able to offer a cheaper, better-quality, and fresher alternative to the food traditionally available in ghetto food stores. Moreover, WLCAC's agricultural operations also opened up new economic opportunities for local residents who could gain practical "experience in the actual operations of commercial farming." [127] In 1972 the Ford Foundation provided extra funding to allow WLCAC to begin its own minority business investment and development corporation to offer the same support opportunities for black businesses in Watts as Restoration and HCC had been doing in New York for several years.[128]

One of WLCAC's most important contributions to the local community was in realizing Watkins's ambition to build a hospital in the Watts-Willowbrook area of South Los Angeles. With no such facilities in a fifteen-mile radius, hospital plans sought to satisfy a long-standing community need and provide a source of jobs for locals too. To that end, WLCAC developed a 140-acre site next to the hospital that included affordable, low-income housing for hospital employees, a shopping center, and recreational community facilities. Furthermore, paramedical and related courses were added to the UREC curriculum, helping ensure that local youth were prepared to take up employment opportunities at the site upon its completion. The new hospital—the Martin Luther King Jr. Medical Center—opened its doors in 1971 and soon became an important source of jobs for local people. To date, Bauman notes, "more Watts residents have worked there than for any other private or public employer in the area." [129]

In Los Angeles, in particular, these organizations also ran social and cultural programs that helped boost local and racial pride. WLCAC built the Watts Happening Coffeehouse, which became a focal point for the performance and discussion of African American music, poetry, art, and literature. The Watts Writers Workshop, which had begun life under Westminster, relocated to Watts Happening Coffeehouse before closing in 1970.[130] OB ran a community workshop theater that toured the state, performed plays exploring the African American experience, and also offered free arts and drama classes for locals.[131] In June 1969 OB refurbished and reopened the Bill Robinson Theater on Central Avenue, the last operational cinema in the whole of South Central, which had been closed for many years.[132]

Perhaps the most significant contribution WLCAC and OB made in this respect, though, was in helping establish the annual Watts Summer Festival, alongside a number of other local organizations, including Westminster and several militant local black nationalist organizations, including Ron Karenga's US Organization and Tommy Jacquette's Self-Leadership for All Nationalities Today (SLANT).[133] Beginning in August 1966, marking the first anniversary of the riots, the festival was intended to signify the area's rebirth by celebrating African American culture and heritage. It went on to become one of the largest black-run events in the whole country, with an estimated highest attendance of 130,000 in 1967. Although focused primarily on the performance of black music and art, the festival was also attended by a wide range of employers with recruitment booths, including many traditionally white city and government agencies (such as the Police and Fire Departments). Moreover, historian Bruce Tyler explains, the festival was a boon for black business and was awash with vendors selling a range of goods, including "candy, ice cream cones, African jewelry, clothes, books, black arts and crafts, barbeque, hot dogs, juice, African clothing and handiworks."

FIGURE 5. Rosanna Wright *(left)*, modeling African-inspired clothing at her clothing shop, Bootstrings, in Los Angeles, California, 1967. Los Angeles Times Photographic Archive, Library Special Collections, Charles E. Young Research Library, University of California, Los Angeles. Used under a Creative Commons Attribution 4.0 International License.

Although it experienced a decline during the second half of the 1970s, it was revived in the 1980s and continues to this day, a lasting symbol of the revival of cultural pride that the Black Power movement brought in African American communities across the nation.[134]

As Restoration demonstrated, the promotion of racial pride and black culture and heritage was often tied to business development. OB, in particular, was a leading exponent of this approach. For example, in late 1967 OB supported former job training graduate Rosanna Wright in expanding her design company, The Boutique (later renamed Bootstrings), which focused on creating women's fashion inspired by traditional African designs and materials. "African culture and black heritage have been lost in our society,"

Wright explained, "and The Boutique is trying to help regain it."[135] In October 1968, in a venture supported by prominent toy manufacturer Mattel Inc., Operation Bootstrap created Shindana (Swahili for "competitor") Toys, a company that produced black dolls, toys, and games. Mattel helped OB obtain a $200,000 start-up loan from Chase Manhattan Bank and provided technical and financial support during the first year of operation, after which OB's new business began an independent life. Based in a factory in Watts and employing local, predominantly unskilled residents, a year into operations Shindana Toys had made $130,000 in sales revenue and distributed its products all over the United States. With plans in place to expand its products into overseas markets, Robert Hall held a birthday celebration for "Baby Nancy," Shindana's best-selling toy, to highlight the company's achievements, which, he argued, proved that "black people can make it in the business world, and that more corporations should give black men opportunity by investing money and training to let them do their thing."[136] By the end of 1971, fellow leader Lou Smith reported that Shindana had U.S. sales totaling just over $1.5 million and had opened distribution agencies in Houston, Chicago, and New York. As a nonprofit subsidiary of Operation Bootstrap, Shindana ploughed all the money it earned from sales back into the various programs that Bootstrap (itself a nonprofit CDC) ran.[137]

At the heart of Shindana's business plan was a fundamental emphasis on racial pride. Whereas black dolls previously, Smith explains, had been "just repainted white dolls" (i.e., black in color but Caucasian in appearance), Shindana was the first company to make dolls with authentic black features. The numerous dolls and toys that the company produced reflected the growing racial and cultural pride among African Americans, as well as a conscious effort to capitalize on it. They were specifically intended to give black children a positive self-image, as well as affirming prominent aspects of changing black culture during the Black Power era. For instance, the most popular girls' toy was the talking doll "Tamu" (meaning "sweet" in Swahili), advertised as having "a real rooted natural afro hairstyle" and with the catchphrase "Can you dig it?" Shindana Toys eventually produced seventeen different dolls representing a wide range of black figures, both male and female, including military men, athletes, musicians, and other entertainment stars. The company's other products also had significant cultural implications. Best-selling items included the "Feel-The-Soul" and "The Jackson-5" board games, which featured black music stars of the period, and the "Afro-American History Mystery" and "The Black Experience" games, which invited youngsters to learn about black history and "live through the setbacks as well as the steps forward" as they played.[138]

In Smith's view, the pursuit of Black Power was inseparable from the development of black businesses. In a statement that drew on the message of men like Malcolm X and Floyd McKissick, Lou Smith wrote in an "Open Letter to Black Power Organizations":

> We must use the system's weapon against it. It is a must that we establish our own economic base from which to finance our struggle. [. . .] Black Power organizations, if they have any hope of surviving, let alone being an influence, must broaden their base to include people who have ideas along economic lines. Our initial ventures should be things directly relating to the black revolution, and should be small enough in the beginning to give some assurance of success. Bar-B-Que pits, Afro-American bookstores, soul food restaurants, and Afro barber shops are a few examples of what I am talking about. All the profits from these ventures should be used to finance the work of the organization as well as creating jobs for our ghetto-trapped brother. With the least amount of imagination you should be able to see how this would open doors to areas not yet explored by our movement. Industries with real growth potential could start to develop once we jump into the economic sea. From this type of thinking, avenues should start to appear that will lead us to where I think we should be headed—a society that allows black people to accumulate the material advantages of the middle-class value system. In short, we must inject the "soul" of the black community into the economic area.[139]

In this edict, Smith captured some of the middle-class-oriented, moderate, and reformist (and gendered) essence that guided the economic development work done by organizations such as Restoration, OB, WLCAC, and HCC. At the core of these endeavors lay a tacit acceptance that America's capitalist free market, private-enterprise system *could* be used to further the goal of social and economic equality and justice. This premise did not mean, however, that they all subscribed to a doctrinaire view of capitalist business enterprise. Indeed, the use of nonprofit business models and the reinvestment of money into new community programs, institutions, and businesses betrayed a quasi-anticapitalist bent. However, at its root, it was this philosophy that made the organizations' vision of Black Power mainstream and that separated them from those who articulated a more radical analysis of the American socioeconomic order and who privileged statist and redistributive politics as the route to black empowerment. As such, it was this philosophy that won them the support—financial and otherwise—of mainstream white politicians, institutions, and businesses.

Although judging these organizations in terms of success or failure is not the main aim here, their achievements must be put in context. Ultimately, their success remained limited for a number of reasons. In the longer term, private enterprise did not commit itself to the solution of urban poverty as Robert Kennedy had envisaged it would. In Bed-Stuy and in black inner-city communities across the nation, the level of private investment required to effect large-scale transformation never materialized. Even if it had, it would likely have taken generations of incremental change to remedy the underlying causes of black urban poverty, despite optimistic political rhetoric at the time predicting its swift elimination. Furthermore, as critics insisted, there was nothing to suggest that increased black capitalist enterprise would prove any more effective in solving black poverty than it had for white poverty. Indeed, economic nationalism among minority groups would always face the issue of a marketplace limited, theoretically, by corresponding population size. Nevertheless, the organizations examined here helped to create, attract, and retain many thousands of jobs in Harlem, Bedford-Stuyvesant, and South Central Los Angeles and brought substantial investment and improvement to their neighborhoods as well. However, poverty still persisted in those communities.

As the state of the national economy worsened during the 1970s, and the American manufacturing sector experienced precipitous decline, the unfavorable financial climate made life increasingly difficult for all of them. The rise of the New Right within the national GOP brought pressure to bear on Nixon's successor, Gerald Ford, and the Republican Party began to back away from its support of minority business in the mid-1970s, a process that was sealed by the election of Ronald Reagan to the White House in 1980.[140] In the absence of large-scale private sector involvement, this change in the political climate meant a severe reduction in funds for most CDCs and spelled the end for many others.[141]

Despite these severe challenges, all these organizations remained committed to making a difference in their communities during a financially challenging period, from the mid-1970s onward, in which political hostility to their aims and methods increased. Not all urban African American communities were as fortunate. Indeed, Restoration proved a pathbreaker, and its legacy lasts far beyond Brooklyn to this day. In addition to HCC and WLCAC, the model set by Restoration has been followed by many others, and estimates suggest there could be as many as eight thousand CDCs currently operating in the United States. The most recent national census of CDCs in America, conducted in 2005, stated that existing CDCs have been responsible for the creation of 774,000 jobs and for housing production totaling over 1.25 million units. Perhaps more significant, as the report suggested, "much of what CDCs do—stabilize communities, change a negative dynamic, give residents hope for the future—cannot be captured by statistics."[142]

The continued vitality of organizations like these is significant for a number of other reasons. First, many are still in operation today, and nearly half a century later they remind us that the fight for black advancement, which took many forms and persisted well beyond the 1970s, is still ongoing. Only Operation Bootstrap did not survive the 1980s, suffering badly during the economic downturn and following the tragic deaths of both the organization's founders in the mid-1970s.[143] Of the others, Restoration is still a vibrant part of Bed-Stuy's social and economic life. CAEHT remains in operation, and a number of the institutions and organizations that it gave rise to under Alice Kornegay's leadership were still playing a vital part in East Harlem community life when she passed away in 1996, and continue to do so today. Though largely absent from the history books, Kornegay's lifetime of achievement and community service is recognized today by a playground bearing her name in a park on Harlem River Drive in East Harlem.[144] HCC continues to thrive, has a significant retail and residential property portfolio in Harlem, and runs, among other programs, a minority business entrepreneurship scheme, a health care academic scholarship program, a free adult education service, and an after-school recreational and educational program for local children.[145] The council is also responsible for the building of Harlem USA, a commercial center housing numerous shops, restaurants, banks, and a nine-screen cinema, which is one of Harlem's biggest economic success stories of the past decade.[146]

In Los Angeles, WLCAC remains a major community institution, running numerous cultural programs, youth-oriented and educational work schemes, extensive local property management (both residential and commercial), and local social services, including building maintenance, senior citizen care, a highly affordable local transportation system, and a young offenders rehabilitation program. In April 2012, the organization was awarded a $5 million grant from the state government to build an urban farm and community center in central Watts, and in late 2015 the organization announced its involvement, along with several other groups, in the planned billion-dollar redevelopment of 103rd Street—the street rechristened "Charcoal Alley" following its devastation during the August 1965 riots.[147] In 1990, Westminster—one of the largest poverty agencies in Los Angeles, with an annual operating budget of $1.6 million, seventy employees, and numerous community facilities—moved into housing development. Working with a local black-owned construction company, it built a $10 million–dollar 130-unit housing development in Watts, the largest such development in the area since the Second World War.[148] These organizations represent perhaps the most vital, most concrete legacy of the civil rights–Black Power era in their communities today. They also complicate conventional narratives of black urban decline during the final decades of the twentieth century, narratives that are, understandably, dominated by the hypersegregation of cities and suburbs, inner-city crack epidemics, gang warfare and skyrocketing murder rates, mass incarceration, failing schools, and the persistence, and even deeper entrenchment, of endemic cyclical poverty.[149] In these tremendously difficult circumstances, such organizations continue to try to ease the socioeconomic pressures of life in the ghetto and to fight for urban improvement.

The late 1960s and early 1970s represented the heyday of these organizations, as they flourished in the window of opportunity that opened between the arrival of new public policies in the mid- to late 1960s and the election of Reagan to the White House in 1980. During that period, they capitalized on the efforts of elected officials and liberal foundations to deal with the urban crisis, using the resources on offer to articulate their own visions for black advancement, and targeting some of the biggest problems that ghetto communities faced, challenges that existing measures had failed adequately to address. As such, these organizations reveal how the negotiation of Black Power unfolded at the local level.

Urban regeneration schemes rehabilitated declining properties, built and sponsored new housing, increased black home ownership, and supplanted the poisonous tenant-landlord relationship that many ghetto residents endured. Other programs designed to create vibrant commercial urban environments helped grow black economic strength by expanding local employment opportunities and business ownership. Efforts to alter discriminatory patterns of lending helped make affordable financing options available to many for the first time. These kinds of programs were simultaneously suffused with an emphasis on black pride, the promotion of racial unity, and the celebration of black history and culture. Last but not least, the creation of new local institutions helped to remake urban environments and enrich community life. In the process, they came to embody a type of Black Power in their communities that, though modest in scope, nevertheless helped to push back against the myriad disadvantages their residents faced.

The value of these institutions as symbols of black progress should not be forgotten, either. Ujima—a black-owned and -run nonprofit development corporation set up in South Central Los Angeles in 1970 that built housing, created and supported local commercial ventures, and provided local services—was described by Congressman Augustus Hawkins as "a bright and inspirational star for black people" and a "symbol that our black children can identify with and be proud of." Furthermore, as "a beautiful black movement," Hawkins continued, Ujima would be "a symbol of black power [. . .] a ray of hope that guarantees the provision of green power, a necessary source if black power is to have significance. It is a symbol that can alter the pattern of exploitation that has historically divided black people and insured a background of poverty and illiteracy." [150]

Operating at the intersection of Black Power, white politicians and institutions, and the urban crisis, these organizations are themselves evidence of the mainstreaming of Black Power. The relative success they enjoyed during the late 1960s and 1970s represented a blueprint for black advancement that resulted from a subtle negotiation of the increasingly turbulent waters of national racial politics, the gender and class biases of policy makers, and the broader battle between liberals and conservatives for the soul of America. As chapter 4 demonstrates, once African Americans began to win elective office these same forces would combine to shape the character and limits of black political power. In the following chapter, however, attention turns to the battles that unfolded in all three cities over local public education.

THREE

Black Power and Battles
over Education

On the afternoon of Wednesday, June 14, 1967, local NAACP branch head Celes King III arrived at Manual Arts High School, a virtually all black public school in South Central Los Angeles, and asked to speak to Robert Denahy, the school's white principal. King wanted to discuss the F grade awarded to Angela Bates, one of the school's African American students, by her white English teacher, Mary Covington. As things stood, the grade would prevent Bates from graduating that school year. With the ceremony just over a week away, King implored the school to change Miss Bates's grade to a D (the lowest passing mark), thereby allowing her to graduate. The student, Principal Denahy and Miss Covington explained, had failed to apply herself and did not deserve a higher mark. The F grade, they insisted, was final. Upon this news, King left, but not before urging them once more to reconsider and warning that if they chose not to cooperate, "there are other ways to handle this problem." In a follow-up letter sent later that day, King reiterated his desire to see Miss Bates "receive her diploma" at the impending graduation ceremony: "In my judgment, a complementary 'D' grade would be a correct and reasonable designation." Aside from her English class, he argued, the student had done well, and that should be recognized "even if Miss Covington does continue to use her standards and insists on a failing grade." Unmoved, Principal Denahy replied that "there is nothing I can do about it. Miss Covington is credentialed and her grade stands." [1]

The following week, just two days before the graduation ceremony, four local Black Power militants (three members of the Community Alert Patrol, along with Westminster's Tommy Jacquette) arrived at Manual Arts High. Making their way past security guards, they stormed into Principal Denahy's office and warned him that Angela Bates would graduate "no matter what."

"We don't give a damn what you or the school board say. If you want trouble, you can have it." Concerned school science teacher Mrs. Georgia Logan decided to visit Celes King, whom she knew as a member of the local NAACP. Reporting back to her fellow teachers, Logan revealed that King had told her that "he had sent the four men and that a 'bigger wrecking crew was available if necessary.'" Manual Arts, he suggested "needed a riot because the Principal does not communicate with the people." Moreover, King explained, Angela Bates's mother had been the victim of a cross-burning after moving in to a white neighborhood, and her daughter's failure to graduate would be another injustice brought against the family by whites that would not be tolerated.[2]

Rumors of a riot planned for the graduation ceremony quickly spread, prompting school board official Isaac McClelland and the mayor's human relations director, Leon Whaley, to intervene. McClelland telephoned King, who told him it was a matter of "white vs black," that he had the backing of "seventeen militant groups" and the local community, and that Angela Bates "would graduate." The NAACP leader's tactics, and the threat of rioting, worked. Still haunted by the specter of the August 1965 Watts riots and strongly committed to avoiding racial conflict at the school, Whaley convinced the Board of Education to pass Bates for graduation over the objections of Manual Arts's predominantly white teaching staff. For King and his supporters, it was a victory over white school administrators whom they had long deemed unresponsive to local peoples' concerns. For the teachers, it was a capitulation to the threat of violence from local militants set on undermining teachers' professional authority and the education system as a whole.[3]

Racial tensions at Manual Arts fitted into the broader struggle of urban blacks nationwide to win control over white-dominated institutions in their communities. Public schools were often an important focal point of that power struggle. Schools in ghetto communities were generally characterized by sharp segregation, dilapidated buildings, outmoded learning resources, overcrowded classrooms, and academic underperformance, and were often under the purview of unhappy, unmotivated, and sometimes overtly racist whites. For many African Americans, then, public schools were monuments to America's still-unfulfilled promise of racial justice and equal opportunity for all.

From the mid-1950s through the mid-1960s, education activists in all three cities pursued an integrationist agenda shaped by the NAACP's landmark victory in *Brown v. Board of Education of Topeka, Kansas* in May 1954, in which the U.S. Supreme Court outlawed segregated schooling. The

NAACP's case rested on the assertion that blacks could receive a high-quality education only if they had access to integrated schools—an assumption that influenced black education activism for decades to come.[4] However, during the mid- to-late 1960s, African Americans in New York, Los Angeles, and Atlanta came to challenge integrationist orthodoxy in the face of changing intellectual currents within the wider black freedom struggle, the hardening of white resistance, and the opening up of political opportunity.

In New York and Los Angeles, antipoverty and Black Power activism inspired calls for community control of local schools—a new, transformative, grassroots-oriented approach to improving black children's education that was founded upon the redistribution of power from established authorities to poor ghetto blacks. First developed and articulated in New York over the course of 1966, community control was presented by African American parents, activists, and students in both cities as a cure for their ailing public schools. Turning control of school policy, hiring, spending, and curriculum over to local parents and community groups would, they argued, democratize the education system, make teachers more responsive, and eradicate racism in their schools. Community control promised to empower minority communities culturally by allowing them to remake local education to reflect local values and to empower them economically by allowing them to control school expenditures.

In Atlanta, on the other hand, Jim Crow laws meant black schools were already largely under African American control. For many of the city's middle-class and elite blacks, whose well-heeled neighborhoods were served by high-quality black-run schools, this was an advantageous situation. Indeed, a significant proportion of the local black middle-class consisted of education professionals who worked in those same schools. This group came to articulate a narrow, class-based, and anti-integrationist vision for educational reform that extended their control over the public schools in their neighborhoods by securing black bureaucratic control over the city's public school system as a whole. This put them directly at odds with grassroots activists in Atlanta's poor black ghetto communities who, led by local black welfare mothers, identified school desegregation and busing as the best way to secure a better education for their children.

Studying education activism in all three cities underscores this book's major arguments by revealing the intimate relationship between black community activism, public policy, and Black Power ideology; the capacity of white interest groups to protect the status quo; and the importance of class interest in dictating the course of black advancement and sociopolitical change.

In New York and Los Angeles, community control movements blurred the lines between civil rights and Black Power activists by uniting students, parent associations, antipoverty workers, church leaders, and community activists of all stripes. In this way, the movements highlight both the flexibility and wide appeal of Black Power ideology and the syncretic, pragmatic approach of local community activists. In Atlanta, although grassroots education activists pursued an explicitly integrationist agenda, their fight for school desegregation emerged from a distinctive Black Power–inflected racial and economic justice politics that was also shaped by the interracial cooperation between black activists, white student volunteers, and white Catholic clergy. Battles for community control in New York and Los Angeles also brought African Americans together with Puerto Ricans, Asian Americans, and Chicanos, illuminating the connections between the black freedom struggle and other racial liberation movements. Taken together, these grassroots movements challenge us to reconsider traditional assumptions about the social, racial, and organizational dimensions of the era's community activism.

The trajectories of grassroots activism in all three cities highlights how the negotiation of Black Power and racial change unfolded through public policy at the local level. Each case underlines this book's overarching conclusion: that the course of black empowerment and socioeconomic change was shaped most decisively by mainstream white interests and their representatives. Community control activism in New York and Los Angeles ultimately foundered on the rock of steadfast white opposition, as white teachers and school administrators—supported by conservative politicians—succeeded in limiting school reform and protecting their professional authority and the educational status quo.

Events in Atlanta—where grassroots organizers also proved unable to realize their ambitions for transformative educational reform—shed a different light on how whites worked to dictate the boundaries of black empowerment. In the face of broad support for school integration among the city's poor and working-class blacks, Atlanta's white elites surrendered administrative control of the city's school system (and the high-ranking jobs it offered) to the local black establishment in return for abandoning the prospect of further school desegregation and busing. By exploiting divergent class interests within the black community, Atlanta's white power structure ensured that school reform worked in its interests and in the process reinforced class and gender inequality in the city.

In each city, the arc of grassroots education activism was tied to the changing landscapes of local politics and school desegregation jurisprudence. After navigating the emergence of these movements from the milieu of civil rights activism, litigation, and antipoverty organizing, this chapter then explores community control activism in New York and Los Angeles. Building on existing historiography, it integrates them into a broader narrative of community control before unpacking their broader significance for our understanding of Black Power organizing, community activism, and public policy. Attention then turns to Atlanta, where an analysis of the legal framework of local school desegregation politics is combined with an exploration of the grassroots community activism that challenged it. We begin by exploring the forces that shaped segregated schooling and African Americans' existing efforts to improve urban education and define the scope of education policy.

THE PURSUIT OF INTEGRATION

The parlous state of 1960s inner-city public education stemmed from endemic discrimination and the spatial and demographic transformation of the United States in the decades following the Second World War. White flight to the suburbs and the resulting creation of economically depressed and overcrowded inner-city black ghettoes produced widespread residential segregation. With school catchment areas tied to housing patterns, this racial separation was replicated in many of the nation's classrooms. Indeed, much white flight was motivated by a desire to avoid integrated education. As historian Kenneth Jackson suggests, the *Brown* decision inclined "millions of families [to] move out of the city 'for the kids' and especially the [. . .] superiority of smaller and more homogenous suburban school systems." There they hoped to find "relief from the pervasive fear of racial integration and its two presumed bedfellows—interracial violence and interracial sex." [5] As black and other nonwhite children became concentrated in inner-city public schools, increasing numbers of white children attended public and private schools in suburban neighborhoods that usually had few, if any, minority students.

With schools funded primarily by local tax revenues, the economic gap between black inner-city and white suburban neighborhoods helped foster educational inequality in their respective public schools. Prosperous white suburban communities generally benefited from well-funded, modern local schools with suitable enrollment levels where students generally performed well under high-quality, motivated teaching staff. The reality for most poverty-stricken black ghetto communities, where underresourced local schools usually offered substandard teaching in dilapidated school buildings, was quite different.[6] Worse still, to cope with severe overcrowding, ghetto schools often divided the day into morning and afternoon sessions and split the student body between the two. Under this arrangement, known as double sessions, children effectively received half of the schooling that their counterparts in schools with normal enrollment levels did. In language reminiscent of Black Power radicals, Watts NAACP leader Edward Warren decried double sessions—a commonplace practice in his community's schools—as tantamount to "educational genocide" against local black children. For many parents—especially single mothers on welfare—double sessions not only undermined their children's education but also restricted their employment opportunities because child care demanded more of their time.[7]

Given the intimate relationship between education and employment prospects, education assumed even greater significance in a postwar national economy and urban landscape transformed by the restructuring of industry, suburbanization, and modernization. Vast numbers of blue-collar industrial jobs had followed migrating whites from the city to the suburb. The relocation of U.S. industry was followed in the 1970s by serious decline, with blue-collar jobs in many sectors disappearing completely as a result of deindustrialization, rapid technological change, economic globalization, and the rise of international competition. As semiskilled and unskilled jobs moved out of reach into the suburbs or into obsolescence, the expansion of white-collar businesses produced an increasingly computerized, office-based urban workplace in which numeracy and literacy were essential prerequisites for employment.

Understanding the importance of quality, modern education to their children's future chances for social mobility and economic security, many black parents were deeply concerned by their local public schools. The inadequacy of inner-city public education, combined with the high dropout rates it produced, meant vast numbers of minority youngsters entered a changing job market without the necessary skills to compete for remunerative employment.[8] With such a chasm in quality and educational achievement between white and black schools, many African Americans understandably viewed integration of the nation's classrooms as the most direct route to securing a better education for black children.

Although historians have debated the impact of the *Brown* decision on the civil rights movement, it certainly stimulated demands for school desegregation across the country, encouraging African Americans everywhere to push back against educational inequality.[9] However, whereas southern blacks challenged a system of segregation mandated in law—de jure segregation—their counterparts in the rest of the country faced a different problem. Outside the Jim Crow South, racially segregated schools were considered the product of de facto segregation—that is, segregation imagined to have resulted not from official law but from a myriad of impersonal market forces and individual choices. The myth of de facto segregation was later rejected by federal courts in the 1970s, as numerous school desegregation cases revealed the broad web of discriminatory practices on the part of white school boards, politicians, realtors, and mortgage lenders that produced racial apartheid in schools outside the South. However, in the immediate wake of *Brown,* African Americans in the North had to constantly battle to prove that segregation of their schools had been deliberately created by local white authorities.[10]

Following the *Brown* ruling, Harlem resident Dr. Kenneth Clark, the noted psychologist whose famous doll test had been used to support the NAACP's case, excoriated New York's Board of Education for implementing policies that, he argued, had produced the segregated and underperforming schools where the vast majority of the city's minority children received woefully inadequate teaching.[11] Clark's public criticism shone a spotlight on the manifest racial inequalities within New York's education system, challenging the city's reputation, now under Democratic mayor Robert Wagner, as a site of enlightened and progressive urban liberalism and harmonious race relations.[12]

In 1955 Reverend Milton Galamison, pastor of one of Brooklyn's most prestigious black churches and a strong proponent of social justice, emerged as the leading figure in efforts to improve teaching standards and the educational attainment of local children through the desegregation of public schools in Brooklyn's two largest black communities, Bedford-Stuyvesant and Brownsville. Galamison fronted the Parents Workshop for Equality in New York Schools, a grassroots organization established in 1956 that held numerous demonstrations and rallies targeting the Board of Education and its members to petition them for integration of the city's schools.[13]

While Galamison and his acolytes targeted the Board of Education, other groups focused on the city's political leaders. In 1957 pioneering civil rights organizer Ella Baker, then head of the Education Committee of the NAACP's New York branch, organized Parents in Action Against

Educational Discrimination, a group made up of local blacks and Puerto Ricans. Demanding school integration and a say for parents in formulating school policy, Baker and her allies put forth a broad vision that extended beyond a narrow interpretation of the *Brown* decision. As historian Barbara Ransby argues, "To insist that parents be empowered to define their children's education was a more substantive and radical demand than simply saying that black and white children should sit next to each other in class." Their activism, Ransby suggests, represented the first steps of the struggle for community control that flourished during the mid- to late 1960s.[14]

The zenith of the southern civil rights movement also brought the high-tide mark in black New Yorkers' bid for integrated schooling. By the start of 1963, national civil rights groups including the NAACP and CORE had joined with local grassroots organizations to form the New York City–Wide Committee for Integrated Schools, led by Reverend Galamison. By the end of that summer, as President Kennedy's civil rights bill was being debated on Capitol Hill, the committee planned to conduct a large-scale school boycott in a bid to force the Board of Education to establish a timetable and blueprint for desegregating New York's schools. With little official action forthcoming, in February 1964 those plans culminated in approximately 465,000 children (including 92 percent of Harlem students, 77 percent of Bed-Stuy students, and 80 percent of students on the Lower East Side) missing school for a day in protest over segregation in the city's schools. It was the single largest civil rights boycott of the period anywhere in the country.[15]

Despite black efforts to bring change to their public schools, the incidence of segregation in schools continued to rise during the decade following *Brown*. Whereas in 1954 the number of schools with nonwhite student enrollment at or above 90 percent in New York was zero, by 1963 that figure had risen to sixty-one. As Martha Biondi argues, a major factor in this trend, besides the continuing white exodus to the suburbs and growing white private school enrollment, was Board of Education policy itself, which served to deepen educational inequality. The board's failure here also resulted from the fierce and often overtly racist resistance of white parents and teachers to policies that would bring meaningful desegregation or educational improvement to ghetto schools, such as school zoning and teacher assignment.[16] New York's school bureaucracy committed itself rhetorically to the goal of school integration, but in practice did more to prevent it than to achieve it.

In Los Angeles, as in New York, school segregation was underpinned by the city's racial geography and reinforced by calculated and discriminatory school board policy. In contravention of its own (supposedly color-blind) student assignment laws, the board allowed whites from racially mixed areas to travel to white schools elsewhere, but denied nonwhite students this right. Housing patterns and school board policy combined to make the city's schools more segregated than the schools in half the southern states. Despite pressure from parent groups and the Los Angeles NAACP to integrate public schools, for most of the decade following *Brown,* local officials brushed school desegregation under the carpet. As in New York, a mixture of leading civil rights and local community groups coalesced to fight for school integration, as the crescendo of the civil rights movement's direct action phase inspired black Angelenos to greater militancy. In May 1963, at the same time that landmark demonstrations were taking place on the streets of Birmingham, Alabama, the United Civil Rights Council (UCRC) formed in Los Angeles. Made up of parents, community activists, leading clergy and black politicians (including future mayor Councilman Tom Bradley), and the local NAACP, CORE, and American Civil Liberties Union (ACLU), UCRC stepped up the fight against educational inequality in the city.[17]

UCRC conducted a series of large marches throughout the summer, one of the last of which came in August 1963 when more than five hundred demonstrators strode through the downtown business district to protest a Board of Education hearing. Accompanied by James Farmer of CORE and James Forman of SNCC, their key demands included the redrawing of school district lines to overturn de facto segregation, as well as teacher transfers and the transportation of students from overcrowded ghetto schools to underutilized white schools. Echoing local white resistance to black demands (and ignoring the board's own discriminatory policies), white board member Charles Smoot rebuked the gathered protesters: "The Negroes want special status and privilege. They want us to gerrymander the school district on a racial basis."[18] Smoot's stance symbolized the board's obfuscation and refusal to take meaningful action. The sit-ins, meetings, marches, hunger strikes, and other acts of civil disobedience conducted by students and civil rights activists over the course of 1963 produced little in the way of results.[19] With protests proving ineffective, the ACLU filed suit against the Los Angeles Unified School District (LAUSD) in August 1963. This landmark case, *Crawford v. Board of Education of Los Angeles,* would ultimately, after a decade-and-a-half-long journey through the legal system, bring the battle to desegregate the city's schools to an end in 1978.[20]

As *Crawford* began in Los Angeles, the NAACP's Legal Defense Fund (LDF) was entering its fifth year of arguing the equivalent case in Atlanta,

Calhoun v. Latimer. With pioneering black female civil rights lawyer (and Thurgood Marshall protégé) Constance Motley Baker as lead counsel, the LDF saw Atlanta—the de facto capital of the South and a bastion of black educational excellence—as a key site in the battle against southern whites' "massive resistance" against the *Brown* ruling. In contrast to the education activism in New York and Los Angeles, the battle against school segregation in Atlanta focused narrowly on the courtroom, featured relatively little popular protest, and was largely removed from the black community itself, especially its poor and working-class members. Indeed, the legal challenge to implement *Brown* in the city was led principally by the LDF, which pursued the case independent of—and at some points in opposition to—important sections of the local black community.

Eventually concluded in 1973 after fifteen years, the *Calhoun* case testified to the power of local whites' resistance to racial change. Throughout the case's trajectory, city school board lawyers provided an object lesson in sophisticated legal maneuvering, creating the appearance of compliance with *Brown* while achieving little of its substance. Ordered by a district court to desegregate the city's schools in 1961, the school board's plan involved a highly convoluted and capricious transfer system that placed the onus on blacks and accomplished barely even token integration. By desegregating a grade per year, the plan threatened to take twelve years to complete the task. Throughout the 1960s, numerous court rulings on school desegregation provided the LDF lawyers with a number of new legal precedents with which to challenge Atlanta's strategy. By meeting those challenges with minimal, piecemeal, and technical changes, the Atlanta school board was able to keep school segregation largely intact. By the end of the decade, as legal scholar Tomiko Brown-Nagin has suggested, although *Calhoun* had ended de jure segregation in the system and brought some integration, it "had not substantially changed the racial make-up of the school system." [21]

WHITE RESISTANCE TO *BROWN*

Deep and pervasive white hostility to school desegregation existed in all three cities. In Los Angeles, pro–school integration marches were often met by counterdemonstrations from local white segregationist groups, including the Committee Against Integration and Intermarriage and the American Nazi Party.[22] Just as 1963 and 1964 witnessed the high tide of the civil rights movement's efforts to integrate New York's public schools, it also brought the emergence of Parents And Taxpayers (PAT), a militant white anti-busing organization set up by outer-borough Jews and Catholics that grew to more than a half million members. PAT overwhelmed the Board of Education with petitions, conducted large-scale demonstrations outside city hall, and established its own separate private academy to circumvent integration, the first such school in any northern city. This united action between two of the city's largest white ethnic groups undermined efforts toward complete integration of New York's schools and would later be revived and cemented in opposition to black residents' demands for "community control" over *their* local schools.[23]

In Atlanta, preserving the existing racial order was a matter of state law. Where school officials in New York and Los Angeles had given vocal, if disingenuous, support to *Brown,* south of the Mason-Dixon Line the decision was greeted with outrage. In March 1956 the region's political leaders published the "Southern Manifesto," in which they dedicated themselves to resisting the "tyranny" of the high court's decision, and every Georgia representative in the U.S. Congress signed it.[24] Under Mayor William Hartsfield, the city's response to the *Brown* decision was guided by the desire to protect Atlanta's reputation as a bastion of biracial cooperation, progress, and harmony. White city fathers had keenly observed the 1957 school desegregation crisis in Little Rock, Arkansas, and the damage it had done to Little Rock's reputation and economy. Resolving to avoid having any such crisis in their city, the first day of school desegregation in Atlanta—in which a mere nine black students enrolled in white schools—was highly policed and coordinated, and it passed without violence. Greeted by the nation's political and media establishment as a shining example of successful integration, the day demonstrated both the city's mastery of public relations and just how limited a school desegregation plan white officials had been able to conjure.[25]

Even this bare minimum of school integration was too much for some white Atlantans, who resorted to a variety of methods to resist change. Once enrolled in white schools, black students' experiences were often extremely negative: at best they were ostracized, and at worst they were subjected to regular verbal and physical attacks from white students and, on occasion, even from staff members. For example, in late 1965, black parents of children at the recently integrated J. Allen Crouch School in central Atlanta complained that the white principal had racially abused their children, that black students had been expelled for defending themselves against violence, and that Ku Klux Klan members had threatened them and their homes.[26] Violence, however, was only one way of discouraging blacks to apply for transfers to white schools. As one local black teacher remembered, there was

> a high school student whose parents I knew. His father was employed as the caretaker of a four-unit apartment complex. This student, without consulting his parents, believed that the landmark decision which eliminated the dual system was law. He marched up to the newly integrated Grady High, and filled out papers to enroll because it was nearer to the white section where his father was living. His application [. . .] was sent to his father's employer. That evening his father was fired immediately and he lost both his livelihood and housing which was provided in his contractual agreement.[27]

Across the nation, many whites, faced with the prospect of school integration, fled inner cities as fast as possible for lily-white suburbs whose racial homogeneity would be reflected in their schools. As Thomas Sugrue suggests, the ability and financial capacity of most middle-class white parents to either withdraw their children from public school or move across school district lines represented a formidable obstacle to blacks' efforts to integrate public schools. As white flight continued, therefore, "the fixity and impermeability of school district boundaries meant most outlying communities were completely unaffected by calls for educational integration." During the 1950s, New York lost more than 800,000 (predominantly middle-class) whites and gained more than 700,000 blacks and Puerto Ricans, the vast majority of whom were poor. As white children moved to suburban or private schools between 1957 and 1964, the number of white students in New York's public schools decreased by nearly a quarter, with some estimates suggesting that approximately 40,000 left the city's schools every year during that period.[28] Atlanta's white population of 300,000 in 1960 declined by 60,000 over the following decade, and a further 100,000 left the city during the 1970s. Consequently, the black proportion of Atlanta's population rose from a third in 1960 to over two-thirds by 1980. Whereas Atlanta's school population had been 70 percent white and 30 percent black when the *Brown* verdict was handed down, by the early 1970s that figure had more than reversed.[29] In Los Angeles, white resistance to integration had been clearly demonstrated by the two-thirds majority vote on Proposition 14 in 1964. Put forward by the white conservative California Real Estate Association, Proposition 14 sought to repeal the Rumford Fair Housing Act of the previous year, which had banned discrimination in the sale and letting of property. Though subsequently declared unconstitutional by the California Supreme Court, the wide public support for Prop 14 demonstrated the considerable depth of white hostility to residential—and by extension, school—integration.[30]

BLACK RESISTANCE TO *BROWN*

While white Americans were broadly hostile to school integration, it was not necessarily welcomed by all African Americans, either. This was especially clear in Atlanta, where, a year after the landmark verdict, more than fifty NAACP leaders from across the country met to discuss the enforcement of *Brown* in the South. The meeting culminated in the "Atlanta Declaration," urging southern branches to petition their local school boards to begin desegregating local schools. However, Atlanta's black leadership elite, led by attorney A. T. Walden, paid this call little heed. According to the city's long-standing pattern of biracial negotiation, the African American community's middle-class core and business leaders defined its interests, and they had long favored negotiation and compromise with the city's white power structure over litigation or direct action. The *Brown* decision did little to change that pattern.[31] Although Walden was listed as co-counsel in *Calhoun*—and the suit was filed in the name of John Calhoun, then Atlanta's NAACP branch head—the case was fought primarily by the LDF with little involvement from the local black power elite.

Perhaps the largest and most influential interest group in black Atlanta consisted of local teachers. As Pearlie Dove, a teacher at Clark College in the Atlanta University Center (AUC), has suggested, in the black community "the teachers were the leaders. They belonged to the NAACP and to the professional organizations. They were the ones who belonged to many of the civil rights groups." However, given their fragile status at the mercy of the city's board of education and white trustees, "they [...] could be scared off very easily." Protecting their own economic interests was, naturally, a high priority for them, and thus it was a high priority for black Atlanta's leadership too.[32] Accordingly, as Brown-Nagin suggests, "Walden, local black teachers, and other leading members of the black middle-class [...] embraced gradualism as the best course for implementing *Brown*."[33]

Historian Adam Fairclough argues that, while many black teachers in the South "endorsed the general principle of Brown," they nevertheless "harbored deep misgivings about the prospect of abandoning segregated schools."

Many black teachers stood to lose far more than they might gain. Recognizing this fear, local white-controlled school boards in Georgia, and across the South, used school desegregation as a way to fire and demote hundreds of black teachers and administrators. Moreover, the prospect of being transferred to work in white schools, in company with deeply hostile white staff and pupils, was naturally unappealing to most black teachers.[34] Furthermore, many rejected the notion that white schools were superior to black schools. The long-established, prestigious cluster of black colleges that made up the AUC testified to the quality of black educational institutions and professional skill. They had not only produced numerous black notables (including Martin Luther King Jr.) but also trained countless African American teachers for the city's schools and, indeed, for black schools across the country.[35]

Black teachers also feared that white schools were highly unlikely to provide black children with a positive educational experience. For example, Alice Holmes Washington, who taught at a number of Atlanta's all-black schools, remembered of her time at South Fulton High that "when youngsters went to that school they met a professional staff of people who were not just teachers but who were friends, who were surrogate parents, who were motivators, inspirers, and disciplinarians and gave to each student the feeling of a sense of worth." Black students, Washington feared, would not be treated that way by southern white teachers. Many black parents shared these concerns, and Washington found herself consoling a number of them, assuring them that school desegregation would not be "the end of the world."[36] Atlanta's black middle class and race leaders were opposed to school desegregation because the schools in their more prosperous neighborhoods were often modern, well-resourced facilities with high-caliber teaching staff. Schools in the city's poor black neighborhoods, on the other hand, were just the opposite, with understaffed, underresourced, dilapidated elementary and high schools, regularly running double sessions to cope with overcrowding.[37]

SCLC leader and future congressman and Atlanta mayor Andrew Young, who lived in a wealthy black neighborhood during the 1960s, explained the interrelationship between the city's black education establishment and its powerful black leadership:

Thanks to the presence of the black colleges in the AUC, black Atlantans were relatively well educated. In fact, when the schools finally were desegregated it was discovered that the average educational level of black teachers in the Atlanta public school system was higher than the average for white teachers. Another result of the strong influence of local higher education was the prevalence of black professionals. Our girls grew up knowing black pediatricians, dentists, and pharmacists, and we kept our accounts at the black bank, Citizens Trust. Jean [Young's wife] endeavored to keep the girls enclosed in a secure world of church, school, and neighborhood on Atlanta's Westside.[38]

Ensconced in the city's salubrious black enclaves, Atlanta's black middle class and elite were fundamentally tied by social and professional networks to the city's black educational establishment. Together, they played a powerful role in defining black interests in Atlanta. For some in the city, the political and economic empowerment that the Black Power movement clamored for was already a reality. Middle-class black Atlantans sought to protect and enhance their status and, as Young's testimony confirms, to isolate themselves from poor communities, just as millions of whites had by leaving the inner cities for the suburbs. Physically separated from the city's poor blacks, as black educator (and later local antipoverty director) Suzette Crank has suggested, Atlanta's black middle class and elite—just like privileged whites—didn't "want their own poor."[39] In the early 1970s the struggle for black control over Atlanta's public school system—an effort led by Atlanta's black teachers and middle class—reinforced this sharp intraracial class divide.

THE ORIGINS OF COMMUNITY CONTROL

In mid-1960s New York City, as white parents and school officials stymied efforts to integrate the city's classrooms, African Americans changed course in the fight for educational equality by seizing upon the prospect of school decentralization legislation as a way both to improve the quality of local education and to empower themselves as parents and as a community at large. John Lindsay's victory in the 1965 mayoral election brought with it the promise of change. Throughout his campaign Lindsay had lamented the impact of educational inequality on the city's poor and minority communities and criticized education officials. Overwhelmed by its responsibility for more than 1 million students, 900 schools, 70,000 teachers, and 43,000 administrators, the Board of Education, he argued, had become a monolithic and unresponsive organization: "For fifteen years every study of our educational system has proclaimed the liabilities of our rigid, over-centralized bureaucracy. 110 Livingston Street, Brooklyn, home of the Board of Education, has become the symbol across the country of an administration almost totally divorced from the schools for which it is responsible." [40] The answer, Lindsay believed, was decentralization. Unlike his predecessor, Mayor Wagner, who had deliberately avoided intervening in school affairs, Lindsay was keen to make his influence felt in education policy. Lindsay's support for decentralization was founded upon his general desire to break down the city's byzantine bureaucracies and give neighborhoods a greater say in the running of their local institutions and services (a philosophy that also underpinned his approach to the War on Poverty).[41] Lindsay's vision for educational change established the political terrain upon which black education activists would strive to shape school reform, ensuring that public policy would again be a primary site of contestation over the scope and direction of black empowerment.

For many black New Yorkers education reform could not come soon enough. In 1966 approximately half of all sixth-graders in the city's public schools failed to meet the minimum standards in reading and mathematics (nearly double the statewide figure), and by the age of twelve, the average black or Puerto Rican student lagged a whole two years behind his or her white equivalent in terms of overall academic performance. By the mid-1960s, with educational results among minority students in steady decline, the need for change appeared to be more pressing than ever.[42] In the eyes of many black parents, the primary obstacles to improving their children's education were the Board of Education and the United Federation of Teachers (UFT), the city's white (and predominantly Jewish) teachers' union. In May 1966, plans to change the teacher transfer system and assign more experienced teachers to ghetto schools were defeated by UFT head Albert Shanker, who argued that "forced transfers" would damage teacher morale. To Isaiah Robinson, head of the Harlem Parents Association (and one of HCC's founders and future co-organizer of the first National Black Power conference), the UFT's opposition to teacher transfer was no different from the PAT's opposition to school integration. Sounding the increasingly militant tone of the battle over education, Robinson warned: "We do not intend to side step a head-on collision with the teachers and the UFT. [. . .] We will not rest until our children are taught to the maximum of their innate abilities. The lives of our children are more precious to us than the UFT realizes. The die is cast." [43]

With black New Yorkers growing insistent in their demands for equal educational opportunities, the opening of a new school in Harlem,

Intermediate School 201 (IS 201), provided the context from which a new approach to school reform emerged. In spite of local opposition, the city's Board of Education elected to build the new $5 million windowless school in the middle of the East Harlem Triangle, a racial ghetto marked by urban blight. By the time the facility was completed in readiness for the new school year in September 1966, community reaction to the new building was overwhelmingly negative. "It looks like a prison instead of a school and it will be segregated," declared one angry local mother.[44] Despite the Board of Education's claims that white students from neighboring Queens, across the Harlem River, would be attracted to the school, very few whites attended. The student body was split between black and Puerto Rican children, reflecting the neighborhood's racial composition. In response, locals formed the Parent and Community Negotiating Committee for IS 201, a group committed to preventing the school from opening unless it was integrated. In September 1966, with the start of the new school year in sight, parents planned to picket the school until their demands were met. However, with the Board of Education refusing to bus white students to integrate IS 201, the group proposed an alternative solution: appoint a black principal and give oversight of the school to a "community council." It was time, they argued, to turn public schools over to the only people who could be entrusted with the educational welfare of African American and other minority students: the parents and local community themselves.[45]

Some East Harlem locals had already pioneered this new empowering philosophy when they established the East Harlem Block Schools (EHBS) in 1965.[46] Growing out of residents' OEO-funded efforts to set up a local nursery school, the parent-controlled EHBS expanded year after year until, by 1971, they offered primary education all the way up to the fifth grade, as well as an after-school tuition program. Also on site was a day care center that by 1970 was the only school operation still receiving public funds. The rest of EHBS's programs relied on a two-dollar weekly student fee and private donations.[47] Although it always faced financial constraints, the school quickly earned a reputation for achieving impressive academic results with so-called "unteachable" children. Parents also benefited from involvement with the school. As a 1971 report explained:

> The parents form the backbone of the administration of the East Harlem Block Schools. The board of directors consists only of parents of children enrolled in the schools; parents have final say over all policy, finance and per-

sonnel decisions. Over half of the full-time staff are parents and community people, many of whom were formerly on welfare. Parents are intimately involved with the daily activities at the schools. Parent-teachers are regarded as on equal footing with professional teachers. All staff meetings include parents and all decisions are made with their full participation.[48]

Still open today, EHBS continues to offer local black and Puerto Rican parents a role in their children's primary education unavailable in the public education system. However, despite being a model of community control, EHBS's example was not widely replicated, largely because of its reliance on private funding. The general lack of financial resources in ghetto communities ensured that public education remained the primary focus of grassroots education activism.

In the wake of the IS 201 imbroglio, the state legislature ordered Mayor Lindsay to prepare a city school decentralization plan by the end of December 1967, a responsibility he entrusted to a group of liberal city elites headed by Ford Foundation president McGeorge Bundy.[49] With the planning in motion, events at a Board of Education budget hearing on December 19, 1966, demonstrated the growing enthusiasm among New York's increasingly militant education activists for a far-reaching and radical vision of school reform. When the black, white, and Puerto Rican community activists in attendance (many of whom had been associated with the IS 201 controversy) insisted that one of their cohort be allowed to speak—in contravention of formal procedure—board officials walked out. Once they left, the activists remained in the chamber, proclaiming themselves the Ad Hoc Board of Education for the People of the City of New York—soon known as the People's Board of Education.

Electing Milton Galamison as their president, the group informed Mayor Lindsay of their actions via telegram and demanded he meet with them. They also insisted he declare a "state of emergency" in New York public education, liquidate the existing Board of Education, and replace it with one that would be "more responsive to parent-community concerns." Resolving to occupy the regular board members' seats until the mayor took action, they remained in 110 Livingston Street for three days until eventually removed by police. Following their ejection from the board's headquarters, the People's Board continued to work and to present themselves as an alternative to the existing official board, conducting hearings of their own, and releasing position papers on school reform and on education and teacher policy. Swiftly setting up offices in poor minority communities across New York, their work would

FIGURE 6. Professor Preston Wilcox *(right)* talking to reporters after having served Dr. Bernard E. Donovan with a show cause order. December 28, 1966. Photo by Barney Stein/New York Post Archives / © NYP Holdings, Inc. via Getty Images.

play a key role in the debate over the meaning and form of school decentralization in the city.[50]

Perhaps the most significant paper released by the People's Board was a late February 1967 publication heavily influenced by the work of African American Columbia University sociologist (and future HCC cofounder) Preston Wilcox, who had been a primary intellectual influence behind the IS 201 demonstrations. The paper called for community-controlled supervisory bodies to be given total control over all aspects of their local schools' finances, curriculum, and education policies, including discretionary power over staff hiring and retention. As historian Vincent Cannato recognizes, it was a blueprint for community control that, if realized, would render the Board of Education and the teachers' union "virtually powerless." This form of community control proved a recipe for racialized controversy, pitting its black and Puerto Rican advocates against the overwhelmingly white teachers' union.[51]

In April 1967, as demands for community control grew louder, New York's superintendent of schools and Board of Education head, Bernard Donovan, sanctioned the creation of three experimental school districts in which to test community control: East Harlem, which included IS 201 and four feeder schools; Ocean Hill–Brownsville, a desperately poor black and Puerto Rican neighborhood in Brooklyn between Bedford-Stuyvesant and Brownsville that included eight schools; and Two Bridges, a community on the Lower East Side that had five schools and a diverse population of blacks, Puerto Ricans, and Asian Americans. The schools in these districts—all with overwhelming nonwhite student populations—were put under the control of locally elected community boards that hired a lead administrator to oversee the running of their district's schools. Endorsed by Mayor Lindsay, funding for the three districts was provided by the Ford Foundation, whose education expert and leading community control theorist, Mario Fantini, was also assigned to the experimental districts as a consultant.[52]

With community control seemingly close at hand, local parents and activists prepared to make the most of the opportunity. Ocean Hill–Brownsville residents elected Reverend C. Herbert Oliver as head of their district's new community board, which quickly appointed Rhody McCoy as unit administrator. Having taught in the New York school system since 1949, McCoy (who had counted Malcolm X among his close friends) brought considerable expertise as well as racial militancy to the role. In East Harlem, David Spencer, a leading People's Board member and community control advocate, was elected to lead the IS 201 district governing board.[53]

The experiment was flawed from the start, however. Locating the demonstration districts in poor minority areas ensured that race remained at the heart of the school reform debate. Moreover, the Board of Education's total failure to properly define the legal boundaries of the three district boards' powers invited conflict. The community control experiment soon descended into a struggle between the community boards and the white, predominantly Jewish UFT. Fought most fiercely in Ocean Hill–Brownsville, this bitter dispute crippled the city's public school system and cast a long shadow over race relations in the city.[54]

As community control activism gathered momentum from mid-1967 onward in New York, so too did demands for school reform on the West Coast. As historian Scot Brown has explained, local cultural nationalist Black Power group US played a leading role in inspiring the first of what became several waves of high school student activism. After the success of their first "Kwanzaa" celebration in December 1966, the organization declared May 19, Malcolm X's birthday, another symbolic black holiday. As the day drew near, US urged black Angelenos to observe "Kuzaliwa," as they called it, by staying away from work and school. Thousands of students from across the city answered their call by missing school, with many congregating in a city park to celebrate instead. The event proved to be the first of several major moments of student activism that year. Over the following months, US remained an important inspiration to protests that evolved at schools across the city. Manual Arts High School, in particular, became an important focal point of dissent.[55]

When teacher Georgia Logan visited the NAACP's downtown office to speak to local branch leader Celes King about the brewing Angela Bates graduation crisis, she was initially prevented from entering the building by Karenga and other US members, who were allies of the NAACP chief.[56] Community discontent with the situation at Manual Arts was only temporarily alleviated by the decision to pass Angela Bates for graduation. With 95 percent black enrollment, Manual Arts was typical of the city's nonwhite ghetto schools: badly overcrowded and underresourced, with low levels of academic achievement. Following the graduation crisis, students, parents, and community activists came together in September and October to picket the school and demand change. Anger was primarily directed at the school's white principal, Robert Denahy, unsanitary school conditions, and the inadequacy of the teaching provided.[57]

The protesters formed the United Parents Council (UPC), headed by Margret Wright, one of the city's most radical advocates of community control. The UPC soon joined forces with the newly formed Black Congress, an umbrella organization of twenty-two local groups that represented a broad cross-section of the local community. Participating organizations included the Black Panther Party, US, CORE, Celes King's NAACP branch, a number of local antipoverty and community groups (including NAPP, Operation Bootstrap, and the Community Alert Patrol), and several local churches. The Black Congress supported the school protests, and many militants—in particular from US—joined the students and UPC on the picket line to demand improved facilities, better instruction, greater community influence on and oversight of school administration, and the firing of Principal Denahy. Demonstrations outside the school soon became violent. Altercations with police, rock throwing, and vandalism resulted in large numbers of arrests, including more than one hundred in just one week. Concerned about intimidation by the protesters, more than half of Manual Arts's teachers went on strike. Their action was also a response to the threat community control posed to their authority, as well as to the presence of Black Power militants in the picket lines—two factors that also motivated teacher strikes in New York the following year. Once the violence abated, the teachers returned and ultimately, as historian Jeanne Theoharis explains, the protesters did achieve some of their aims. More teachers and guidance counselors were transferred to the school, and various committees were set up to give parents a greater say in school affairs. Principal Denahy, the object of considerable ire, transferred to another district. At the same time, the school board increased the number of security guards in the school, a development that angered students and parents. Subsequent school protests in 1968 and 1969 were driven first and foremost by students, who were then joined by the community, in contrast to the actions conducted by New York's more parent-and-community-activist-led school reform movement.[58]

COMMUNITY CONTROL, THE WAR ON POVERTY, AND BLACK POWER

The War on Poverty's capacity for inspiring racial identity politics and invigorating community activism (including welfare rights activism) was especially clear in grassroots movements for educational change in all three cities. Demands for community control were firmly rooted in experience with the antipoverty program. Energizing and emboldening community activism in cities such as New York and Los Angeles, the War on Poverty's endorsement of "maximum feasible participation" of the poor both encouraged and legitimized poor black communities' struggle for self-determination. As Thomas Sugrue observes, while Black Power provided the intellectual foundations for community control, the War on Poverty's Community Action Program provided a model for its implementation.[59]

In New York in particular, community antipoverty and CDC-type organizations and their leaders, who benefited from the organizational resources and funding provided by the OEO, were vital in mobilizing and sustaining grassroots movements for community control. For example, some of the most prominent education activists in the city included Helen Testamark, head of HARYOU-ACT's education committee; Community Association of the East Harlem Triangle leader Alice Kornegay; and Evelina Antonetty, a People's Board founder and head of the OEO-funded United Bronx Parents (UBP), a multiracial (though predominantly Puerto Rican) school advocacy group.[60] East Harlem Block Schools—the most successful vision of community control realized in New York—began with OEO funds. Leading community control advocates Preston Wilcox, Isaiah Robinson, and Roy Innis were all founding members of HCC. As chapter 2 reveals, Restoration's Sonny Carson and Albert Vann were both prominently involved in education activism in Brooklyn. This profound interrelationship was undoubtedly shaped by Mayor Lindsay, who opened New York's War on Poverty to minority groups. In Los Angeles, where Mayor Yorty was less supportive of antipoverty organizing in the black community, the relationship was less pronounced. The community control movement in Los Angeles became predominantly student-driven, but was backed by a large group of Black Congress–associated local community groups. Operation Bootstrap, in particular, gave strong support to education activism in the city.

The War on Poverty also boosted the fight for community control in New York and Los Angeles by providing important motivation. The struggle over local education was guided by the desire to undermine the dominant white narrative that blamed educational underperformance among minority students on an apparent cultural indisposition toward learning and academic work on the part of nonwhites. This idea had been reinforced and given a veneer of scientific legitimacy by the "culture of poverty" theory that arose from anthropologist Oscar Lewis's 1958 study of poor Mexican American communities. As historian Adina Back explains, although Lewis intended to emphasize the importance of environmental determinism in shaping poor communities, his theory was all too easily subverted to explain poverty as a result of cultural weakness—a loose assumption that underpinned much liberal policy making in the 1950s and 1960s, including the War on Poverty. The notion of limited black educational ability was evident in local white conservatives' response to Los Angeles's student protesters. Rejecting black calls for more Afrocentric curricula on the grounds that they were "useless to upward mobility," they urged the students to instead "make better use of high schools, apprenticeship programs, trade and technical schools. It is through these doorways that blacks will progress." These racist assumptions were a powerful motivation to school reform activism in minority communities that utterly rejected the notion that they were somehow responsible for the underperformance of their schools and that they did not value education. Demands for community control reflected their belief that chronic under-resourcing of public schools and the inadequacy of white teaching staff were to blame for the schools' failure; these demands were proof positive that minority groups cared deeply about education.[61]

The emergence of Black Power ideology also critically influenced educa-tion activism. Grassroots organizers' embrace of community control in New York and Los Angeles was part of a wider shift in the black freedom struggle then under way, from integrationist goals and moderate, conciliatory rhetoric toward more forthright and critical demands for the political and economic empowerment of African American communities. Stokely Carmichael and Floyd McKissick—perhaps the two most prominent Black Power advocates in the country at the time—joined protesters on the picket line outside IS 201 on the first day of school in September 1966, illustrating the relevance of the struggle for New York's schools to the nascent Black Power movement. Similarly, a year later, black militants from US, the Black Panther Party, and other local Black Power organizations joined with student protesters in Los Angeles to push for school reform. Rooted in the demand for greater black self-determination, community control was a natural component of the emerging Black Power ideology. As Carmichael declared, "Negroes have a right to run schools in their areas. White people do. They run the schools in the suburbs where they live and it should be the same in Harlem. It is their right."[62] The core principle of community control was not, of course, neces-sarily limited to schools. As the "Community Control of City Services" rally held at IS 201 in November 1968 highlighted, the demand for community control could extend over a range of existing urban institutions. Speakers at the rally emphasized the need for local control over not only schools but also welfare centers, the Police Department, and city social services.[63]

Community control also resonated with other core aspects of Black Power philosophy. Authority over school policy, spending, and teacher hiring all offered the prospect of developing local black economic strength in a number of ways. First, as minority community control advocates from across New York agreed, control over school finances would allow community school boards to direct school spending toward black and other nonwhite contrac-tors or suppliers. Whether it be repairing a school building or purchasing new teaching materials, school expenditure represented a chance to strengthen the local community's economic base by making local nonwhite companies and their employees the beneficiaries.[64]

Second, community control could increase black employment opportunities by addressing the proportional underrepresentation of black teachers in both cities. In the mid-1960s, minority student enrollment in New York's public schools exceeded 50 percent, but only 8 percent of teachers and 3 percent of administrators were black. By early 1968, over 40 percent of all students in Los Angeles's schools were nonwhite, nearly evenly divided between the city's two largest minority groups, African Americans and Hispanics. At the same time, only around 14 percent of teachers and 6.1 percent of school administrators were black (though this was better than the case for Hispanics, who made up just 3 percent and 1.3 percent respectively).[65] The hiring of black teachers and administrators in proportional numbers was a demand rooted in a civil rights movement vision of racial equity that Black Power radicals, students, and others imbued with greater militancy during the late 1960s. Control over staff selection also promised to make teachers more accountable and responsive to the local community. Existing white teachers were often seen as uncaring, uninterested (and, in some cases, openly racist) educators concerned more with their paychecks than with educating black children. Many African Americans understandably believed, therefore, that control over hiring teachers and staff—regardless of their color—offered the best hope for positive and collaborative teacher-community relations in the future.

Third, control of school policy, educational programs, and teacher hiring could help improve black students' future economic prospects. In mid-November 1967, in response to the Manual Arts protests and growing discontent among black and Chicano students over the state of their schools, the Los Angeles city school board created a special Communications Task Force, which aimed to improve school-community relations in South Los Angeles. This task force gave students a chance to air their grievances away from the picket line. In late January 1968, Glanville Lockett, a former student counselor at all-black Jordan High School, attended a meeting with a large group of local high school students arranged by Lou Smith, head of the local organization Operation Bootstrap. Mirroring Manual Arts students' demands, these students expressed concern over the quality of the instruction they received and its failure to prepare them for further education and high-wage employment.[66] Figures indicating the underenrollment of minorities in professional training courses in the city supported their claims. For example, of 392 registered students at UCLA's medical school in late 1968, only 2 were black and none were Mexican American.[67]

California assemblyman Victor Vesey, head of an assembly select committee set up in 1968 to investigate campus disturbances at the state's universities, agreed with the students, finding that minority access to higher education in California had been severely limited by "inadequate schools and poor counseling together with false and artificial entrance requirements" that together had "systematically screened out even gifted youths from minority communities."[68] Students believed that being taught by more committed, sympathetic, and skilled staff would improve their ability to access more lucrative career opportunities in the future.

Furthermore, community control activists' demands for black history courses to be taught in schools also overlapped and reflected another central pillar of the Black Power mission: the importance of education as a tool of black liberation. This was evident throughout the late 1960s and 1970s as Black Power radicals established private, independent Pan Africanist schools, covering among them all levels of education, in cities across the country. These institutions, as historian Russell Rickford has shown, provided their students with an alternative Afrocentric education they hoped would shape a new generation of young activists committed to the liberation and empowerment of black people across the world.[69]

African Americans also fought to remake white-dominated educational institutions. In early November 1968, as community control controversies raged in New York and Los Angeles, black students at San Francisco State College went on strike, demanding the creation of the first Black Studies program.[70] The emergence of Black Studies as an academic discipline during the late 1960s was a direct outgrowth of militant Black Power protest, especially by students on university campuses across the nation. Black Studies programs reflected an effort not only to establish greater black independence and authority in the nation's white-dominated university system (a sphere in which it was traditionally absent) but also to create an academically recognized body of knowledge on the African American experience. That knowledge was intended to inform the redefinition and celebration of black identity, history, and culture, which, in turn, would serve as the basis for building greater racial pride, solidarity, and consciousness. As Maulana Karenga, now a leading Africana Studies scholar, explains, "Black studies [. . .] came into being in the midst of the black freedom movement as an emancipatory project that sought to be both an ongoing and profound critique and corrective, both intellectually and socially."[71]

The clamor for Black Studies courses was therefore a natural corollary to community control of local schools and curricula. As New York high school student James Toponwey of the African American Students Association argued, "integrated" schools would not change the substance of public education, which had come to mean "You [whites] force your culture on us and deny us a relevant education."[72] Redefining black identity and celebrating black culture could be woven into African American children's education during their early, formative years, instilling racial pride, consciousness, and solidarity in black youth in a way that the "whitewashed" and inferior education they received in public schools never could. In this way, community control was seen by some as crucial to the broader struggle for Black Power. As Operation Bootstrap leader Robert Hall argued, "We can't have a black revolution, we can't build black dignity, we can't build a black nation if every year [the schools] are turning out a generation of ignorant black children."[73]

The black demand for a more culturally relevant public education naturally reinforced the demand for more black teachers and administrators. As historian Peter Novick explains, the question of racial authenticity and perspective in education and academia became a central theme of Black Power–era criticism of white-authored scholarship and curricula. How could white teachers, from their racially privileged and dominant position, educate African American children about a black past defined by a racial oppression that they could never truly understand? Only black scholars and teachers, some argued, could be entrusted with the tasks of writing black history and of informing black children about their cultural identity and heritage and the society in which they lived. These concerns were evident among Jordan High students who, during a meeting with Lockett at OB headquarters, expressed deep skepticism about the prospect of having their apparently "insensitive" and "racist" white teachers deliver the black history courses that they were seeking. Hiring more black teachers, they insisted, was the only solution.[74]

Community control also promised to place the social and psychological development of black children in the hands of teachers whose shared racial identity made them, in theory, the best candidates for the job. For Les Campbell, a leader in the Afro-American Teachers Association (AATA), an organization at the heart of black militancy in the community control movement in Ocean Hill–Brownsville, Brooklyn, this was an inescapable truth. The AATA first formed as the Negro Teachers Association in March 1964, largely in reaction to Albert Shanker and the UFT's unwillingness to publicly back the public schools boycott led by Reverend Galamison the previous month. In 1966, the group changed its name as black teachers Albert Vann and Les Campbell, both militant Black Power advocates, gave the organization an explicitly ideological focus.[75] According to Campbell, there was a fundamental, insurmountable difference between the AATA and the white teachers' union.

The UFT's primary concern, he argued, was teachers' pay, benefits, and teaching conditions and not the quality of teaching they provided or the well-being of their black students. Only the AATA, Campbell reasoned, could be a teachers' organization genuinely "centered around the question of providing a better educational opportunity for black youth." With many of its members teaching in the district, the AATA strongly endorsed community control at its 1966 annual convention and worked closely with the Ocean Hill–Brownsville Governing Board and Unit Administrator Rhody McCoy.[76] Support for community control among black teachers was not limited to New York. In September 1968—with the Ocean Hill–Brownsville experiment under way—a four-day conference held in Chicago and attended by more than eight hundred black teachers and academics from thirty-seven states culminated in the creation of the National Association of Afro-American Educators, an organization that made black control of black schools its primary goal and sought to attract black teachers away from the two largest teachers' organizations in the country, the National Educational Association and American Federation of Teachers (AFT).[77]

As we have seen, the demand for community control in New York and Los Angeles, which resonated with broad sections of local black communities, strongly reflected and overlapped the philosophy and organizing of Black Power militants. However, the bold and radical vision that community control activists in both cities championed required a redistribution of power guaranteed to meet resistance from those most directly threatened by it.

COMMUNITY CONTROL NEGATED, COMMUNITY CONTROL DEFEATED

The ultimate defeat of community control in both New York and Los Angeles revealed the power of white teachers and city officials to resist calls for transformative educational change. Unlike their counterparts in

New York, grassroots activists in Los Angeles received no support from the city, whose leading officials were united in their determination to preserve the status quo. In late January 1968, a few months after the Manual Arts protests, Superintendent of Schools Jack Crowther delivered a report explaining his vision for public education reform in the city. Among other recommendations, Crowther proposed "an aggressive and forward-looking program which, although not limited to members of minority groups, would especially encourage and help prepare minority personnel for high administrative roles." The proposal was a tacit acknowledgement and acceptance of black and Latino demands for more nonwhite principals and administrators in their local schools. Referring to events in New York, Crowther worried that "an impression that 'the schools don't care about us and don't respond to our needs,'" had been allowed to prevail in some urban areas, leading to demands for decentralization and, worse still, calls "to turn the schools over completely to the community." "I would plead," he urged, "that this false impression not be allowed to gain a foothold in our school communities." Crowther had no intention of allowing community control in Los Angeles and was confident that, if the school board provided "greater flexibility for local school staffs to adapt to local needs," and ensured that the lines of communication between schools and the community were made more open, "this attitude can be headed off."[78]

The Board of Education endorsed Crowther's position, as its response to the Manual Arts protests demonstrated. When demands for community control of schools—this time led by students—stepped up again in March 1968, the board responded accordingly. After students at six high schools (one predominantly black, five Chicano) staged walkouts to protest the condition and inadequacy of their schools—again supported by the UPC and Black Congress—the board swiftly acceded to a number of their demands. Black students from Jefferson High School got the African American principal, vice-principal, and guidance counselor they had demanded, as well as a commitment from the board to create teacher-student committees and begin teaching black history in city schools. Protests by black students at Fremont High School in December later that year yielded similar results. While these developments were victories of sorts, they resulted in little substantive change. As students came to discover, the appointment of black administrators did not necessarily bring the educational improvements they expected. The outcomes were bittersweet in other ways as well. Following these protests, the Board of Education, just as it had at Manual Arts, increased security in the schools, which became a point of contention among students.[79] African American congressman Augustus Hawkins petitioned Governor Reagan to use community people instead of professional law enforcement officers in the schools as a way to ease tensions, but was ignored, and the police presence in the city's predominantly nonwhite schools remained.[80]

Ultimately, community control activism in Los Angeles did secure some changes, satisfying demands for more black history courses, better college preparation, improved teacher-student communications, and in some instances, the appointment of more black staff. Community pressure resulted in the removal of white principals from four black high schools.[81] However, officials had ceded no real power over school affairs or policy, and in the years that followed, students increasingly resented the growing security presence in their schools. Disturbances at the city's schools from mid-1969 to mid-1970 resulted in nearly $500,000 in damages to public and private property and injury to sixty-one police officers. Mayor Yorty pointed the finger squarely at "student and militant group violence."[82] Indeed, the breakdown of order in the city's minority schools seemed to get progressively worse from this point. As NAPP's education consultant, Edward "Abie" Robinson, lamented in early 1973, "Guns on junior and senior high schools campuses, senseless gang shooting and killing, [. . .] drugs and high school vandalism" had come to characterize the urban school experience for many black Angelenos.[83]

In New York the city's decision to put community control to a test ensured that the city's schools would prove to be an even more volatile site of activism than had those in Los Angeles. Nowhere did the experiment create more controversy than in Ocean Hill–Brownsville, where in the absence of clearly defined limits to its powers, the racially militant community governing board claimed complete control over all school operations. On May 8, 1968, the governing board dismissed thirteen white teachers and six white administrators on the basis of their poor teaching performance and negative attitudes toward community control. Outraged at what he considered a violation of the teachers' legal rights and the denial of due process by the community school district leaders, UFT leader Albert Shanker demanded their reinstatement. Later that month 350 white teachers walked out of the district's schools in protest of the sackings. As the schools broke for the summer holiday, the governing board began hiring replacement teachers despite the UFT's protests. Convinced that McCoy and the governing board lacked the legal authority to dismiss teaching staff at will (infringing a teachers' right protected by civil service law), Shanker planned a strike for the first week of the new term, in September 1968. The UFT's opposition and the mass teacher walkout seemed only to confirm the governing board and local community's belief that their schools' white teachers were more interested in destroying community control than they were in educating black children.[84] Three strikes took place between September and late November. At points, the strikes went citywide and saw more than two-thirds of New York's teachers walk out of school.[85] In between, ugly scenes marked by violent reprisals, death threats, and anti-Semitic and racist abuse were witnessed in schools across the Ocean Hill–Brownsville district. By the strike's end, the radical vision of school reform that community activists had pushed so hard for was destroyed.

The UFT prevailed, and the School Decentralization Act, passed by the state legislature in April 1969, felt like a comprehensive defeat for New York's community control advocates. The new legislation divided the city into thirty-two school districts with each of the three demonstration districts subsumed into larger districts. While each of the thirty-two districts would elect its own community board, that board would have virtually no power over teachers or curriculum. Final authority over most aspects of the schools' affairs remained with a reconfigured, smaller Board of Education under the direction of a schools chancellor.[86] Bearing the clear imprimatur of its conservative Republican authors, the new law, as leading black education activist Isaiah Robinson lamented, did "not provide community control, only administrative decentralization."[87] Anger and disillusionment led many, including UBP head Evelina Antonetty and the AATA's Albert Vann, to boycott the process, resulting in very low turnout for the first community board elections held under the new legislation.[88]

The UFT had initially supported decentralization, believing it offered a chance to increase both parents' commitment to schools and teachers' authority over education. However, as historian Daniel Perlstein explains, the teachers' union came to see community control as a radical threat to job security, established procedure, and unbiased, quality education. Ultimately it became "a clash between black community activists and white teacher unionists that transformed decentralization from an experiment aimed at increasing parent participation and improving school efficiency into a shattering struggle for the redistribution of political power."[89]

The decision to locate demonstration districts only in poor minority communities and the Board of Education's failure to properly define the legal boundaries of the districts' powers undermined the community control experiment from the start.[90] These mistakes were recognized in Los Angeles, where in January 1969 African American assemblyman Bill Greene proposed school decentralization legislation (ultimately unsuccessful) to break up the Los Angeles Unified School District into ten autonomous districts. Mindful of events in New York, Roger Segure, executive secretary of AFT Local 1021, declared that the key issue in decentralization would be "the measure of control given to local communities, and under what conditions." It would be essential, he continued, to "carefully delineate lines of authority" and to ensure that community spokesmen were "truly representative." Recognizing the travails of their New York counterparts, Segure made it clear that teachers would not accept any arrangement that left them with "an inferior or impotent status," and he guaranteed that the union would fiercely oppose the barring of teachers on a racial basis (i.e., the removal of white teachers from black districts).[91]

The following year, South Los Angeles's black state assembly representatives introduced another school decentralization bill, this time to experiment with community control in three black districts, as had happened in New York. They hoped to find support from local whites in the wake of Judge Alfred Gitelson's decision to mandate citywide busing in Los Angeles's school desegregation case. As one black proponent argued, not only would blacks welcome the proposed new community control measure, but conservative whites could support the bill too, "because they don't want any part of the Gitelson decision."[92] This new approach, however, did not work. Although student activists and black politicians had fought to put community control on the agenda, they ultimately failed. In Los Angeles, school reform was carefully managed and involved little change in the power of established educational officials. Speaking in late 1971, Crowther's successor as superintendent, William J. Johnston, explained that school decentralization in Los Angeles aimed only to "minimize the unresponsiveness of [school] bureaucracy" and "enhance the opportunity for community and staff involvement in school programs." "Overall policy and administration with regard to personnel selection and placement, pupil housing, transportation and assignment, and broad curriculum requirements," he concluded, would "continue to reside with the Board of Education and the Superintendent."[93]

Grassroots movements for community control in New York and Los Angeles fell short in their battles to define the shape and meaning of school reform. In New York, despite having the tacit endorsement of Mayor Lindsay and the support of the Ford Foundation, activists came up against a white union that staunchly defended the rights of its members and turned the civil rights movement's language of anti-discrimination and color-blindness against community control advocates. Antagonism between the two groups cut across racial and ethnic lines, devolving into outright hostility, occasional violence, and lasting bitterness. In Los Angeles, student activists and their allies came up against school officials and state politicians who, conscious of developments in Harlem and Brooklyn, skillfully deflected and absorbed protests, granting largely superficial change and preserving the status quo. In both cities, activists lacked the political power to displace entrenched educational power structures, finding that without the support of teachers, a vision of school reform as radical as community control was unlikely to ever be fully realized. Educational change would proceed along the lines dictated by white, not black and minority, interests.

THE LESSONS OF COMMUNITY CONTROL
FROM THE BOTTOM UP

Despite the controversy that community control engendered in New York and Los Angeles, it proved to be an important site of unity, blurring the lines traditionally drawn between black moderates and militants and illuminating the flexibility and broad appeal of Black Power as a philosophy and organizing tool. Manual Arts High School demonstrations had brought together students with parents, Black Power militants, antipoverty activists, clergymen, civil rights leaders, and even elected officials.[94] In Harlem, the struggle over local education led to the creation of the Harlem Board of Education Organizing Committee, a similarly diverse collection of local interest groups, organizations, and individuals who united to lobby for the creation of an independent and locally controlled school system in Harlem. Black Power militants on the committee included Floyd McKissick and Roy Innis of CORE. Alongside them were local leaders of moderate or conservative groups such as the NAACP and the Urban League, as well as local antipoverty agency leaders, parent groups, and education professionals. Like their counterparts in Los Angeles, local black politicians state senator Basil Patterson and assemblyman Charles Rangel were also involved, submitting two, ultimately unsuccessful bills for the creation of an autonomous Harlem school district.[95] In Brooklyn, not long after the UFT had called its first strike in

September 1968, the breadth of community support for the militant stance of the experimental districts' governing board was demonstrated at a public meeting in Ocean Hill–Brownsville. Chairman Reverend C. Herbert Oliver read out letters of support he had received from four local chapters of the Black Panther Party, nineteen different New York–based NAACP branches, a number of the city's antipoverty agencies, interdenominational faith alliances, and various local parent associations.[96]

Community control enjoyed a broad and diverse base of support in both cities, reflecting the potential it offered for improving public education and empowering local people, and demonstrating the black community's willingness to appropriate ideas, tactics, and establish associations whenever they promised to be useful and deliver results. Although Black Power radicals played a prominent, often controversial role in community control movements in both cities, they were far from the sum of their parts. Many supporters saw community control differently from their more militant associates.[97] Community activists often took a syncretic, pragmatic approach to their activism, appropriating the elements of community control they found most appealing and most likely to improve their children's education. Many agreed that the classroom was the perfect place to teach black children about African American culture and heritage and to reshape black identity, but disagreed with black radicals' emphasis on class perspective and believed that Afrocentric educational programs were too narrow and limited in scope. Black education, they thought, could be both culturally empowering and directed toward advancement in white-dominated American society. As one local educator argued, "We're not interested in teaching middle-class values, but neither are we concerned with educating people to keep them in the ghetto."[98]

As a natural extension of Black Power ideology, community control was flexible and open to interpretation. This was evident in May 1968 when national NAACP leader Roy Wilkins backed school decentralization in New York in spite of its association with Black Power militancy and its unlikeliness to advance school integration, one of the organization's primary goals.[99] At the NAACP's annual convention the following year, the two thousand delegates seemed to agree, passing a resolution endorsing community control. Underlining the concept's flexibility and broad appeal, the resolution read: "We strongly support the concept of community control of public schools, particularly in the North and West, as a means of achieving fundamental changes in the schools and insuring accountability of public schools for public achievement. We do not believe that community control and desegregation are inherently incompatible or in conflict unless they are made to be by the advocates, white or black, of racial separatism." [100]

The wide appeal and malleability of community control as a premise were also visible in Milton Galamison's journey from ardent integrationist to community control advocate. As Clarence Taylor explains, Galamison was completely opposed to black separatism, which he equated with white supremacist ideology. His support for community control was founded on the scope it offered for greater black self-determination, the chance it gave African American parents and communities to improve their children's future prospects, and the importance of the classroom as a place to build character and pride in black heritage and culture.[101] In this view, a Black Power–oriented community control philosophy was completely compatible with an integrationist one: they both aimed at giving black children a better chance of succeeding in mainstream American society.

For over a decade after the *Brown* decision, education activists in New York pushed for school integration because at the time it represented the best chance for improving the quality of education available to their children. However, through 1966, as political changes in the city brought the prospect of school reform—and in the face of obdurate white resistance to school desegregation—parents and community activists latched on to an emerging Black Power message to foreground a new solution to the problems they faced in their local schools, and to shape the course of education reform in the city. Black parent and community groups forged alliances with Black Power militants because they shared considerable common ground in their vision of community control and offered valuable support and energy. In the earliest days of the community control movement, integrationists and Black Power militants had protested side by side outside IS 201 in September 1966.[102] When in early 1967 the People's Board of Education was looking for a location in Harlem in which to set up, SNCC, a Black Power organization, gave the board space within its Harlem offices.[103] Black Power advocates, typically cast as the extreme edge of black activism, were at the heart of a diverse, community-wide movement.

Community control also proved fertile ground for positive interracial cooperation between blacks and other minority groups (as well as some whites), in contrast to the racial antagonism that characterized antipoverty program organizing in the two cities. New York's community control movement, though dominated by African Americans, was certainly multiracial. Minority group solidarity was founded on their common target: improving the quality of their children's education. As a Chinese American mother from the Two Bridges experimental district declared, "We Asian Americans know our fate lies with the Black and Puerto Rican parents. We realize as much as they that our Chinese children are being subjected to inferior education. We join them in their fight." [104] Other minority groups also recognized the power of education to shape cultural identity. Urging the creation of an exclusively Puerto Rican school district, Julio Morales of the East Harlem Coalition for Community Control argued that such a district would help Puerto Rican children "to gain a sense of identity" and allow their parents to "program education for Puerto Rican kids who have distinctly different requirements to the blacks of Central Harlem and the white middle-class of Yorkville." [105] In Los Angeles, 1968 witnessed large-scale school protests in Latino communities, where students had similarly embraced Black Power militants' language of cultural empowerment and drawn inspiration from African American protests in Manual Arts High at the end of the previous year.[106] Students, parents, and activists in both communities recognized the inadequacies of their local public schools and engaged in overlapping protests to force change.

Community control activism in New York and Los Angeles reminds us that the black struggle for empowerment took place in a multiracial environment and overlapped and intertwined with other racial liberation efforts. The cross-fertilization between militant activism in both cities makes this especially clear. In New York the radical group the Young Lords, the Puerto Rican equivalent of the Black Panther Party, declared their "support for all battles for community control of schools." In a message to Puerto Rican students the Young Lords echoed the militancy of some of the city's Black Power advocates: "If your school is messed up, if the administrators and teachers don't care and don't teach—don't let them force you to drop out. Throw them out. The schools belong to us, not them. [. . .] Make revolution inside the schools. If the schools don't function for us, they shouldn't function at all!" [107]

In Los Angeles, the student-led walkouts in black and Mexican American schools were related and mutually supportive phenomena. As Theoharis explains, although the Manual Arts protests predated the widespread student strikes in East Los Angeles's Mexican American high schools throughout 1968, African American students' 1968 walkouts began, in part, as a sympathetic action in solidarity with their Latino counterparts. The Chicano school walkouts—or "blowouts," as Chicanos referred to them—remain a celebrated aspect of local Latino history and resulted from the collaboration between students and militants who shaped school protest together. Again, significant similarities existed between the situations that black and Latino students faced. As Carlos Montes, a prominent leader of the revolutionary nationalist Brown Berets (the era's most militant Chicano liberation group), has recounted:

> Our schools were old and in bad condition, with high drop-out, or push-out, rates and racist administrators and teachers. Over time, we started agitating for bilingual education, better school conditions, Chicano studies and more Chicano teachers. We attended community, school and youth meetings to raise demands for better educational and school conditions. This finally led to the historic East L.A. Blowouts in March of 1968, where thousands of high school Chicano youth walked out of the four predominantly Chicano high schools in the Eastside over a two week period. The Brown Berets were the first to run in to the high schools, yelling, "Walk out! Walk out!" We eventually won bilingual education, Chicano studies, better school conditions and Chicano teachers and administrators.[108]

Other minority groups were influenced in their freedom struggles by the emergence of Black Power. As historian Jeffrey Ogbar explains, the Black Power movement "had a profound effect on the symbolism, rhetoric, and tactics of radical activism outside of the African American community" in the late 1960s. "Radical ethnic nationalism and new constructions of ethnic identity" (evident in groups such as the Brown Berets and Young Lords) were heavily influenced by black radical groups, especially the Black Panthers.[109] Indeed, as historian Laura Pulido's study of Los Angeles reveals, the Black Panther Party "created the political space and inspiration for other activists of color to pursue more militant and radical forms of political action."[110] However, in advancing as radical a vision of school reform as community control, activists inevitably came into conflict with entrenched interests reluctant to concede power. In both cities, militancy and confrontational politics had far-reaching and injurious consequences.

In New York the schools crisis accelerated the decline of support for liberalism among the city's lower-middle- and middle-class white voters, many of whom agreed with Albert Shanker when he blamed the dispute on the permissiveness of liberals (embodied by Mayor Lindsay and the Ford Foundation) who had privileged the demands of disruptive, violent black militants over the legal rights of the city's hardworking white citizens. The law-and-order rhetoric of conservatives like Richard Nixon and Ronald

Reagan seemed particularly apt in the face of the violent and tense scenes that characterized the New York school crisis. To many white New Yorkers, they seemed another symptom of liberal politicians' apparent preference for minority groups and of their inability to preserve order and protect white interests in a changing urban political economy. Furthermore, by badly souring the relationship between the city's blacks and Jews, the school controversy helped to reshape the city's ethno-religious landscape. The fallout from the schools crisis saw race overtake religion as the city's key divide, as working- and middle-class Jews joined the white ethnic revival under way in the city and moved closer to New York's Irish, Italian, and Eastern European Catholic populations, which had previously been their rivals.[111] As Podair explains, this process fatally weakened the "informal political alliance between Jews, blacks, and white Protestants in New York that had defined the city's culture since the end of World War II." The new conservative alliance between Catholics and Jews made its influence on city politics felt for much of the following three decades, orchestrating a shift to the right that elected a succession of conservative mayors.[112] Moreover, this decisive new political coalition soon turned the language of community control against the very communities that had first used it, making it a rationale for the expansion of white community power. During the late 1970s, as New York experienced its greatest postwar fiscal crisis, white outer-borough voters joined with Manhattan elites to elect Ed Koch as mayor, supporting his program of severe cuts to the city's social service and welfare spending that had the heaviest impact on New York's minority communities.[113]

In Los Angeles, while community control protests brought a degree of change, the specter of violence and racial militancy on the picket line also resulted in an increasingly problematic relationship between police and security personnel and students in city schools. Worse still, when black efforts to secure community control in Los Angeles fell well short of success, similar demands by other local minority groups—once mutually supportive—were turned against wider African American efforts for educational equality. By deciding in the *Crawford* case in favor of the ACLU in 1970 and ordering the LAUSD to submit a plan for desegregation, Judge Alfred Gitelson brought a long-standing contradiction within multiracial school activism to the surface. By including black and Chicano children in his order, historian Mark Brilliant argues, Gitelson extended the meaning of *Brown* "beyond the black/white binary racial categories in which it had been originally cast." The result pitted Mexican American activists' primary target of bilingual education—which relied on the maintenance of predominantly Chicano schools—against the prospect of court-ordered busing to desegregate the city's schools (desired by many blacks), which critically undermined it. Seeking the Latino vote during his campaign for reelection in 1970, Governor Ronald Reagan used the issue of bilingual education (as distinct from community control) to bolster opposition to school desegregation. Adopting a fiercely anti–"forced busing" platform, Reagan strongly supported bilingual education while on the campaign trail and continued to do so once reelected. Reagan appropriated bilingual education to once again turn interest group identity politics against black Californians' efforts to desegregate their cities, just as he had used the language of "freedom of association" and property rights to oppose the Rumford Fair Housing Act in 1966.[114]

Ultimately, community control was too inimical to entrenched white interests to succeed. As the preceding chapters establish, the trajectory of black empowerment was vitally influenced by both public policy and the political support (or lack thereof) of whites. The War on Poverty's potential for mobilizing and empowering poor black communities brought decisive reactions from established urban power structures, which sought to nullify that threat and maintain the clientelist bent of urban politics. CDCs and other black economic development policies enjoyed a measure of success because they were deliberately distinct from the redistributive economic principles of welfare state liberalism and existing antipoverty policies, support for which among white voters had badly eroded. Although community control initially enjoyed the support of Mayor Lindsay and the Ford Foundation, it was defeated by a white middle-class labor union who's economic and professional interests it threatened. The UFT was able to exert its considerable power to kill the experiment and to conclusively define the parameters of education reform in the city as members saw fit. In Los Angeles, demands for community control were skillfully absorbed and deflected and, when school decentralization did later occur, it did so in a way that strengthened the power of teachers and education officials, but did virtually nothing to increase community influence over school affairs.[115] As the following section explains, events in Atlanta demonstrated the ways in which the cause of black empowerment could be furthered when white and black interests aligned and when it promised to reinforce, rather than weaken, class privilege.

In early February 1970 Preston Wilcox delivered an address on the virtues of community control in front of Atlanta's black establishment. Speaking at the Butler Street YMCA—the unofficial "Black Chamber of Commerce"—he was a world away from the IS 201 protests in Harlem, where the theory had originated. Wilcox spoke to a room filled with powerful individuals, including wealthy, independent, and highly influential black business leaders, educators, professionals, and ministers. It was a group whose star was on the rise. In the year leading up to Wilcox's visit, black political power in the city had grown sharply, and African Americans now held one-third of all elective offices in the city. Maynard Jackson had become the city's first black vice-mayor. Recent elections had considerably increased the black presence on the city's powerful aldermanic council. Revered local educator Dr. Benjamin E. Mays headed the city's Board of Education, one of three black board members out of a total of ten.[116] "Now is the time," Wilcox announced, "for the communities to take charge of the education of their children as to what they should study and by whom these books are taught." "Community control," he concluded, "promotes better schools, aids in the selection of administrators, teachers, school curricula and eliminates the self-hatred of the black youth."[117] However, whereas community control activists in New York and Los Angeles sought the transfer of educational authority to parent and grassroots activist–led councils, Atlanta's black leadership elite instead sought to build on their growing influence by securing themselves administrative control of the city's school system. Their efforts to take over the apparatus of public education in Atlanta would triumph at the expense of grassroots education activism in the city's poor black neighborhoods, reflecting an intraracial struggle in which both gender and socioeconomic class played a defining part.

Class interests had long dictated the course of racial progress in Atlanta. Following the Second World War, the city's black community was effectively led by the Atlanta Negro Voters' League (ANVL), an organization that Alton Hornsby has described as "a handful or two of black aristocrats who spoke for black Atlantan politics and civil rights matters for two decades." At the top of the pile were men like A. T. "Colonel" Walden, an attorney and legendary political operator, and Reverend William Holmes Borders, the "dean of the City's black preachers" and pastor of the prestigious Wheat Street Baptist

Church. Favoring negotiation and gradualism over protest and litigation, the concessions that Walden and his allies won from the city's white power structure rarely benefited Atlanta's poorest blacks. The student movement that exploded out of Atlanta in 1960 shook the city's black establishment, and after Walden's death in 1965 the remaining members of ANVL joined forces with the new generation of aspiring black city leaders. This new coalition combined several elderly ministers of large churches, a number of black college professors, some older businessmen, and a number of young professionals and ambitious businessmen and -women. As the decade progressed, these leaders (who, Hornsby explains, came to be known as the New Black Power Structure) continued—as had the ANVL before them—to try to ensure that Atlanta remained "a middle-class black haven."[118] Local education reform became an important target of their efforts. The antipathy of the city's black leaders to school integration reflected the concern it had caused Atlanta's black education professionals and its middle- and upper-class blacks, who treasured the high-quality black-run schools that served their neighborhoods. As the city's school desegregation fight dragged on into the late 1960s, pupil desegregation became a secondary, even incidental, concern for these groups. Instead, Brown-Nagin explains, the campaign morphed into a struggle "over employment discrimination and socioeconomic class as much as a fight about race and pupil education." Driven by Atlanta's black teachers, these developments underlined their position as one of the city's most powerful black interest groups, a role they had enjoyed for many decades.[119]

Horace Tate, head of the Georgia Teacher and Education Association (GTEA) and school board member, explained his constituents' position on school desegregation in mid-1969. As faculty desegregation in the city had failed to allay teachers' fears about discrimination, especially for the school system's top jobs, Tate argued: "Our people believed in integration. But by now they see it's placing the Negro in the worst position he's ever been in."[120] Board of Education president Benjamin Mays echoed Tate's narrow, sectional view of black interests when he chided black students outside the South protesting for Black Studies courses at their universities. Their demands, he argued, would lead northern universities to poach southern black colleges' best academics. "With the scarcity of black scholars," Mays complained, "this would only mean the weakening of black colleges. If we are as concerned as we say we are about blackness, black control, black power, and the like—we should be against any move that would weaken what is definitely our own."[121] These sentiments, articulated by two of the city's most influential education officials (irrespective of race), revealed the high level of support given to protecting and increasing black teachers' power, as well as the underlying assumption that what was good for black teachers was good for the black community as a whole.

With greater power over the city's school system firmly in their sights, Atlanta's black establishment was soon presented with an excellent opportunity to advance its interests. In April 1971 the Supreme Court's ruling in *Swann v. Charlotte-Mecklenburg Board of Education* raised the prospect of court-ordered busing to accelerate school desegregation. The implications of the *Swann* decision for the outcome of *Calhoun*, the city's ongoing school desegregation case, gave Atlanta's black leaders a bargaining chip with which to force the hand of the city's white power structure.[122] The city's black leaders, including Mays and Tate, entered into negotiations with local white counterparts keen to settle *Calhoun*. Begun in secret, these talks produced an agreement that secured Atlanta's black elite immediate control over the city's school system in return for bringing the *Calhoun* suit to a close, thereby ending the prospect of busing. Subsequently known as the Atlanta Compromise, the settlement proposed an organizational restructuring that guaranteed local blacks twenty-five of thirty-seven public school system administration posts (twenty-one of which would be newly created). Furthermore, the settlement reserved eight of the fifteen most senior positions for African Americans. The whole process reflected the broader acceptance among the city's black and white leaders of an affirmative action–inflected proportional distribution of power based on race. However, just like the federal contract set-asides for minority-owned businesses that the Nixon administration developed, the designation of high-level city jobs for African Americans promised primarily to help the black middle class and elite and not the poor, who generally lacked the education and training that such positions demanded. Furthermore, the plan was designed to minimize future pupil desegregation, and left approximately two-thirds of Atlanta's 153 public schools virtually all black. What busing the plan did include involved less than 3 percent of the total student body, none of which would include students from the city's upper- and middle-income black neighborhoods.[123]

The decision to settle *Calhoun* was contrary to the wishes of Atlanta's poor and working-class blacks, a majority of whom favored busing as a method for desegregating the city's schools. The class politics that informed the school board's position did not escape local black newspaper editor and social justice advocate J. Lowell Ware, who strongly criticized the board's stance after negotiations became public. "Blacks living in swanky middle-class neighborhoods," he complained, "no longer worry about their poor brothers who must fight the rats. Blacks who have good schools in their neighborhoods are not aiding the less fortunate blacks who need busing to get a decent education for their children." Atlanta's black elite, he argued, were "more interested in political status than in racial equality for all people. [. . .] It makes the sons of Robert E. Lee and the richer sons of Fred Douglass partners in keeping the peace by destroying the power of civil rights." [124] The Atlanta Compromise, however, did not go unchallenged.

THE FIGHT FOR SOCIAL JUSTICE AND EDUCATIONAL EQUALITY IN ATLANTA'S GHETTOS

The battle to invalidate the *Calhoun* settlement and make busing the primary weapon in the fight for educational equality in Atlanta, emerged from a diverse base of grassroots community activism rooted in Peoplestown, one of the city's poorest black neighborhoods. At the heart of it all was Emmaus House, a local social service and community support center established in 1967 by the Diocese of Atlanta. The center's operations were run by local blacks alongside the predominantly white church staff, as well as unpaid workers (often white northern college students), all under the leadership of white Catholic priest Father Austin Ford. Emmaus House sought primarily to empower the local poor by making them aware of their rights and helping them to fight for positive change in their community.[125] Strongly committed to their cause, Emmaus House became perhaps the greatest wellspring of African American grassroots activism for social and economic justice in the city.

In mid-July 1968, inspired by a visiting NWRO spokeswoman from Washington, D.C., five local black welfare mothers established the neighborhood's first NWRO branch. The group elected one of their number, Ethel Mae Matthews, as president. Matthews soon emerged as one of the most committed and hardworking leaders and advocates for social and economic justice in Atlanta. Led by Matthews, and with the help of Emmaus House staff, the group's membership quickly swelled to more than 150.[126] Emmaus House offered vital organizational support to burgeoning local welfare rights activism by providing both a space for meeting and transport to and from meetings for those involved, and with Emmaus House's help a number of other NWRO chapters formed in nearby disadvantaged black neighborhoods. The following year, along with several local black ministers, Emmaus House worked with public housing residents to start the citywide tenants' rights organization Tenants United For Fairness (TUFF), which, like local NWRO branches, was predominantly female-led. Over time, TUFF's battles with the Atlanta Housing Authority resulted in significant victories for poor local blacks. These included improved leases, better housing code enforcement, and the establishment of a grievance review procedure that was the first of its kind and that later became a requirement in public housing nationally.[127] Together with the local welfare rights groups (with which there was considerable membership overlap), these organizations represented the city's most energetic grassroots community activism.

Emmaus House's commitment to economic and social justice led it to play a central role in the battle for integrated local education. In October 1969 the Supreme Court's decision in *Alexander v. Holmes County Board of Education* forced the Atlanta school board to adapt once more to the changing terrain of school desegregation jurisprudence. In *Alexander,* Chief Justice Warren Burger decreed that dual school systems were to be eradicated immediately, invalidating long timetables for desegregation despite the protestations of the Nixon Department of Justice. Accordingly, the city devised a new plan that did increase desegregation of both pupils and faculty but limited racial change by increasing black enrollment in white schools and white enrollment in black schools by less than 10 percent. In spite of its modest scope, white Atlantans (including large teacher and student protest groups) opposed the new plan vociferously, and the ongoing white exodus from the city's public schools accelerated as a result.[128] The new plan also included a provision allowing for students in schools where they were in a racial majority to apply for transfers to schools where they would be in a minority. Deliberately unpublicized, this rule required a minimum of thirty children to be signed up before the city would provide transport. As an Emmaus House worker suggested, this requirement "effectively disenfranchised a lot of parents who would like for their child to transfer because they didn't have the organizational capacity to get up a bus load of kids. [. . .] so Emmaus House filled that gap."[129]

Emmaus House workers, alongside Matthews and her fellow community activists, canvassed local parents (capitalizing on the growing welfare and tenants' rights activist network they were cultivating) to garner support for utilizing the school transfer provision. The response was emphatic. As Father Ford remembered, "There were a lot of housing projects, and they were all teeming with women who were desperate to improve their situation and help their children. There wasn't any problem with recruiting." Their first organizing efforts resulted in nearly four hundred local black children applying for a transfer. Beyond seeking a better education for local children, the effort was also a deliberate, symbolic challenge to the racial and economic dimensions of educational inequality in Atlanta. As Father Ford explained: "We were determined not to send them just to scatter them around but to have enough of those children in a school so they wouldn't feel isolated. And so we went to E. Rivers and [Morris] Brandon and [Warren T.] Jackson [Elementary Schools]—all the posh schools in town. You know, they operate like private schools, and only rich white people could get there."[130] Emmaus workers targeted high-performing, well-resourced schools in wealthy white neighborhoods in North Atlanta, which were almost always under capacity, while schools in poor black neighborhoods like Peoplestown ran at double, and sometimes even triple, sessions to cope with overcrowding. Despite the anger of many white parents in North Atlanta (including some Emmaus House donors who withdrew their support in protest), the Peoplestown students attended the white schools with little incident. The Emmaus House–local-welfare-rights activist coalition sought to build on this initial success and make busing available to more of Atlanta's underprivileged black children.[131]

In Peoplestown, the fight for school desegregation resulted naturally from grassroots black community activism that flowed through Emmaus House. What began in mid-1968 as welfare rights and tenants' rights activism became a much broader struggle for social and economic justice and self-determination. As one Emmaus House worker remembered, local activists had initially focused on "basic rights such as obtaining higher welfare payments and using formal grievance hearings to dispute termination or reduction of benefits or other improper decisions by their caseworkers." Over time, as they "developed confidence in speaking out, and other leadership capacities," they came to address other issues such as "better pay for black workers, securing better housing and food, and electing better government officials."[132] As historian Rhonda Williams's work on female-led black public housing tenant activism in Baltimore has suggested, this kind of activism was influenced by the grassroots organizing spirit and philosophy evinced by radical Black Power groups like the Black Panthers.[133] It was part of a Black Power–oriented agenda concerned primarily with transformative social and economic justice politics, the redistribution of power and resources from the top downward, the democratization of local institutions, and resistance against racial and gender oppression. Unlike more mainstream, middle-class visions of Black Power cultivated by some white politicians, black community organizations, and Black Power advocates, it attributed far less value to the pursuit of economic nationalism and was less attached to the symbolic value of black ownership. Black empowerment—political or economic—was valuable only to the extent that it served the greater cause of reforming and democratizing American institutions and society in the pursuit of social, economic, and racial justice for all.

Emmaus House was a vital space where this local vision of community empowerment was supported and developed. One room was dedicated to the Poverty Rights Office (PRO), which helped local people deal with practical problems they faced. As one staff member explained: "The kind of work that they [the PRO] did, we did on a walk-in basis: somebody's electricity was cut off, somebody needed to apply for welfare or get Social Security benefits, somebody was having a housing issue, all sorts of things like that, and we'd just go out and do." [134] Not unlike the "community survival" programs run by the Black Panther Party, Emmaus House ran free baby-feeding and food surplus programs. A food cooperative also existed at the center for several years during the early 1970s.[135] Beyond community support, the PRO also helped develop local activism by printing and distributing the *Poor People's Newspaper*. Appearing every six weeks, the *Poor People's Newspaper* carried articles that enumerated and explained local people's rights, as well as relevant developments concerning a wide range of agencies, organizations, and issues such as welfare, housing, Supreme Court decisions, and prisoners' rights. The newsletter was a vital organizational tool, and Ethel Mae Matthews's regular opening articles helped make her an influential and widely respected local leader.[136]

Emmaus House also facilitated local efforts to win political power. On top of voter registration and education work, the organization sponsored candidates from the community to run for local office and supported their campaigns. In 1969 and 1973 Matthews ran for a seat on the city council. Although unsuccessful on both occasions, her candidacy did lead to the removal of the city's $500 candidate filing fee requirement, which, Matthews had argued, unduly penalized the poor and restricted their ability to stand in local elections. In 1972 local black resident and Emmaus House volunteer Margret Griggs (whose daughter participated in the center's busing program) was persuaded by Father Ford to run for election to the Board of Education, and she won later that year.[137]

The center also had direct links to Black Power radicalism. Gene Ferguson, a leading figure at Emmaus House, was one of the small but committed cadre

FIGURE 7. Ethel Mae Matthews, the founder of the Atlanta Welfare Rights Organization, during a welfare rights march in downtown Atlanta, Georgia, 1976. Boyd Lewis Collection, Kenan Research Center at the Atlanta History Center.

of local Black Panther Party activists. When he was not running the BPP's local free breakfast and other survival programs, Ferguson was teaching local children at Emmaus House about black history and running numerous other programs. Along with Columbus Ward (a former BPP member and fellow Emmaus House organizer), Ferguson ran an after-school children's club called "Liberators" that provided meals; ran educational field trips to city government buildings, museums, and elsewhere; and engaged local children in dramatic and other artistic activities.[138] As an institution, Emmaus House embraced Black Power, just as the people they worked with had. As staff member Sister Marie Bodell remembered, she and her colleagues felt part of "a great community-building opportunity. Gene, of course, helped lay out black history, and we had Sister Mary Joseph who made a beautiful sign that was in the front entrance for decades that said, 'black is beautiful.' 'Black power' and 'I'm black and I'm beautiful' were chants that the kids would say all the time." [139]

While the relationship between Emmaus House and Black Power activism and ideology is far from typical of white religious groups—especially Catholics—parallels did exist elsewhere (in cities such as Milwaukee, Wisconsin, and Louisville, Kentucky), though they were few and far

FIGURE 8. Community activist Gene Ferguson *(far right)* speaks to a group of young people at Emmaus House in the Peoplestown community of Atlanta, Georgia, 1975. Boyd Lewis Collection, Kenan Research Center at the Atlanta History Center.

between.[140] Ultimately, the interracial and faith-based Black Power organizing evident in Atlanta was unusual. Indeed, Catholics are more often identified with opposition to civil rights and social justice activism. For example, the McCarthyite anticommunist populism of the early Cold War was rooted in broad Catholic support, and William F. Buckley and L. Brent Bozell Jr., two key antiliberal, conservative ideologues of the 1950s, were also Catholics.[141] In northern cities such as New York, Chicago, and Detroit, white Catholic working- and lower-middle-class ethnic groups such as Italian and Polish Americans were often associated with fierce resistance to integration and black civil rights legislation during the 1960s and afterward.[142] Along with similar activism in Milwaukee, the partnership between Emmaus House and local black community activists complicates the dominant image of the relationship between white Catholic groups and the black freedom struggle.

The Supreme Court's April 1971 decision in *Swann v. Charlotte-Mecklenburg Board of Education*—which prompted biracial negotiations among city elites to settle the *Calhoun* case—presented Emmaus House and its local allies with an opportunity to realize their vision of school reform. By endorsing busing and rezoning as methods to achieve a degree of racial balance in school districts, *Swann* encouraged community activists in Peoplestown to file a lawsuit of their own. As Emmaus House worker David Morath has explained:

> Charlotte-Mecklenburg had a [metropolitan] school district, and we had looked and thought probably more could be done if we looked at Atlanta on a metropolitan basis [rather] than just the city of Atlanta. There were areas on the edge of the city of Atlanta where there were more opportunities for whites and blacks to mix. So, the NAACP, which had the original court case, was not interested in pursuing this because the Atlanta school board had just turned majority black. So the city school district was in black control and we were starting to get into the black power verses integration debate. [Instead of pursuing the NAACP as a partner,] we picked up with ACLU. Margie Pitts Hames was the attorney, and we signed up plaintiffs to sue for [desegregating as a] metropolitan school district.[143]

The resulting case, *Armour v. Nix,* was led by Hames, a leading civil rights lawyer with a history of fighting important poverty and women's rights cases. The *Armour* plaintiffs—the majority of whom were local black welfare mothers—were firmly convinced of the need for school desegregation. As Ethel Mae Matthews explained to the court in 1973, "What we are searching for is equality for our children and the Metro suit is the only way to get it." [144] By demanding a broader jurisdictional scope for school desegregation remedies in Atlanta, a victory in *Armour* would supersede the *Calhoun* settlement that negotiations between the city's black and white leaders would soon produce.[145] The courts would ultimately decide which of the two opposing visions of black empowerment would prevail.

BLACK CONTROL TRIUMPHANT

The filing of *Armour* on June 8, 1972, ensured that the ongoing *Calhoun* settlement talks were expeditiously concluded a few weeks later. On the white side of the negotiating table sat, among others, several school board members, including the superintendent of schools, John Letson. On the black side sat Benjamin Mays and other black school board members, Atlanta Urban League head Lyndon Wade, and insurance company executive Jesse Hill Jr., Atlanta's most influential black businessman. This prestigious group was led by local NAACP chief Lonnie King, a celebrated former SNCC activist and former leader of the city's student sit-in movement.

King was especially important to the process because the city's school desegregation case had been filed in 1958 by John Calhoun, then the Atlanta NAACP branch president. Even though the case had been led by the Legal Defense Fund ever since, and local involvement had always been limited, King was able to use his position as Calhoun's successor—and, therefore, the case's de facto sponsor—to wrestle control of *Calhoun* away from the LDF. After much legal maneuvering (which included temporarily firing LDF as counsel), King and his fellow negotiators eventually presented the court with their agreed settlement in February 1973, which sacrificed further busing in return for putting administrative control of the public school system in black hands. Hames immediately filed an objection to the settlement and argued for the right of those affected to have their voices heard, securing her clients the chance to testify before the *Calhoun* district court judges. In early March, a series of hearings gave Atlanta's poor black community the chance to speak out in favor of busing and to challenge the notion that Lonnie King spoke for all black Atlantans. Despite impassioned testimony from poor and working-class blacks, including Ethel Mae Matthews, Edward Moody, and prominent tenants' rights leader Eva Davis, the judges ultimately approved the settlement, once more declaring Atlanta's school system unitary.[146]

The settlement's main protagonists were quick to defend their work. Lonnie King argued, "What we've come up with is a compromise, but it's the only solution that could be negotiated that will guarantee quality education for blacks." King also stressed that large numbers of middle-class black parents had demanded he bring the school desegregation saga to an end. Not only was the ongoing turmoil unsettling for their children, they argued, but they also feared that black students would get the short straw and be bused long distances. Many others, King suggested, were not convinced their children would get a better education in white schools than they already received in their local black school. Board of Education president Benjamin Mays explained his backing of the compromise a different way, framing it as part of the broader economic interests and public relations image of a city in which African Americans were starting to gain political hegemony:

> 20 years ago or so when school desegregation was just starting in the South, Atlanta schools were 70% white and 30% black. Now they're 80 percent black and 20 percent white. It's a matter of white flight and private schools, the old story. Massive busing would be counterproductive at this point. We'd end up with no whites to bus. Then what would happen to Atlanta and all this

progress and growth we're always bragging about? Even with the compromise, it may be too late.[147]

Other local black leaders also backed the settlement, insisting the plan had strong local support. Recently elected congressman Andrew Young celebrated it as an opportunity for blacks to gain more power in city government, while state representative Billy McKinney praised the fact that it would not "disturb" black neighborhoods. Reverend J. E. Lowery, chairman of the SCLC board, argued that it was the best plan the city could come up with because it kept twenty-five thousand black children from being bused. "Busing just to have a certain number of black students sitting with whites is not meaningful and borders on being racist." Although SCLC moved quickly to distance itself from this view, Lowery remained firmly behind the compromise. Reverend Joseph Boone, a close ally of Father Ford of Emmaus House, and the city's welfare rights groups offered a dissenting voice. Boone, a consistent advocate of Atlanta's disadvantaged, decried the settlement as "anti-black" and a product of black political "busybodies" who had ignored the wishes of the city's poor African Americans.[148]

The settlement's impact reverberated far beyond the city. Developments in Atlanta dismayed officials at the NAACP's New York national headquarters, who swiftly suspended King and his fellow local branch officials. As one national board member asserted, "We're fighting for the integrity of our national policy, and that integrity must be maintained. There are compromises and there are compromises, but we cannot repudiate our national policy." Nathaniel R. Jones, general counsel for the NAACP's national office, argued that the Atlanta Compromise represented a dangerous new policy that threatened to "turn the clock back to segregated schools." Indeed, he noted, it had already set a precedent: the *Calhoun* settlement was quickly brought into school desegregation case proceedings by city lawyers in Grand Rapids, Michigan, and Knoxville, Tennessee. The national NAACP leadership's response was unequivocal. In August 1973, following an inquest, the national office expelled all the Atlanta branch members and started the organization afresh.[149]

After the schools compromise was upheld by the courts, the only case that threatened it, *Armour v. Nix,* resumed. If successful, the ACLU's suit would require a metropolitan-wide school desegregation initiative that would invalidate Atlanta's existing arrangements. The prospects for success, however, were severely damaged by events elsewhere. In June 1974 a Supreme

Court dominated by conservative Nixon appointees overturned the lower-court decision in *Milliken v. Bradley*. In *Milliken*, Detroit district court judge Stephen Roth, having found the city's residential segregation to be the result of both public policy and the discriminatory practices of realtors, had mandated large-scale interdistrict busing to integrate white and black schools across the metropolitan area. The Supreme Court's rejection of Roth's findings effectively absolved suburban whites of any responsibility for desegregation, seemingly dooming efforts toward metropolitan-wide school integration. *Armour* dragged on until May 1980, when the Supreme Court endorsed the local court's late-1979 decision to dismiss the case. With defeat came the end of further court-ordered busing as a solution for desegregating Atlanta's public schools.[150]

DIFFERENT PATHS, DIFFERENT OUTCOMES

Struggles over public education unfolded differently in all three cities, with each revealing the various ways Black Power translated into, and helped reshape, black community activism. Battling to define the scope of public policy, activists in New York and Los Angeles foregrounded a vision of public education reform intended to transform existing power arrangements. These grassroots movements for community control proved to be a fertile ground for cooperation between moderates and militants alike. Black Power radicals worked alongside civil rights advocates, clergy, students, antipoverty workers, and parents in the fight to improve local education, blurring the lines traditionally drawn between them. The fracturing of the black freedom struggle that supposedly followed the emergence of the "Black Power" slogan in mid-1966 did not translate so readily into community control activism in New York and Los Angeles. In Atlanta, grassroots education activism was supported by Emmaus House, a local faith-based community organization headed by a white Catholic priest. Uniting local black residents, Black Power activists, female welfare and tenants' rights advocates, and white church staff and student volunteers, the Black Power–inflected social and economic justice activism channeled through Emmaus House illuminates a fascinating and understudied example of interracial cooperation. Almost entirely interdependent, Emmaus House staff and local blacks fought collectively for a vision of education reform that sought to empower local poor black mothers and challenge the black middle class's claims to speak on behalf of the black poor.

Education activism in all three cities reveals several significant trends. First, it underscores the importance of public policy as a site of political contestation and community activism upon which Black Power—and African Americans' attempts to secure greater self-determination and economic power and opportunity more broadly—was negotiated. Second, the diversity of school reform movements demonstrates the wide appeal of Black Power ideology (in part, if not completely) at the grassroots level, as well as its influence across racial lines. Black Power's flexibility was matched by the pragmatism of grassroots activists' approaches to protest and militancy. Third, it broadens the list of actors involved in Black Power's development at the everyday, community level. As Theoharis suggests, the place of high school students on the front line in Los Angeles (a largely neglected aspect of the city's history) shows us how "Black Power evolved at the grassroots from years of struggle around issues of schools, jobs, and housing." [151] Similarly, the extensive involvement of antipoverty groups in community control activism in New York makes clear the War on Poverty's role in providing an organizational and intellectual framework within which grassroots visions of black empowerment were incubated. Community activism in Atlanta revealed the ways in which local people and institutions could come together across racial boundaries to forge their own brand of Black Power politics, one in which race, class, and gender oppression were inseparable.

Finally, and perhaps most significantly in the context of this book, the defeat of grassroots education activism in all three cities underlines the success of white mainstream politicians, institutions, and organizations in absorbing, deflecting, subverting, and defeating African American movements for transformative and redistributive political and socioeconomic change. The course of educational reform in Atlanta also highlighted how narrower visions of black empowerment, skewed toward the economic and political interests of black and white elites, were able (with the endorsement of local white leaders) to prevail. While pressure for black control of public education in New York and Los Angeles came predominantly from the grass roots, in Atlanta the opposite was true. The settlement of *Calhoun* in 1973 must be understood as part of the broader trend toward increasing black power in Atlanta, a work in progress that was gathering momentum in the early 1970s. As Atlanta gradually became a majority-black city, its African American elite stepped up their efforts to gain full administrative control of the city and its institutions. As Lonnie King explained at the time, "It's a chess game. The school compromise was just one move." [152]

Brown-Nagin is right to suggest that the Atlanta case "powerfully illus-trates how the black middle-class's aspiration to consolidate not only political power, but also their economic power, shaped events." What is less tenable, however, is her suggestion that it should be seen as a movement for commu-nity control.[153] Atlanta's school desegregation politics was guided by a view of black empowerment informed primarily by professional and class con-cerns, and predicated on increasing and concentrating power in the hands of the privileged groups that already held it. Atlanta's black establishment came to covet control of the city's school system, seeing it as a source of jobs and as a way to protect the professional rights of the city's large contingent of black teachers. The gendered implications of the episode, though never explicitly articulated at the time, were also clear. As the city's largely male, professional elite negotiated to foreclose the possibility of substantial busing, they subor-dinated the interests of the city's welfare rights groups and their overwhelm-ingly poor female leadership, which supported busing and school desegrega-tion. Their actions were thus fundamentally antithetical to those of community control movements in New York and Los Angeles that demanded the redistribution of power from the top downward, to the powerless and disadvantaged.

The trajectory of education reform in each of the three cities reinforces the overarching argument of this book: that opportunities for black progress were made available where they privileged middle-class values and leadership and where they endorsed (or did not threaten) white interests and the exist-ing socioeconomic and political order. As the final chapter demonstrates, this trend became especially clear—and even more pronounced—in Atlanta and Los Angeles under black city leadership during the 1970s. Public policy would again be at the heart of this development.

FOUR

Black Mayors and Black Progress

THE LIMITS OF BLACK POLITICAL POWER

On September 25, 1972, Atlanta mayor Sam Massell gave his "Fear to Eternity" speech at the city's prestigious Emory University. Meditating on the theme of growing black political power—a theme that had characterized his speeches for the past year—Massell warned his audience:

> We are beginning to see signs of self-confidence on the part of the have-nots who are getting their first taste of affluence [...] the fear of losing security because others are gaining it causes a class struggle quite costly to the very prosperity the rich want most to preserve. [...] Perhaps the most significant switch of fear from one group to another is that which is taking place in many major cities between blacks and whites. The transition from second class citizenship by the black community, the members of which have been suppressed all their lives, to a status of equality with whites in all walks of life, is difficult to cope with, even by the most conscientious.[1]

Although Massell was talking about blacks and whites in general, he was also talking about himself. A charismatic young liberal and the city's first-ever Jewish mayor, Massell had been elected in 1969 and was seeking reelection in 1973. Elected largely on the strength of black support, Massell had done a great deal during his time in office to increase black participation in city government, increasing local African Americans' share of municipal jobs appreciably. While happy to run the city in partnership with the local black elite, Massell still envisaged them as the junior partner. However, as Atlanta became a majority-black city at the start of the 1970s, its black leaders were increasingly inclined toward becoming the senior partner. Maynard Jackson, the city's first-ever African American vice-mayor, had been elected alongside Massell in 1969. By 1973, many felt it was time for a black candidate to take the reins at city hall. Concerned by this shift in city politics, Massell cautioned that

> the young, the poor, the black have a heavy responsibility. Adjustment to the use of rights long denied is in and of itself taxing of mind and body, but conquering that alone is not enough. Those who move into formerly forbidden territories must take care lest they rush the entire structure. [. . .] If you are black and have become powerful, you must be able to think white to understand their needs. To do less will destroy all that has been gained by the struggles up to this point.[2]

Massell argued that unless blacks were willing to "think white" and govern in the interests of middle-class whites and white businesses, whites would continue to abandon the city for surrounding suburbs, further eroding the city's already declining tax base and putting Atlanta's economic future in jeopardy. The insinuation was clear: black control of city hall was likely to exacerbate these trends. Continuing to work in partnership with a white mayor, he insisted, would therefore be in the best interests of the whole city—black and white.

Pointedly, Massell first delivered this message in October 1971 at the Butler Street YMCA, the city's premier black community forum. His speech was not well received. Waiting newsmen heard former SNCC activist John Lewis express his disappointment: "It is wrong for the mayor of a city like Atlanta to suggest that black people should not be concerned about their own political destiny." African Americans, Lewis continued, "should have an interest in controlling this city. We are a majority of this city, and we should control it." Another audience member declared that the implication that black conduct, rather than white racism, was to blame for white flight was "an insult to all blacks who think. [. . .] We are not responsible for white folks running from the city of Atlanta." African American city alderman Henry Dodson also disagreed with Massell, insisting he didn't have to "think white to get along in this society. I can think black and get along in this society."[3]

Massell's words did little to soften local black leaders' resolve to secure the political power they coveted by running a black mayoral candidate at the next election. While black representatives in Congress and state legislatures were in a position to influence the direction and scope of public policy, power over the decisions that affected the most immediate circumstances of daily life for urban black communities often resided at the local level, in city hall. Local public education, city development and urban renewal projects, welfare and public housing, law enforcement and public transit, and municipal and social services all, generally speaking, came under the authority of city government. Large numbers of African Americans were elected to office at the local level from the mid-1960s onward, precisely because control of city politics offered black voters the chance to remedy problems such as unchecked urban decay, housing code violations, inadequate sanitation services, police brutality, street repair and maintenance, and underresourced and failing public schools.

However, once in charge, black mayors found addressing the socioeconomic issues facing their black constituents very difficult. At the root of this difficulty lay the fundamental truth that Massell had touched upon in his speech, and that underpins this book as a whole: the importance of white concerns, demands, and pressures to the vitality and direction of African American protest, politics, empowerment, and progress. Bringing together this book's major themes, this chapter assesses how the longer-term development of public policies intended to co-opt and modify Black Power, along with white resistance to redistributive city policy more generally, affected the scope and nature of black progress and empowerment under black city leadership through the 1970s. These themes are explored by focusing primarily on events in Los Angeles and Atlanta during the 1970s, two cities that in 1973 elected their first black mayors—Tom Bradley and Maynard Jackson.[4] (As I am interested primarily in the result of black political control, this chapter does not explore New York City politics in depth, because the city's first black mayor, David Dinkins, was not elected until 1989.)

Scholarship on African American mayors commonly identifies the numerous factors that conspired to limit black political power. The first wave of black mayors, including Carl Stokes in Cleveland and Richard Hatcher in Gary, Indiana (both elected in 1967), and Kenneth Gibson in Newark (elected in 1970), represented what can be seen as an "idealistic" brand of black city politics. Their efforts to compensate for years of black exclusion by realigning resources and power in favor of their African American constituents encountered strong resistance—especially where those efforts were designed to benefit the black working class and poor in particular. Often opposed by white voters, local and state governments and bureaucracies, and city departments (especially police departments), such efforts were further hamstrung by fiscal difficulties, which were exacerbated by continuing white flight. Confronted with these issues, these mayors' options were limited. While Stokes declined to run for a third term in 1971 and withdrew from city politics, Hatcher and Gibson adjusted their sights and programs to the political and economic pressures they faced. In both cases they significantly retrenched their social welfare spending and curbed efforts to help working-class and poor black communities.[5]

The experiences of this first wave of African American mayors was instructive for subsequent black city politicians who, with few exceptions (most notably Harold Washington in Chicago and Coleman Young in Detroit), have since tended to distance themselves from issues primarily affecting poor black and other minority communities. As political scientist J. Phillip Thompson III has explained, most have presented themselves as race-neutral technocrats and have advanced fiscally conservative agendas that have privileged the interests of private business and the middle class and elite (both white and black) and done little to challenge existing patterns of inequality. While the black poor have gotten poorer, the black middle class and elite have generally enjoyed increasing opportunity and prosperity and have (unlike their poor and working-class counterparts) become more fully integrated into the nation's political and economic mainstream. As a result, in the eyes of many political scientists, black political power during this period has resulted predominantly in a significant backward step in the pursuit of social and economic justice.[6]

Bradley's and Jackson's mayoralties throughout the 1970s provide two important, contrasting examples of how black political power evolved at the city level, and of the forces that guided its development. Like other "idealistic" black mayors before him, Jackson began his tenure as a strong racial advocate who supported a more redistributive course for city politics. Bradley, on the other hand, was a forerunner of the race-neutral, technocratic black politician who came to dominate in the 1980s and after. Committed to the principles of color-blind democracy, Bradley believed deeply that increasing opportunity, rather than redistributing wealth, was the key to alleviating black poverty.

Despite the differences between Bradley's and Jackson's respective initial political profiles and platforms, both of their administrations had, broadly speaking, the same impact on their black constituents: they delivered substantial gains to middle-class and elite blacks and reinforced many of the disadvantages facing poor and working-class blacks. A pattern of increasing inequality came to characterize the black experience under both Jackson and Bradley, though in different ways. While this pattern was powerfully shaped by the myriad economic and political pressures that Bradley and Jackson faced when in office, black progress made under their leadership was also a legacy of mainstream white efforts to negotiate Black Power's meaning and to dictate the pace and direction of black empowerment. Black middle-class success, therefore, was in part a result of a political project shaped by white interests and resistance to socioeconomic change that was endorsed by, and that flourished under, black city leadership.

For both Jackson and Bradley, affirmative action city hiring and municipal contract disbursement were the most viable methods for advancing black interests that they were able to employ during their tenures at city hall. Grounded firmly in the pro–private enterprise and black capitalist politics advanced by Robert Kennedy and Richard Nixon, the opportunities these policies presented had the effect, intentionally or otherwise, of promoting intraracial inequality and class division in the black community. At the same time, reorienting city policy to address the concerns of working-class and poor blacks proved virtually impossible. As such, with the benefit of hindsight, black city leaders can be seen to have presided over an early stage of what Thompson has referred to as the "programmatic abandonment" of America's inner-city poor, at all levels of government, that underpinned conservative national government under Ronald Reagan during the 1980s.[7]

After first examining the different factors that drove the growth of black political power, and the contest to define a black political agenda at the national level, this chapter explores the election campaigns and mayoralties of Tom Bradley and Maynard Jackson and the developments, political debates, and policies that guided their leadership during the 1970s. The two men operated in significantly different political landscapes and, in some key respects, articulated divergent political messages. However, the ultimate legacy of their time in office was a pattern of black progress and city policy heavily advantageous to the interests of middle-class whites and blacks and of downtown economic elites. Their mayoralties thus underscore both the longer-term impact of white engagement with Black Power and the powerful sway that white interests and mainstream political discourses held over the direction and scope of black political power.

THE GROWTH OF BLACK POLITICAL POWER

In June 1974 a number of African American politicians south of the Mason-Dixon Line came together to found the Southern Conference of Black

Mayors (SCBM), choosing to headquarter the organization symbolically in downtown Atlanta, a historic center of black power and prestige. The SCBM stood as testament to the rapid increase since the late 1960s in the number of black elected officials. Just six years earlier, at the start of 1968, there were no black mayors in the South, and there had been none since Reconstruction. By the end of 1974 there were sixty-six. A year later the figure climbed to eighty-two. In a region where white supremacy and racial terrorism had kept the vast majority of African Americans shut out of the political process for over a century, it seemed nothing short of a political revolution. This seismic change was not confined to the South. In November 1967, Carl Stokes in Cleveland, Ohio, and Richard Hatcher in Gary, Indiana, became the first African Americans to be elected mayor of major American cities. A decade later more than two hundred black mayors had been elected, and by 1990 that figure exceeded three hundred. Nationwide, the number of black officeholders—from Congress down to local school boards, judgeships, and a range of local governance positions—rose from 1,124 in March 1969, to 3,499 by May 1975. As SCBM chairman (and recently elected first black mayor of Atlanta) Maynard Jackson argued, African Americans had come to the realization that "the methods for achieving equal rights are changing, and that the dominant battleground lies at the ballot box and through city hall."[8]

The upsurge in the number of black elected officeholders during the late 1960s and 1970s was driven by various overlapping factors that converged and entwined with the emergence of vociferous demands for "Black Power" from mid-1966 onward. Perhaps the most fundamental of these were the powerful demographic forces that had transformed the nation's urban and racial geography over the previous three decades. The 1970 U.S. Census revealed that over half of African Americans lived in urban centers, with a third of all blacks residing in just fifteen cities. New York City claimed the largest number of black residents—1.6 million—which accounted for 21.2 percent of its population. Los Angeles had the sixth largest at just over half a million, approximately 17 percent of local residents. Atlanta's black community, though half the size of Los Angeles's, represented a numerical majority in the city (51.3 percent).[9] As black migration to the cities and white flight continued, the concentration of blacks in America's inner cities naturally created strong black electorates that helped in turn to deliver black candidates to office. The voting strength of urban black communities outside the South was also boosted by a different demographic trend. One estimate suggested that the birth rate among black urban migrants increased 150 percent between 1940 and 1960, a development leading to a sharp increase in the number of voting-age blacks, from 10.3 million to 13.5 million between 1964 and 1972.[10]

The landmark legislation that long-standing voter registration activism and civil rights protest had helped to deliver also underpinned increasing black political power. As political scientist Charles Hamilton has explained, the 1965 Voting Rights Act helped to more than double the number of registered black voters in the South, from 1,530,634 in 1965 to 3,448,565 in 1972.[11] Upon its expiration in 1970, President Nixon signed into law a revised version of the five-year act—authored principally by moderate and liberal Republicans and Democrats—which ensured that the act covered the whole nation, not just the South. During the 1970s, the Supreme Court viewed the revised legislation through the prism of federal commitment to affirmative action, producing rulings that allowed for the creation and protection of majority–black (and other racial minority) voting districts. The result was significant. As Kotlowski has explained, the 1970 Voting Rights Act did a great deal to "enhance minority voting strength and office holding."[12]

Bringing African Americans into the electoral process had been a long-standing, central goal of twentieth-century civil rights activism, and demands for black voting rights during the early to mid-1960s were another vital factor behind the increase in black political representation in subsequent years. In particular, the voter registration work undertaken by SNCC, CORE, and the NAACP, often in tandem with the Southern Regional Council's Voter Education Project (backed by the Kennedy administration and several northern liberal foundations), not only dramatized the need for voting rights legislation but also inspired rural southern blacks to embrace electoral politics.[13] SNCC took this a step further by helping to organize grassroots efforts to remake American democracy by supplanting local white supremacist Democratic Party formations. The Mississippi Freedom Democratic Party (MFDP), in particular, encapsulated SNCC's ethos of participatory democracy and its belief that black communities had to be allowed to develop their own leadership skills and define their own agendas, free from outside influence, so that they could use the democratic process to effect meaningful socioeconomic change. These efforts had highly significant consequences. The MFDP's attempt to unseat the regular, lily-white state delegation at the Democratic National Convention in Atlantic City in August 1964, though unsuccessful, was a vital step toward growing minority representation within the apparatus of the Democratic Party.[14]

Similarly, SNCC-inspired black political organizing in Lowndes County, Alabama, produced the Lowndes County Freedom Organization (LCFO), which was committed to voter registration, political education, and community organizing and ran indigenous black candidates for every type of local office. In the process, the symbol of the black panther, which was emblazoned across LCFO insignia, became a powerful new icon in the black freedom struggle—one soon irrevocably identified with Black Power. Both the MFDP and the LCFO highlighted the importance to SNCC activism of organizing for political power, and the experience of both organizations was important in SNCC's transformation into a Black Power group in the mid-1960s.[15]

Black political empowerment was a fundamental goal of mid-to-late-1960s Black Power organizing, as two of the slogan's earliest advocates made clear. Speaking in July 1966, CORE's Floyd McKissick suggested that the emergence of Black Power represented "phase two" of the civil rights movement, in which securing political power became vital to consolidating the movement's hard-won legal victories and ensuring that they were "actually translated into more earning power, better education, and adequate housing." [16] Black Power, Stokely Carmichael explained in September 1966, was fundamentally concerned with giving blacks their rightful share of political power and making the promise of democracy a reality:

> Black Power is not being in charge of something white people control. Black Power is when we pick the person and put him into place and make sure he is responsive to our needs. In its simplest form it is the demand for majority control in areas where black people are the majority and a proportional share of key decision making posts in areas where they are in the minority [. . .] it is a way for [black people] to come together to stop oppression by any means necessary. It is a way they can force government, white liberals, and other structures, to attend to their problems. It is a way that black people can come together and get themselves out of the bag.[17]

Growing demands for "Black Power" from mid-1966 succeeded in sharpening the focus of black communities across the nation on the task of electing blacks to public office. As political scientist Cedric Johnson has suggested, they "effectively reoriented the terms of black public debate from the task of attaining equal constitutional protection, which framed local struggles against desegregation since the landmark 1954 *Brown* decision, toward the actual seizure of state power." [18] Fundamentally committed to increasing black political power, Black Power activists were an important and active part of electoral politics, campaigning for black candidates for public office. Recent scholarship has revealed the important role that Black Power advocates played—often as part of broader community-wide political activism—in efforts to elect African Americans to office in cities such as Cleveland, Newark, Greensboro, Philadelphia, and Oakland.[19] Where the civil rights movement had focused on winning legal and political rights, the Black Power movement shifted the emphasis toward increasing African Americans' direct access to resources and the levers of power; and, on the surface, the results were spectacular.

Although New York wouldn't elect its first black mayor—David Dinkins—until 1989, the mid-1960s and 1970s did see the growth of black political influence in the city, especially at the state level. While, from the early 1960s onward, Dinkins was building his career in Harlem—a long-standing seat of African American power in city politics and the Democratic Party in New York—there were relatively few black elected representatives in other parts of the city, such as Brooklyn, Bronx, and Queens. By the mid- to late 1970s that situation had begun to change, thanks in part to the efforts of Mayor Lindsay. Seeking to unite the city's sizable minority groups with white liberals and progressives in a new political coalition of his own, Lindsay brought talented individuals from the city's poor black and Puerto Rican communities into city government, and its official antipoverty apparatus in particular. Significant numbers of those individuals later became elected officials at the city, state, and national level. By creating opportunities for politically ambitious individuals from the city's minority communities, Lindsay played an important role in increasing the number of black candidates who ran for public office in New York from the early 1970s onward. The expansion and normalization of black political power in the city during the 1970s helped pave the way for Dinkins's election in the longer term. In the shorter term, however, the city's 1975 fiscal crisis (discussed later in this chapter) led to a radical shift in city politics that disproportionately affected New York's minority poor. From the mid-1970s through the 1980s, conservative Democrat mayors Abe Beame and Ed Koch abandoned the Lindsay administration's redistributive agenda, and local black elected officials found it very difficult to limit the deleterious impact that changes in city policy had on their constituents.[20]

During the early 1970s, African American efforts to acquire power at the local level were joined by unprecedented political organizing at the national level that aimed to unite African Americans across the country behind a so-called black political agenda. The attempt to create a strong and independent black third-party political formation that could leverage black influence over the Democratic Party brought to the surface important tensions within the wider black political community. Chief among these was the relationship between, on one hand, Black Power radicals and grassroots community organizers advocating a social democratic and progressive vision of black politics and, on the other, those black politicians already working within the two-party system, tied to the Democratic Party and constrained by the boundaries of mainstream political discourse. Disagreement between these two groups not only undermined efforts to build independent black politics but, as this chapter's subsequent sections reveal, remained a critical factor affecting black city leadership under both Bradley and Jackson (albeit one that shaped and constrained their political programs in different ways).

The leading figure in efforts to unite black Americans nationwide politically was prominent cultural nationalist and Black Arts Movement leader Amiri Baraka.[21] As historian Komozi Woodard reveals, the poet cum political activist fused a Pan-Africanist Black Nationalist philosophy with a firm commitment to electoral politics and community organizing. Indeed, Baraka had been a key figure in the election of Newark's first black mayor, Kenneth Gibson, in 1970. At the same time, Baraka had helped create the Congress of African People (founded in Atlanta in 1970), a leftist Black Nationalist organization dedicated to establishing links with, and raising support for, anticolonial liberation movements and black political groups and governments in Africa, the Caribbean, and the Middle East.[22] Alongside his efforts to foster transnational links with black radical movements and governments across the world, Baraka was also highly concerned with building black political power and unity in the United States. As he explained in a letter to Black Panther Party leader Huey Newton in May 1971, "For the past few months I have been in conversation with various well-known black leaders throughout the country. Subject of these dialogues has been the pressing need for a National Black Leadership Conference." Inviting Newton's participation, Baraka announced his aim to "bring together all those black people we feel, or any who you feel, constitute legitimate leadership for black people." He sought ultimately to develop a united, insurgent black political force that could begin to transform the economic and political principles and institutions that underpinned racial inequality in America.[23]

African American elected officials were a key driving force behind broad-based political organizing at the national level. At the forefront was Detroit congressman Charles Diggs, who in 1969 led the formation of the Democratic Select Committee, a grouping of all nine black congressmen intended to facilitate united black political action on Capitol Hill. In April 1971, with the number of black legislators in the House of Representatives up to thirteen, the group became the Congressional Black Caucus (CBC) and declared its opposition to the Nixon administration, which it branded both antipoor and antiblack.[24] Diggs and Baraka, along with Richard Hatcher, African American mayor of Gary, Indiana, coordinated a number of meetings among black politicians, elected officials, organizational leaders, and other prominent black figures from cities across the country. The most decisive of these occurred in Northlake, Illinois, in September 1971, where agreement was reached to hold the first "National Black Political Convention" the following March. Gary—a seat of black political power under Mayor Hatcher—was chosen to host the event.[25]

Approximately three thousand official delegates and another nine thousand other convention attendees descended on Gary over the weekend of March 10–12, 1972. The largest black political meeting in U.S. history to that point, the Gary convention brought together a broad range of community activists, elected officials, and business and civic leaders, covering, as Manning Marable has explained, "revolutionary nationalist, cultural nationalist, moderate integrationist, and Black Capitalist tendencies." With the 1972 presidential election on the horizon, the convention, Peniel Joseph explains, was an effort to combine the many strands of black politics in a "pragmatic coalition" that could define a "black" political platform as a basis for coordinated future action on the part of a decisive electoral bloc.[26] After three days of in-depth discussion and negotiation, the convention resulted in the "National Black Political Agenda," a sixty-two-page document that for the most part strongly reflected a radical social democratic and progressive vision of black politics, couched in uncompromisingly militant language. Mainstream American politics, the agenda's authors declared, was "a decaying and unsalvageable system." The Gary convention sought "fundamental, far reaching change in America" that would lead to the broader "empowerment of the black community," and "not simply [of] its representatives." The radical vision that the so-called Gary Agenda outlined included, among other objectives, the institution of a "steeply progressive income tax" as part of a "long-run policy of redistribution of wealth"; the seizure of rural land by the federal government and its transfer to the black community; a guaranteed minimum income of $6,500 (rising to $7,200 in three years) for a family of four and a substantial increase in the minimum wage; and the halving of both the national defense and space budgets and of the tax allowances and federal subsidies to large-scale agriculture and oil companies, with the funds saved redirected to social programs, education, housing, and economic development in rural and urban areas. It also called for Social Security payments for people over age fifty to be doubled and for targeted tax increases to "end forever the inter-generational perpetuation of ownership of unearned white fortunes." [27]

The agenda's radical and redistributive "politics of social transformation" was unmistakably dominated by Black Nationalist and Black Power sentiment (as the convention itself had been). As the NAACP's Roy Wilkins complained, "Any reading of statements and positions of the Gary group clearly show [sic] a separatist thrust." [28] In particular, there were resolutions calling for the right of all black communities to "determine whether or not they wish to become independent political entities (cities, villages, etc) when they deem it politically and administratively desirable." Another pledged a plebiscite for the Black Belt of the Deep South, offering the chance of formal statehood and independence from "the captive sovereignty of the U.S." Black political power was to be guaranteed by an affirmative action–oriented distribution of political offices at the federal, state, and local levels, proportionally by race. The agenda's education policy strongly denounced busing ("a bankrupt, suicidal method of desegregating schools') and included resolutions calling for community control of black schools and the protection of black colleges and universities from the "threat" of integration. Black elected officials were required to pledge support to black community control over "the police, schools, and all other institutions that affect the lives of black people." Prison rights—a key theme among some radical Black Power groups—was also targeted under criminal justice reform that included the release of "all black political prisoners and draft resisters." Foreign policy proposals reflected the Pan-Africanist and Third World liberation motif of Black Power radicalism by supporting nonwhite liberation struggles worldwide (including, controversially it would prove, support for Palestinians' right to self-determination), demanding a halt to U.S. imperialism, and urging support for the economic development of indigenous-led governments in Africa. [29]

Despite the agenda's strong anticapitalist overtones, calls for more mainstream black capitalist development were also a key feature, with a demand that the federal government support a massive program of black economic development and business support (funded with $10 billion over the first five years). There was also a strong focus on economic nationalist measures, including a plan to form a nationally coordinated black pressure group to solicit from white corporations and financial institutions greater private investment in the black community and black businesses. In sum, the Gary agenda called for a massive redistribution of wealth and power in the name of social, economic, and racial justice, and of black political empowerment and capitalist development, reflecting the broad spectrum of Black Power politics represented at the convention.[30]

It was not long, however, before the apparent unity between militants and moderates in Gary broke down. The militant and radical tone of the convention's adopted platform, and its strong emphasis on the need for black political organization independent of the nation's two main political parties, conflicted with the more pragmatic agenda of the black elected officials. On one side of the divide, Joseph explains, were local organizers who "stressed issues of accountability, social justice, and public policy that remained focused on the redistribution of American wealth toward the inner-city and rural areas dominated by poor blacks." On the other were black elected officials who, encumbered by the practical constraints of urban politics, were more concerned with consolidating and entrenching black power within the Democratic Party.[31]

Some Black Power militants had already cautioned against working with black politicians within the two-party system. Before a large rally held in the LA Sports Arena on February 18, 1968, SNCC chairman H. Rap Brown had warned: "Two of the most dangerous Negroes in this country are Democrats [Richard] Hatcher and [Carl] Stokes. Now understand this—their allegiance is not to the black community, it is to the Democratic Party headed by Lynch'um Johnson."[32] The aftermath of the Gary convention underlined the powerful sway of the two-party system over the direction and tone of black political engagement. Most black elected officials rejected the call for blacks to form an independent third political party—embodied in the "National Black Political Assembly," established to carry the convention's work forward—because it threatened their own power in the Democratic Party. By mid-1972, black elected officials (most prominently members of the CBC) had publicly broken with the Gary Agenda and the radical Black Power milieu that had reigned at the convention. On June 1 the CBC released the "Black Bill of Rights," which outlined a platform of social democratic and progressive liberal policies, many of which had appeared on the Gary Agenda. These included federal job creation and full employment policies; greater federal aid to the cities for housing, education, and health care; constructive welfare reform; minority business support; affirmative action and equal-opportunity hiring legislation; and pro-African and anti-racist foreign policy. The CBC's proposals, however, as the *New York Times* explained, "were mild compared with the National Black Political Agenda" set forth at Gary. By explicitly rejecting Gary's anti-busing and pro-Palestine rhetoric, the CBC widened the breach between its members and the convention's radical Black Power set. The split worsened over time. The National Black Political Assembly's third and final meeting, held in Cincinnati, Ohio, in 1976, drew a crowd of barely one thousand attendees that included few black elected officials.[33]

The swift dissolution of the consensus at Gary highlighted how the demands of party loyalty and the realities of interest group politics in a pluralist, multiracial democracy informed the approach of black elected officials. If the Gary Agenda had evinced the spirit of radical Black Power, what kind of Black Power politics—if any—would be realized in cities under the control of black mayors? The following sections explore the mayoralties through the 1970s of Tom Bradley in Los Angeles and Maynard Jackson in Atlanta, assessing what black political power meant for African Americans in both cities, first by examining how their electoral campaigns and respective political platforms were shaped by local political and social conditions and by national political discourses and developments.

RACE AND RUNNING FOR OFFICE: THE CASE OF TOM BRADLEY IN LOS ANGELES

The realities of running for office and governing at a time of ongoing conservative political realignment had a powerful effect on the ability of black municipal politicians such as Bradley and Jackson to address the needs of their poorest constituents. Deepening white racial resentment over the welfare system made pursuing redistributive city policy once in office, or promising it while on the campaign trail, problematic for all politicians. Given the strong racial overtones that permeated debates over welfare state liberalism, it was even less viable for black politicians, especially for those running in majority-white cities. In Los Angeles, where African Americans made up just

17 percent of the city's population—only the second-largest local minority group—it would have been very difficult, perhaps impossible, for Bradley to be elected advocating issues such as redistributive social and city spending that were so strongly identified with poor inner-city blacks. His electoral success owed much to the fact that he did not attempt to do so.

As political scientist Raphael Sonenshein explains, the trajectory of Bradley's own career—up from poverty to the top levels of mainstream American life—played an important role in forging his public image and political philosophy. Bradley's own experiences of excelling and breaking the color line—first as a star athlete at UCLA, then as the first black police lieutenant in the LAPD, and then as the first African American to sit on the city council—made his life a powerful story of an individual's ability to overcome discrimination through hard work and talent. This image appealed to whites as well as blacks. Bradley was celebrated in particular by the city's black middle-class establishment (of which he became a leading member during his three-decade rise to the top). Bradley himself seemed to lend weight to the mainstream narrative, constructed through the public policies analyzed throughout this book, that black progress would come from efforts to facilitate greater black self-reliance and individual initiative, and not through government social welfare programs that encouraged dependency. However, as Sonenshein suggests, while Bradley's life became a symbolic metaphor for "black upward mobility in the face of great odds," it could also "obscure the conditions of those blacks unlikely to rise up as well." Although Bradley had always criticized racial discrimination, he was firmly convinced that African Americans could overcome the obstacles they faced and realize the American Dream if they worked hard enough, just as he had. Consequently, Bradley's leadership at city hall was guided by the belief that increasing opportunity, rather than redistributing wealth, was the way forward for African Americans.[34]

Bradley's outlook was also attuned to the political realities of running for office in a multiracial, white-majority city. Elected in 1963 as a city councilman for the Tenth District (a section of the city approximately 50 percent white, 35 percent black, and 15 percent Asian American), Bradley was well versed in presenting himself as a race-neutral candidate committed to governing in the interests of all. As he constantly reminded the city's multiracial electorate: "I am not the Negro candidate for mayor. I am the candidate for mayor deeply committed to a liberal Democratic philosophy, who is black."[35] Although blacks gave Bradley significant support at the ballot box, he relied on other groups more heavily, especially the wide base of white support he developed during his time on the city council. As Bradley's campaign manager, Maury Weiner, explained, this support base stretched citywide in the mayoral elections and consisted predominantly of the city's white liberal (and mainly Jewish) middle- and upper-middle-income voters, many of whom were members of the leading statewide Democratic organization, the California Democratic Council.[36]

Bradley's political platform strongly reflected the interests of his middle-class white supporters who, though broadly supportive of liberal social and civil rights policies, were profoundly concerned with the rising tax burden they faced as property owners. Federal—not local—government, Bradley believed, should bear the cost of providing social welfare support. Consequently, Bradley prioritized tax relief for the city's home owners. He also campaigned on administrative matters such as pursuing fiscal responsibility, eliminating government waste, and eradicating the Yorty administration's apparent culture of graft. Although Bradley lamented urban inequality, he rarely addressed issues affecting the black poor explicitly. When he did speak about their problems or more generally about black advancement, it was almost always in terms of community development and minority business support and affirmative action—approaches to solving inequality that did not threaten to increase either taxes or welfare spending. He was especially keen to enlist business in the effort to solve urban poverty, believing that private enterprise could "teach poverty communities about how the system works, that it can work and to develop a stake in it."[37] In doing so, Bradley echoed and wholly endorsed the principles and policies that Kennedy and Nixon had espoused, underlining their entrenchment in mainstream political discourse and urban policy.

In 1969 Bradley ran for city hall against incumbent conservative Democrat Mayor Sam Yorty. Bradley's strong identification with taxpayers' interests meant Yorty was unable to exploit white concerns over the prospect of black city leadership leading to greater social spending on black ghetto communities. Yorty instead labeled Bradley a black radical sympathizer and played to white voters' fears over the supposed threat that black militants posed to law and order. Black Power had long been associated by opponents and the mainstream media with dangerous, volatile militancy and political radicalism. No group seemed to better fit this stereotype than the BPP, a group whose spectacular rise in Oakland, California, from late 1966 onward to regional and national prominence helped mark the Golden State as a vital site of Black

Power radicalism.[38] Branded by FBI chief J. Edgar Hoover as "the greatest threat to the internal security of the nation," the Black Panthers became the main target of the bureau's Counterintelligence Program (COINTELPRO), a brutal campaign of state-sponsored repression orchestrated by the Nixon administration and directed against Black Power, New Left, and countercultural radicals.[39]

As a 1976 Senate-led inquiry into the FBI's conduct revealed, the Panthers were the subject of 233 of COINTELPRO's 295 operations. Often conducted in league with local law enforcement agencies, these operations comprehensively disrupted and undermined the activities of BPP branches nationwide.[40] In Los Angeles, the FBI deliberately exacerbated an existing feud between the local chapter of the Panthers and Ron Karenga's US organization, which resulted in the killing of two Panther leaders by US members on the UCLA campus in January 1969, as well as numerous other beatings and shootings.[41] On December 8, 1969, heavily armed LAPD squadrons raided three Panther buildings, resulting in the arrest and trial of eighteen party members. One of the raids, at the Panther's Central Avenue offices, resulted in a five-hour-long fire fight during which three policemen were wounded and the police dynamited the building's roof.[42]

The repression of the BPP and other radicals was a powerful statement in the era's fierce ongoing contest over the meaning and nature of American culture. As Nixon lauded "Middle America" for its patriotism, respect for authority, and faith in the traditional, Christian values of American political and social life, he simultaneously endorsed the repression and vilification of dissenting radicals whose lifestyles and politics were branded deviant and "anti-American." The message being sent by the FBI, the Nixon administration, and local and state authorities was clear: there was no place in mainstream American society and politics for leftist protest and dissent.

Tom Bradley's campaigns for city hall in Los Angeles revealed the degree to which Black Power radicalism was successfully demonized during the late 1960s. Bradley emerged in early 1969 as a genuine contender to unseat Yorty. As election day drew near and Yorty found himself behind in the polls, he began to exploit white prejudice and fear by alleging that his opponent had connections to black radicals. Yorty claimed that were Bradley elected, "the militants would come down and intimidate the city council [. . .] and then what could the police do? How are they going to handle the black militant friends of the mayor who are there to back him?'[43] Yorty devoted his entire final pre-election press conference to reciting a nine-page paper listing the various accusations he had made about Bradley and his apparent association with Black Power militants and "extreme liberals." The most damaging charge (later proved untrue) was that Bradley's campaign coordinator, Don Rothenberg, had "presided over a meeting to raise money to buy guns for the Black Panther Party" in the Bay Area in July 1967.[44] On the defensive, Bradley retorted: "Day after day he has injected into this campaign the lowest and vilest element in American politics today. Day after day he has appealed to the fear and doubts which lurk in many minds. His appeal is irrational, divisive and hateful. But I am convinced it is the last gasp of a desperate man, seeking to salvage victory from the bitter dregs of the past."[45]

In a state where Black Power radicalism was a prominent current issue, Yorty's tactics proved especially effective. On election day, 80 percent of the city's voters turned out to hand Yorty a 53 to 47 percent victory. While Bradley had enjoyed massive majorities in the city's black districts, voters in many of the city's white precincts (and a number of Chicano districts too) changed their minds and, having voted for him in the Democratic primary, switched to Yorty at the ballot box instead.[46] Yorty's victory did come at something of a cost, as he attracted opprobrium from journalists and commentators across the nation. Yorty rebuked one critic—the prominent African American and UN diplomat Ralph Bunche—by saying that it had been "the Bradley camp who FIRST introduced racism into the Los Angeles Mayoralty campaign" through their "calls for black bloc voting power" and "efforts to form a black-brown coalition." However, Yorty's protestations did little to undo the lasting damage he had done to his reputation.[47]

When Bradley challenged Yorty again four years later, he encountered similar attacks. Once more, Yorty spent his final press conference before voters went to the ballot boxes branding Bradley a "radical left-winger" and "sort of a black nationalist." Erroneously identifying one of Bradley's campaign volunteers, John Floyd, as a member of the Black Panther Party, Yorty also argued that his opponent, like the BPP, was "very antipolice."[48] Bradley had not been helped by a public endorsement from Black Panther Party leader Huey Newton. His swift response to Newton's support was unequivocal: "I did not seek, do not want, and I reject the endorsement." It was, Bradley suggested, "an obvious, desperate trick by the Yorty campaign because he is trailing so badly in the polls." It was all too reminiscent, he complained, of the time when "thousands of 'Black Power' bumper stickers" appeared in the predominantly white San Fernando Valley in the final days of the 1969 election. "We later learned," Bradley explained, "that those stickers were ordered,

paid for and distributed by the Sam Yorty Campaign Committee." [49] Yorty responded by arguing that Newton endorsed Bradley because "his activity in the past would warrant the endorsement." [50] This time, however, Bradley won a convincing victory.

If Yorty's victory in 1969 had demonstrated the degree to which the demonization and repression of Black Power radicalism that intensified under the Nixon administration had helped to delegitimize leftist politics, his loss in 1973 reflected different political realities. First, the fallout that followed Yorty's 1969 campaign tactics played an important role in limiting their effectiveness in 1973, especially in light of four years of relative urban peace (whereas 1969 had been proceeded by several summers of urban rioting). Second, Bradley had spent the intervening time reinforcing his political image and message as a friend and advocate of middle-class and business interests, successfully establishing the distance between his own agenda and radical black politics.[51] Last, by 1973 the BPP—having experienced sustained state repression, the incarceration of multiple leaders, and a high-profile internal schism—had moved to a more moderate and conciliatory position. This shift included an active and formal engagement in the political process, with Chairman Bobby Seale and Information Minister Elaine Brown running for mayor of Oakland and a seat on the Oakland city council, respectively.[52] Put simply, the BPP of 1973 was a different proposition from the BPP of 1969, making Yorty's scaremongering less resonant than it had been previously.

Overall, for African Americans, the broader message of black radicals' repression was clear. At the same time that groups like the Panthers were being vilified, organizations such as Restoration and WLCAC, and black capitalist ventures, were getting support from the state and were giving a more mainstream, middle-class, and reformist face to the pursuit of Black Power, starkly underlining the type of Black Power politics that would be tolerated. Indeed, Tom Bradley's own political outlook demonstrated this narrative's dominance within black Democratic politics and national political discourse. Bradley was a cheerleader for the kind of pro-business development, middle-class–oriented vision of Black Power that politicians like Nixon and Kennedy had sought to encourage. As Bradley had explained when setting out his bid to become the city's first black mayor in 1969, in his eyes Black Power meant "economic power; the quest for economic opportunity and economic growth; political power; voter registration and education about the political process to develop confidence it will really work; and intellectual power through equal opportunity in education. All of the foregoing lead to a stake in society for the black man necessary for the preservation of peace and due to every man in a country such as ours." What his vision of Black Power did not include, he was at pains to emphasize, was any association with "violence and disorder." [53] As Bradley explained in a letter to a supporter, "There is no place in a democratic society for the motto 'by any means necessary.'" [54] At the polls on election day in 1973, Bradley's middle-class–oriented, pro-taxpayer platform secured him the multiracial, cross-sectional support he needed for victory. Indeed, Bradley's multiracial coalition was so broad that even without the votes of the city's two largest black voting districts, he would still have won. In terms of votes, therefore, his election owed more to white and Latino support than it did to local African Americans.[55]

RACE AND RUNNING FOR OFFICE: THE CASE OF MAYNARD JACKSON IN ATLANTA

In Atlanta, Maynard Jackson's political image and message were also shaped by the political climate in which he operated. Whereas Tom Bradley adhered to a race-neutral, middle class–oriented political philosophy in part dictated by Los Angeles's demography, Jackson began his political career as a forth-right advocate of black empowerment and economic justice. This choice was not only a matter of personality (Jackson having little of Bradley's faith in the promise of color-blind democracy) but also a product of local racial politics and demographics. As a majority-black city in early 1970, Atlanta offered Jackson far greater scope for campaigning on so-called "black" interests than had Los Angeles for Bradley (had he been inclined to do so). Moreover, Atlanta's black community expected black city leaders to work for their interests. This sentiment was especially pronounced among Atlanta's well-established and politically influential black elite, who saw the election of a black mayor as the path to (at the very least) genuine biracial control over local decision making and a greater share in the city's economic fortunes. As the local schools compromise suggested, firm progress toward these goals was already being made before Jackson's election.

Jackson's political career was characterized from the beginning by forth-right racial advocacy. Unswerving opposition to racial discrimination inspired his first foray into electoral politics in 1968 when the bold young attorney challenged U.S. senator Herman Talmadge. Although he failed to unseat the staunch segregationist former state governor, Jackson did not have to wait long for his first taste of political success. The following year he was elected as vice-mayor alongside Sam Massell, the young Jewish candidate for mayor who had been vice-mayor under outgoing incumbent mayor Ivan Allen. Like Allen, Massell was a liberal with a reputation for progressive racial views. Despite Massell's close connections with Allen (who had consummated the relationship between downtown economic elites and city hall), the local white business elite backed a different candidate—white moderate Republican state representative Rodney Cook. Massell's victory was achieved thanks to winning 96 percent of the black vote, along with the support of Atlanta's Jewish voters. Citywide, he claimed just 18 percent of the white vote. The election of a young black liberal vice-mayor and a young liberal Jewish mayor seemed to underscore Atlanta's reputation for racial harmony and progress.[56]

The fact that the black vote, growing in proportional strength as white flight continued, had been so decisive in the election did not go unnoticed in the black community. An ambitious man, Jackson used his position as vice-mayor to build his image and enhance his political reputation. Unlike Bradley in Los Angeles, Jackson consistently offered strong, vocal support to the city's poor black communities throughout his time as vice-mayor. This became evident when, just two months into Massell's tenure, three thousand of the city's sanitation workers (75 percent of whom were black) threatened to strike, demanding a 4.5 percent pay increase for those in the city's lowest salary bracket (where most of them were). Having been brought to power primarily by the black vote, Massell's political loyalties were immediately tested. Massell rejected the demands of local and national representatives from the American Federation of State, County, and Municipal Employees (AFSCME) union, insisting that the city lacked the money for salary increases. In response, the sanitation workers commenced industrial action. While local black leaders tried to negotiate a compromise behind the scenes, local welfare rights activists joined the striking workers on the picket line in solidarity. Lasting over a month, the strike was brought to an end when the city agreed to drop pending legal action against the union pickets and reinstate those workers it had fired during the strike. The pay raise offered, however, was far below what the workers had demanded.[57] Jackson vociferously backed the sanitation workers and lambasted Mayor Massell's compromise, arguing that the city had "a responsibility to anticipate its needs, so that its employees could receive a living wage."[58]

Although Jackson firmly endorsed black economic empowerment policies (such as minority business development and affirmative action, policies he pursued enthusiastically during his tenure as mayor), he did not share Bradley's faith that such initiatives could remedy racial and urban inequality. As he explained to the Urban League National Conference in 1970: "We have to understand, I believe, that Black Capitalism is not our panacea [. . .] in order for it to make any difference in all our lives, it would, I believe, have to have a significant and lasting corrective effect on the lives of the masses of Black Americans and not just the talented tenth."[59] Atlanta's poor black citizens needed better social services, neighborhood improvement projects, and jobs, Jackson insisted. As vice-mayor, Jackson was also especially vocal about the need for police reform. He called for more black police officers and criticized police brutality and the department's failure to enforce the law in ghetto neighborhoods. This criticism underlined his image as a politician with a deep concern for Atlanta's deprived black communities, not just its middle class and elite. Championing his commitment to "the politics of unbought and unbiased social change," Jackson announced his candidacy in early 1973, and black Atlanta began to eagerly and confidently anticipate the prospect of electing the city's first African American mayor.[60] As Jackson would discover, however, his strong identification with the black poor and

FIGURE 10. Atlanta vice-mayor Maynard Jackson *(center)* campaigning for mayor on election day in downtown Atlanta, 1973. Boyd Lewis Collection, Kenan Research Center at the Atlanta History Center.

support for redistributive social spending would be far less popular among white Atlantans.

Throughout the late 1960s and 1970s, America's lower-middle- and middle-class white voters became ever more hostile toward footing the cost of increasing welfare enrollment. Conservative politicians exploited this powerful and growing sentiment. Few captured taxpayer disillusionment and resentment better than California governor Ronald Reagan, who chided liberals for creating a "welfare never, never land" and lamented the injustice of "redistributing the earnings of the productive to the non-productive until we achieve the monotonous mediocrity of the ant heap."[61]

Anger over the fiscal and moral politics of Great Society welfare liberalism was bound up with a broader set of interconnected concerns white voters had regarding the direction in which the nation was heading. Faced with a maelstrom of campus unrest, antiwar demonstrations, urban riots, countercultural protest, and rising crime, a growing sense of anger deepened among many whites already resentful toward distant Washington liberal elites whom they blamed for encouraging challenges to traditional gender and racial hierarchies. Collectively, these issues helped inspire the realignment of working-class and lower-middle-class white voters to the Republican Party in both the North and South.[62]

The increasingly divisive national debate over redistributive liberal social policy, in particular, was magnified by the Nixon administration's proposed welfare reform policy, the Family Assistance Plan (FAP). Introduced in August 1969, the FAP promised to replace the existing, much disparaged AFDC program with a guaranteed national income which would ensure that no family received less than $1,600 annually. It was a proposal that pleased virtually no one. Supporters of a guaranteed minimum income, including many liberal Democrats, antipoverty fighters, civil rights and Black Power organizations, and many on the Left, argued that the baseline figure was far too low—not even half of what was broadly considered to be the "poverty line." Welfare rights activists and their allies insisted on the need for a minimum of $5,500 per year and lambasted work provisions included in the FAP (labeling them 'workfare'), which obliged welfare recipients to undertake designated employment opportunities as a condition of continued enrollment.

FAP's opponents, on the other hand, rejected it for very different reasons. As historian Gareth Davies suggests, in the eyes of conservatives and many of the nations' white working- and middle-class voters, the theory and rhetoric of "entitlement" that underpinned the concept of a guaranteed minimum income was antithetical to the nation's core values. In their view, Davies argues, a guaranteed income would undermine peoples' work ethic and individuals' accountability for their own lives, as well as representing an unconscionable extension of government responsibility.[63] Opposition to the welfare rights movement and its supporters was further inflamed by the NWRO's strong rejection of FAP's financial and work proscriptions and its militant and uncompromising demands for "More Money Now!" which outraged conservative sensibilities. In Washington, D.C., the American Conservative Union, a lobbying group, resolved to stand up to the NWRO and "the professional welfare organizations," dedicating itself to "an all-out fight for taxpayers who are sick and tired of having their hard-earned tax dollars squandered by demonstrating welfare recipients."[64]

By having proposed to extend the reach of federally mandated public assistance, the FAP has been held up by some historians as proof of a liberal streak in the domestic policy of a president popularly considered to be ideologically conservative.[65] However, although FAP certainly complicates our understanding of Nixon's political philosophy, the broader aim that motivated it placed it firmly in Nixon's rhetorical politics of racial polarization, betraying his underlying conservative spirit. As historian Bruce Schulman argues, despite its liberal dimensions, at its heart the FAP "pursued an authentically conservative objective," namely, to "dismantle the welfare system and the agencies and programs that administered it, eliminate the social workers who ran them, and starve the liberal networks they nourished."[66]

After three years of debate and dispute, liberals failed to overcome conservative opposition or, indeed, even to reach agreement among themselves over either the scope of the FAP or its funding, and it died in the Senate in late October 1972. As historian Felicia Kornbluh suggests, by ending with "combative conservatives ascendant, Republican liberals marginalized, and Democrats divided," the FAP's defeat fit a pattern that would characterize U.S. politics for a generation to come.[67] The crushing defeat of liberal Democratic nominee Senator George McGovern in the 1972 presidential race confirmed the rising tide of voter discontent with liberalism and redistributive social and economic justice politics. Dismissing McGovern's economic program (which included federal job programs for full employment, progressive tax reform, and a generous guaranteed minimum income) as "socialist dogma," Nixon romped to victory with nearly 61 percent of the popular vote, one of the largest margins in U.S. history.[68]

As the Atlanta mayoral race wore on, the supposedly liberal Massell sought to exploit white welfare backlash politics. Jackson's support for the city's poor and working-class blacks left him vulnerable to charges that, if elected, he would favor African Americans over the city's white taxpayers. With Atlanta becoming a majority-black city in early 1970, near the start of his tenure, Massell recognized the changing political climate and expected to face an African American challenger at the next election. From mid-1971 onward, Massell began warning of the dangers of black political control of the city. This message, encapsulated in his "Fear to Eternity" speech, remained a dominant theme of the mayor's rhetoric throughout 1972. As Massell continually portrayed growing black political power as a threat to white interests, he also pursued other methods to highlight this issue and to try and nullify growing black electoral strength. In December 1971 Massell submitted a proposal to the state assembly that would, without a referendum, have expanded the city limits to take in an extra fifty thousand people, practically all of whom were white, in time for them to participate in the 1973 mayoral election. Despite its clear racial overtones, Massell maintained the plan was not racially motivated; nevertheless, it was subsequently defeated in the state senate.[69]

As the election drew near, Massell's rhetoric became ever more alarmist, portraying Jackson as a militant racial advocate, perhaps even a black racist, who would be incapable of governing the city impartially. African American control, he asserted, would inevitably be aggressively antiwhite. Jackson's advocacy of the black poor and redistributive politics, he insinuated, would see city resources, services, and jobs redirected to the black community. "One can almost see them," he stated provocatively, "dancing in the streets in anticipation of a black takeover." Black control of city hall, he insisted, would be disastrous for the local economy. Whites would flee the city in greater numbers, and "real estate would really drop to the bottom." Jackson, dismayed by his opponent's attempts to exacerbate racial fears and tensions, lamented: "He's in the gutter with this type of attack."[70] Massell's message was reinforced by his campaign slogan—"Atlanta—Too Young to Die"— which was accompanied, Jackson recalls, by television commercials "that made Atlanta look like an abandoned Western mining town, with tumbleweed blowing through the streets ... Atlanta's too young to die."[71] Massell's tactics, however, did not bring him victory. In a run-off election, Jackson won handily, taking over 95 percent of the black vote and, importantly, nearly 18 percent of the white vote, predominantly from white liberals based in north Atlanta's middle- and upper-middle-income enclaves.[72]

Bradley and Jackson's campaigns demonstrated the different ways in which race and broader mainstream political discourses concerning black radicalism and redistributive politics influenced the nature of local politics. Different racial and political landscapes in both cities played an important part in shaping the tone and content of Bradley's and Jackson's political platforms. As a black candidate in Los Angeles, where less than one-fifth of the population was African American, Bradley sought to present himself as a race-neutral, nonpartisan liberal—a position to which he had a deep and genuine philosophical commitment. He entered office at the start of 1974 with a program focused primarily on relieving the property tax burden on local home owners and improving city government in the interests of all. Bradley catered first and foremost to the concerns of middle- and upper-income whites because they composed the main part of his electoral coalition. As a result, Bradley downplayed and avoided redistributive social and economic justice politics and touted safer, more politically viable strategies such as economic development and affirmative action hiring instead. In Atlanta, where blacks were a far more significant part of the electorate, the liberal Jackson was able to win election while advocating the reorientation of city policy toward Atlanta's disadvantaged black communities, as well as endorsing a proportional share of economic and political power for the local black middle class and elite.

Consequently, while race proved a controversial and divisive electoral issue in both cities, specific local contexts in each saw it exploited in subtly different ways. In Los Angeles, where Yorty primarily targeted voter concerns over law and order and black radicalism, his attempts to play on fears of racially biased black political control were only half-hearted. This result was due largely to Bradley's success in cultivating a race-neutral, pro-taxpayer political image and message. The fact that blacks were a relatively small minority in terms of local demography also made such fears less immediate. In Atlanta, on the other hand, a southern city that had recently become majority black, and against a vocal racial advocate like Maynard Jackson, the threat of antiwhite black governance promised to resonate with white Atlantans. In this scenario, the supposedly liberal Massell proved just as willing to exploit racial fears as the conservative Yorty. Racial fearmongering, it seemed, was a political tool used by conservatives and liberals alike. Although both Bradley's and Jackson's victories required a significant proportion of nonblack votes (especially so in the case of Bradley), the solid electoral bloc of white working-, lower-middle-, and middle-class voters who opposed them confirmed the deepening, racial polarization of American politics.

Finally, as historian Heather Ann Thompson has suggested, both victories also demonstrated the enduring strength of liberalism as a political force at the city level. The elections of liberal black mayors such as Bradley and Jackson, and others in the 1970s through the 1980s (for example, Coleman

Young in Detroit and Harold Washington in Chicago) undermines the dominant and declensional narrative of liberalism during this period which, largely seen through the prism of national politics, projects a pattern of zenith followed by precipitous and lasting decline from the mid-to-late 1960s. However, well into the 1980s, at a time when conservatives were firmly ascendant in Washington D.C., white and minority voters aligned in so-called "rainbow coalitions" to bring liberal black politicians to power in cities across America, underlining the complexities and the local and regional fault lines of the nation's ongoing political realignment in the process.[73]

Exactly what kind of politics that liberal, rainbow coalition–supported black mayors would bring about, however, was another question entirely. How would Bradley's and Jackson's different platforms translate into political action when faced with the realities of municipal control? And to what extent would black Angelenos and Atlantans benefit under African American city government? The following two sections examine how and why black city leadership in Los Angeles and Atlanta under Bradley and Jackson, irrespective of their divergent political platforms and approaches, broadly delivered the same result: racial progress characterized by growing opportunity and prosperity for the black middle class and deepening disadvantage for their poor and working-class black constituents.

DEFERRING THE DREAM: BLACK MAYORS AND THE URBAN POOR

Throughout their campaigns, Bradley and Jackson had received overwhelming support from local African Americans. Their momentous victories pushed black expectations sky-high. In Los Angeles, over the month and a half following Bradley's election, leading local black newspaper the *Los Angeles Sentinel* ran a five-part editorial special on the victory. Under the banner "Bradley's Victory Ends Plantation Years," the paper's leading political commentator, Booker Griffin, envisaged a new era of independent black politics in the city. Bradley's election, Griffin declared, meant that "the black community is liberated from the plantation yoke and is free to seek its own directions and own dynamics."[74] South of the Mason-Dixon Line, in Atlanta, the response was even more exuberant. As Jackson has recalled, the feeling abounded that "overnight, Valhalla will be found, heaven will come on earth and it's all because the Black mayor has been elected." However, as

Jackson continued, "things just don't work that way."[75] While some African Americans in Atlanta and Los Angeles benefited significantly from black control at city hall, poor and working-class black neighborhoods generally fared badly. A range of interlocking and mutually reinforcing economic and political pressures—some of which were beyond the mayors' control—guided and constrained Bradley's and Jackson's approaches to the problems of the urban poor, approaches that often exacerbated the continuing decline of inner-city ghetto neighborhoods.

Global and national macroeconomic shifts had a profound effect on poor and working-class American families of all races during the 1970s. A broad range of economic problems stemmed from persistent inflation that, building from the start of the decade, reached drastic proportions in the mid-1970s when the price of crude oil doubled following the Arab Oil Embargo of 1973. Inflationary pressures accelerated the decline of American manufacturing. Faced with rising costs driven by inflation, and with prices held down by the growth of global competition (in particular from Japan and Germany), corporations saw their profits plummet and many corporate leaders in the United States began downsizing their workforce or relocating their operations to cheaper labor markets overseas.[76] These trends had serious consequences for workers in cities such as Los Angeles and Atlanta. For example, in Los Angeles, the steel, rubber, and automobile industries contracted massively during the 1970s and 1980s, with ten major corporations shutting their local plants during that period. One estimate suggested that 70,000 blue-collar jobs disappeared from the city between 1978 and 1982.[77] In Atlanta, where industry was on a smaller scale than in Los Angeles, the same trend was apparent, with Department of Labor statistics revealing a loss of more than 8,000 jobs from the city in the single year ending in February 1976. The loss of low-skilled industrial jobs was largely offset by the growing number of white-collar, skilled employment positions created by the ongoing shift toward increasingly technological and office-based work environments (which demanded high-level literacy and numeracy) and low-paid jobs in the expanding service sector (which often held little hope for career progression).[78]

The massive loss of blue-collar jobs caused by economic recession and industrial restructuring was especially injurious to the national black community, already locked in a severe unemployment crisis. According to Department of Labor figures, black unemployment rose from 9 percent in June 1974 to nearly 15 percent in just twelve months. During the same period, total unemployment had risen from 5.2 percent to 9.2 percent as the number of jobless jumped by over 3 million. These statistics struck some as conservative. As National Urban League (NUL) head Vernon Jordan argued, the government's numbers were misleading because official definitions of the labor force omitted millions of people who "by any measure, other than the official one, are unemployed." The NUL's "Hidden Unemployment Index," Jordan explained, put the black unemployment rate at 26 percent, a figure that reflected a joblessness rate of two-thirds among black teenagers.[79]

Federal policy did little to help poor Americans during the 1970s. Caught in the trap of stagflation (inflation coupled with recession and high unemployment), the Nixon administration introduced wage and price controls in a bid to control inflation. These controls, however, were not designed to decrease unemployment and had the effect of increasing the economic squeeze on all poor and working-class Americans, regardless of race. This approach, Jordan later argued, was tantamount to "economic warfare on poor and working people." Black groups such as the NUL and the Congressional Black Caucus (CBC) urged the government to pursue instead full employment measures as a way to deal with economic problems, including the revival of massive federal employment programs last seen under the New Deal, progressive reform of the tax code, and incentives for private businesses to hire. However, both the subsequent Gerald Ford and Jimmy Carter administrations responded to persistent inflationary and unemployment pressures with economic policies that predominantly sought to cut taxes and federal spending, rather than increase them.[80]

Economic problems not only made life harder for poor and working-class Americans but also made it harder for black elected officials to pursue city policies that would improve the lot of their poor black constituents. In the tough inflationary economic climate of the 1970s, government social spending came under ever greater attack from conservatives who sought to exploit taxpayers' concerns over such policies and their own economic well-being. At the same time that redistributive city policies were becoming less politically viable, the continuation of deleterious trends that weakened city finances also made them less fiscally feasible. Escaping the tax burden of mounting social welfare costs—seen by many as an unjust use of their tax dollars—was one of myriad factors that inspired continuing white flight (of both families and businesses) to the suburbs, where whites successfully insulated themselves from the cost of inner-city government. This, in turn, further eroded the tax base of many cities, making it very difficult, if not impossible, to maintain existing social service provision in what were predominantly poor minority inner-city communities.[81] In the case of New York in the early 1970s, dwindling fiscal resources and spiraling costs pushed the city toward the brink of bankruptcy. In 1975, leading executives of the financial institutions that held most of the city's mountainous debt orchestrated an extraordinary and radical restructuring of city finances that drastically reduced the city's social spending and public assistance programs. This episode not only highlighted the power of entrenched white economic interests but, in hindsight, as political scientist David Harvey has explained, proved a pivotal moment in global economic history. As the first major example of the kind of aggressive corporate-interest–driven economic restructuring that compelled the retrenchment of state responsibility for social welfare provision, it was a landmark step on the road toward the global neoliberal economic revolution led by the Reagan administration and other conservative governments worldwide during the 1980s and afterward.[82]

Although New York's experience was not typical, dealing with entrenched economic interests seeking to dictate the direction of city government was a problem faced by many municipal leaders during the 1970s. As insurgents within existing urban power arrangements, black city executives often had to contend with white business elites who, intent on maintaining their influence in local politics, could pose a significant problem for them, depending on the agenda that the mayors sought to pursue once in office. Since the New Deal, as Thompson has explained, public policy in the nation's cities had been strongly influenced by a broad coalition of business interests, including real estate developers, major business leaders, banking and insurance executives, lawyers, and construction firms. Sharing a common interest in securing federal subsidies for "public infrastructure to promote private investment and economic growth," their broad vision of "pro-growth" politics dictated that city government should be dedicated to maintaining and developing downtown business districts, ensuring law and order in the central city, improving transportation infrastructure, and encouraging private enterprise and greater profitability through pro-business fiscal policy. At a time when white flight meant city resources were increasingly sparse, business leaders became even more hostile toward policies (such as city spending on poor neighborhoods) that did not meet their demands, either directly or indirectly. Indeed their staunch opposition to redistributive politics had underpinned the creation of inner-city ghettos since the 1930s, which, in turn, highlighted the dominance of pro-growth urban politics during the four decades after the Great Depression.[83]

The economic crises of the 1970s, and broader white public resentment of redistributive politics, continued to put even greater pressure on black mayors to defer to the interests of downtown economic elites. Pursuing policies that might exacerbate white flight, such as increasing taxes to fund city social spending, not only was discouraged by pro-growth interests but also threatened to exacerbate urban decline and confirm prejudiced white predictions of economic catastrophe under black city leadership. In Los Angeles, however, Tom Bradley's own fiscal conservatism and political outlook meant that his program was already broadly in tune with that of local white taxpayers and economic elites. By the end of his first term Bradley boasted of having kept his promises on taxes: he had cut government spending by $200 million, presented three balanced city budgets, vetoed various proposed tax increases, and secured a 10 percent cut in the property tax rate.[84]

Bradley's political program, however, did not ignore the city's poor minority neighborhoods entirely. After he pledged to avoid tax increases, his efforts to address the severe housing, unemployment, and social problems that beset South Central and East Los Angeles rested on securing greater federal funds for the city, an endeavor in which he met considerable success during his first administration. Whereas federal grants to the city sat at $80 million when Bradley took office in 1973, they grew to $400 million within two years and reached nearly $900 million by the end of the decade. Part of this additional revenue was directed toward efforts to improve the lives of the city's poorer citizens. Among these were after-school educational programs, efforts to address housing shortages, and increased police patrols. His administration also worked with financial institutions to combat redlining and ran a scheme (similar to that run by Restoration in Brooklyn) that sold rehabilitated properties at affordable prices to local residents in poor communities via advantageous mortgage arrangements. In keeping with Bradley's political philosophy, his administration favored pro-business and economic development–oriented solutions for tackling local urban poverty.[85] This approach was designed— just as Kennedy's and Nixon's had been—to maximize opportunity for and aid to poor minorities with minimum political risk.[86]

Bradley's firm faith in the capacity of pro–capitalist development politics to deal with economic inequality and recession led him to actively increase the influence of the city's economic elite on city hall. In April 1974 Bradley established the Ad Hoc Economic Development Committee, composed almost entirely of representatives from the private sector. Almost a year later, in March 1975, as unemployment and inflation worsened, Mayor Bradley, along with the city council, created an economic development structure within the city government based on the recommendations made by the Ad Hoc Economic Development Committee.[87] One long-term result of this effort was the redirection of federal community development block grant (CDBG) funds away from the city's poor neighborhoods toward the central business districts. This shift was justified with the assertion that investment in the downtown area would produce trickle-down benefits to the city's poor neighborhoods via the extra jobs such investment might be expected to produce. In reality, few jobs resulted from such development, and the loss of funds only accelerated the decline of the city's ghettos.[88] Furthermore, Bradley's partnership with the city's economic elites—who were highly concerned with the maintenance of law and order—disinclined him from effectively challenging the LAPD (an organization he had poor relations with throughout his five terms in office). Bradley's failure to pursue police reform aggressively was a severe disappointment for many poor and working-class black Angelenos for whom the issue of police brutality was especially important. As Sonenshein has explained, committed first and foremost to making Los Angeles a "world class city," Bradley pursued a political agenda throughout his five terms strongly oriented toward the interests of downtown business elites and middle-class taxpayers.[89]

Bradley's programs for helping the city's poor black communities did little to stem the decline of South Central, which was being ravaged by large-scale corporate disinvestment and urban decay. The jobs created by his administration's business-oriented economic development programs did little to redress the imbalance. Worse still, their reliance on expanded federal funding streams made them vulnerable to conservative tax and spending measures that shook both California and the nation from the late 1970s onward. The passage of Proposition 13, a property tax limitation measure approved by two-thirds of California voters in 1978, cut $7 billion from state government funds, greatly impacting city finances and necessitating severe cutbacks in essential services. This trend was exacerbated by the massive reductions in federal support for urban social welfare spending that followed the election of Ronald Reagan to the White House in 1980, precipitating the hyperdecline of ghetto communities such as South Central Los Angeles over the following decades.[90]

Whereas Bradley's mainstream political and economic credos aligned him with Los Angeles's white downtown power structure, Maynard Jackson's political vision put him in direct opposition to Atlanta's white business elite, an effectively organized group accustomed to holding sway over city government since the 1940s. Business interests were represented by Central Atlanta Progress (CAtP), a nonprofit development corporation comprising more than two hundred local downtown property holders, business leaders, and executives who were concerned with public policy, land use, and investments in the central city. CAtP had enjoyed a very close partnership with Mayor Ivan Allen (who had been head of the city's Chamber of Commerce prior to his election), and worked productively with his successor, Mayor Massell. Jackson's forthright racial advocacy, however, threatened to disrupt the existing power arrangements so favorable to the city's white economic elite. As political scientist Clarence Stone explains, Jackson set out under the assumption that his election was "a mandate for social reform which the business leaders as well as other sectors of the community" should support. Jackson soon realized that his efforts to deliver on his campaign promises to tackle the problems facing Atlanta's poor black neighborhoods and pursue his ambitious program for black empowerment would not go unchallenged. CAtP would mount the most formidable resistance.[91]

Fiscal constraints further undermined Jackson's efforts to increase social spending. To counteract budgetary shortfalls and avoid cutting services and laying off city workers, Jackson proposed increasing local taxes (primarily property taxes) by $6.2 million. It was vital, he argued, that the city's middle class and elite accept a greater tax burden. "We've cut down below the bone. We're down to the marrow [. . .] you can't go anymore unless you kill the victim." However, his proposal was soundly rejected (six-to-one) by the city council's finance committee, which found revenue instead by cutting city employee pay.[92] Faced with limited finances, Jackson reprioritized the use of existing city funds. CDBG money previously earmarked for downtown business district redevelopment was redirected toward revitalizing the city's poor black neighborhoods, including housing construction and rehabilitation, improving sanitation, street maintenance, recreation facilities, and social services.[93]

Furthermore, Jackson pursued a two-pronged approach to reforming the Atlanta Police Department. The first initiative involved significantly increasing the number of black police officers, which jumped from 23 percent of the force when he took office to over 35 percent by the end of his first term. The second involved the symbolic removal of white police chief John Inman, a pariah in the black community. Atlanta police acquired a reputation for brutality under his command, as twenty-three African Americans died at the hands of police officers between July 1973 and July 1974.[94] Local Black Panthers were especially critical of Inman, lambasting him as the "trigger-man" for "powerful, wealthy racist right wing elements" in Atlanta hell-bent on stopping "black and poor people gaining control of their lives." After local courts stymied Jackson's attempts to fire Inman, he used an administrative reorganization (a revised city charter) to circumvent Inman's authority by subordinating the police department and its leaders under a public safety commissioner (a position to which Jackson appointed an African American, Reggie Eaves). For local blacks, it was a welcome victory that brought a sig-nificant reduction in the incidence of police brutality; for white business leaders, it was an alarming and unwelcome development under the city's brash new African American mayor.[95]

Jackson's bold city leadership, weighted toward the concerns of poor local blacks, brought a hostile response from the city's white business elite and their allies throughout his first year in office. Local corporate leaders were angered by the redirection of funds away from the central business district, especially as CAtP was planning a number of major downtown redevelop-ment projects for which it expected the city's fiscal support.[96] For the first half of his administration, Jackson has recalled, the city's newspapers were "almost hysterical." [97] One local journalist described Jackson's redistributive policies as "demagogic action on behalf of poor blacks." The new mayor's police reforms and his strong commitment to affirmative action in city gov-ernment hiring and contracts were seen by others as proof that Jackson was unable to govern the biracial city evenhandedly.[98] In September 1974, CAtP sent an open letter to the mayor and the city council president warning that many of its members were contemplating leaving the city because of an increasing crime rate, Jackson's apparent disrespect for the police department (evidenced by Inman's sacking), the changing racial balance in the city's workforce, and the "perceived attitude of the mayor as anti-white." [99]

Jackson understood that his vision for black progress and his combative approach would unsettle the city's white economic elites. He also believed they would ultimately adjust to and accept his commitment to reorienting city policy toward the interests of the black community. As he recalls, "I [. . .] fervently wanted the business community to work hand-in-glove with me as we went through this transition. I didn't want to do it in a confrontational way. [. . .] But my job was to do it, one way or the other." It soon became clear that Jackson's initial confidence that they wouldn't "walk away from the relationship" was "dead wrong." "Times got hot, even some of the closest friends I had in the business community [...] said, 'Maynard, that was the dumbest thing I've ever seen, and goodbye.' [...] So, I miscalculated." [100] By the end of his first term in office, Jackson came to appreciate fully the necessity of having downtown leaders' support. Not only could they make life very difficult through political pressure and negative publicity, but as city tax resources continued to decline, they represented a vitally important source of private investment in the city. In that sense, they were the primary bulwark against the city's insolvency. Pursuing an agenda that failed to meet their demands proved untenable in the longer term, and as he prepared to run for reelection in 1977, Jackson began to change tack accordingly. Although he remained strongly committed to advancing black interests through affirmative action and city contract disbursement and black business support, he drastically curtailed the redistributive aspects of his political program for Atlanta.[101]

The shift in policy direction, historian Ronald Bayor explains, "was abrupt." In 1977, Jackson responded to the pressure and criticism from local business leaders by establishing the Mayor's Office of Economic Development, dedicated to maintaining a strong central business district. From that point on, Jackson largely abandoned his redistributive spending on poor black neighborhoods, reinstating public works improvement projects in the downtown area as the top priority for CDBG funds. Jackson also removed a number of his own black appointees to city government who had earned the disapproval of CAtP leaders. Nothing more clearly underlined Jackson's change in emphasis than his response to the city's sanitation workers when, in March 1977, they threatened to strike unless they were given a fifty-cent-per-hour pay increase. As vice-mayor seven years earlier, Jackson had offered the workers strong support during their battle with Mayor Massell. Faced with the same situation as mayor, however, Jackson did exactly what his predecessor had done: refused their demands, insisting that the city had no money for raises. Jackson promptly fired nearly one thousand city employees—the vast majority of whom were low-income blacks—when they decided to go on strike. Although many were rehired over the following year, Jackson had delivered an unmistakable message about the city's new priorities. His administration's commitment to issues affecting poor and working-class blacks was over. Economic and class interests would once again come to define politics and progress in Atlanta.[102]

Bradley and Jackson's mayoralties reveal a great deal about the powerful influence that white interests—and the mainstream political discourses, ideas, issues, and policies that those interests supported—had on black city politics. Despite the different approaches each took to addressing the needs of the black poor on the campaign trail and once in power, they both eventually occupied the same position. Redistributive policies were either avoided or abandoned in favor of pro-business and economic development programs tailored to the needs and interests of economic elites. Their ability to help disadvantaged blacks was constrained by a number of factors: broader white taxpayer backlash politics; ongoing economic trends and difficulties at city, national, and global levels; and, perhaps most decisively, the pervasive and powerful influence of white economic elites.

For many African Americans, black political power proved far less beneficial than they had hoped. In particular, city spending cuts on inner-city black neighborhoods impacted the black community unevenly, along lines of class and gender. At a time when the incidence of single-parent, female-headed families in ghetto communities was increasing, this trend in urban policy ensured that poor and working-class black mothers and their children continued to be most heavily affected by governmental retreat from urban social spending. At the same time, Bradley's and Jackson's pro-business, economic development policies did little to remedy inner-city ghetto decline. However, while Bradley was reluctant, and Jackson proved unable, to sustain a commitment to the interests of their poor and working-class black constituents, their political programs proved highly advantageous to other sections of the black community in Los Angeles and Atlanta.

THE PATH OF LEAST RESISTANCE: CLASS INTEREST, AFFIRMATIVE ACTION, AND MINORITY BUSINESS SUPPORT UNDER BLACK CITY LEADERSHIP

In Los Angeles, Tom Bradley's pro-business stance and failure to identify with the issues affecting the inner-city poor drew significant criticism from social and economic justice advocates and disadvantaged local blacks. In Atlanta, Dorothy Bolden, a prominent community organizer who as head of the National Domestic Worker's Union (NDWU) represented thousands of low-income black women in the city, captured the disappointment that Jackson's leadership generated among Atlanta's once hopeful black poor. Mayor Jackson, she lamented, "started off being" a good choice but "ended being a bad one. [. . .] He didn't do what I thought he was going to do." [103]

Middle-class and upper-income blacks in both cities had an altogether different perspective on their mayor's records, heralding Bradley and Jackson as
valuable and inspiring symbols of black progress who did what they could to
advance black interests in extremely challenging circumstances. Accordingly,
they urged the black poor and working class to join with them in full support
of their African American political representatives. However, as this section
argues, black middle-class and elite solidarity with Bradley and Jackson
rested less on race than it did on the fact that African American city leadership generally served their interests by widening their access to political and
economic opportunity.[104] Black progress under Bradley and Jackson owed a
great deal to the policy shift (explored in chapter 2) that sought to channel
black demands for empowerment through greater integration into the mainstream economy. As those policies and the assumptions that underpinned
them were developed, adapted, and further entrenched in local and national
politics, they skewed opportunities for black advancement firmly toward the
black middle class and elite.

In one respect, as Marable points out, an apparent class bias within black
politics is unsurprising. After all, the vast majority of African American
elected officials tended to be drawn from the ranks of the black middle class
and professional elite, and their "ideological outlook and basic political practices tended to align them more with other parvenu elites than with the black
working-class." [105] At a time when middle-class and wealthy whites were
increasingly demanding tax relief and smaller, pro-business government,
there is no reason to think that their black counterparts would not also favor
such an approach. While Bradley's consistently middle-class, pro-business
agenda suggests this kind of innate class bias, Jackson's initial commitment
to redistributive politics complicates our view of him in this respect. Both
pursued the most politically viable opportunities available to them. Whereas
growing resistance to redistributive politics among white voters and business
interests severely constrained black elected officials' scope for helping poor
and working-class African Americans, the entrenchment of affirmative
action and minority business development in federal policy under the Nixon
administration helped foster a political climate in which city employment
and contracts policy became the primary and most legitimate means to
advance black interests. The economic opportunities these policies opened
up to the black community—as the cases of both Los Angeles and Atlanta
demonstrate—were fundamentally skewed toward benefiting the black middle class and elite (and men in particular).

Although affirmative action policy reached its zenith under President Nixon, when it was installed (alongside minority business development) as one of the primary federal approaches to meeting black demands for equality, it emerged from two decades of African American protest and organizing and federal-government–led fair employment practice legislation aimed at eradicating racial discrimination in the workplace.[106] The fundamental aim underlying affirmative action—to accelerate the integration of minorities (and especially unemployed black men) into the nation's economic mainstream—was also at the heart of Robert Kennedy's CDC blueprint. Not only did Kennedy's plan seek to bring the private sector further into the battle against endemic black unemployment, poverty, and urban decay, but its provisions mandating tax incentives for businesses that boosted black employment (by locating operations in ghetto areas and employing locals) were tantamount to affirmative action. Having long insisted upon the need for proactive policy that would help to remedy past discrimination, African American leaders welcomed affirmative action, hoping it could overcome the "institutional racism" that restricted nonwhites to low-wage employment and kept many in poverty.[107]

Keen to reorient federal civil rights policy toward advancing economic opportunity for minorities, Nixon took affirmative action a stage further by carrying forward an existing pilot scheme that applied Johnson's September 1965 Executive Order 11246 (which forbade employment discrimination on the part of federal contractors) to a number of federally funded construction projects in Philadelphia. The "Philadelphia Plan" sought to undermine the racially biased practices of the city's labor unions by stipulating increased minority hiring as a precondition for involvement on any construction project receiving federal funding. In developing the Philadelphia Plan, Kotlowski explains, Nixon introduced the setting of "goals and timetables" for affirmative action, thereby allowing progress toward overturning employment bias to be measured and monitored. Under the plan, the city loosely adhered to a theory of proportional representation that had emanated from civil rights groups' efforts to discern whether or not a company's hiring policies were discriminatory. If the proportion of a company's staff who were black was significantly lower than the proportion of the local population that was black, this was deemed likely to indicate racial discrimination. The principle of proportional representation became an important one in civil rights and Black Power discourse about political and economic empowerment. Demands for a proportional share of jobs, contracts, and political offices were nothing more than demands for blacks to be given their "fair share." This principle would play a significant role in shaping both black expectations and black progress under African American city leadership.[108]

Under Nixon, affirmative action became a vital part of the policy shift with which this book is concerned, the approach intended to co-opt and modify Black Power. The pragmatic Nixon backed affirmative action in part because, like his theory of black capitalism, it did not threaten to offend broader public opinion among the "Silent Majority" in the same way that welfare state liberalism did. Affirmative action did not require the direct redistribution of wealth (via increased taxes or social spending on the poor) or the expansion of government's scope or responsibility through federal government public employment programs. Rather, it sought to channel minority employment demands into the mainstream economy and existing government employment structures. Furthermore, by seeking to open up the American workplace to minorities, it ostensibly chimed with core aspects of the nation's work ethic and success myth, and fit into the politics of the welfare backlash. Affirmative action would help increase minority employment; those who found jobs could then provide for themselves and their own families and would not be dependent on government. In these ways affirmative action perfectly complemented the president's black capitalism initiatives, as did the establishment of federal contract set-asides for minority businesses.

Affirmative action also resonated with Nixon's own meritocratic principles. A person's potential to succeed, he believed, should be governed only by his ability and willingness to work. In this sense, Nixon found denying black people the opportunity to reach their potential because of their race as offensive as the advantages enjoyed by many privileged white liberal elites by virtue of their social connections. Affirmative action would, therefore, help eradicate a false and unjust barrier to personal success and individual initiative. Finally, just as Nixon's support of black business development was designed to grow the black middle class and win them over to the Republican fold, affirmative action was similarly intended to offer African Americans the scope for greater upward mobility. Widening employment opportunities in public and private sector employment promised first and foremost to benefit those blacks best prepared to take advantage of those opportunities. This often meant those most qualified and best educated. Furthermore, affirmative action opened up the nation's universities to greater minority participation, further widening the educational gap between disadvantaged blacks and their middle-class counterparts. Affirmative action did not, therefore, offer great potential for tackling endemic unemployment among the nation's growing black urban underclass. In this way, it dovetailed with the middle-class tilt of Nixon's approaches to dealing with the black demand for economic empowerment.[109]

Many conservatives objected to affirmative action, for a number of reasons. First, affirmative action seemed a blatant violation of the very color-blind anti-discrimination provisions set down in Title VII of the 1964 Civil Rights Act that it was intended to make a reality. Here lay the fundamental contradiction between the civil rights movement's vision of a color-blind society and affirmative action. In seeking to eradicate racial discrimination through positive action toward the hiring of minority workers, affirmative action explicitly required employers to consider race as a fundamental and decisive factor in their hiring process. For many conservatives, therefore, affirmative action by definition constituted unfair racial discrimination (often called reverse discrimination) because it gave minorities preferential treatment, predominantly at the expense of whites. Second, anger over "goals and timetables" revolved around the notion that such devices really represented "quotas." This, in turn, raised the prospect of race trumping aptitude in the selection process—a corruption of core meritocratic American ideals that threatened a decline in workplace standards. Third, many businesspeople argued that government dictates concerning employment policy infringed on their freedom to run their businesses as they saw fit. In doing so, they concluded, the government was overstepping its bounds by interfering in the free-market mechanism and artificially jeopardizing a company's performance. Finally, many business owners were also concerned that their white employees would be hostile to the prospect of working alongside nonwhites. In all cases, the underlying concern (apart from racial prejudice) was the fear that businesses might lose money through affirmative action, a concern magnified by national economic strife during the 1970s.[110]

Despite the opposition and controversy engendered by the Nixon administration's endorsement of goals and timetables, affirmative action became established at the heart of the federal government's attempts to tackle discrimination in the job market specifically, and economic inequality more generally, during the early 1970s. Strongly supported by liberals in the Democrat-controlled Congress, affirmative action was advanced by the Equal Employment Opportunity Act (EEOA) they helped to pass in January 1972. A landmark piece of legislation, the EEOA revised Title VII of the 1964 Civil Rights Act (which outlawed discrimination against nonwhite and female workers) by increasing federal enforcement powers and extending its coverage to include a greater percentage of private businesses and, for the first time, both state and local government as well. This provided the legal ground upon which black elected officials such as Bradley and Jackson operated when they sought to boost the number of African Americans and other minorities employed by city hall.[111]

Once in office both Bradley and Jackson pursued vigorous affirmative action programs in city employment. While on the city council, Bradley had, alongside fellow black councilman Billy Mills, fought for stricter enforcement of the "Greater Los Angeles Plan," the city's own version of the Philadelphia Plan.[112] One of the most important tasks Bradley faced as he began his administration was appointing the city commissioners who would put his political stamp on, and establish his influence within, the city's bureaucracy. As historian Heather Parker explains, Bradley had 140 of these appointments to make and retained only seventeen Yorty appointees, none of whom sat on the most important boards. By appointing twenty-one African Americans, thirteen Latino Americans, and ten Asian Americans, Bradley made city government far more racially diverse and representative than it had ever been. Bradley's first act as mayor was to issue Executive Order No. 1, which established a forthright affirmative action policy for city government hiring and contracts. Although Bradley himself rarely spoke about affirmative action as a black issue, framing it more broadly as a way to increase minority and female employment in general, he appointed African American Bill Elkins, a strong racial advocate, to oversee its development and implementation. Results were impressive, and blacks were the racial group that benefited most from the city's affirmative action programs under Bradley during his five terms as mayor from 1973 to 1992. During that period, as Parker has shown, the number of blacks in high-paying municipal positions—where they had been severely underrepresented—went up dramatically, doubling in many categories. By 1992, when blacks represented only 13 percent of the city's population (down from 17.9 percent in 1973 thanks to the growing Latino population), they represented 21.2 percent of the city's employees.[113]

In Atlanta, Jackson set out to make city government truly biracial, as fast as possible. During his first year in charge, Bayor explains, African Americans accounted for 80 percent of all new city hires and nearly 60 percent of those appointed to the two highest-paid job grades. Of the twenty-seven leadership positions in city departments and agencies that Jackson filled, fifteen were given to blacks and the remaining twelve to whites. Considerable progress was made in increasing the black share of municipal employment. In 1970, under Jackson's predecessor Mayor Massell, just over 38 percent of the city workforce was African American, which included 7 percent of its administrators and 15 percent of city professionals. By the start of Jackson's second term in 1978, nearly 56 percent of city employees were black, and the percentage of African American administrators and professionals had risen to 32 and 42 percent, respectively.[114]

Both Bradley and Jackson also used city contracts and spending as a way to leverage change in private sector employment patterns, in the same way that federal affirmative action policy did. However, this was not easy. In Los Angeles, Bradley met resistance from several corporate business leaders, especially those from major local car manufacturers General Motors, Ford, and Chrysler, who refused to sign the Bradley administration's affirmative action pledge, arguing that the goals and timetables it set were too demanding. Bradley responded by terminating city procurement from those firms. Remaining steadfast in his promise not to do business with them, despite a vehicle shortage crisis in the police department, Bradley reached a negotiated settlement, and the automobile giants accepted the city's new hiring policy. For Bradley, it was an important and symbolic victory: "I think it set a principle that if we could take on the biggest corporations in the country on affirmative action and win and preserve our ordinances, they were going to be secure against any attack by any other companies. [. . .] That was, I think, the major breakthrough. It was important not only to Los Angeles but to other cities that had similar kinds of affirmative-action ordinances. As a consequence, now every company willingly and quickly agrees to this approach."[115]

In Atlanta, Maynard Jackson targeted the local downtown banks as a sector in which business executives could do more to promote minority employment. In this case, the city held nearly $600 million of its tax funds in six major white-run downtown banks. Jackson was especially keen that those banks begin hiring and promoting blacks to middle and senior management positions, where they were almost entirely absent. Through informal negotiations with the banks during the first year and a half of his tenure at city hall he hoped to prod them into action. As Jackson recalls, taking this soft approach resulted in "zero" being accomplished. "I don't mean almost zero. I mean, zero." Jackson subsequently adopted a new strategy, advising the banks they had thirty days to comply with the city's affirmative action policy or face losing the city's accounts. With only one bank, the First Georgia Bank, having come to terms with the city before the deadline, the mayor made good on his threat. The remaining five banks soon acquiesced. As Jackson explains, "On day 31, we moved the smallest account we could find from uncooperative bank A; it was a $500,000 account, just a half million dollar account, moved that into First Georgia Bank, and I think, ah, the message was heard." [116]

Boosting black businesses was the other main way in which African American mayors were able to successfully and consistently cater to black interests. This was done through the disbursement of city contracts and resources, an approach to remedying racial and economic inequality that, again, emerged from mainstream white engagement with Black Power and that was firmly established and legitimized under the Nixon administration. Through the Office of Minority Business Enterprise (OMBE), Nixon increased the value of federal procurement from black businesses from approximately $9 million when he took office to $250 million by 1975. In the process, the Nixon White House initiated what became known as contract set-asides. As economist Thomas Boston explains, these set-asides fused affirmative action with minority business development by designating an increasing proportion of federal contracts to minority-owned businesses. As with affirmative action hiring, the underlying goal was the integration of blacks into the nation's economic mainstream. Between 1968 and 1977, $2.2 billion in federal contracts was awarded to minority businesses under this scheme. As minority businesses expanded their operations thanks to increased federal revenues, they became more viable entities within the broader mainstream economy. During the same period (1969–75) the total purchases made from minority-owned businesses increased by over 250 percent, rising to $475 million. A similar effect was seen with black-owned banks as the Nixon administration increased the amount of federal funds held with them from $35 million in 1971 to $80 million in 1973. Over that period, the total amount of both public and private investments in those banks more than doubled, from approximately $400 million to over $1 billion. [117]

To an even greater degree than affirmative action city hiring, minority business development tended primarily to benefit the black middle class and elite, the groups from which entrepreneurs tended to emerge and whose access to educational opportunity gave them a distinct advantage over poor and working-class blacks in the free-market economy. As chapter 2 demonstrates, the fundamental principle that underpinned pro-capitalist business venture and economic development policies was that support for black business and increasing mainstream economic opportunity for African Americans would boost the black middle class. This, in turn, would help lift up the black poor. Directing greater revenues to black-owned business enterprises was intended to put more money into black communities indirectly via the hands of black business owners and then on to their employees. This faith in the capacity of the American private enterprise system to reduce economic inequality, rather than exacerbate it as its critics complained, would prove misplaced in the longer run, especially when neoliberal economic restructuring during the 1980s and afterward did much to further widen the poverty gap.

Just as the ongoing retrenchment of federal and city social spending on the nation's ghetto communities disproportionately affected poor black women and children, business development policies skewed toward the black middle class and elite tended, first and foremost, to benefit black men. The world of mainstream American business had always been a bastion of white male privilege and power (a fact that remains largely true today). The assumption and fact of male dominance characterized the black business world as much as it did the white. This reality was clear in the testimony of Norman Hodges, chairman of the National Association of Black Manufacturers and director of the Green Power Foundation Inc., a Los Angeles–based minority business development and support organization, when he spoke before an SCLC convention in Chicago in 1973. Profiling the type of black entrepreneur who could achieve prominence in the world of American business, Hodges explained:

> He's a black man who's got the drive of Henry Ford, trying to develop a safe and sound automobile that can be afforded by all people in this country. He's as committed as Carnegie, developing an industry of steel. He's got the vision of a Vanderbilt, breaking through the mountain paths to establish the Trans-American railroad, and in 1960, he has the taste of Colonel Sanders making a fortune selling fried chicken that blacks have been frying for over a hundred years. The list could also include men like Edison, Rockefeller, and Woolworth.[118]

While policies aimed at developing black businesses, therefore, certainly had the capacity to increase wealth throughout the black community and could help make those businesses (as Robert Kennedy had foreseen) a generator of urban improvement, they also predominantly concentrated economic benefits among a restricted class. Those who gained most from such policies tended to be black men from the middle class and elite. While this fundamental gender and class bias was not always an explicit part of discourses surrounding white efforts to negotiate Black Power and the scope and direction of black progress, it was always there. Channeling black advancement and empowerment through the nation's mainstream political and economic institutions necessarily rested on the same gender and class dynamics and values that dominated white American society.

Whereas Tom Bradley did not advocate funneling city contracts to black businesses (largely because of his race-neutral stance), he firmly believed in and practiced the politics of black economic development, and during his first term set up the Office of Small Business Assistance, which offered financial and technical help to minority and other disadvantaged businesses in the city.[119] Maynard Jackson, on the other hand, was firmly committed to "leveling the playing field" for black businesses in Atlanta. When he came to office in 1973, Jackson discovered that of $33 million in city contract expenditure, just $41,500 went to black-owned firms. In a majority-black city, he argued, black businesses ought to have a fair share in that city's economic success. Jackson's election signaled the end of white businesses' monopoly on Atlanta's city spending. Indeed, perhaps more than any other black elected official in the country, Jackson made boosting black businesses through city contract disbursement a major focal point of his political program for black advancement.[120]

In giving black businesses a prime role in Atlanta's growth and development, Jackson overcame considerable resistance from local white elites. No single project showcased Jackson's commitment to supporting black businesses and bringing them into the city's economic life better than the construction of Atlanta-Hartsfield International Airport during his first term in office. Given that the airport was the largest capital construction project in the South at the time, worth an estimated $1 billion, Jackson insisted that 25 percent of all project-related contracts go to black-owned businesses. Despite fierce, sustained criticism from white business leaders and the local white press, who argued that his plan was too aggressive and unfair to local white businesses, the project was a stunning success. Finished on time (despite Jackson's decision to hold up the project until the black business contract target was met), the construction project was widely praised for its effective administration and smooth completion. As Boston explains, the project was hugely significant for black businesses in Atlanta and beyond (many black companies from across the United States worked on it), allowing many of them to break into nontraditional industries, while others worked on new economies of scale or diversified, leading to rapid growth and increasing profitability.[121]

Atlanta's black business development and support efforts also helped to further entrench minority business development in federal policy. On the heels of Jackson's successful airport project, the Public Works Employment Act and Omnibus Small Business Act, passed in 1977 and 1978, respectively, set percentage targets for the first time by requiring that minority-owned businesses receive a minimum of 10 percent of federal procurement contracts and 10 percent of the business related to federally funded public works projects. At the same time that the Carter administration cut social welfare spending, it wrote support for minority business more boldly into law through federal contract set-asides. Under the Reagan administration, which decimated federal support for social welfare spending, federal procurement from minority businesses continued to rise. In 1981 minority businesses received 3.4 percent of all federal procurement expenditures. By 1994, they received 8.3 percent, or $14.4 billion.[122] As policies that primarily benefited poor and working-class blacks (and women in particular) were being pared back aggressively, alternative political approaches designed to bolster and expand the black middle class became ever more tightly fixed in national policy.

BLACK POWER, BLACK POLITICS, AND BLACK PROGRESS

Some black politicians saw political power as an opportunity to challenge and transform the nation's existing dominant white political cultures and philosophies, and to pursue the radical democratic transformation sought by welfare rights activists and groups like the Black Panthers. As African American state representative for South Central Los Angeles Mervyn Dymally explained to his fellow black elected officials at the California Black Leadership Conference held in Los Angeles in June 1971:

> White political power has failed in the quest to establish a just society. Black political leadership may be the last tool sharp enough to do the job. For, in the final analysis, black politics has become the new cutting edge of the Black Power movement. And, unlike most white politics, black politics has justice as its ultimate goal [...] justice for the masses of people whose dignity has been dwarfed by the contradictions of a system that is in need of reform.[123]

For the majority of African Americans in Los Angeles and Atlanta, however, black city leadership was anything but a generator of improvement and social and economic justice. Under Tom Bradley, who was elected mayor in 1973 and served five consecutive terms, South Central Los Angeles declined precipitously as unemployment worsened, disinvestment continued apace, and gang warfare and a crack cocaine epidemic ravaged the area throughout the 1980s. Mayor Bradley's pro-growth corporate- and middle class–interest politics, along with the cuts in city services that followed the passage of Prop 13 in 1978, served only to worsen this decline. While the local black middle class and elite experienced unprecedented gains under his leadership, Bradley's last year in office was marked, somewhat poignantly, by the riots of 1992, which dramatized the simmering discontent and social disaffection bred by the decline of local ghetto communities he had simultaneously over-seen.[124] Deep disillusionment with Bradley's policies and his failure to iden-tify with the black poor and the issues they faced, Thompson explains, had the effect of demobilizing large numbers of black voters. From Bradley's first campaign for mayor in 1969 to the end of his five terms in 1993, black voter turnout in the city decreased by 38 percent.[125]

In Atlanta, Maynard Jackson's first two terms vitally shaped the future course of black city politics. Beginning with his successor, former SCLC leader and congressman Andrew Young, in the decades since 1980 Atlanta's black political leadership has taken Jackson's pro-growth politics and close cooperation with the business community to ever greater levels.[126] During that period, as Grady-Willis explains, intraracial inequality in Atlanta has only deepened, with the city's wealthy black suburbs expanding steadily over the past three decades (thanks in part to many northern black professionals relocating to the city to take advantage of the economic opportunities avail-able). The poor, however, have become ever more marginalized in the city's political affairs (a trend that worsened sharply during Young's mayoralty). Despite this, cross-class racial solidarity in Atlanta has seen black voters con-tinue to elect pro-growth black mayors in the Jackson and Young mold throughout the three decades since. The result, Grady-Willis concludes, is that today there are "two Black Atlantas, one middle-class to affluent and the other working-class to destitute."[127]

The pro–black business development policies examined in this and previ-ous chapters—which emerged from white engagement with Black Power—constituted only one of many factors that worsened wealth inequality. It is, however, an important factor. Atlanta offers an especially telling example. In November 1985, the Atlanta chapter of the National Association of Minority Contractors held a banquet in Maynard Jackson's honor. Elliot Marsh, the group's president, praised Jackson for maintaining his commitment to affirmative action. As a group, black businesses had a great deal to thank him for. Since 1976 they had received a quarter of a billion dollars in city contracts. When Jackson had entered office, less than 0.2 percent of city contracts went to black-owned businesses. By the end of his second term, they received more than a third. When he rose to speak, Jackson thanked the audience and spoke of his pride at having run "the most successful affirmative action program in the history of this nation." Jackson's successor, Mayor Andrew Young, was also there to pay tribute: "We thank you for taking on those hard battles and dealing with those issues when the way was lonely." [128]

In reality, while Jackson's policies had proved very beneficial for a select group of African American business leaders, they had done little for the majority of the city's black citizens. As Emma Darnell, head of the city's affirmative action program, acknowledges:

> The initiative which we undertook in the 70s to open up the government to minority workers and businessmen led to success for a few, but for the great majority of minority businessmen in Atlanta, our initiatives had no effect at all. Our unemployment rates were as high before we instituted the affirmative action program as they were afterwards. And of course that is because government alone cannot do the job. We had enormous successes. We saw during the seventies in Atlanta blacks moving into positions all over downtown where they'd never been before. That's because the city had forced businesses to hire them in order to do business with the city [. . .] but overall, if you looked at the real economic condition of the average Black person in Atlanta, [. . .] not those in the clique, but the everyday working class black during this period, [they] simply did not see the benefits of what we tried to do.[129]

It is here that the success, and longer-term consequences, of white engagement with Black Power is illuminated. As this chapter—and this book more broadly—argues, the efforts of white politicians, institutions, and organizations to control the meaning of Black Power, and to define the political parameters within which racial progress could occur, played a vital and understudied role in guiding black advancement during the Black Power era. The underlying emphasis of public policy—authored by whites and supported by many blacks—on creating economic opportunity for the middle class and promulgating middle-class social and political values played a tangible and underappreciated role in making possible the progress that the black middle class made during the 1970s and afterward. Along with broader white resistance to redistributive liberalism and socioeconomic change, the policy shift intended to co-opt Black Power also helped sow the seeds of greater economic inequality. Rather than challenge the class and gender biases in mainstream American society, black politics—as it came to be defined by the political opportunities and pressures created by white interests and opposition—served primarily to reinforce them. Black city politicians, such as Bradley and Jackson, were often important actors in these developments. The vision of Black Power that many black mayors helped to realize, therefore, was one that had been powerfully shaped by mainstream white America.

Conclusion

In 1966 Stokely Carmichael argued that American democracy required radical transformation if African Americans were ever to attain social, economic, and racial justice. Existing civil rights remedies, he explained, had failed to challenge structural inequalities in the American economy and society. Black Power, as he envisaged it, would bring about the necessary transformation by redistributing power and wealth down to the poor, oppressed, and disenfranchised.[1] For Carmichael, Black Power was fundamentally about reorienting the black freedom struggle to serve the interests of America's black urban and rural poor: "a means for the black poor to get together, define their needs, and put people in power to achieve them." The new slogan thus represented "a call, perhaps the last call, to the black middle-class to come home. It is a demand that black haves make common cause with the black have-nots."[2] In Carmichael's view, the black middle class had to look beyond narrow class interest and individual aspirations for the greater good. Seeking assimilation into the mainstream American middle class—a "perpetuator of black oppression" and the "backbone of institutional racism"—he argued, would do nothing to serve the broader cause of black liberation from white oppression and exploitation.[3] As this book suggests, however, Carmichael's grassroots-oriented vision of Black Power—as a force for transformative political change and social and economic justice—was only one of many. Black Power was a flexible and ambiguous concept, and the goals it broadly encompassed—black political, economic, and cultural empowerment—had wide appeal among African Americans. Defining no single path for achieving those goals, Black Power was open to interpretation. In the tumultuous, highly charged urban political landscapes of mid-1960s America, Black Power's meaning was constantly being contested and was always evolving and being adapted to suit different needs and contexts. As this book argues, mainstream white politicians, institutions, and organizations played a vital yet understudied role in that process.

At the center of white engagement with Black Power ideology—and white efforts to define the scope and character of black progress and socioeconomic change more broadly—lay the tool of public policy. It was through public policies and battles to define them that mainstream white politicians and institutions sought to both cultivate and appeal to an alternative interpretation of Black Power more oriented to middle-class interests and more conservative than that articulated by racial agitators such as Carmichael. This book maps the developmental arc and longer-term impact of these efforts through close analysis of key public policies, including the Johnson administration's War on Poverty, Robert Kennedy's CDC program, Richard Nixon's black capitalism initiatives, and local education reforms in all three cities. By exploring how black community activists in New York, Los Angeles, and Atlanta contested and used public policies, and how policies impacted the communities they targeted, this book has illuminated several significant themes.

First, it has more fully revealed the War on Poverty's significance in both the short and long term. This book confirms what other historians have recently argued: that the War on Poverty had a catalyzing effect on black community activism.[4] Furthermore, its close analysis of black community organizations such as CAEHT and WLCAC, and of grassroots movements for community control in New York and Los Angeles, makes clear how the War on Poverty became an important site of Black Power's development at the local level as it merged with, and helped transform, existing black activism and protest. However, the War on Poverty's effects beyond the black community were even more significant—though this point is yet to be fully recognized in the historiography. As the first major federal policy since the New Deal explicitly intended to deal with economic inequality, the War on Poverty helped expand grassroots movements for social and economic justice and inadvertently triggered an expansion of the nation's welfare rolls. In the process, the antipoverty program played a vital part in stimulating broader political controversies and developments that reshaped the nation's political landscape. The debates, welfare backlash politics, and white racial resentment that the War on Poverty helped generate played a critical role in inspiring alternative political solutions to dealing with economic inequality and meeting the challenge of Black Power (solutions that shared the War on Poverty's innate class and gender biases). It is only by excavating the War on Poverty's longer-term consequences that the full extent of its significance for U.S. politics and the course of future reform is revealed. By outlining the antipoverty program's impact on future landscapes of reform from which white political engagement with Black Power emerged, this book sheds light on an underappreciated aspect of the War on Poverty's history.

Second, this book underscores the malleability of Black Power by exploring how and why mainstream white politicians and institutions and black community activists and organizations interpreted and adapted Black Power ideology in varying ways to suit their needs. Inspired by the emergence of Black Power radicalism and the limitations (and the gendered and class politics) of the War on Poverty, Robert Kennedy and Richard Nixon established policies intended to co-opt and modify Black Power that were designed to appeal to the more conservative strands of its ideology.[5] Seeking to cultivate a mainstream, middle-class interest–oriented brand of Black Power politics that aimed to reinforce the nation's existing political and social order, these public policies were adapted to the political sensibilities of an increasingly conservative white voting public. White mainstream engagement with Black Power rested on the fact that many African Americans simply did not share the political worldview of Carmichael and other Black Power and social and economic justice advocates. Indeed, rather than questioning middle-class values and the institutions of American society, many African Americans endorsed them. Instead of radical, transformative political change, many blacks wanted fuller inclusion in American life as it was; they wanted a chance to realize the "American Dream" for themselves and their families.[6]

Kennedy's and Nixon's policy initiatives aimed to channel African American energy through business, economic development, and urban regeneration programs; grow the black middle class; and draw inner-city communities away from protest, radical and redistributive politics, and violent extremism. In the process they offered a path for black empowerment that was intended to endorse and strengthen the status quo. Black Power and radical politics did not always go hand in hand. Exploring how black communities used these policies illuminates how the negotiation of Black Power, and the fight for black advancement in general, unfolded at the local level. Close examination of organizations such as Restoration, Operation Bootstrap, and the Harlem Commonwealth Council reveals the different local institutional forms and legacies of the civil rights–Black Power era, some of which survive today. Such organizations—the existence of which undermines truncated narratives of the 1960s and 1970s black freedom struggle—remain a relatively neglected aspect of Black Power's history. Analyzing these groups, along with grassroots education activism in all three cities, reveals how Black Power ideology translated into the lives and activism of ordinary African Americans at the local level. By tracing the roots, contours, and differing trajectories of the fight against racial discrimination in each of the three cities, this book also complicates the relationship between the civil rights and Black Power phases of the struggle, forcing us to blur the lines traditionally drawn between the two.

Third, this book highlights the enduring power of whites to dictate the course and character of black progress during the Black Power era. Efforts to defend the racial and socioeconomic order and maintain white privilege—through public policy, political power structures and institutions, and professional and community organizations—were prevalent, powerful, and often decisive. Established authorities' opposition to the redistribution of political and economic power was evident in their efforts to stymie the War on Poverty's potential for mobilizing and empowering poor communities. The defeat of grassroots education activists in all three cities further underscores how whites successfully resisted African Americans' demands for transformative and redistributive political change. In the case of Atlanta, the course of educational reform revealed how mutual class interest could be exploited, and black advancement channeled, through solutions that bolstered or at best modified the existing socioeconomic and political order, rather than challenging it. This trend became especially clear in Los Angeles and Atlanta under black political leadership during the 1970s.

Speaking at the Congressional Black Caucus annual dinner in October 1974, Maynard Jackson admonished the $100-a-plate audience that black political power had to serve the broader cause of black liberation. It had to work, he argued, in the interests of all African Americans. Black elected officials, he pleaded, must not forget about their "Brothers and Sisters who are still locked in the dungeons of deprivation." It was no good if black political leadership helped only to "open up a handful of $20,000 a year jobs in business and government. The fight is for freedom."[7] However, the direction of city policy in Los Angeles under Tom Bradley and in Atlanta under Maynard Jackson followed the very pattern Jackson had criticized, though in different ways. Their respective approaches to city government stemmed from their differing ideas about how best to serve the interests of their African American constituents, and their cities at large. Whereas both agreed on increasing opportunity for black businesses and middle-class professionals, the two mayors differed on how to tackle black poverty. Jackson fought to realign city resources toward Atlanta's poor black neighborhoods—a fight he eventually abandoned in the face of white resistance and pressure. Bradley, on the other hand, was a standard-bearer for mainstream pro-business approaches to solving inequality that were fundamentally linked to pro-black middle-class policies and that had been forged in the negotiation of Black Power by dominant white interests set on dictating the direction of socioeconomic change. Black progress in both cities during the 1970s underlines the decisive role played by whites in both limiting the scope of redistributive city policies addressing the needs of disadvantaged blacks, and in expanding political and economic opportunity for middle-class and elite blacks. As this book argues, perhaps the most significant factors guiding the direction of black politics and the pace and character of racial change during this period were the ways in which mainstream white politicians, institutions, and organizations were able to successfully defend and assert their interests in the face of African Americans' efforts to win greater political and economic power.

This leads us to the final and broadest, overall theme: the implications of the negotiation of Black Power through public policy—along with white resistance to socioeconomic and political change more broadly—for African American society in the longer term. In sum, white efforts to influence the direction and scope of racial and socioeconomic change and black empowerment were highly successful. The policies established by Kennedy and Nixon represented an important moment in 1960s public policy that further cemented middle-class advantage within the federal government's approach to tackling economic inequality. Reflecting a desire to reconfigure existing political solutions for tackling economic and racial inequality, these policies represented a political project to co-opt and nurture Black Power and boost the black middle class, an approach tailored to the ongoing conservative realignment. As such, they mark a critical moment and transitional stage in the retreat from liberal social policy, and the turn to domestic neoliberalism that accelerated under President Ronald Reagan during the 1980s and following decades. The potential of these policies to advance the interests of the black middle class was magnified under black political leadership in both Los Angeles and Atlanta. As the black middle class and elite enjoyed unprecedented levels of prosperity, poor and working-class communities endured precipitous decline. While the deepening of intraracial inequality under black city leadership cannot be attributed solely to those public policies, they nevertheless played an important part in the process. As such, they provide a perspective on Black Power and its relationship to mainstream politics that has been overlooked by much of the existing historiography of the period.[8]

Overall, therefore, this book incorporates the story of black middle-class success into our understanding of Black Power's impact on American society and politics. In the process, it challenges normative ideas about the relationship between middle-class success and Black Power (as it is popularly understood; i.e., as a radical and militant ideology). As the black middle class continued to make progress during the mid- to late 1960s through the 1970s—through the Black Power era—the apparent tension between the two was perfectly captured by African American *Chicago Tribune* journalist Leanita McClain. In her article "The Middle-Class Black's Burden," which appeared in *Newsweek* in October 1980 and catapulted her to national prominence, McClain explained:

> I am a member of the black middle-class who has had enough of being patted on my head by white hands and slapped in my face by black hands for my success. Here's a discovery that too many people will find startling: when given opportunities at white collar pencil pushing, blacks want the same things from life that everyone else does. These include the proverbial dream house, two cars, an above average school and a vacation for the kids at Disneyland. We may, in fact, want these things more than other Americans because most of us have been denied them so long. Meanwhile the folks we left behind in the "old country," commonly called the ghetto, and the militants we left behind in their antiquated ideology can't berate the black middle-class enough for "forgetting where we came from." We have forsaken the revolution we are told, we have sold out. We are Oreos, they say, black on the outside, white within. The truth is we have not forgotten; we would not dare. We are simply fighting on different fronts.[9]

This notion—that black middle-class success and Black Power were somehow in conflict—is at issue here. Indeed, rather than viewing black middle-class success as a betrayal of "the revolution," this book reveals the ways in which they were in fact related. It was precisely because of the emergence of radical Black Power and its advocacy of the politics of "revolution" that mainstream white politicians, institutions, and organizations sought to engage with Black Power through the public policies examined in this book. At the core of that engagement with Black Power was an appeal to the sentiment among African Americans that McClain had expressed so clearly: the desire to be part of the American mainstream, to share in the American Dream and enjoy the comforts and opportunity of middle-class life.

In this sense, McClain's suggestion that the black middle class was "fighting" on a "different front" from those committed to the "revolution," is especially apt. Indeed, this book can be thought of as an exploration of how mainstream whites participated in the battles to negotiate Black Power's meaning and to define the scope of racial progress, on those different fronts—in support on one and in opposition on the other. Their success on both fronts underlines the extent to which African Americans' progress toward two of the main goals that Black Power encompassed—political and economic empowerment—was shaped most powerfully by white interests. Ultimately, therefore, the most decisive force in the negotiation of Black Power was white power.

Epilogue

In mid-August 2015 the Watts Labor Community Action Committee (WLCAC) staged a number of events to mark the fiftieth anniversary of the 1965 Watts riots, the momentous uprising that precipitated the organization's founding. The Watts Village Theater Company put on a production of *Riot/ Rebellion,* a play that revisited the turmoil of mid-August 1965 through firsthand accounts from those involved. Another event, a symposium entitled "Voices of Rebellion," brought local people of all ages together with other community institutions and elected officials to reflect on the link between the neighborhood's past, present, and future.[1]

Commemorating Watts's turbulent history was supposed to offer a chance to celebrate the progress that had been made in the area over the previous fifty years. However, recent events beyond Los Angeles cast a shadow over the proceedings. Almost exactly a year earlier the fatal shooting of unarmed African American teenager Michael Brown by white police officer Darren Wilson in the city of Ferguson, Missouri, had precipitated the largest wave of urban unrest in the United States since the Los Angeles riots of 1992. In the months that followed, the unrest spread to other cities across the nation as a number of African Americans died at the hands of law enforcement officers in other states.[2]

To the veterans of the 1965 Watts rebellion taking part in WLCAC's half-centenary retrospective, the present must have seemed all too like the past. The conditions that inspired rioting in black inner cities from the mid- to late 1960s—including police brutality—have persisted and in some respects worsened over the past five decades. Race relations are at their lowest point since the 1960s. By almost every socioeconomic indicator, black America today is in the midst of crisis. The poverty rate among African Americans today stands at 26 percent—two and a half times the rate among whites (10 percent). At nearly 14 percent, the black unemployment rate is more than double the white unemployment rate, as it has been for much of the past sixty years. Most African Americans live in racially segregated—and often poor—neighborhoods where economic opportunity is scarce. Recent analysis has confirmed a strong correlation between residential segregation and a range of poor health outcomes including "infant and adult mortality, and a wide variety of reproductive, infectious, and chronic diseases." Grossly disproportionate numbers of African Americans are languishing either in prison or on the streets. Despite being only 13 percent of the U.S. population, nearly 40 percent of America's 2.6 million prison inmates are black, as are just over 40 percent of its homeless shelter users.[3]

To say that African Americans have seen little progress since the 1960s, however, would be to overlook the very real advances that have been made in that time. In the field of education, 86 percent of black adults aged twenty-five and older today have completed high school. In 1964 the figure was only 27 percent. The number of black high school graduates undertaking post-secondary education has increased significantly too, from 45 percent in 1972 to 70 percent in 2014.[4] When the Office of Minority Business Enterprise (now the Minority Business Development Agency) was established in 1969, there were 163,000 black-owned businesses that took in $4.5 billion in sales revenue. There are currently nearly 2.6 million black-owned firms in the United States (9.4 percent of all businesses nationally), with combined gross sales receipts of $150 billion.[5] New York, Atlanta, and Los Angeles are three of the most significant sites of black business ownership in the country.[6] The pursuit of educational and economic opportunity has translated into real black income gains. Between 1970 and 2014 the percentage of African Americans earning at least $75,000 a year more than doubled to 21 percent. The number making at least $100,000 nearly quadrupled, to 13 percent.[7]

African Americans have also enjoyed continued success in electoral politics. New political ground was broken in 2008 with the election of Barack Obama, the nation's first president of African descent. Four years later he was convincingly reelected to a second term in office. Obama's ascent to the Oval Office capped nearly five decades of sustained black political representation at all levels of government, in towns, cities, and states across the nation. Whereas the Congressional Black Caucus began in 1971 with thirteen members, it now counts forty-six.[8] The 2014 U.S. Congress was the most racially diverse in the nation's history, with representatives of color constituting

17 percent of House members, the majority of whom were black.[9] African Americans still wield political power in Atlanta—in both city hall and on the city council—as they have in a virtually unbroken line since the election of Mayor Maynard Jackson in 1973. In both Los Angeles and New York, blacks continue to broadly enjoy at least proportional representation in the major institutions of city and state government.[10]

However, even these seemingly positive developments and statistics obscure as much as they reveal. African Americans may be attending college in higher numbers than ever, but a college education is no guarantee of economic prosperity. Indeed, blacks with college degrees in the United States today tend to have only around two-thirds of the wealth of whites who failed to finish high school.[11] Although black business income is far higher today than it was in 1969, that income is not evenly spread. Nearly 96 percent of black-owned firms in the United States today are small businesses that have no paid employees. The average annual gross receipts of black-owned businesses is just $58,119—the lowest of any minority group, barely one-third of the national average for minority businesses ($173,552), and only just over 10 percent of the average figure for nonminority businesses ($552,079).[12]

Worse still, black economic progress since the 1970s has proved especially vulnerable in recent times. Although millions of Americans of all colors were hit hard by the subprime mortgage crisis of late 2008 and the so-called Great Recession that followed, African Americans—who held a disproportionate amount of the nation's subprime and high-cost mortgages—suffered worst of all. Hundreds of thousands lost their homes, life savings, or pensions. Indeed, the Great Recession wiped out post-1960s increases in black home ownership completely.[13] As a result, the racial wealth gap has widened during the post-recession recovery. In 2010 median white household wealth was eight times that of black households. By 2013 it was thirteen times greater—the widest racial wealth gap since 1989, when the figure for whites was seventeen times higher.[14]

In an era marked by downward social mobility for Americans in general, African Americans face especially bleak prospects for the future. Black children are more than twice as likely as their white counterparts to be raised in a single-parent family, a phenomenon that studies have linked strongly to a child's chances of future success. Moreover, nearly three-quarters of black students attend majority-nonwhite public schools—schools far more likely statistically to be underresourced and to underperform academically than majority-white public schools—meaning that vast numbers of black children leave high school ill-prepared for further education and poorly placed to compete for well-paid employment.[15] As a result, half of blacks born into poverty today are likely to remain in poverty at the age of forty (compared to a rate of 23 percent for whites). Worse still, the children of black middle-class parents are more likely to fall into a lower economic group as adults than children of any other racial group in the United States.[16]

These kinds of stark racial disparities are all clearly visible in Los Angeles, Atlanta, and New York. In Los Angeles, the estimated median net worth of white households ($355,000) is nearly one hundred times that of African American households ($4,000). Nowhere were African American home owners hit harder by foreclosures during the Great Recession than in Atlanta. Of those black Atlantans who managed to keep their homes, many are still burdened with negative equity (up to three-quarters of home owners in some black neighborhoods). And despite performing better than average on some economic indicators, black New Yorkers are more likely to live in a segregated neighborhood, be unemployed, underperform academically at school, spend time in prison, and die earlier than any other racial group in the city.[17]

Ultimately, millions of African Americans find themselves mired in poverty and trapped in a world shaped by post-industrial urban decline and the retrenchment of the welfare state, their chances for a better future severely constrained by the failure of public education and the persistence of discriminatory practices in employment, housing, credit and insurance markets, the criminal justice system, and a range of public institutions. Having more African Americans holding elected office, working in corporate management positions, owning their own businesses, or working and studying on college campuses over the past few decades has not substantially undermined structural inequality or cyclical black poverty.

Politicians in particular have offered disadvantaged blacks little succor since the 1970s. The race-conscious employment and economic development policies fashioned to engage with and co-opt Black Power helped open the doors of opportunity for African Americans in higher education and the domestic and international economy. However, they have tended to concentrate opportunities and wealth in the hands of the black few. Given the innate middle-class bent of policies such as affirmative action, black business and economic development programs, and minority contract set-asides, it is hardly surprising that they have generally helped upwardly mobile African Americans more than they have poor and working-class blacks.[18] For example, socioeconomic disparities persist in college attendance rates. Eighty-two percent of high school graduates from high-income families currently enroll in college, with only 52 percent of high school graduates from low-income families doing so, and affirmative action has failed to correct this trend. Business ownership—though not an especially lucrative enterprise for the vast majority of African American businesspeople—remains the pursuit primarily of educated middle-class blacks, with more than three-quarters of black entrepreneurs today owning their own home and having either a bachelor's degree or at least some college education.[19]

While the policies that Robert Kennedy and Richard Nixon advanced during the mid- to late 1960s operated in the hope that an expanded black middle class would lift up the black poor—in part by establishing businesses and employing poor and working-class blacks—the business mechanism has proved especially ineffective at reducing inequality. With just 4.2 percent of black-owned firms employing staff, black business ownership has done very little to either meaningfully reduce African American joblessness or generate urban improvement.[20]

As the 1970s gave way to the 1980s and brought arch-conservative Ronald Reagan to the presidency, political conditions deteriorated even further for many African Americans. Through the 1980s and 1990s, ascendant conservatives decimated federal support for the nation's cities and committed themselves to dismantling the welfare state and rolling back the gains of the black freedom struggle. Their efforts were supported by a "color-blind" conservative ideology which insisted that the enactment of civil and voting rights legislation in the mid-1960s eradicated institutional racism, thereby making America a free, fair, and color-blind society. Under this logic, from that point onward African Americans competed on an equal basis with everyone else. If racial inequality persisted, therefore, it could be the result only of African Americans' own cultural failings and behavioral pathologies—characteristics exacerbated by decades of interventionist Democratic Party liberalism and the very social welfare policies that conservatives sought eagerly to eliminate.[21]

In emphasizing small government; lauding middle-class values such as hard work, individual initiative, and self-reliance; and championing free-market solutions to racial inequality, Kennedy's and Nixon's policies chimed with the pro-taxpayer and aggressive anti–welfare state and anti–big government rhetoric that came to dominate mainstream American politics increasingly from the 1970s onward. Economic development–focused urban policies—with which Kennedy's and Nixon's thinking also dovetailed—have continued to prevail over redistributive polices in cities across the nation over the past four decades, and as a recent study makes clear, they continue to have a significant negative impact on segregated and predominantly nonwhite cities in particular.[22]

However, despite their resonance with core conservative principles and dominant urban policy, the explicitly race-conscious nature of the Kennedy and Nixon policies meant they too were targeted by conservatives during the 1980s and 1990s. Affirmative action—which offended the sensibilities of color-blind conservatives and a great many white American voters—came under particularly fierce attack.[23] Rather than helping push back against the damaging conservative rhetoric and policies in recent decades, many of the African Americans who have become part of the nation's economic, political, and cultural mainstream during that time have either tacitly or explicitly supported them.

Black politicians have proved especially willing to accept prevailing conservative orthodoxy. Since the 1970s a now dominant black political tradition has developed in which increasing numbers of highly credentialed technocratic black candidates have been elected to public office by multiracial voter coalitions that often include significant numbers of white middle-class liberals and African Americans. They have typically won election by adopting a race-neutral stance, supporting pro-growth policies that favor dominant white business interests, and campaigning on issues such as good government and fiscal responsibility. At the same time, black politicians in this mold generally avoid discussing race and racism or identifying with supposedly "black" issues such as economic inequality, redistributive politics, or social welfare spending. These politicians rarely offer forthright racial advocacy and routinely tout universal (rather than race-specific) policies instead. Los Angeles mayor Tom Bradley was something of a pioneer in this tradition.[24]

Not only have black elected officials in the post–Black Power era generally endorsed conservative rhetoric and policies responsible for reifying racial inequality, but so have much of the black middle class and elite. Some prominent black conservatives during the 1980s and 1990s, including economist Thomas Sowell and Supreme Court justice Clarence Thomas, joined white conservatives on the front lines in their battle against race-conscious policies such as affirmative action. Race neutral, pro-growth black politicians have historically enjoyed strong support from their black middle-class and elite backers, who regularly defend them from the criticism of poor and working-class blacks and social justice advocates, often by championing their importance, above all else, as inspirational symbols of black success and achievement. As political scientist Michael Dawson argues, along with their black elected representatives the black middle class and elite have abandoned "traditional notions of black politics centered on mass mobilization, and egalitarian, state-centered, and contentious politics." [25]

An important part of the ideological union between black politicians and the black middle class and elite in recent decades, Dawson suggests, has been their growing acceptance of the white conservative assertion that black poverty "is primarily the result of pathological behaviors of communities and individuals," rather than of institutional racism or an unfair economy.[26] Historian Michael Eric Dyson points to celebrated black entertainer Bill Cosby as an example of the extent to which black elites—who, like Cosby, are often steadfastly race-neutral in their outlook—have peddled this rhetoric increasingly since the 1980s. In 2004 Cosby used the occasion of the NAACP's *Brown v. Board of Education* fiftieth anniversary gala dinner to publicly excoriate low-income black families and their children. The central theme of his message was that "the miserable condition of the black poor" was the result of "their own destructive behavior." This view, Dyson explains, is shared by many others in a black elite "composed of lawyers, physicians, intellectuals, civil rights leaders, entertainers, athletes, bankers and the like" who criticize regularly "the pernicious habits of the black poor." [27] To an extent, this is not a new phenomenon. As political scientist Fredrick Harris explains, African American elites have put a new spin on an old trope of black political and cultural discourse: the politics of black respectability. However, whereas black elites in the early twentieth century sought to "uplift the race" by "correcting the 'bad' traits of the black poor," today's version of respectability politics "commands the blacks left behind in post–civil rights America to 'lift up thyself.'" [28]

If either Robert Kennedy or Richard Nixon were alive today, they might well conclude that their efforts to help expand and cultivate a black middle class that embraced the dominant political, economic, and social values of mainstream American society had been a success. Indeed, they could look no further than the nation's first black president. When Barack Obama was elected in 2008, his victory was greeted with optimism by African Americans, many of whom expected great things of their new commander in chief. Once in office, however, those hopes (which he did much to raise on the campaign trail) were largely unfulfilled. That is not to say, however, that Obama's presidency was without its successes. Obama supporters, such as Harvard sociologist William Julius Wilson, have defended the president's record, arguing that parts of the administration's stimulus and recovery spending programs and the Patient Protection and Affordable Care Act—often called "Obamacare"—"far exceed any legislation beneficial to low-income Americans passed during the Carter, Ford, Reagan, George H. W. Bush, Clinton, or George W. Bush administrations." [29]

However, Obama generally did not deliver the kind of policies or the kind of leadership that many racial advocates and poor and working-class blacks would have liked. In part this is because for most of Obama's time in office he was confronted with a deeply hostile white conservative opposition—most clearly in the form of Tea Party Republicanism—which is in large part funded and orchestrated by conservative foundations and billionaire white businessmen. This opposition zealously committed itself to obstructing Obama's legislative program at every opportunity (as their resistance to Obamacare demonstrates). The power of entrenched white economic and political interests to constrain and limit socioeconomic and racial change—a core theme of this book—remains undimmed and, since the mid-1970s, has become increasingly well coordinated and assertive at the national level. (It seems likely at this writing that the influence of this group on U.S. domestic policy will only increase under Obama's successor, Donald Trump.) [30]

More important, however, Obama did little to either address inequality or challenge structural racism, because he was a centrist Democrat who was not, and had never been, ideologically committed to transformative socioeconomic and racial justice politics. Like Robert Kennedy, Obama was wholly convinced of the virtues of American capitalism and believed that solutions to inequality should be embedded within the framework of the free-market enterprise system. At his political core, then, Obama was another in the long line of post-1960s race-neutral, technocratic black politicians—in the Tom Bradley mold—who strive to avoid race as an issue and reject race-specific policies, offering instead universalist solutions in the belief that "a rising tide lifts all boats." [31] As Obama explained in an interview with *Black Enterprise* magazine when asked if his administration's business development policies were aimed at African Americans: "I'm not the president of black America. I'm the president of the United States of America [. . . but] I'll put my track record up against anybody in terms of putting in place broad-based programs that ultimately had a huge benefit for African American businesses." [32]

For some, Obama's presidency will have brought few surprises. Back in April 2008, when the Illinois senator's campaign for the Democratic nomination was well under way, black political scientist Adolph Reed described Obama as "a vacuous opportunist, a good performer with an ear for how to make white liberals like him," whose "fundamental political center of gravity, beneath an empty rhetoric of hope and change and new directions, is neoliberal." Nine years later, Reed's analysis rings true with those of growing numbers of African American critics who have come to see the limits of Obama's political style.[33]

Perhaps the most troubling hallmark of Obama's presidency, as historian Eddie Glaude Jr. explains, was his consistent invocation of "the idea of black criminality, of black people looking to government for handouts instead of working hard, of black parents failing to raise their children properly, and of false cries of racism as the excuse for troubles that are of their own making."[34] Whatever good President Obama did for African Americans must be weighed against his willingness to publicly and repeatedly rehearse the deeply negative racial narratives that conservatives have used both to explain away the persistence of racial discrimination and the widening of racial inequality over the past three and half decades, and to justify their retrenchment of the welfare state.

Whenever Obama was taken to task for his problematic rhetoric on African American society, black elites—including civil rights leader Reverend Al Sharpton, radio personality Tom Joyner, media mogul Oprah Winfrey, and music artist Jay-Z—were quick to defend him, habitually emphasizing Obama's importance as an inspirational symbol of black potential and achievement (exactly the same defense that middle-class and elite blacks in Los Angeles and Atlanta offered when poor and working-class African Americans criticized Tom Bradley or Maynard Jackson).[35]

Obama also received criticism over his halting and limited responses to the proliferation of police killings of African Americans, especially during his second term in office. Encumbered by the constraints of the office and the weight of national leadership, Obama did not speak out against police brutality or racial injustice, or in support of the black community, as strongly as many African Americans wanted him to. However, when Obama has failed to address issues of racial inequality and state violence boldly, others stepped into the breach.

Out of the August 2014 unrest in Ferguson came a renewal of radical black protest and politics, marking a new phase in the struggle for racial equality. Leading the struggle today is the Black Lives Matter (BLM) movement: a grassroots, youth activist–dominated movement that focuses on institutional racism, especially in the criminal justice system.[36] Operating largely outside the black church, BLM has in many respects reignited the flame of 1960s and 1970s Black Power radicalism, consciously appropriating its symbols, language, and militant style as it emphasizes the need for racial pride and solidarity and articulates a similarly piercing critique of American society and its political culture.[37]

And just as in the mid-1960s when the specter of radical black activism and protest had American liberals searching for ways to engage with—and control—that radicalism, the same has proved true in the wake of BLM's emergence in late 2014. As historian Keeanga-Yamahtta Taylor explains, major philanthropic foundations (including the Levi Strauss Foundation, the Barr Foundation, the Hill Snowden Foundation, billionaire George Soros's Open Society Foundation, and the Ford Foundation) were quick to involve themselves in funding BLM's organizing and advocacy activities.[38] The political effort to co-opt BLM was led by President Obama himself. In the immediate aftermath of unrest and mass demonstrations in Ferguson in August 2014, Obama met with some of the young activists involved. Counseling gradualism and pragmatism, he warned them that "change is incremental and hard." Protesters could make ambitious demands, he argued, but had to be content with any kind of progress: "Shoot for the sky, but 'better' is [still] good."[39]

Just as in mid-1966 when Robert Kennedy looked to bring young Black Power radicals together with older middle-class black leaders in Bedford-Stuyvesant in the hope they would exert a moderating influence over their younger counterparts, so too Obama tried to bridge the marked ideological and generational gap in the black activist community today. In February 2016 the Obama administration arranged a conference at the White House on criminal justice reform that it called the "first of its kind." Inviting three of the most prominent BLM activists (Brittney Packnett, Ainslin Pulley, and DeRay McKesson), Obama used the summit to try to bring the new young generation of militant BLM activists into conversation with the more moderate and conciliatory older 1960s generation of black civil rights leaders and politicians.[40]

For their part, BLM activists appear to be well aware of the potential pitfalls of engaging with the president. Ainslin Pulley declined the invitation, arguing that she "could not, with any integrity, participate in such a sham that would only serve to legitimize the false narrative that the government is working to end police brutality and the institutional racism that fuels it."[41] Brittany Packnett did attend but reminded the White House that BLM sought its own path. As Packnett explained in the wake of earlier criticism from Oprah Winfrey, who had chided the young protesters for not having nominated leaders or devised a clear strategy as 1960s civil rights organizations did: "We very purposefully have been a leaderless movement. [...] We've been doing that intentionally because we know absolute power corrupts absolutely. That ensures we remain about the heart of the movement rather than certain personalities."[42]

BLM activists' refusal to conform to traditional organizational models or expected modes of behavior, or to allow themselves to be dictated to by their elders, frustrated the president. Two months after the White House summit, as BLM protests continued throughout early 2016 in the wake of further African American deaths at the hands of white police officers, Obama criticized the movement's apparent unwillingness to engage with politics and the political process: "Once you've highlighted an issue and brought it to people's attention and shined a spotlight, and elected officials or people who are in a position to start bringing about change are ready to sit down with you, then you can't just keep on yelling at them. And you can't refuse to meet because that might compromise the purity of your position." For Obama—every inch the consensus politician—the very purpose and meaning of BLM should have been to engage with the political establishment: "The value of social movements and activism is to get you at the table, get you in the room, and then to start trying to figure out how is this problem going to be solved."[43]

Politicians today face a very different task in their efforts to engage with and co-opt radical movements than did politicians in the past. As BLM's experience to date makes clear, political activism and organizing are being transformed by social media and technology. Moreover, BLM's lack of clear leadership figures, its flat organizational structure, and its diffuse and mobile centers of activity mean it may prove to be a movement impossible to co-opt. Only time will tell. What we can be certain of, though, is that there will always be some mainstream politicians and institutions that are trying to do just that.

NOTES

INTRODUCTION

1. Andrew J. Young Papers, Subseries C, Box 8, Memorandum for Att. Gen. Nicholas Katzenbach from Roger Wilkins, December 18, 1967.

2. Jack Jones, "NAACP Director Condemns Moves for 'Black Power,'" *Los Angeles Times,* July 6, 1966, p. 16; "Dr. King Denounces 'Black Power' Talk," *Los Angeles Times,* June 21, 1966, p. 7; Don Irwin, "Johnson critical of Black Power Crusades," *Los Angeles Times,* July 6, 1966, p. 6; William Van Deburg, *New Day in Babylon: The Black Power Movement and American Culture, 1965–1975* (Chicago: University of Chicago Press, 1992), 11–22 (quotation on 11).

3. Memorandum for Att. Gen. Nicholas Katzenbach from Roger Wilkins, December 18, 1967, pp. 7, 9–10, 12.

4. This book builds on the work of Devin Fergus and Karen Ferguson, the only two historians who have explored the relationship between Black Power and mainstream politics in any serious depth. Fergus's pathbreaking 2009 work focuses on the "interplay" between liberals and Black Power in North Carolina and challenges the normative interpretation that Black Power "ran amok over liberalism and contributed to, if not instigated, the political and social unraveling of America." See Devin Fergus, *Liberalism, Black Power, and the Making of American Politics, 1965–1980* (Athens: University of Georgia Press, 2009). Karen Ferguson's excellent 2013 study, *Top Down,* focuses on New York and examines the role played specifically by the Ford Foundation in the mainstreaming of Black Power and the shaping of a new racial liberalism. See Karen Ferguson, *Top Down: The Ford Foundation, Black Power, and the Reinvention of Racial Liberalism* (Philadelphia: University of Pennsylvania Press, 2013).

5. Ferguson, *Top Down,* 11.

6. Peniel E. Joseph, "The Black Power Movement: A State of the Field," *Journal of American History,* Vol. 96, No. 3 (December 2009), 4.

7. The malleability of Black Power as a concept has been recognized by historians such as William Van Deburg and Manning Marable. See, for example, Van

Deburg, *New Day in Babylon*, 11–28; Manning Marable, *Race, Reform, and Rebellion: The Second Reconstruction and Beyond in Black America, 1945–1982* (Jackson: University of Mississippi Press, 1983), 104–10.

8. Julius Lester, *Revolutionary Notes* (New York: Richard W. Baron, 1969), 104.

9. As historian William Chafe has argued, an essential trait of twentieth-century postwar liberalism's relationship with the black freedom struggle (and other insurgent movements for socioeconomic and political change) was its "desire to channel [the movements'] protests into existing political processes and to deny them the resources and support to attack policies from below or outside." See William Chafe, *Never Stop Running: Allard Lowenstein and the Struggle to Save American Liberalism* (Princeton: Princeton University Press, 1998), 467.

10. For important recent scholarship on the Black Panther Party, see Joshua Bloom and Waldo E. Martin, *Black against Empire: The History and Politics of the Black Panther Party* (Berkeley: University of California Press, 2012); Jama Lazerow and Yohuru Williams, eds., *In Search of the Black Panther Party: New Perspectives on a Revolutionary Movement* (Durham, NC: Duke University Press, 2006); Curtis J. Austin, *Up against the Wall: Violence in the Making and Unmaking of the Black Panther Party* (Fayetteville: University of Arkansas Press, 2006); Jane Rhodes, *Framing the Black Panthers: The Spectacular Rise of a Black Power Icon* (New York: W. W. Norton, 2007); Judson Jeffries, ed., *On the Ground: The Black Panther Party in Communities across America* (Jackson: University of Mississippi Press, 2010); Charles E. Jones, ed., *The Black Panther Party Reconsidered* (Baltimore: Black Classic Press, 1998). For a recent, comprehensive discussion of the politics of the broader antipoverty and welfare rights coalition, see Gordon K. Mantler, *Power to the Poor: Black-Brown Coalition and the Fight for Economic Justice, 1960–1974* (Chapel Hill: University of North Carolina Press, 2013). For discussion of the evolution of Martin Luther King's political philosophy, see, for example, Thomas F. Jackson, *From Civil Rights to Economic Rights: Martin Luther King Jr. and the Struggle for Economic Justice* (Philadelphia: University of Pennsylvania Press, 2007).

11. This book adds to a growing body of work (often local case studies) that has explored the War on Poverty and revealed in particular the impact of America's antipoverty battle (and especially the Community Action Program) on minority communities and their struggles for racial and economic justice and political empowerment in cities and communities across the nation. See, for example, Annelise Orleck and Lisa Gayle Hazirjian, eds., *The War on Poverty: A New Grassroots History, 1964–1980* (Athens: University of Georgia Press, 2011); Susan Youngblood Ashmore, *Carry It On: The War on Poverty and the Civil Rights Movement in Alabama, 1964–1972* (Athens: University of Georgia Press, 2008); Robert Bauman, *Race and the War on Poverty: From Watts to East L.A.* (Norman: University of Oklahoma Press, 2008); William S. Clayson, *Freedom Is Not Enough: The War on Poverty and the Civil Rights Movement in Texas* (Austin: University of Texas Press, 2010); Kenneth S. Jolly, *Black Liberation in the Midwest: The Struggle in St. Louis, Missouri, 1964–1970* (New York: Routledge, 2006); Lisa Gayle Hazirjian, "Combating NEED: Urban Conflict and the Transformations of the War on Poverty and the

African American Freedom Struggle in Rocky Mount, North Carolina," *Journal of Urban History*, Vol. 34, No. 4 (May 2008), 639–64; Guian A McKee, *The Problem of Jobs: Liberalism, Race, and Deindustrialization in Philadelphia* (Chicago: University of Chicago Press, 2008); Annelise Orleck, *Storming Caesars Palace: How Black Mothers Fought Their Own War on Poverty* (Boston: Beacon Press, 2005); Mantler, *Power to the Poor;* Rhonda Y. Williams, *The Politics of Public Housing: Black Women's Struggles against Urban Inequality* (New York: Oxford University Press, 2004).

12. Moynihan quoted in Michael Javen Fortner, *Black Silent Majority: The Rockefeller Drug Laws and the Politics of Punishment* (Cambridge, MA: Harvard University Press, 2015), 133.

13. Rhonda Y. Williams, *Concrete Demands: The Search for Black Power in the Twentieth Century* (New York: Routledge, 2015), 167–68.

14. A number of grassroots historical studies have undermined the once dominant idea that the civil rights and Black Power phases of the black freedom struggle were fundamentally distinct, even oppositional, by blurring the line between them, revealing their interconnectedness, and challenging the geographical and temporal boundaries traditionally imposed on them. See, for example, Tim Tyson, "Robert F. Williams, 'Black Power,' and the Roots of the African American Freedom Struggle," *Journal of American History*, Vol. 85, No. 2 (Sept. 1998), 540–70; Jacquelyn Dowd Hall, "The Long Civil Rights Movement and the Political Uses of the Past," *Journal of American History*, Vol. 91 No. 4 (March 2005), 1233–63; Simon Hall, "The NAACP, Black Power, and the African American Freedom Struggle, 1966–1969," *The Historian*, Vol. 69, No. 1 (March 2007), 49–82; Jeanne Theoharis, "Black Freedom Studies: Re-imaging and Redefining the Fundamentals," *History Compass*, Vol. 4, No. 2 (March 2006), 348–67; Heather Ann Thompson, "All across the Nation: Urban Black Activism, North and South, 1965–1975," in *African American Urban History since World War II*, ed. Kevin Kusmer and Joe Trotter (Chicago: University of Chicago Press, 2009), 181–202. Two of the most important collections of essays that explore this argument include Jeanne Theoharis and Komozi Woodard, eds., *Freedom North: Black Freedom Struggles outside the South, 1940–1980* (New York: Palgrave Macmillan, 2003), and Charles M. Payne et al., eds., *Groundwork: Local Black Freedom Movements in America* (New York: New York University, 2005).

15. See, for example, Allen Matusow, *The Unraveling of America: A History of Liberalism in the 1960s* (New York: Harper & Row, 1984); Gareth Davies, *From Opportunity to Entitlement: The Transformation and Decline of Great Society Liberalism* (Lawrence: University of Kansas Press, 1996); Maurice Isserman and Michael Kazin, *America Divided: The Civil War of the 1960s* (New York: Oxford University Press, 1999); William L. O'Neill, *Coming Apart: An Informal History of America in the 1960's* (1971; repr., Chicago: Ivan R. Dee, 2005).

16. Lester, *Revolutionary Notes*, 106–7.

17. Political scientist Michael Javen Fortner makes this very point with respect to the passage of draconian drug laws in New York State during the early 1970s. These laws—proposed by state governor Nelson Rockefeller—were, Fortner argues,

supported by the black middle class and elite in Harlem who were as concerned over increasing drug use, violence, crime, and immoral behavior as their white counterparts. See Fortner, *Black Silent Majority*.

18. Black Power has had several important legacies for American society and politics. It played an important part in fostering public discourses of multiculturalism that have helped make overt racism largely taboo in mainstream American life. It redefined black identity and provided a linguistic and stylistic blueprint that inspired a broader revolution in affirmative cultural and identity politics among many other minority groups. Black Power's cultural legacy can also be found in hip-hop and rap music, the most dominant cultural and artistic form in contemporary black America. Finally, the trenchant critique of American society articulated by many radical Black Power activists in the 1960s and 1970s still survives, echoed in social and political activism and dissent today. See Joseph Tilden Rhea, *Race Pride and American Identity* (Cambridge, MA: Harvard University Press, 1997), 102–17; Peniel E. Joseph, *Dark Days, Bright Nights: From Black Power to Barack Obama* (New York: BasicCivitas Books, 2010), 30–32.

19. This is a phrase that Brinkley applied to scholarship on the American Right in his 1994 essay on the relative paucity of literature on postwar U.S. conservatism. See Alan Brinkley, "The Problem of American Conservatism," *American Historical Review*, Vol. 99, No. 2 (April 1994), 409.

20. This book adds to a vibrant and evolving body of Black Power scholarship. Since the early 2000s, an increasing number of historians have worked to rescue Black Power from the normative, declensional narrative of the 1960s in which the march of a noble nonviolent southern civil rights movement (and, indeed, of the nation at large) toward racial equality was derailed by an ill-disposed, violent, and angry northern Black Power movement. Two significant trends in recent scholarship have helped to undermine this simplistic view of the Black Power movement. First, radical Black Power organizations have begun to have their historical reputation rehabilitated. Second, greater study of Black Power has begun to reveal its many dimensions, demonstrating that the movement comprised much more than just the radical elements with which it is most commonly identified. Consequently, Black Power's evolution has now been more effectively historicized and its impact more accurately mapped. This book enhances the increasingly sophisticated, expansive, and evolving picture of Black Power now evident in the historiography.

For recent work (in addition to the Black Panther Party scholarship listed in note 10) that has enriched and brought balance to our understanding of radical Black Power groups, see, for example, Scot Brown, *Fighting for US: Maulana Karenga, the US Organization, and Black Cultural Nationalism* (New York: New York University Press, 2003); Bettye Collier-Thomas and V. P. Franklin, eds., *Sisters in the Struggle: African American Women in the Civil Rights–Black Power Movement* (New York: New York University Press, 2001); Dayo F. Gore et al., eds., *Want to Start a Revolution? Radical Women in the Black Freedom Struggle* (New York: New York University Press, 2009). For work on the Black Studies movement in particular, see, Martha Biondi, *The Black Revolution on Campus* (Berkeley: University of California

Press, 2012); Ibram H. Rogers, *The Black Campus Movement: Black Students and the Racial Reconstitution of Higher Education, 1965–1972* (New York: Palgrave Macmillan, 2012); Fabio Rojas, *From Black Power to Black Studies: How a Radical Social Movement Became an Academic Discipline* (Baltimore: Johns Hopkins University Press, 2007). For important recent scholarship that has broadened our understanding of Black Power's origins and the breadth of its impact on American politics and society, see, for example, Peniel E. Joseph, *Waiting 'til the Midnight Hour: A Narrative History of Black Power in America* (New York: Henry Holt, 2007); Jeffrey O. G. Ogbar, *Black Power: Radical Politics and African American Identity* (Baltimore: Johns Hopkins University Press, 2005); Cedric Johnson, *Revolutionaries to Race Leaders: Black Power and the Making of African American Politics* (Minneapolis: University of Minnesota Press, 2007); Fergus, *Liberalism, Black Power, and the Making of American Politics;* Ferguson, *Top Down;* Komozi Woodard, *A Nation within a Nation: Amiri Baraka (LeRoi Jones) and Black Power Politics* (Chapel Hill: University of North Carolina Press, 1999); Williams, *Concrete Demands.*

CHAPTER 1: "A MOUTHFUL OF CIVIL RIGHTS
AND AN EMPTY BELLY"

1. California State Office of Economic Opportunity Records (hereafter California State OEO Records), Series F3751, Box 9, Folder 181, Department of Health, Education, and Welfare Press Release, May 18, 1967. Funding for the project was handled and approved by a team of officials working across the Department of Health, Education, and Welfare and the Office of Economic Opportunity.

2. California State OEO Records, Series F3751, Box 9, Folder 181, Community Alert Patrol Press Release, May 24, 1967.

3. California State OEO Records, Series F3751, Box 9, Folder 181, Senator George Murphy Press Release, June 5, 1967.

4. California State OEO Records, Series F3751, Box 9, Folder 181, Ronald Reagan to Sargent Shriver, June 12, 1967; Sam Yorty Papers, Box C-0280, F: Mayor's Letters 1967, Yorty to Lyndon Johnson, May 26, 1967, p. 2.

5. California State OEO Records, Series F3751, Box 9, Folder 181, Thomas W. Edmonds to Ronald Reagan, May 25, 1967.

6. California State OEO Records, Series F3751, Box 9, Folder 181, Memorandum from Jim Barber to Jackie Beam, June 20, 1967, p. 3.

7. Peter Edelman, "The War on Poverty and Subsequent Federal Programs: What Worked, What Didn't Work, and Why? Lessons for Future Programs," *Clearinghouse REVIEW Journal of Poverty Law and Policy* (May–June 2006), 10; Annelise Orleck, "Introduction: The War on Poverty from the Grass Roots Up," in *The War on Poverty,* 6.

8. For a list of recent scholarship on the War on Poverty, see the introduction, note 11.

9. Edelman, "The War on Poverty and Subsequent Federal Programs," 10.

10. Paul Weeks, "Voices of Poverty Are Being Heard—And City Halls across U.S. Quail," *Los Angeles Times,* August 9, 1965. Representative Gibbons floor-managed the $1.9 billion extension of the antipoverty program to a 254–158 victory in the House in August 1965.

11. Orleck, "Introduction: The War on Poverty from the Grass Roots Up," 5.

12. John Kenneth Galbraith, *The Affluent Society* (Boston: Houghton Mifflin, 1958); Michael Harrington, *The Other America: Poverty in the United States* (New York: Macmillan, 1962).

13. Irwin Unger, *The Best of Intentions: The Triumphs and Failures of the Great Society under Kennedy, Johnson, and Nixon* (New York: Doubleday, 1996), 65–66. Kennedy's own personal interest in tackling poverty had first been sparked by witnessing firsthand the extreme poverty of white Appalachian coal-mining communities while he was on the campaign trail for the Democratic nomination in rural West Virginia in 1960. See Thomas Kiffmeyer, *Reformers to Radicals: The Appalachian Volunteers and the War on Poverty* (Lexington: University Press of Kentucky, 2008), 1, 37.

14. Guian McKee, "'This Government Is with Us': Lyndon B. Johnson and the Grass-Roots War on Poverty," in *The War on Poverty,* 35; Lyndon B. Johnson, State of the Union Address, 1964, Public Broadcasting Service, http://www.pbs.org/wgbh/americanexperience/features/primary-resources/lbj-union64/.

15. Daniel P. Moynihan, *Maximum Feasible Misunderstanding: Community Action in the War on Poverty* (New York: Free Press, 1969), pp.21–37.

16. Hubert Humphrey, *War on Poverty* (New York: McGraw-Hill, 1964), p. 96.

17. Ibid., 19, 49, 95–98; Appendix Table A1: Race and Hispanic Origin for the United States, 1790–1990, in "Historical Census Statistics on Population Totals by Race, 1790 to 1990, and by Hispanic Origin, 1970 to 1990, for Large Cities and Other Urban Places in the United States," U.S. Census Bureau, https://www.census.gov/population/www/documentation/twps0076/twps0076.html.

18. Johnson, State of the Union Address, 1964.

19. Vincent J. Burke, "Congress Urged to Help Negroes out of Poverty," *Los Angeles Times,* April 15, 1964, p. 10.

20. Tomiko Brown-Nagin, *Courage to Dissent: Atlanta and the Long History of the Civil Rights Movement* (New York: Oxford University Press, 2011), 258.

21. Johnson, State of the Union Address, 1964; Robert Thompson, "Johnson Asks Negroes to Help Battle Poverty," *Los Angeles Times,* January 19, 1964, D15.

22. Anthony Badger, *The New Deal: The Depression Years, 1933–1939* (Chicago: Ivan R. Dee, 2002), 254–255, 301; Cornelius L. Bynum, *A. Philip Randolph and the Struggle for Civil Rights* (Urbana: University of Illinois Press, 2010), 164; Alan Brinkley, *Liberalism and Its Discontents* (Cambridge, MA: Harvard University Press, 2000), 76–77.

23. Alice Kessler-Harris, *In Pursuit of Equity: Women, Men, and the Quest for Economic Citizenship in 20th Century America* (New York: Oxford University Press, 2001), 4.

24. Nancy MacLean, *Freedom Is Not Enough: The Opening of the American Work Place* (New York: Russell Sage Foundation; Cambridge, MA: Harvard University Press, 2006), 6.

25. Glenda Elizabeth Gilmore, *Defying Dixie: The Radical Roots of Civil Rights, 1919–1950* (New York: W. W. Norton, 2008), 361–64.

26. Franklin D. Roosevelt, Annual Message to the Congress on the State of the Union, January 11, 1944, Franklin D. Roosevelt Presidential Library and Museum, http://www.fdrlibrary.marist.edu/archives/address_text.html.

27. Lizabeth Cohen, *A Consumers' Republic: The Politics of Mass Consumption in Postwar America* (New York: Random House, 2003), 7, 11.

28. Adam Fairclough, "Race and Red-Baiting," in *The Civil Rights Movement: Rethinking History,* ed. Jack E. Davis (Oxford: Blackwell, 2001), 102.

29. Thomas J. Sugrue, "Affirmative Action from Below: Civil Rights, the Building Trades, and the Politics of Racial Equality in the Urban North, 1945–1969," *Journal of American History,* Vol. 91, No.1 (June 2004), 149.

30. Bynum, *A. Philip Randolph,* ix.

31. David W. Southern, *Gunnar Myrdal and Black-White Relations: The Use and Abuse of An American Dilemma, 1944–1969* (Baton Rouge: Louisiana State University Press, 1987), 261–65.

32. Johnson, State of the Union Address, 1964.

33. Bauman, *Race and the War on Poverty,* 18.

34. Alice O'Connor, "Community Action, Urban Reform, and the Fight against Poverty: The Ford Foundation's Gray Areas Programs," *Journal of Urban History,* Vol. 22, No. 5 (July 1996), 588.

35. Moynihan, *Maximum Feasible Misunderstanding,* 45–50.

36. Unger, *Best of Intentions,* 58–59.

37. O'Connor, "Community Action," 599.

38. McKee, "'This Government Is with Us,'" 36. For an in-depth discussion of the place of community action within the broader sweep of social science history in the twentieth century, see Alice O'Connor, *Poverty Knowledge: Social Science, Social Policy, and the Poor in Twentieth-Century U.S. History* (Princeton: Princeton University Press, 2001), esp. 124–37.

39. Orleck, "Introduction: The War on Poverty from the Grass Roots Up," 9.

40. O'Connor, "Community Action," 593–595, 599.

41. Henry Hazlitt, "How to Cure Poverty," *Newsweek,* January 27, 1964.

42. Gefland, ed., The War on Poverty, 1964–1968 [microfilm], Ex WE-9, Reel 1, "Waging War on Poverty," AFL-CIO Executive Committee Statement, February 21, 1964.

43. Marisa Chappell, *The War on Welfare: Family, Poverty, and Politics in Modern America* (Philadelphia: University of Pennsylvania Press, 2010), 40; Unger, *Best of Intentions,* 74–75.

44. Andrew J. Young Papers, Series 1, Subseries A, Box 5, Folder PPC, OEO 1968, OEO Pamphlet: "The Watershed: A New Look at the War on Poverty," n.d. (1968), p. 1.

45. Robert Self, *All in the Family: The Realignment of American Democracy since the 1960s* (New York: Hill & Wang, 2012), 18–21. For a discussion of how black veterans were denied full GI Bill benefits, see Cohen, *Consumers' Republic,* 167–73.

46. James T. Patterson, *Freedom Is Not Enough: The Moynihan Report and America's Struggle over Black Family Life, from LBJ to Obama* (New York: Basic Books, 2010), 14–18.

47. McKee, "'This Government Is with Us,'" 40–41, 57. For a detailed discussion of Johnson's experiences in the NYA and its impact on his views on race and poverty, see Robert A. Caro, *Master of the Senate,* vol. 3 of *The Years of Lyndon Johnson* (New York: Alfred A. Knopf, 2002), 734–37.

48. For example, blacks in Alabama and Mississippi used antipoverty programs to good effect, though not without serious resistance from local whites. See Ashmore, *Carry It On;* David C. Carter, *The Music Has Gone Out of the Movement: Civil Rights and the Johnson Administration, 1965–1968* (Chapel Hill: University of North Carolina Press, 2014).

49. Gefland, ed., The War on Poverty, 1964–1968 [Microfilm], Ex WE-9, Reel 2, Paul Weeks, "U.S. Shows Gain in Poverty War," *Los Angeles Times,* n.d.

50. McKee, "'This Government Is with Us,'" 34.

51. William Clayson, "'The Barrios and the Ghettos Have Organized!': Community Action, Political Acrimony, and the War on Poverty in San Antonio," *Journal of Urban History,* Vol. 28, No. 2 (January 2002), 158.

52. Biondi, *To Stand and Fight,* 221, 240.

53. "Poverty and Patronage," *New York Times,* April 17, 1965, p. 18.

54. Lindsay and Cloward, quoted in Sterling Memorial Library, Yale University, John V. Lindsay Papers (hereafter cited as SML Lindsay Papers), Box 130, Folder 738, News Clippings, Woody Klein, "Key to Poverty's Cure—Power," *New York Herald Tribune,* April 4, 1965.

55. Warren Weaver, "Powell Threatens Cutoff in Antipoverty Aid to City," *New York Times,* April 16, 1965, p. 1.

56. "Coordinating Council Warring on Poverty," *New York Amsterdam Times,* December 5, 1964, p. 30.

57. SML Lindsay Papers, Box 104, Folder 250, "Statement by Congressman John Lindsay, 6 August 1965," p. 1; Nicole P. Marwell, *Bargaining for Brooklyn: Community Organizations in the Entrepreneurial City* (Chicago: University of Chicago Press, 2007), 29.

58. Paul Montgomery, "Governor Vetoes Agency to Direct City Poverty Aid," *New York Times,* July 1, 1965, p. 1.

59. SML Lindsay Papers, Box 96, Folder 126, News Clippings, "Report on Clubhouse Politics," *New York Herald Tribune,* May 10, 1965.

60. Bauman, *Race and the War on Poverty,* 18–19.

61. George Goodman, "Wider Scope for Poverty Bill Seen," *Los Angeles Sentinel,* September 3, 1964, A1.

62. Bauman, *Race and the War on Poverty,* 21–22.

63. Ray Herbert, "Poverty Funds Control Problem, Stirs Dispute," *Los Angeles Times,* October 26, 1964, A1.

64. Bauman, *Race and the War on Poverty,* 23, 32–33.

65. Ibid., 23–25; "Outsiders Running War on Poverty," *Los Angeles Sentinel,* May 27, 1965, A11; "Eastside Residents Seek Poverty Housing Funds," *Los Angeles Sentinel,* May 20, 1965, B12.

66. For a definitive account of the August 1965 Watts riots, see Gerald Horne, *The Fire This Time: The Watts Uprising and the 1960s* (Charlottesville: University Press of Virginia, 1995).

67. "Committee to Urge Poverty War Merger," *Los Angeles Times,* May 28, 1965, A8; Bauman, *Race and the War on Poverty,* 43–47.

68. Lindsay, quoted in SML Lindsay Papers, Box 130, Folder 738, News Clippings, Woody Klein, "Key to Poverty's Cure—Power," *New York Herald Tribune,* April 21, 1965.

69. SML Lindsay Papers, Box 77, Folder 632, John Lindsay speech at the University of Illinois, April 30, 1968, p. 2–3.

70. Vincent Cannato, *The Ungovernable City: John Lindsay and His Struggle to Save New York* (New York: Basic Books, 2001), 109.

71. Municipal Archives, New York City Hall, Mayor John V. Lindsay Papers, 1966–1973, Vol. 1, Subject Files, Reel 14, Box 27, Folder 475, Executive Order 28, August 16, 1966, pp. 2, 7; Timothy Costello Papers (not yet inventoried), Folder: Poverty 1966, Donald Elliot to Timothy Costello, July 26, 1966.

72. Community News Service Records, 1969–1976 (hereafter cited as CNS Records), Reel 1, Doris Roldan, "Black-Puerto Rican Conflict Stalls South Bronx Program," October 10, 1969.

73. CNS Records, Reel 1, "Badillo Says Appointing Blacks and Puerto Ricans throughout City Government Is Answer to Conflict over Jobs," January 24, 1970.

74. "NAPP Fights Poverty with Total Grass-Roots Approach," *Los Angeles Sentinel,* July 15, 1965, A10.

75. Bauman, *Race and the War on Poverty,* 47, 52–55, 57–59, 63. As the following chapter shows, when the Nixon administration set out to divest the War on Poverty of its most controversial elements, the CAP was at the top of its list of targets.

76. Ibid., 66.

77. NAACP Western Regional Office Records (hereafter cited as NAACP-WRO Records), Carton 46, Folder 11, Opal Jones keynote address, "We are Angry," May 22, 1972, p. 1.

78. NAACP-WRO Records, Carton 13, Folder 32, Leonard Carter to Augustus Hawkins, June 8, 1972.

79. Paul Weeks, "Atlanta Sets Pace in War on Poverty," *Los Angeles Times,* August 12, 1965, p. 2.

80. Robert F. Kennedy Senate Papers, 1964–1968 (hereafter cited as RFK Papers), Box 17, Folder 2, "Poverty Funds in Atlanta," *Atlanta Journal,* August 16, 1966, p. 15.

81. Frankie V. Adams Collection, Series B, Box 1, Folder 26, *EOA Inc. Newsletter,* Vol. 1, No. 1 (July 1965), 1; "Negro Leaders Rally around Summit," *Atlanta Inquirer,* July 24, 1965, p. 1.

82. Georgia Government Documentation Project (hereafter cited as GGDP), Series P, Folder 6, Interview with Dan Sweat, November 20, 1996, pp. 16–17.

83. "Summit Conference Holds Breakfast Meet," *Atlanta Inquirer,* February 6, 1965, pp. 1, 13.

84. Harold H. Martin, *Atlanta and Environs: A Chronicle of Its People and Events,* vol. 3, *Years of Change and Challenge, 1940s–1970s* (1987; reprinted, Atlanta: Atlanta Historical Society; Athens: University of Georgia Press, 2011), 437.

85. Eliza K. Paschall Papers, 1932–1988, Series IV, Box 16, Folder 18, Atlanta All-Citizens Poverty Meeting Agenda, November 19, 1965; "Grassroots Leaders Term EOA Action a 'Slap in the Face,'" *Atlanta Inquirer,* November 27, 1965, p. 2; Brown-Nagin, *Courage to Dissent,* 259.

86. Ralph Martin Cloud, "The Management of an Antipoverty Program: A Case of Economic Opportunity Atlanta, Incorporated" (unpublished thesis, University of Georgia, Athens, 1967), 2, 107, 110; GGDP, Series P, Folder 6, Interview with Dan Sweat, November 22, 1996, pp. 14–16.

87. "Atlanta Receives Grants to Expand EOA Program," *Atlanta Inquirer,* September 25, 1965, p. 7. For material explaining the operation and programmatic focus of Atlanta's NSCs, see the numerous reports compiled by Community Council of Atlanta worker Ella Mae Brayboy available in Community Council of the Atlanta Area Records, 1960–1974, Box 10.

88. "Group to Fight Exclusion of Aides from Disputed EOA Pension Plan," *Atlanta Inquirer,* October 9, 1965, pp. 1, 11.

89. "EOA Aides Charge Discrimination, Low Pay," *Atlanta Inquirer,* December 11, 1965, p. 11.

90. Eliza K. Paschall Papers, 1932–1988, Series IV, Box 16, Folder 18, Edward Moody to Charles Emmerich, September 26, 1966.

91. A wage garnishment requires an employer to redirect a fixed amount of an individual employee's wage to a debtor to force the process of debt repayment, which is often stipulated by a legal ruling.

92. AFL-CIO Civil Rights Department, Southern Office Records, 1964–1979, Series I, Subseries B, Box 1595, Folder 38, W. H. Montague Statement: "Operational Policies of the EOA Merit System Committee," November 27, 1967, pp. 1–2.

93. J. Lowell Ware, "Poverty Fight Goes Nowhere," *Atlanta Voice,* Vol. 6, No. 42 (October 16, 1971), 1.

94. Much of the best-organized activism in Atlanta came under the direction of SNCC activists who ran the Vine City Project during the mid- to late 1960s. See Winston A. Grady-Willis, *Challenging U.S. Apartheid: Atlanta and Black Struggles for Human Rights, 1960–1977* (Durham, NC: Duke University Press, 2006), 83–113.

95. Paul Weeks, "Voices of Poverty Are Being Heard—And City Halls across U.S. Quail," *Los Angeles Times,* August 9, 1965.

96. Gefland, ed., The War on Poverty, 1964–1968 [microfilm], Ex WE-9, Reel 2, Memorandum from Charles Schultz to President Johnson, September 18, 1965, pp. 2–3.

97. Gefland, ed., The War on Poverty, 1964–1968 [microfilm], Ex WF-9, Reel 2, Memorandum from Hubert Humphrey to President Johnson, December 2, 1965, p. 2; ibid., "The Office of Economic Opportunity and Local Community Action Agencies," United State Conference of Mayors Report, p. 2.

98. McKee, "'This Government Is with Us,'" 34, 40, 41, 57. McKee's work has, through analysis of hitherto unstudied telephone conversations, revealed an interesting new perspective on Johnson's view of the War on Poverty and the CAP. Jackson, From Civil Rights to Economic Rights, 194.

99. SML Lindsay Papers, Box 61, Folder 91, Memorandum from Jim Carberry to John Lindsay, June 3, 1966, p. 1.

100. Major Owens, interview with author, November 8, 2010.

101. Thomas Sugrue, Sweet Land of Liberty: The Forgotten Struggle for Civil Rights in the North (New York: Random House, 2008), 373. Sugrue gives the example of Chicago as one city where strong top-down municipal control of the War on Poverty was seen to result in an effective, timely, and efficient delivery of programs.

102. Augustus F. Hawkins Papers, 1935–1990, Box 94, Folder: OEO—Compton-Willowbrook-Enterprise CAA, Charles Knox to Augustus Hawkins, October 2, 1967.

103. Paul Weeks, "Grasp of Poverty Gradually Eases," Los Angeles Times, August 13, 1965.

104. Gefland, ed., The War on Poverty, 1964–1968 [microfilm], Ex-FG 11–15, Reel 8, Additional testimony of Sargent Shriver before the Senate Subcommittee on Executive Reorganization, August 19, 1966, pp. 5–6.

105. Gefland, ed., The War on Poverty, 1964–1968 [microfilm], Ex-FG 11–15, Reel 8, Lyndon B. Johnson, Message to Congress, June 22, 1967, p. 2.

106. Gefland, ed., The War on Poverty, 1964–1968 [microfilm], Ex-FG 11–15, Reel 11, "Congress and Poverty," Atlanta Journal, November 17, 1967, p. 18.

107. Martin Luther King Jr., Where Do We Go from Here: Chaos or Community? (Boston: Beacon Press, 1967), 35–36.

108. Gefland, ed., The War on Poverty, 1964–1968 [microfilm], Ex-FG 11–15, Reel 8, Memorandum to the President from Robert Kintner, October 13, 1966.

109. Gefland, ed., The War on Poverty, 1964–1968 [microfilm], Ex WE-9, Reel 3, Memorandum to the President from Charles Schultz, November 7, 1966.

110. Gefland, ed., The War on Poverty, 1964–1968 [microfilm], Ex-FG 11–15, Reel 11, Confidential Report: "Analysis of 1966 Congressional Elections Re OEO Legislative Position" n.d. (1966), pp. 1–3.

111. Sam Yorty Papers, Box D-0025, Folder OEO 1966, Sam Yorty to Sargent Shriver, November 29, 1966, p. 1.

112. Frankie V. Adams Collection, Series B, Box 2, Folder 1, Charles Emmerich to Richard Boone, December 20, 1966, p. 1.

113. Orleck, "Introduction: The War on Poverty from the Grass Roots Up," 17.

114. For a discussion of the ways in which ideas of motherhood both shaped and were shaped by welfare rights activism, see Gina Denton, "'Neither guns nor

bombs—neither the state nor God—will stop us from fighting for our children': Motherhood and Protest in 1960s and 1970s America," *The Sixties,* Vol. 5, No. 2 (2012), 205–28.

115. Premilla Nadasen, *Welfare Warriors: The Welfare Rights Movement in the United States* (New York: Routledge, 2005), 143–46.

116. Gefland, ed., The War on Poverty, 1964–1968 [microfilm], Ex-FG 11–15, Reel 8, Additional testimony of Sargent Shriver before the Senate Subcommittee on Executive Reorganization, August 19, 1966, pp. 7–8.

117. See, for example, Felicia Ann Kornbluh, *The Battle for Welfare Rights: Politics and Poverty in Modern America* (Philadelphia: University of Pennsylvania Press, 2007); Chappell, *The War on Welfare;* Nadasen, *Welfare Warriors.*

118. Richard Cloward and Frances Fox Piven, "The Weight of the Poor: A Strategy to End Poverty," *The Nation,* May 2, 1966, http://www.thenation.com/article /weight-poor-strategy-end-poverty#.

119. Congress on Racial Equality Papers (hereafter cited as CORE Papers), Part 3, Series A, Reel 10, George Wiley to Marvin Rich, July 25, 1967.

120. Chappell, *War on Welfare,* 50–51.

121. Felicia Kornbluh, "'Who Shot FAP?' The Nixon Welfare Plan and the Transformation of American Politics," *The Sixties,* Vol. 1, No. 2 (December 2008), 125–50.

122. Gefland, ed., The War on Poverty, 1964–1968 [microfilm], Ex WE-9, Reel 1, Memorandum to the President, "The Poverty Program vs. the Middle Class," December 30, 1963, pp. 2–4.

123. Kevin Phillips, *The Emerging Republican Majority* (New Rochelle, NY: Arlington House, 1969).

124. John Lindsay, *The City* (New York: W. W. Norton, 1970), 48 (italics in the original).

125. Yvonne Braithwaite Burke Papers, LP69:14, Telford L. Smith to Yvonne Braithwaite Burke, May 20, 1970.

126. Gefland, ed., The War on Poverty, 1964–1968 [microfilm], Ex WE-9, Reel 7, Victor Riesel, "Revolutionizing the Streets," *Publishers Hall-Syndicate,* September 19, 1968.

127. Craig Steven Wilder, *A Covenant with Color: Race and Social Power in Brooklyn* (New York: Columbia University Press, 2000), 176.

128. For an in-depth exploration of the urban riots of the 1960s, see Robert M. Fogelson, *Violence as Protest: A Study of Riots and Ghettos* (New York: Anchor Books, 1971).

129. Gefland, ed., The War on Poverty, 1964–1968 [microfilm], Part V, White House Central Files, WE9–1, Reel 17, Lester Maddox to Lyndon Johnson, July 10, 1968, p. 1.

130. Gefland, ed., The War on Poverty, 1964–1968 [microfilm], Ex-FG 11–15, Reel 8, Memorandum to all OEO Regional Directors from Sargent Shriver, July 20, 1967.

131. Gefland, ed., The War on Poverty, 1964–1968 [microfilm], Ex WE-9, Reel 5, Memorandum to President Johnson from Sargent Shriver, September 12, 1967; ibid., "Summer Program Inspection 1967 Report"; ibid., "OEO and the Riots—

A Summary," p. 2. The "EOA CAP Centers" that Mayor Allen refers to are the Neighborhood Service Centers (NSCs) discussed earlier in this chapter.

132. Lindsay quoted in Gefland, ed., The War on Poverty, 1964–1968 [microfilm], Ex WE-9, Reel 7, Memorandum to Joe Califano from Jim Gaither, July 11, 1968, p. 2.

133. California Republican Assembly Records, Box 10, CRA Newsletters, 1969–1970, "CRA News," Dec 67–Jan 68, Vol. 2, Nos. 4 and 5, p. 14.

134. Ira Katznelson, City Trenches: Urban Politics and the Patterning of Class in the United States (New York: Pantheon Books, 1981), 4.

135. Dan T. Carter, The Politics of Rage: George Wallace, the Origins of the New Conservatism, and the Transformation of American Politics (Baton Rouge: Louisiana State University Press, 2000), 11, 304.

136. Katznelson, City Trenches, 2.

137. CORE Papers, Part 1, Reel IV, Architects' Renewal Committee in Harlem, Inc., Memorandum to CORE on Rent Supplement Program, June 27, 1967, p. 4; Robert B. Semple, "$40 Million Voted for Rent Subsidy by Senate Panel," New York Times, August 29, 1967, p. 1; Dennis Hevesi, "Paul Fino, Politician Who Battled Lindsay, Dies at 95," New York Times, June 19, 2009, A25.

CHAPTER 2: COMMUNITY DEVELOPMENT
CORPORATIONS, BLACK CAPITALISM, AND
THE MAINSTREAMING OF BLACK POWER

1. "Boro Cry to RJK, JVL: We're Tired of Waiting," New York Amsterdam News, February 12, 1966, p. 23; "New Look Coming to Bed-Stuy," New York Amsterdam News, December 17, 1966, p. 28; RFK Papers, Box 2, Folder 3, "Robert Kennedy Address to Second Borough President's Conference of Community Leaders," January 21, 1966, p. 10. Kennedy's efforts in Bedford-Stuyvesant have been relatively neglected by historians, overshadowed in accounts of his life by his opposition to the war in Vietnam and his bid for the Democratic Party presidential nomination in 1968. Only the recent work of historian Edward Schmitt has examined Kennedy's role in Restoration's genesis in any serious depth. See Edward R. Schmitt, President of the Other America: Robert Kennedy and the Politics of Poverty (Amherst: University of Massachusetts Press, 2010). The discussion of Restoration in this chapter has appeared in Tom Adam Davies, "Black Power in Action: The Bedford-Stuyvesant Restoration Corporation, Robert F. Kennedy, and the Politics of the Urban Crisis," Journal of American History, Vol. 100, No. 3 (December 2013), 736–60.

2. Fergus, Liberalism, Black Power and the Making of American Politics, 12.

3. Ford Foundation Papers: Inventory of the Bedford Stuyvesant Restoration Corporation (hereafter cited as Ford Foundation Papers), Box 2, Folder 1, Ford Foundation Policy Paper, Community Development Corporations: A Strategy for Depressed Urban and Rural Areas (New York: Ford Foundation, 1972), 3–5. The foundation's program of nationwide CDC funding is detailed on pp. 1–27.

4. Nixon White House microfiche, Part 6, President's Office Files, 1969–1974 (hereafter cited as NWHM Part 6), 8–51, D.P. Moynihan, Progress Report to the President on Activities of the Urban Affairs Council, April 1969, pp. 2–4.

5. Andrew Young, *An Easy Burden: The Civil Rights Movement and the Trans-formation of America* (New York: HarperCollins, 1996), 443.

6. Andrew J. Young Papers, Series 1, Subseries A, Box 5, Folder: PPC, Dept. of Labor, Ralph Abernathy to Willard Wirtz, April 29, 1968, p. 1

7. Gerald McKnight, *The Last Crusade: Martin Luther King, Jr., the FBI, and the Poor People's Campaign* (Boulder, Colo.: Westview Press, 1998) p.7

8. See, for example, Matthew Countryman, *Up South: Civil Rights and Black Power in Philadelphia* (Philadelphia: University of Pennsylvania Press, 2006); Fergus, *Liberalism, Black Power and the Making of American Politics;* Self, *American Babylon;* Sugrue, *Sweet Land of Liberty;* Woodard, *A Nation within a Nation;* Yohuru Williams, *Black Politics/Whitepower: Civil Rights, Black Power, and the Black Panthers in New Haven* (St. James, NY: Brandywine Press, 2000); McKee, *The Problem of Jobs;* Patrick D. Jones, *The Selma of the North: Civil Rights Insurgency in Milwaukee* (Cambridge, MA: Harvard University Press, 2009); Clarence Lang, *Grassroots at the Gateway: Class Politics and Black Freedom Struggle in St. Louis, 1936–75* (Ann Arbor: University of Michigan Press, 2009).

9. For work on identifying the intellectual and political roots of black capitalist policies, see Robert E. Weems Jr., with Lewis A. Randolph, *Business in Black and White: American Presidents and Black Entrepreneurs in the Twentieth Century* (New York: New York University Press, 2009). Robert E. Weems Jr.'s other work in this field includes *Desegregating the Dollar: African American Consumerism in the Twentieth Century* (New York: New York University Press, 1998); and "The Revolution Will Be Marketed: American Corporations and Black Consumers during the 1960s," *Radical History Review,* Vol. 54 (Spring 1994), 94–107. For scholarship on the place of black capitalism within the shifting currents of Black Power and GOP politics during the late 1960s and 1970s and within the political philosophy and career of Richard Nixon, see Fergus, *Liberalism, Black Power, and the Making of American Politics,* 196–231; Devin Fergus, "Black Power, Soft Power: Floyd McKissick, Soul City, and the Death of Moderate Black Republicanism," *Journal of Policy History,* Vol. 22 (2010), 148–92; Dean J. Kotlowski, *Nixon's Civil Rights: Politics, Principle, and Policy* (Cambridge, MA: Harvard University Press, 2001).

10. See Laura Warren Hill, "FIGHTing for the Soul of Black Capitalism: Struggles for Black Economic Development in Postrebellion Rochester" (pp. 42–67); Nishani Frazier, "A McDonalds That Reflects the Soul of a People: Hough Area Development Corporation and Community Development in Cleveland" (pp. 68–92); Julia Rabig, "'A Fight and a Question': Community Development Corporations, Machine Politics, and Corporate Philanthropy in the Long Urban Crisis" (pp. 245–72); Andrea Gill, "'Gilding the Ghetto' and Debates over Chicago's Gatreaux Program" (pp. 184–214)—all in *The Business of Black Power: Community Development, Capitalism, and Corporate Responsibility in Postwar America,* ed. Laura Warren Hill and Julia Rabig (Rochester, NY: University of Rochester Press, 2012).

11. Kenneth T. Jackson, *Crabgrass Frontier: The Suburbanization of the United States* (New York: University of Oxford Press, 1985), 195–203.

12. Wilder, *A Covenant with Color,* 185–95.

13. David M. P. Freund, *Colored Property: State Policy and White Racial Politics in Suburban America* (Chicago: University of Chicago Press, 2007), 116. For an in-depth discussion of New Deal housing policies and their role in the development of segregation across America, see ibid., 97–138.

14. Wilder, *A Covenant with Color,* 185.

15. RFK Papers, Box 89, Folder 9, "Consumer Action Programs' Staff Report to the Senate Subcommittee on Employment, Manpower, and Poverty," June 13, 1967, p. 1.

16. Jonathan J. Bean, "'Burn, Baby, Burn': Small Business in the Urban Riots of the 1960s," *Independent Review,* Vol. 5, No. 2 (Fall 2000), 165–87.

17. SML Lindsay Papers, Box 91, Folder 83, Milton Mollen, "Report on the Lindsay Team's Program for Housing Code Enforcement in New York City: An Effective Attack on Slums," October 21, 1965, p. 68.

18. Grady-Willis, *Challenging U.S. Apartheid,* 114.

19. CORE Papers, Part 2, Reel XIV, George Schiffer, "Ending the Landlord-Tenant Relationship in the Slums," February 5, 1965, p. 5.

20. RFK Papers, Box 2, Folder 3, "Robert Kennedy Address to Second Borough President's Conference of Community Leaders," January 21, 1966, p. 10.

21. "Social Service Agency Seeks New Members," *Los Angeles Sentinel,* May 9, 1963, B3.

22. "Tutorial Services Offered in Watts," *Los Angeles Sentinel,* May 28, 1964, E6; "Westminster Success," *Los Angeles Sentinel,* March 24, 1966, A6.

23. "Westminster Success."

24. "Youth Training Program Falling behind Schedule," *Los Angeles Sentinel,* February 3, 1966, D1; "Westminster YTEP Student in Key Job," *Los Angeles Sentinel,* April 7, 1966, D4.

25. "Parkside Manor Improvement Council," *Los Angeles Sentinel,* September 2, 1965, C6.

26. Noel A. Cazenave, *Impossible Democracy: The Unlikely Success of the War on Poverty Community Action Programs* (Albany: State University of New York Press, 2007); Augustus F. Hawkins Papers, 1935–1990, Box 94, Folder: Labor—Westminster Neighborhood Association, Inc., George Broadfield, "Syllabus for Staff Training Institute of the WNA," February 1966, p. 1. HARYOU-ACT sent five officials, who were joined by two from Youth-In-Action, the Bedford-Stuyvesant antipoverty agency.

27. Archie Hardwick, "Westminster Report on Watts," *Los Angeles Sentinel,* November 3, 1966, A6; Budd Schulberg, "Watts '67—Unfinished Business," *Los Angeles Times,* July 2, 1967, A6; Daniel Widener, *Black Arts West: Culture and Struggle in Postwar Los Angeles* (Durham, NC: Duke University Press, 2009), 94. For Widener's in-depth discussion of the trajectory of cultural liberalism in Watts and its relationship to the development of the local Black Arts Movement, see ibid, 90–115.

28. "Watts Credit Union Issued State License," *Los Angeles Sentinel*, April 14, 1966, A7.

29. Rucker, quoted in "Poverty Executive Sees Watts Gain," *Los Angeles Sentinel*, December 7, 1967, B10.

30. Warren, quoted in "Gov. Defends Mormon Church Racial Position," *Los Angeles Sentinel*, September 28, 1967, A8.

31. Jacquette, quoted in Schulberg, "Watts '67—Unfinished Business."

32. RFK Papers, Box 2, Folder 3, "Robert Kennedy Address to Second Borough President's Conference of Community Leaders," 8.

33. Arthur M. Schlesinger Jr., *Robert F. Kennedy and His Times* (London: Heinemann, 1978), 784.

34. RFK Papers, Box 2, Folder 3, "Robert Kennedy Address to Second Borough President's Conference of Community Leaders," 7.

35. "New Look Coming to Bed-Stuy," *New York Amsterdam News,* December 17, 1966, p. 28.

36. Thomas M. C. Johnston Papers, 1936–2008 (hereafter cited as Thomas Johnston Papers), Box 3, Folder 1, "Special Impact Project Proposal Paper," February 16, 1967, pp. 4, 6–7.

37. Joseph Palermo, *In His Own Right: The Political Odyssey of Senator Robert F. Kennedy* (New York: Columbia University Press, 2001), 168.

38. Schlesinger, *Robert F. Kennedy and His Times,* p.781; Schmitt, *President of the Other America,* 122.

39. Ford Foundation Papers, Box 1, Folder 1, Robert Goldmann, "Performance in Black and White: An Appraisal of the Development and Record of the Bedford-Stuyvesant Restoration and Development and Services Corporations," February 1969, pp. 4, 135.

40. Kennedy, quoted in Schmitt, *President of the Other America,* 153.

41. Huey P. Newton, *Revolutionary Suicide* (New York: Writing and Readers Publishing Inc., 1973), 110; Bobby Seale, *Seize the Time: The Story of the Black Panther Party and Huey P. Newton* (London: Hutchinson, 1970), 80.

42. For other examples of Kennedy's efforts to reach out to young black militants, see Schmitt, *President of the Other America,* 208; and Schlesinger, *Robert F. Kennedy and His Times,* 908–9.

43. RFK Papers, Box 2, Folder 6, "Statement of Senator Robert F. Kennedy before Committee on Government Operations, Subcommittee on Executive Reorganization," August 15, 1966, p. 13.

44. Fergus, *Liberalism, Black Power, and the Making of American Politics,* 10–11.

45. Thomas Johnston Papers, Box 1, Folder 2, "The Bedford-Stuyvesant Community" Report, n.d., p. 1. For a detailed discussion of the impact of New Deal housing policies on ghetto formation in Brooklyn in particular, see Wilder, *A Covenant with Color,* 175–217.

46. Ford Foundation Papers, Box 1, Folder 1, Goldmann, "Performance in Black and White," 4; Thomas Johnston Papers, Box 2, Folder 4, "Grant Proposal to Ford

Foundation," February 1967, pp. 1–2; ibid., Box 1, Folder 2, "The Bedford-Stuyvesant Community" Report, 2.

47. Among the other foundations that committed funds to Restoration were the Astor Foundation, the Tatonic Foundation, the Rockefeller Brothers Foundation, the Stern Family Fund, the Field Foundation, and the JM Kaplan Fund. For foundations' desire for bipartisan support, see, for example, Thomas Johnston Papers, Box 2, Folder 2, Astor Foundation Press Release, March 26, 1967, p. 1; ibid., David Stern to Robert Kennedy, October 13, 1966, p. 1; Ford Foundation Papers, Box 1, Folder 1, Goldmann, "Performance in Black and White," 14–15, 17–19, 22–23.

48. "New Look Coming to Bed-Stuy," *New York Amsterdam News,* December 17, 1966, pp. 28–29; Thomas Johnston Papers, Box 1, Folder 3, Thomas Johnston, memorandum, November 20, 1967, p. 5; Ford Foundation Papers, Box 1, Folder 1, Goldmann, "Performance in Black and White," i.

49. RFK Papers Box 1, Folder 1, "Robert Kennedy Address to Independent Order of Oddfellows," August 18, 1965, p. 5; "Brooklyn Leaders Get Support from RFK," *New York Amsterdam News,* October 22, 1966, p. 25.

50. Schmitt, *President of the Other America,* 152; Ford Foundation Papers, Box 1, Folder 1, Goldmann, "Performance in Black and White," 25, 31, 33–34.

51. Angela Y. Davis, *Women, Race, and Class* (New York, 1983), 13; Steve Estes, *I Am a Man! Race, Manhood, and the Civil Rights Movement* (Chapel Hill: University of North Carolina Press, 2005), 107; Steven V. Roberts, "800 Demand Vote on Renewal Unit," *New York Times,* April 7, 1967, p. 49.

52. Thomas Johnston Papers, Box 2, Folder 8, Earl Graves, memorandum, May 22, 1967, p. 4; ibid., Box 1, Folder 13, Thomas Johnston to Lionel Payne, April 4, 1967, p. 2.

53. Thomas Johnston Papers, Box 1, Folder 7, Earl Graves, memorandum, May 27, 1967, p. 2; Ford Foundation Papers, Box 1, Folder 1, Goldmann, "Performance in Black and White," 34.

54. Thomas Johnston Papers, Box 1, Folder 14, Eli Jacobs to Louis Winnick, June 20, 1967; "City Bank Ups Black," *New York Amsterdam News,* December 19, 1970, p. 40.

55. C. David Heyman, *RFK: A Candid Biography* (London: Heinemann, 1998), 423; Schmitt, *President of the Other America,* 154; Heyman, *RFK,* 422.

56. Elsie Richardson later enjoyed a number of different positions within Central Brooklyn Model Cities, and Lucille Rose became the head of the city's Department of Employment. See, for example, Elsie Richardson, "Open Letter," *New York Amsterdam News,* April 15, 1972, C1; "Lucille Rose Given Powell Award," *New York Amsterdam News,* November 10, 1973. Concerning the composition of the two boards, see Ford Foundation Papers, Box 1, Folder 1, Goldmann, "Performance in Black and White," 141–43; ibid., Box 2, Folder 2, *Restoration Newsletter,* Vol. 11, No. 1 (1981), 1.

57. NWHM Part 6, 173–32, Maurice Stans, memorandum to John Ehrlichman, September 15, 1971, p. 2.

58. Kotlowski, *Nixon's Civil Rights,* 130. The SBA was established in 1953 by the Eisenhower administration to provide assistance to small-business owners.

59. NWHM Part 6, 173–32, Maurice Stans, memorandum to the president, July 24, 1971, pp. 4–5.

60. NWHM Part 6, 123–41, Leonard Garment, memorandum to Bob Haldeman, February 22, 1971.

61. Ford Foundation Papers, Box 2, Folder 1, Ford Foundation Policy Paper, *Community Development Corporations*, 7.

62. Rick Perlstein, *Nixonland: The Rise of a President and the Fracturing of America* (New York: Scribner, 2008), 91–95, 202.

63. Michael W. Flamm, "The Politics of 'Law and Order,'" in *The Conservative Sixties,* ed. David Farber and Jeff Roche (New York: Peter Lang, 2003), 149, 145.

64. Robert E. Weems Jr. and Lewis Randolph, "The National Response to Richard M. Nixon's Black Capitalism Initiative: The Success of Domestic Détente," *Journal of Black Studies,* Vol. 32, No. 1 (September 2001), 66–68.

65. Laura Warren Hill and Julia Rabig, "Toward a History of the Business of Black Power," in *The Business of Black Power,* ed. Laura Warren Hill and Julia Rabig (Rochester, NY: University of Rochester Press, 2012), 15–20.

66. Ogbar, *Black Power,* 194. As Ogbar explains, in black communities across America, the NOI built and sustained petty capitalist enterprises and aimed to secure local control over economies in black neighborhoods.

67. Malcolm X, "The Ballot or the Bullet," in *Malcolm X Speaks: Selected Speeches and Statements,* ed. George Breitman (New York: Grove Press, 1994), 39.

68. Angela Dillard, "Malcolm X and African American Conservatism," in *The Cambridge Companion to Malcolm X,* ed. Robert Terrell (New York: Cambridge University Press, 2010), 92.

69. Malcolm X, quoted in Estes, *I Am a Man!* 106.

70. Andrew J. Young Papers, Series 1, Subseries A, Box 5, Folder: PPC, Statements, 1968, Robert F. Kennedy Statement: "Solutions to the Problems of Welfare," May 19, 1968, p. 2.

71. Kotlowski, *Nixon's Civil Rights,* 126.

72. Timothy J. Minchin, *From Rights to Economics: The Ongoing Struggle for Black Equality in the U.S. South* (Gainesville: University Press of Florida, 2007), 59–81; Fergus, *Liberalism, Black Power, and the Making of American Politics,* 196–231. While Minchin posits the development of Soul City as an extension of civil rights activism, Fergus frames it more effectively as "federally-subsidized Black nationalism" and draws out the project's broader significance to the growing ascendancy of the New Right within Republican politics in North Carolina (led by conservative senator Jesse Helms) and, subsequently, within the GOP nationally.

73. Black Panther Party Collections, Box 1, Folder 21, Earl Ofari, "Black Capitalism: Salvation or Sell Out?" December 5, 1968, pp. 1–2. Perhaps the most famous contemporary criticism came from African American scholar Robert Allen in the form of his book *Black Awakening in Capitalist America: An Analytic History* (Garden City, NY: Doubleday, 1969).

74. Eldridge Cleaver, "An Open Letter to Stokely Carmichael" (July 1969), in *The Black Panthers Speak,* ed. Philip S. Foner (New York: Da Capo Press, 1995), 105–6.

75. Ogbar, *Black Power,* 194.

76. Black Panther Party Harlem Branch File, 1969–1970, Box 1, Cheryl Foster Writings, 1970.

77. Huey P. Newton, "Black Capitalism Re-analyzed: June 5, 1971," in *The Huey P. Newton Reader,* ed. D. Hilliard and D. Weise (New York: Seven Stories Press, 2002), 229, 231.

78. In a similar vein, as historian Dean Kotlowski has explained, Nixon's other major policy for black advancement was the funneling of federal funds to support and preserve black colleges. Promoting black control of their own separate institutions again signaled the federal government's move away from integrationist goals under Nixon. Validating African Americans' cultural and ethnic independence also fit with Nixon's endorsement of the broader revival of white ethnic identity politics that, as Matthew Frye Jacobsen has argued, formed an important cultural dimension of the white backlash against African American gains during the civil rights–Black Power era. See Kotlowski, *Nixon's Civil Rights,* 14, 60 (see 15–42 and 151–155 for in-depth discussion of these matters); Matthew Frye Jacobson, *Roots Too: White Ethnic Revival in Post–Civil Rights America* (Cambridge, MA: Harvard University Press, 2006).

79. Nixon White House microfiche: Part 2, President's Meeting File, 1969–1974 (hereafter cited as NWHM Part 2), 69-3-2, B5-C6, John Ehrlichman, memorandum for the President's Personal File, March 14, 1969, pp. 2–3.

80. CNS Records, Reel 1, "Community Calendar," May 8, 1970.

81. Laura Warren Hill and Julia Rabig, "Introduction," in *The Business of Black Power,* ed. Laura Warren Hill and Julia Rabig (Rochester, NY: University of Rochester Press, 2012), 6.

82. NWHM Part 6, 173–32, George Schultz, memorandum to the president, September 17, 1971, p. 2.

83. Thomas Johnston Papers, Box 2, Folder 12, Franklin A. Thomas to D&S Board, January 1967, p. 1.

84. "New Guy in Town," *New York Amsterdam News,* January 13, 1968, p. 21; Robert F. Kennedy Oral History Collection, Franklin A. Thomas Oral History Interview, RFK #1, March 23, 1972, pp. 8–9; Thomas Johnston Papers, Box 1, Folder 7, "Minutes of Development & Services Corporation Board Meeting," February 5, 1968, p. 4; Ford Foundation Papers, Box 1, Folder 1, Goldmann, "Performance in Black and White," 118.

85. Thomas Johnston Papers, Box 1, Folder 1, "Minutes of Development & Services Corporation Board Meeting," March 8, 1967, p. 8; Franklin Thomas, quoted in Ford Foundation Papers, Box 2, Folder 1, *Black Enterprise,* June 1975, p. 1.

86. Ford Foundation Papers, Box 1, Folder 5, "Annual Home Improvement Program," *New York Recorder,* May 11, 1974; Schmitt, *President of the Other America,* 162.

87. Ford Foundation Papers, Box 1, Folder 1, Goldmann, "Performance in Black and White," 93–94; ibid., Box 1, Folder 3, "Minutes of Development & Services Corporation Board Meeting," July 26, 1971, p. 5.

88. Thomas Johnston Papers, Box 1, Folder 1, "Minutes of Development & Services Corporation Board Meeting," March 8, 1967, p. 54; Ford Foundation Papers,

Box 1, Folder 1, Goldmann, "Performance in Black and White," 56–58; Dawnyielle Peeples, "Workers Use a Buyout to Buy In," *Black Enterprise,* January 1994, archived at Questia, http://www.questia.com/library/1G1-14779706/workers-use-a-buyout-to-buy-in-6-5-million-lbo-turns.

89. Ford Foundation Papers, Box 2, Folder 2, "Spotlight on Economic Development," *Restoration Newsletter,* Vol. 2, No. 3 (October. 1972), 1; "First McDonalds Store in Bed-Stuy Going Up," *New York Amsterdam News,* October 16, 1971, D1; Ford Foundation Papers, Box 1, Folder 1, Goldmann, "Performance in Black and White," 59.

90. Ford Foundation Papers, Box 2, Folder 2, "Spotlight on Economic Development"; Joseph, "The Black Power Movement," 4.

91. Ford Foundation Papers, Box 1, Folder 6, "Design Works," *Downtown Brooklyn,* April 1974; ibid., Box 1, Folder 7, "Designing an Idea," *Black Enterprise,* November 1974.

92. "Historic Weeksville to Be Preserved by Bed-Stuy Rest Corp," *New York Amsterdam News,* June 23, 1973, C1; Ford Foundation Papers, Box 2, Folder 2, *Restoration Newsletter,* Vol. 3, No. 2 (September–October 1973), 2–3. See also "History," *Weeksville Heritage Center,* http://weeksvillehc.tumblr.com/ (accessed August 16, 2013).

93. See, for example, "Bed-Stuy 'Soul Sunday,'" *New York Amsterdam News,* May 1, 1971, p. 23; Ford Foundation Papers, Box 1, Folder 1, Goldmann, "Performance in Black and White," 70–72.

94. Ford Foundation Papers, Box 1, Folder 1, Goldmann, "Performance in Black and White," 72; ibid., Box 2, Folder 2, "Tenant Aid," *Restoration Newsletter,* Vol. 3, No. 1 (April 1973), 5; ibid., "Free Tax Clinic Reopens," *Restoration Newsletter,* Vol. 2, No. 4 (April 1973), 3–4; ibid., Debra Walton, "My Experiences Working for the Bedford-Stuyvesant Restoration Corporation This Summer," *Restoration Newsletter,* Vol. 2, No. 3 (October 1972), 6.

95. "Bedford-Stuyvesant Was the Newer World of RFK," *New York Amsterdam News,* June 15, 1968, p. 17. For Restoration's cultural programs, see, for example, Ford Foundation Papers, Box 2, Folder 2, "'Beauty of the Ghetto' Exhibition at Restoration," *Restoration Newsletter,* Vol. 5, No. 5 (Winter 1975), 1; ibid., Box 1, Folder 5, Albert Jones, "What Makes a Ghetto?" *Antillean Caribbean Echo,* November 10, 1973; ibid., Mel Tapley, "Cultural Center—Home of Dreams," *New York Amsterdam News,* May 4, 1974; ibid., "Local Artist Returns Home to Brooklyn," *New York Amsterdam News,* January 1, 1978.

96. Ford Foundation Papers, Box 1, Folder 1, Goldmann, "Performance in Black and White," 44–47.

97. Albert Vann, "View of the Black Teachers Conference," *New York Amsterdam News,* May 20, 1972, A5; Ford Foundation Papers, Box 2, Folder 2, "The African American Teachers Association and Its Search for Black Talent," *Restoration Newsletter,* Vol. 1, No. 5 (June 1971), 4–5.

98. "Launch Crispus Attucks Democratic Club," *New York Amsterdam News,* February 1, 1975, C1.

99. Schmitt, *President of the Other America,* 162; Ford Foundation Papers, Box 1, Folder 1, Goldmann, "Performance in Black and White," 119–20. Regarding the 2000 board merger, see "Bedford-Stuyvesant Restoration Corporation Profile," PlaceMatters, para. 6, http://www.placematters.net/node/1028; "Doar Quits; Restoration Will Still Have 2 Boards," *New York Amsterdam News,* December 29, 1973, C1.

100. For an excellent account of the school crisis, see Jerald Podair, *The Strike That Changed New York: Blacks, Whites, and the Ocean Hill–Brownsville Crisis* (New Haven: Yale University Press, 2002); "Sonny Carson Faces DA Charges," *New York Amsterdam News,* July 28, 1973, A1; "Sonny Carson Back to Brooklyn," *New York Amsterdam News,* March 11, 1978, B1.

101. Dasun Allah, "Sonny Carson Dies," *Village Voice,* December 31, 2002, para. 7, http://www.villagevoice.com/2002-12-31/news/sonny-carson-dies.

102. Ford Foundation Papers, Box 2, Folder 2, "Restoration of Confidence in Bedford-Stuyvesant's Future," *Restoration Newsletter,* Vol. 11, No. 1 (1981), 4.

103. "Alice Kornegay Triangle," May 5, 1998, NYC Parks, http://www.nycgovparks.org/about/history/historical-signs/listings?id=6397; "Grassroots Group in Own Headquarters," *New York Amsterdam Times,* February 26, 1966, p. 7.

104. "For the Harlem Commonwealth Council Growing Up Means Buying Up," *Black Enterprise,* November 1978, p. 59. As the following chapter shows, Wilcox was the primary academic theorist behind the city's movement for community control of public education, and Robinson (along with Kornegay) was also a leading figure in the movement.

105. Bauman has done more than any other historian to advance our understanding of WLCAC. See, Bauman, *Race and the War on Poverty,* 69–89.

106. "Labor Group Urges Action Programs," *Los Angeles Sentinel,* September 9, 1965, A8; Ford Foundation Papers, Box 2, Folder 1, Ford Foundation Policy Paper, *Community Development Corporations,* 20; Bauman, *Race and the War on Poverty,* 70.

107. Ernie Sprinkles, "Watts Riots in Review: What Good Did It Do?" *Los Angeles Sentinel,* May 20, 1971, D10.

108. Lou Smith, letter to editor, *Black Enterprise,* January 1973, p. 6.

109. "'Operation Bootstrap' Shows How Training Is the Key to Progress," *Los Angeles Sentinel,* June 22, 1967, F7.

110. Charles E. Brown, "Operation Bootstrap Prepares," *Jet,* December 21, 1967, pp. 16–22.

111. Jerri Moore, "A Will to Make Ideas Work," *Los Angeles Sentinel,* July 4, 1968, A3.

112. "Reagan Visits Ghetto Areas, Lauds Self-Help," *Los Angeles Sentinel,* February 3, 1966, A1.

113. Architects' Renewal Committee in Harlem, Inc., *East Harlem Triangle Plan: Prepared for the Community Association of the East Harlem Triangle and New York Housing and Development Administration* (October 1968), 3.

114. "Grass Roots Group in Own Headquarters," *New York Amsterdam News,* February 26, 1966, p. 7.

115. "East Harlem Center Opening," *New York Amsterdam News,* June 29, 1974, B7.

116. "For the Harlem Commonwealth Council Growing Up Means Buying Up," 76.

117. Bauman, *Race and the War on Poverty,* 77–79; Marshall Lowe, "WLCAC: Changing Face of Community," *Los Angeles Sentinel,* May 20, 1971, D1.

118. Black Panther Party Collections, Box 2, Folder: "Watts 1960s," "Watts Labor Community Action Committee" brochure, n.d. (1972).

119. Marshall Lowe, "WLCAC: Changing Face of Community," *Los Angeles Sentinel,* May 20, 1971, D1.

120. Bauman, *Race and the War on Poverty,* 74–75.

121. William Russell Ellis, *People Making Places: Episodes in Participation, 1964–1984* (Berkeley: University of California, 1987), 172–73.

122. "Ruth Warrick Teaches Trainees in Bootstrap's Self-Help Course," *Los Angeles Sentinel,* February 24, 1966, C8; Charles E. Brown, "Operation Bootstrap Prepares," *Jet,* December 21, 1967, pp. 16–22.

123. Barry Grier, "Whites Surpass Blacks in Purchasing 'Black Doll,'" *Los Angeles Sentinel,* May 31, 1973, p. 5.

124. Roy Innis, "Separatist Economics: A New Social Contract" (1969), in *Modern Black Nationalism: From Marcus Garvey to Louis Farrakhan,* ed. William L. Van Deburg (New York: New York University Press, 1997), 179.

125. "Freedom Bank Seeks More 'Big' Depositors," *New York Amsterdam Times,* June 18, 1966, p. 14; "For the Harlem Commonwealth Council Growing Up Means Buying Up," 62, 65, 67.

126. Black Panther Party Collections, Box 2, Folder "Watts 1960s," "Watts Labor Community Action Committee" brochure; Bauman, *Race and the War on Poverty,* 74; Eldridge Cleaver Papers, 1963–1988, Carton 27, Folder 9, Confidential FBI Internal Memorandum, June 24, 1968, p. 3.

127. Black Panther Party Collections, Box 2, Folder "Watts 1960s," "Watts Labor Community Action Committee' brochure.

128. Bauman, *Race and the War on Poverty,* 74–75.

129. Ibid., 76; Ford Foundation Papers, Box 2, Folder 1, Ford Foundation Policy Paper, *Community Development Corporations: A Strategy for Depressed Urban and Rural Areas,* 21; Marshall Lowe, "WLCAC: Changing Face of Community," *Los Angeles Sentinel,* May 20, 1971, D1.

130. Widener, *Black Arts West,* 97.

131. See, for example, "Community Calendar," *Los Angeles Sentinel,* September 21, 1967, B10.

132. "Business-Financial News," *Los Angeles Sentinel,* June 5, 1969, C7.

133. Bauman, *Race and the War on Poverty,* 80–81.

134. Bruce M. Tyler, "The Rise and Decline of the Watts Summer Festival, 1965–1986," *American Studies,* Vol. 31, No. 2 (Fall 1990), 64, 61; Bauman, *Race and the War on Poverty,* 84; Widener, *Black Arts West,* 108–9, 157.

135. Mary Crosby, "Africa Spreads Her Wings in Fashion," *Los Angeles Sentinel,* December 7, 1967, D1.

136. "Happy Birthday to Shindana," *Los Angeles Sentinel,* October 16, 1969, D1.

137. "Toy Making Profitable for Bootstrap Company," *Los Angeles Sentinel,* December 23, 1971, A3.

138. "Toys That Build Pride," *Ebony,* November 1975, p. 137; Shindana Toys Advertisement, *Ebony,* November 1975, p. 140.

139. Smith, quoted in Ellis, *People Making Places,* 174–75.

140. Fergus, "Black Power, Soft Power," 171–74.

141. Kimberley Johnson, "Community Development Corporations, Participation, and Accountability: The Harlem Urban Development Corporation and the Bedford-Stuyvesant Restoration Corporation," *Annals of the American Academy of Political and Social Science,* Vol. 594 (July 2004), 121.

142. Schmitt, *President of the Other America,* 166; "Reaching New Heights: Trends and Achievements of Community-Based Development Organizations," 5th National Community Development Census, National Congress for Community and Economic Development, p. 4, archived at community-wealth.org, http://community-wealth.org/content/reaching-new-heights-2005-ncced-census-trends-and-achievements-community-based-development.

143. Ellis, *People Making Places,* 175–78. Robert Hall died following an illness in 1973, and Lou Smith was killed in a car accident in 1976.

144. "Alice Kornegay Triangle."

145. See "Health Career Educational Scholarships," Harlem Community Council, https://www.harlemcommonwealth.org/index/program/health-career-educational-scholarships.

146. See "Harlem USA," Grid Properties, Inc., http://www.gridproperties.com/projects-harlemusa.html.

147. See "WLCAC Wins $4.9 Million Prop 84 California State Parks Award!" WLCAC (WordPress), posted April 11, 2012, http://wlcac.wordpress.com/2012/04/11/wlcac-wins-4-9-million-prop-84-california-state-parks-award/. For WLCAC's current programs see "Our Future," WLCAC, www.wlcac.org/our-future.htm.

148. Glenn F. Bunting, "'Amazing Grace' Hits Rough Waters," *Los Angeles Times,* September 5, 1990, http://articles.latimes.com/1990–09–05/local/me-462_1_amazing-grace.

149. Dowd Hall, "The Long Civil Rights Movement and the Political Uses of the Past," 1261.

150. Augustus Hawkins, "Ujima—Black Ownership," *Los Angeles Sentinel,* December 4, 1969, A6.

CHAPTER 3: BLACK POWER AND BATTLES OVER EDUCATION

1. NAACP-WRO Records, Carton 15, Folder 47, Celes King III to Robert Denahy, June 14, 1967; ibid., Memo from the Office of Principal Denahy, June 19, 1967.

2. NAACP-WRO Records, Carton 15, Folder 47, "A Chronological List of the Events in the Angela Bates Graduation Case, As Compiled by the Manual Arts Faculty Association," June 26, 1967, pp. 1–4.

3. NAACP-WRO Records, Carton 15, Folder 47, "Report on the Meeting with the Los Angeles City School Board and Representatives of the Manual Arts Faculty Association," June 26, 1967, pp. 1–2.

4. Raymond Wolters, *Race and Education, 1954–2007* (Columbia: University of Missouri Press, 2008), 3.

5. Jackson, *Crabgrass Frontier,* 289–90.

6. Sugrue, *Sweet Land of Liberty,* 468.

7. NAACP-WRO Records, Carton 15, Folder 13, Press Release, Watts Branch NAACP, June 7, 1967, p. 1.

8. Ibid., p. 450.

9. Clayborne Carson, "Two Cheers for *Brown v. Board of Education," Journal of American History,* Vol. 91, No. 1 (June 2004), 27. See also Sugrue, *Sweet Land of Liberty,* 450–92.

10. Matthew F. Delmont, *Why Busing Failed: Race, Media, and the National Resistance to School Desegregation* (Oakland: University of California Press, 2016), 6–8.

11. "Study of Negroes in Schools Hailed," *New York Times,* July 15, 1954, p. 23.

12. Clarence Taylor, "Robert Wagner, Milton Galamison, and the Challenge to New York Liberalism," *Afro-Americans in New York Life and History: An Interdisciplinary Journal,* Vol. 31, No. 2 (July 2007), http://www.nyc.gov/html/cchr/justice /downloads/pdf/robert_wagner.pdf.

13. Clarence Taylor, *Knocking at Our Own Door: Milton A. Galamison and the Struggle for School Integration in New York City Schools* (New York: Columbia University Press, 1998), 3. See also Daniel Perlstein, *Justice, Justice: School Politics and the Eclipse of Liberalism* (New York: Peter Lang, 2004), esp. 97–98.

14. Barbara Ransby, *Ella Baker and the Black Freedom Movement: A Radical Democratic Vision* (Chapel Hill: University of North Carolina Press, 2003), 149, 155.

15. Taylor, *Knocking at Our Own Door,* 142; Sugrue, *Sweet Land of Liberty,* 463.

16. Biondi, *To Stand and Fight,* 247–48; Taylor, *Knocking at Our Own Door,* 116; Cannato, *Ungovernable City,* 268–70.

17. Josh Sides, *LA City Limits: African American Los Angeles from the Great Depression to the Present* (Berkeley: University of California Press, 2004), 159, 163.

18. "Integrationists March on Board of Education," *Los Angeles Times,* August 9, 1963, p. 2.

19. Jeanne Theoharis, "W-A-L-K-O-U-T! High School Students and the Development of Black Power in L.A.," in *Neighbourhood Rebels: Black Power at the Local Level,* ed. Peniel Joseph (New York: Palgrave Macmillan, 2010), 110.

20. Sides, *LA City Limits,* 168.

21. On white officials' resistance to school desegregation in Atlanta, see Kevin Kruse, *White Flight: Atlanta and the Making of Modern Conservatism* (Princeton: Princeton University Press, 2006), 131–61; Brown-Nagin, *Courage to Dissent,* 307–409 (quote on 351).

22. "Integrationists March on Board of Education," *Los Angeles Times,* August 9, 1963, p. 2.

23. For a discussion of PAT's development and its impact on local and national civil rights politics, see Delmont, *Why Busing Failed,* 23–53; Podair, *The Strike That Changed New York,* 23–26.

24. Kruse, *White Flight,* 132.

25. Brown-Nagin, *Courage to Dissent,* 324–25; Kruse, *White Flight,* 146–52; Wolters, *Race and Education,* 113–19.

26. "Integrated School, 'Hotbed of Hate,'" *Atlanta Inquirer,* November 13, 1965, pp. 1, 5.

27. GGDP, Series J, Folder 2, Interview with Pearlie Dove, April 9, 1992, pp. 32–33.

28. Sugrue, *Sweet Land of Liberty,* 457–461, 467; Cannato, *Ungovernable City,* 268.

29. Kruse, *White Flight,* 5, 234; B. Drummond Ayers, "Atlanta Strikes Integration Bargain," *New York Times,* April 25, 1973, p. 89.

30. Mark Brilliant, *The Color of America Has Changed: How Racial Diversity Shaped Civil Rights Reform in California, 1941–1978* (New York: Oxford University Press, 2010), 220–24.

31. Stephen G. N. Tuck, *Beyond Atlanta: The Struggle for Racial Equality in Georgia, 1940–1980* (Athens: University of Georgia Press, 2001), 100.

32. GGDP, Series J, Folder 2, Interview with Pearlie Dove, April 9, 1992, p. 40.

33. Brown-Nagin, *Courage to Dissent,* 308.

34. Adam Fairclough, *A Class of Their Own: Black Teachers in the Segregated South* (Cambridge, MA: Belknap Press of Harvard University Press, 2007), 357–58.

35. Marian Wright Edelman, *Lanterns: A Memoir of Mentors* (Boston: Beacon Press, 1999). Edelman's memoirs give an account of her life and education at Spelman College, the all-female black college within the AUC, and provides fascinating insight into the institutions that make up the center.

36. GGDP, Series J, Folder 6, Interview with Alice Holmes Washington, April 15, 1993, pp. 25, 45.

37. Community Council of the Atlanta Area Records, 1960–1974 (hereafter CCAA Records), Box 10, Folder: Atlanta Community Foundation. This folder contains numerous survey reports compiled by community advocate Ella Mae Brayboy between 1965 and 1966 from a wide range of Atlanta's poor black neighborhoods. A number of the reports detail the precarious condition of local public schools at all grade levels.

38. Young, *An Easy Burden,* 196.

39. GGDP, Series J, Folder 1, Interview with Suzette Crank, April 12, 1993, 57.

40. SML Lindsay Papers, Box 91, Folder 79, "White Paper on Education, October 20, 1965," 11.

41. Cannato, *Ungovernable City,* 268–69, 275.

42. Ibid., 272, 290; Taylor, *Knocking at Our Own Door,* 185.

43. "Parents Score UFT," *New York Amsterdam News,* May 14, 1966, p. 31.

44. "Parents Fight Transfer," *New York Amsterdam News,* June 18, 1966, p. 35.

45. Diane Ravitch, *The Great School Wars: A History of the New York City Public Schools* (Baltimore: Johns Hopkins University Press, 2000), 296–98.

46. One book has been written on EHBS and its genesis. See Tom Roderick, *A School of Our Own: Parents, Power, and Community at the East Harlem Block Schools* (New York: Teachers College Press, 2001).

47. CNS Records, Reel 1, "At East Harlem Block Schools the Major Problem Is Survival," April 22, 1970.

48. Far West Laboratory for Educational Research and Development, "The East Harlem Block Schools: Program Summary," November 1971, pp. 7, 6, 5, http://www .eric.ed.gov/ERICWebPortal/detail?accno=ED125746.

49. Podair, *The Strike That Changed New York,* 77–78.

50. Taylor, *Knocking at Our Own Door,* 181–86.

51. Cannato, *Ungovernable City,* 282; Perlstein, *Justice, Justice,* 14–31.

52. Cannato, *Ungovernable City,* 298–299; Podair, *The Strike That Changed New York,* 80–81.

53. Perlstein, *Justice, Justice,* 5–6; Podair, *The Strike That Changed New York,* 64.

54. Cannato, *Ungovernable City,* 299.

55. Brown, *Fighting for US,* 77.

56. NAACP-WRO Records, Carton 15, Folder 47, "A Chronological List of the Events in the Angela Bates Graduation Case, as Compiled by the Manual Arts Faculty Association," June 26, 1967, p. 2.

57. NAACP-WRO Records, Carton 15, Folder 13, Annual Report of Jesse Scott, Field Director, November 28, 1967, pp. 9–10.

58. Brown, *Fighting for US,* 82–84; Theoharis, "W-A-L-K-O-U-T!" 111–13, 116.

59. Sugrue, *Sweet Land of Liberty,* 474.

60. Les Matthews, "Commissioners Visit Harlem and Get an Earful," *New York Amsterdam News,* March 19, 1966, p. 7; Ravitch, *The Great School Wars,* 295.

61. Adina Back, "'Parent Power': Evelina Lopez Antonetty, the United Bronx Parents, and the War on Poverty" in Orleck and Hazirjian, eds., *The War on Poverty,* 184–208 (see esp. 185–91); California Republican Assembly Records, Box 10, CRA Newsletters, 1969–1970, "CRA News," Vol. 3, No. 3 (June 1969), 9; Theoharis, "W-A-L-K-O-U-T!" 118–21.

62. "'Black Power' Moves into Harlem School Battle," *New York Amsterdam News,* September 24, 1966, p. 1.

63. CORE Papers, Series C, Part III, Reel 7, "Tell It Like It Is," *NWRO Newsletter,* Vol. 15, No. 2 (November 7, 1968).

64. CORE Papers, Series B, Part III, Reel 4, Memo from Gardinia White to Dr. Marilyn Gittel, November 13, 1968.

65. MacLean, *Freedom Is Not Enough,* 195; Councilman Tom Bradley Records, Box D84, Folder: School—Community Relations, Board of Education Folder, "Los Angeles City Schools Public Information Office: Racial and Ethnic School Survey Results," March 20, 1968, p.1, 5.

66. Councilman Tom Bradley Records, Box D84, Folder: School—Community Relations, Board of Education, Glanville A. Lockett, "Views on my meeting at Bootstrap."

67. Kenneth Hahn Collection, Schools, General, 1968–1969, Box 273, Folder 2b, Kenneth Hahn to Chancellor Charles Young, November 26, 1968.

68. Yvonne Braithwaite Burke Papers, LP 68:24, Assemblyman Victor Vesey Press Statement, n.d., p. 2.

69. See Russell Rickford, *We Are an African People: Independent Schools, Black Power, and the Radical Imagination* (New York: Oxford University Press, 2016).

70. Rojas, *From Black Power to Black Studies,* 22.

71. Maulana Karenga, "Black Studies: A Critical Reassessment," in *Dispatches from the Ebony Tower: Intellectuals Confront the African American Experience,* ed. Manning Marable (New York: Columbia University Press, 2001), 163–64.

72. CNS Records, Reel 1, "Racial Composition Emerges as Key Issue on Experimental District 19," April 17, 1970.

73. Stanley G. Robertson, "Two Sides of a Perplexing Coin," *Los Angeles Sentinel,* June 8, 1968, A7.

74. Peter Novick, *That Noble Dream: The "Objectivity Question" and the American Historical Profession* (New York: Cambridge University Press, 1988), 474–77; Councilman Tom Bradley Records, Box D84, Folder: School—Community Relations, Board of Education, Glanville A. Lockett, "Views on my meeting at Bootstrap."

75. Podair, *The Strike That Changed New York,* 153, 155.

76. Les Campbell Interview, November 3, 1988, Eyes on the Prize II Interviews, Washington University Digital Gateway Texts, http://digital.wustl.edu/e/eii/eiiweb/cam5427.0642.028marc_record_interviewee_process.html.

77. *Great Speckled Bird,* Vol. 1, No. 14 (September 13–19, 1968), 9.

78. Councilman Tom Bradley Records, Box D84, Folder: School—Community Relations, Board of Education, Jack Crowther, "Perspective and Direction: Address to Los Angeles School Board," January 25, 1968, pp. 11–12.

79. NAACP-WRO Records, Carton 57, Folder 71, "Emergency Closing of School," Memorandum from Jack Crowther to Los Angeles Board of Education, March 14, 1968; Theoharis, "W-A-L-K-O-U-T!" 118–21.

80. Yvonne Braithwaite Burke Papers, LP 68:24, Augustus Hawkins to Ronald Reagan, March 10, 1969.

81. NAACP-WRO Records, Carton 46, Folder 9, "Presentation of Senate Committee on Education" July 21, 1970, p. 2.

82. Sam Yorty Papers, Box D-0011, Folder: Assembly Bills, 1970, Mayor's Office Press Release, June 18, 1970, p. 1.

83. NAACP-WRO Records, Carton 14, Folder 32, Edward Robinson to Leonard Carter, February 15, 1973.

84. Podair, *The Strike That Changed New York,* 1–8; Martin Mayer, "Frustration Is the Word for Ocean Hill," *New York Times,* May 19, 1968, SM28.

85. Sugrue, *Sweet Land of Liberty,* 476.

86. Cannato, *Ungovernable City,* 348; Podair, *The Strike That Changed New York,* 152.

87. Lesly Jones, "IS Schools Making It; McCoy 'Reads' Execs," *New York Amsterdam News,* March 21, 1970, p. 23.

88. CNS Records, Reel 1, "Community Reactions Mixed on School Board Elections," January 21, 1970.

89. Perlstein, *Justice, Justice,* 5, 2.

90. Cannato, *Ungovernable City,* 299.

91. "School Decentralization Plan Probed," *Los Angeles Sentinel,* January 23, 1969, B1.

92. "Blacks Back Bill for Local School Control," *Los Angeles Times,* April 9, 1970, C2.

93. William J. Johnston, "Integration and Decentralization in Los Angeles," *Equity and Excellence in Education,* Vol. 9, No. 6 (1971), 12.

94. Theoharis, "W-A-L-K-O-U-T!" 111.

95. "Want Autonomous School system," *New York Amsterdam News,* January 25, 1969, p. 1.

96. Sara Slack, "Angered People Vow to Keep Teachers Out of School," *New York Amsterdam News,* October 5, 1968, p. 1.

97. For a discussion of the pedagogical techniques used in the Ocean Hill–Brownsville experimental district, see Rickford, *We Are an African People,* 50–56.

98. CNS Records, Reel 1, "Racial Composition Emerges as Key Issue on Experimental District 19," April 17, 1970; Les Campbell Interview, November 3, 1988, Eyes on the Prize II Interview; Sugrue, *Sweet Land of Liberty,* 474.

99. "New School System in City Is Supported," *New York Times,* May 14, 1968, p. 44.

100. Thomas A. Johnson, "NAACP Scores 'Hostile' Nixon Acts," *New York Times,* July 6, 1969, p. 32.

101. Taylor, *Knocking at Our Own Door,* 176–80.

102. "'Black Power' Moves into Harlem School Battle," *New York Amsterdam News,* September 24, 1966, p. 1.

103. Taylor, *Knocking at Our Own Door,* 186.

104. Quoted in Sara Slack, "School Hearings: Bronx Wins; Manhattan, Brooklyn Lose??" *New York Amsterdam News,* December 13, 1969, p. 1.

105. CNS Records, Reel 1, "East Harlem Puerto Ricans Seek Separate School District," October 17, 1969.

106. See Theoharis, "W-A-L-K-O-U-T!" 110–31.

107. Richie Perez, "H.S. Revolt!" *Palante,* Vol. 2, No. 13 (October 16, 1970), reprinted in *The Young Lords: A Reader,* ed. Darrel Enck-Wanzer et al. (New York: New York University Press, 2010), 127.

108. "The Brown Berets: Young Chicago Revolutionaries" (Carlos Montes, interview with Fight Back!), n.d., US History Documents, San Francisco University High School, http://inside.sfuhs.org/dept/history/US_History_reader/Chapter14/brownberets.htm.

109. Ogbar, *Black Power,* 159.

110. Laura Pulido, *Black, Brown, Yellow, and Left: Radical Activism in Los Angeles* (Berkeley: University of California Press, 2006), 6.

111. See Joshua M. Zeitz, *White Ethnic New York: Jews, Catholics, and the Shaping of Postwar Politics* (Chapel Hill: University of North Carolina Press, 2007).

112. Jerald Podair, "The Ocean Hill–Brownsville Crisis: New York's *Antigone*" (conference paper presented at the Conference on New York City History, City University of New York, New York, October 6, 2001), 2–3, archived at https://www.researchgate.net/publication/237650298_The_Ocean_Hill-Brownsville_Crisis_New_York%27s_Antigone.

113. Podair, *The Strike That Changed New York,* 184.

114. Brilliant, *The Color of America Has Changed,* 228, 231, 236.

115. Priscilla Wohlstetter and Karen McCurdy, "The Link between School Decentralization and School Politics," *Urban Education,* Vol. 25, No. 4 (January 1991), 408–11.

116. Alton Hornsby, *Black Power in Dixie: A Political History of African Americans in Atlanta* (Gainesville: University Press of Florida, 2009), 128–29; Tuck, *Beyond Atlanta,* 212.

117. "Community Must Control Schools, Says Forum Speaker," *Atlanta Voice,* February 22, 1970, p. 22.

118. Grady-Willis, *Challenging U.S. Apartheid,* xiii, 12–13; Hornsby, *Black Power in Dixie,* 119, 124.

119. Brown-Nagin, *Courage to Dissent,* 348.

120. "Tate Sees Problem," *Atlanta Voice,* May 11, 1969, p. 3.

121. Benjamin Mays, "Black Students—Helping? Hurting," *Atlanta Voice,* May 25, 1969, p. 5.

122. Brown-Nagin, *Courage to Dissent,* 363, 368.

123. Ibid., 382–83; Paul Delaney, "The Choice: Integration or Power; Black Pragmatism," *New York Times,* July 15, 1973, p. 17.

124. Southern Regional Council Collection, 1944–1977, Box 14, "Busing Problem Is U.S. Contradiction," *Atlanta Voice,* October 9, 1971, p. 2.

125. The following discussion of Emmaus House is based primarily on an oral history project run by Kennesaw State University titled "The Peoplestown Project." All the interviews referred to here were conducted by Dr. LeeAnn Lands and can be found online at http://thepeoplestownproject.com/oral-histories/.

126. Grady-Willis, *Challenging U.S. Apartheid,* 136–37.

127. Dennis Goldstein, interview, July 31, 2009, http://thepeoplestownproject.com/2011/dennis-goldstein/. A detailed collection of official correspondence, news clippings, and tenants' rights organizational material can be found in CCAA Records, Boxes 12–16.

128. Brown-Nagin, *Courage to Dissent,* 360–62. For an in-depth discussion of white resistance to school desegregation in Atlanta, see Kruse, *White Flight,* 131–79.

129. Tom Erdmanczyk, interview, August 31, 2009, http://thepeoplestownproject.com/2011/emmaus-house-oral-history/.

130. Father Austin Ford, interview, March 6, 2009, http://thepeoplestownproject.com/2011/austin-ford/.

131. David Morath, interview, August 10, 2009, http://thepeoplestownproject.com/2011/david-morath/.

132. Dennis Goldstein, interview, July 31, 2009.

133. Rhonda Y. Williams, *The Politics of Public Housing: Black Women's Struggles against Urban Inequality* (New York: Oxford University Press, 2004), 191.

134. David Morath, interview, August 10, 2009.

135. Margret Griggs, interview, August 31, 2009, http://thepeoplestownproject.com/2011/margaret-griggs/.

136. For example, the January 28, 1971, issue discusses tenants' rights, free school lunch programs, changes to prison visiting procedures, income tax return filing advice, Medicaid, Legal Aid representation changes, and housing code enforcement. For the PPN repository, see Muriel Lokey Papers, MSS 967; and Dennis Goldstein, interview, July 31, 2009.

137. Grady-Willis, *Challenging U.S. Apartheid,* 138; "Mrs. Matthews Sues to Enter Council Race," *Atlanta Daily World,* May 3, 1973, p. 1; Margret Griggs, interview, August 31, 2009.

138. Grady-Willis, *Challenging U.S. Apartheid,* 177–78, 210; Silvia Griggs Britt, interview, August 16, 2009, http://thepeoplestownproject.com/2011/silva-griggs-britt/.

139. Sister Marie Bodell, interview, July 23, 2009, http://thepeoplestownproject.com/2011/mimi-sister-marie-bodell-2/.

140. Two broadly analogous examples of Black Power–Catholic co-organizing can be found in scholarship on Milwaukee and Louisville. See Patrick Jones, "'Not a Color but an Attitude': Father James Groppi and Black Power Politics in Milwaukee," in *Groundwork: Local Black Freedom Movements in America,* ed. Jeanne Theoharis and Komozi Woodard (New York: New York University, 2005), 259–81; Tracy K'Meyer, *Civil Rights in the Gateway South: Louisville, Kentucky, 1945–80* (Lexington: University of Kentucky Press, 2009).

141. Patrick Allitt, "American Catholics and the New Conservatism of the 1950s," *U.S. Catholic Historian,* Vol. 7, No. 1 (Winter 1988), 15–37; Lisa McGirr, *Suburban Warriors: the Origins of the New American Right* (Princeton: Princeton University Press, 2001), 18, 107.

142. See, for example, Alan B. Anderson, *Confronting the Color Line: The Broken Promise of the Civil Rights Movement in Chicago* (Athens: University of Georgia Press, 1986); Thomas J. Sugrue, *The Origins of the Urban Crisis: Race and Inequality in Postwar Detroit* (Princeton: Princeton University Press, 1996); Jonathan Rieder, *Canarsie: The Jews and Italians of Brooklyn against Liberalism* (Cambridge, MA: Harvard University Press, 1985).

143. Brown-Nagin, *Courage to Dissent,* 364; David Morath, interview, August 10, 2009.

144. Marcia Cross-Briscoe, "Atlanta Metro School Suit: A Search for Equality," *Southern Changes,* Vol. 1, No. 2 (1978), 11–12, archived at http://beck.library.emory.edu/southernchanges/article.php?id=sc01-2_005.

145. Brown-Nagin, *Courage to Dissent,* 373.

146. Ibid., 373–74, 382. For a detailed discussion of how King gained control of the case, see 376–82.

147. Boone quoted in B. Drummond Ayers, "Atlanta Strikes Integration Bargain," *New York Times,* April 25, 1973, p. 89.

148. Ibid.; David Morath, interview August 10, 2009.

149. Paul Delaney, "Atlanta NAACP Faces Expulsion," *New York Times,* July 9, 1973, p. 69; Paul Delaney, "Spread of Atlanta School Plan Reported by NAACP Aide," *New York Times,* July 22, 1973, p. 19; Brown-Nagin, *Courage to Dissent,* 399–400. For a detailed discussion of the hearing, see ibid., 395–400.

150. Sugrue, *Sweet Land of Liberty,* 486–87; Brown-Nagin, *Courage to Dissent,* 425–26. For a detailed discussion of the *Armour v. Nix* proceedings, see ibid., 409–29.

151. Theoharis, "W-A-L-K-O-U-T!" 123.

152. King quoted in B. Drummond Ayers, "Atlanta Strikes Integration Bargain," *New York Times,* April 25, 1973, p. 89.

153. Brown-Nagin, *Courage to Dissent,* 358.

CHAPTER 4: BLACK MAYORS AND BLACK PROGRESS

1. Sam Massell Jr. Papers, Box 27, Folder 26, "Fear to Eternity: Remarks at Emory University," September 25, 1972, p. 4.

2. Ibid., 6.

3. WSB-TV news film clip of African Americans reacting to a speech by Mayor Sam Massell, Atlanta, Georgia, October 6, 1971, Civil Rights Digital Library, http://crdl.usg.edu/cgi/crdl?action=retrieve;rset=002;recno=5;format=_video; WSB-TV news film clip of African Americans reacting negatively to Mayor Sam Massell's speech on politics and government, Atlanta, Georgia, October 6, 1971, Civil Rights Digital Library. http://crdl.usg.edu/cgi/crdl?format=_video&query=id%3Augabma_wsbn_64296&_cc=1.

4. While both historians and political scientists have looked at the mayoralties of both Bradley and Jackson, there is not an overabundance of studies on either. The only major study that looks specifically at Bradley's tenure is Raphael Sonenshein, *Politics in Black and White: Race and Power in Los Angeles* (Princeton: Princeton University Press, 1993). No such study yet exists for Maynard Jackson. However, a number of scholars have written about Los Angeles and Atlanta, covering Bradley and Jackson's mayoralties in the process. This scholarship—which this chapter builds upon—includes Sides, *LA City Limits;* Heather Parker, "Tom Bradley and the Politics of Race," in *African-American Mayors: Race, Politics, and the American*

City, ed. Jeffrey Adler and David Coburn (Urbana: University of Illinois Press, 2001), 153–77; Ronald Bayor, *Race and the Shaping of Twentieth Century Atlanta* (Chapel Hill: University of North Carolina Press, 1996); Hornsby, *Black Power in Dixie;* J. Phillip Thompson III, *Double Trouble: Black Mayors, Black Communities, and the Call for Deep Democracy* (New York: Oxford University Press, 2006); Clarence Stone, "Partnership New South Style: Central Atlanta Progress," *Proceedings of the Academy of Political Science,* Vol. 36, No. 2 (1986), 100–110; Mack Jones, "Black Political Empowerment in Atlanta: Myth and Reality," *Annals of the American Academy of Political and Social Science,* Vol. 439 (September 1978), 90–117.

5. See Leonard N. Moore, *Carl B. Stokes and the Rise of Black Political Power* (Urbana: University of Illinois Press, 2002); James B. Lane, "Black Political Power and Its Limits: Gary Mayor Richard G. Hatcher's Administration, 1968–1987," in *African-American Mayors: Race, Politics, and the American City,* ed. Jeffrey Adler and David Colburn (Urbana: University of Illinois Press, 2001), 57–79; Woodard, *A Nation within a Nation.*

6. See, for example, Thompson, *Double Trouble;* Adolph Reed Jr., *Stirrings in the Jug: Black Politics in the Post-segregation Era* (Minneapolis: University of Minnesota Press, 1999); Michael C. Dawson, *Not in Our Lifetimes: The Future of Black Politics* (Chicago: University of Chicago Press, 2011), 63–135; Robert C. Smith, *We Have No Leaders: African Americans in the Post–Civil Rights Era* (Albany: State University of New York Press, 1996). For discussion of Harold Washington and Coleman Young, see Manning Marable, *Black Leadership* (New York: Columbia University Press, 1998), 127–46; Heather Ann Thompson, "Rethinking the Collapse of Postwar Liberalism: The Rise of Mayor Coleman Young and the Politics of Race in Detroit," in *African-American Mayors: Race, Politics, and the American City,* ed. David Colburn and Jeffery Adler (Urbana: University of Illinois Press, 2001), 223–48.

7. Thompson, *Double Trouble,* 14.

8. Twenty-First Century Foundation Papers, Box 8, Folder 3, Bernard Porche to Robert Browne, November 7, 1974; Jeffrey Adler, "Introduction," in *African-American Mayors: Race, Politics, and the American City,* ed. Jeffrey Adler and David Colburn (Urbana: University of Illinois Press, 2001), 1; Marable, *Race, Reform, and Rebellion,* 134; Randall Harber, "Black Mayors Report New Shift in Movement," *Los Angeles Sentinel,* November 21, 1974, A8.

9. Jack Rosenthal, "One-Third of Blacks Found in Fifteen Cities," *New York Times,* May 19, 1971.

10. Richard L. Stevens Papers, 1964–1969, Box 4, Folder 6, Charles E. Silberman, "'Beware the Day They Change Their Minds!'" *Fortune* (November 1965), 154; Marable, *Race, Reform, and Rebellion,* 134.

11. Charles V. Hamilton, *The Bench and the Ballot: Southern Federal Judges and Black Voters* (New York: Oxford University Press, 1973), vii.

12. Kotlowski, *Nixon's Civil Rights,* 87–94.

13. Manfred Berg, *The Ticket to Freedom: The NAACP and the Struggle for Black Political Integration* (Gainesville: University Press of Florida, 2005), 181–85.

14. For detailed discussion of the MFDP challenge, see, for example, John Dittmer, *Local People: The Struggle for Civil Rights in Mississippi* (Urbana: University of Illinois Press, 1994), pp. 273–302; and James Forman, *The Making of Black Revolutionaries* (Seattle: University of Washington Press, 1995), 386–400.

15. Hasan Kwame Jefferies, *Bloody Lowndes: Civil Rights and Black Power in Alabama's Black Belt* (New York: New York University Press, 2009), 5; for discussion of LCFO and Black Power, see ibid., 143–206. In describing his and his fellow SNCC activists' evolution toward Black Power, Cleveland Sellers has described the importance they attributed to the defeat of the MFDP challenge. The whole episode at Atlantic City, he asserted, "was to the civil rights movement what the civil war was to American history: afterward, things would never be the same." Cleveland Sellars and Robert Terrell, *The River of No Return: The Autobiography of a Black Militant and the Life and Death of SNCC* (Jackson; University Press of Mississippi, 1990), 111.

16. Student Nonviolent Coordinating Committee Papers (hereafter cited as SNCC Papers), A:VIII:170, "Black Power Impact," *Wall Street Journal,* July 22, 1966.

17. Lerone Bennett Jr., "Stokely Carmichael: Architect of Black Power," *Ebony* (September 1966), 26–27.

18. Johnson, *Revolutionaries to Race Leaders,* xx.

19. See, for example, Moore, *Carl B. Stokes and the Rise of Black Political Power;* Woodard, *A Nation within a Nation;* Countryman, *Up South;* William H. Chafe, *Civilities and Civil Rights: Greensboro, North Carolina, and the Black Struggle for Freedom* (New York: Oxford University Press, 1980); Self, *American Babylon.*

20. On Dinkins's political career and his administration, see Thompson, *Double Trouble,* 155–263; Roger Biles, "Mayor David Dinkins and the Politics of Race in New York City," in *African American Mayors: Race, Politics, and the American City,* ed. Jeffrey Adler and David Coburn (Urbana: University of Illinois Press, 2001), 130–52.

21. For a discussion of Amiri Baraka's place as one of the leading African American thinkers of the 1960s and 1970s, see Daniel Matlin, *On the Corner: African American Intellectuals and the Urban Crisis* (Cambridge, MA: Harvard University Press, 2013).

22. Woodard, "Amiri Baraka, the Congress of African People, and Black Power Politics from the 1961 United Nations Protest to the 1972 Gary Convention," in *The Black Power Movement: Rethinking the Civil Rights–Black Power Era,* ed. Peniel Joseph (London: Routledge, 2006), 72–74. Also see Woodard, *A Nation within a Nation.*

23. Huey P. Newton Foundation Records, Series 2, Box 53, Folder 5, Amiri Baraka to Huey Newton, May 20, 1971, p. 1.

24. Marable, *Race, Reform, and Rebellion,* 136.

25. Shirley Chisholm, *The Good Fight* (New York: Harper & Row, 1973), 24–36. Brooklyn congresswoman Shirley Chisholm, a member of the CBC and attendee at

the Northlake meeting, explains the evolution of this black political organizing—as well as its patriarchal and misogynist overtones.

26. Marable, *Race, Reform, and Rebellion,* 137; Peniel E. Joseph, *Dark Days, Bright Nights: From Black Power to Barack Obama* (New York: BasicCivitas Books, 2010), 173.

27. Andrew J. Young Papers, Series 2, Subseries B, Box 4, Folder: National Black Political Convention, 1972, "National Black Political Agenda," May 1972, pp. 4, 7, 8, 35–38.

28. NAACP-WRO Records, Carton 9, Folder 6, Roy Wilkins, "Monthly Summary Reports" (April 24, 1972), 1–2.

29. Andrew J. Young Papers, Series 2, Subseries B, Box 4, Folder: National Black Political Convention, 1972, "National Black Political Agenda," May 1972, pp. 10, 13–15, 19–21.

30. Ibid., 12, 34.

31. Joseph, *Dark Days, Bright Nights,* 174.

32. SNCC Papers, A:I:73, H. Rap Brown Speech, February 18, 1968.

33. Andrew J. Young Papers, Series 2, Subseries B, Box 4, Folder: Congressional Black Caucus, 1971–76, "The Congressional Black Caucus: Special Issue," *Focus* (Joint Center for Political Studies), Vol. 5, No. 8 (August–September 1977), 6–8; Paul Delaney, "House Caucus Lists 'Black Bill of Rights,'" *New York Times,* June 2, 1972, p. 22; Marable, *Race, Reform, and Rebellion,* 150. For the CBC, strongly worded anti-busing resolutions caused controversy, first, because they appeared to abandon Democratic liberals' nominal commitment to school integration (many liberals in fact avoided the question of busing because of its unpopularity among whites). Second, support for Palestinian self-determination and criticism of Israel threatened to alienate Jewish American groups that had long supported the civil rights movement, and the Democratic Party more broadly. Many of the Black Power radicals who had predominated at the convention not only sympathized with the plight of the Palestinians but also chafed at Israel's economic links with the apartheid regime in South Africa. The CBC's highly public endorsement of Israel following the Gary Convention, therefore, did much to sour relations between the black radicals and elected officials involved with the national black political movement. Marable, *Race, Reform, and Rebellion,* 150.

34. Sonenshein, *Politics in Black and White,* 59–60.

35. Tom Bradley Papers, Box 1434, Folder 2, Tom Bradley Campaign Speakers Manual, July 1969, p. 7; ibid., Box 1434, Folder 3, Position Papers, 1969, Tom Bradley Statement, March 5, 1969.

36. State Government Oral History Program: Mervyn Dymally Interview, Vol 1 (1996–97), 221; Parker, "Tom Bradley and the Politics of Race," 159.

37. Tom Bradley Papers, Box 1434, Folder 2, Tom Bradley Campaign Speakers Manual, July 1969, p. 21.

38. On the BPP's development in Oakland, see Donna Murch, *Living for the City: Migration, Education, and the Rise of the Black Panther Party in Oakland, California* (Chapel Hill: University of North Carolina Press, 2010); Self, *American Babylon,* 217–56.

39. U.S. Senate, *Supplementary Detailed Staff Reports on Intelligence Activities and the Rights of Americans, Book III: Final Report of the Senate Select Committee to Study Governmental Operations with Respect to Intelligence Activities* (Washington, DC: U.S. Government Printing Office, 1976), 20.

40. Ibid., 187–88.

41. Ibid., 188–91. For a detailed discussion of the feud between the BPP and US, see Brown, *Fighting for US,* 107–30.

42. David Hilliard and Lewis Cole, *This Side of Glory: The Autobiography of David Hilliard and the Story of the Black Panther Party* (Chicago: Lawrence Hill Books, 2001), 271; Black Panther Party Collections, Box 1, Folder 13, Leaflet by Committee to Defend the Panthers: "Support the Panthers" (n.d.).

43. Parker, "Tom Bradley and the Politics of Race," 158.

44. Sam Yorty Papers, Box C-2080, Folder: Mayor's Letters 1969, John Chamberlain, "These Days," *Kings Features Syndicate,* June 13, 1969, pp. 1–2; Kenneth Reich, "Yorty Confines Response to 2 Subjects at News Conference," *Los Angeles Times,* May 22, 1969, p. 1.

45. Tom Bradley Papers, Box 1685, Folder 3, Tom Bradley Speech, May 16, 1969.

46. NAACP-WRO Records, Carton 10, Folder 41, Richard Bergholz, "White Voters Made the Difference: Precinct Tallies Show How Bradley Lost," pp. 1–4.

47. Sam Yorty Papers, Box C-2080, Folder: Mayor's Letters 1969, Mayor Yorty to Ralph Bunche, June 4, 1969.

48. Richard Bergholz, "Yorty Declares Foe as 'Radical Left Winger,'" *Los Angeles Times,* May 24, 1973, D1.

49. "Bradley Denounces Newton's Backing as Campaign Trick," *Los Angeles Times,* May 21, 1973, p. 3.

50. Richard Bergholz, "Newton's Support of Bradley Is Warranted, Yorty Declares," *Los Angeles Times,* May 22, 1973, p. 3.

51. See Sonenshein, *Politics in Black and White,* 101–13.

52. See Murch, *Living for the City,* esp. 191–228; Self, *American Babylon,* 298–316.

53. Tom Bradley Papers, Box 1434, Folder 2, Tom Bradley Campaign Speakers Manual, July 1969, p. 17.

54. Ibid., Box 1434, Folder 3, Tom Bradley to Claudia Room, April 22, 1969.

55. Parker, "Tom Bradley and the Politics of Race," 160.

56. Hornsby, *Black Power in Dixie,* 125, 128.

57. Ibid., 130–31; Grady-Willis, *Challenging U.S. Apartheid,* 170–71.

58. Jones, "Black Political Empowerment in Atlanta," 115.

59. Urban League of Northeastern New York Papers, Series 3, Box 1, Maynard Jackson Speech, National Urban League Conference, July 22, 1970, p. 5.

60. Hornsby, *Black Power in Dixie,* 139–43; Grady-Willis, *Challenging U.S. Apartheid,* 187, 189.

61. California Republican Assembly Records, Box 10, CRA Newsletters, 1969–1970, "CRA News," Vol. 4, No. 3 (May 1970), 3, 11.

62. While race was a critical factor in the realignment of American democracy during the late 1960s and 1970s—especially in the South—it was not the only factor.

See Byron E. Schafer and Richard Johnson, *The End of Southern Exceptionalism: Class, Race, and Partisan Change in the Postwar South* (Cambridge, MA: Harvard University Press, 2006).

63. See Davies, *From Opportunity to Entitlement,* 4.

64. ACU member and Republican senator John Williams quoted in Howard Samuels Gubernatorial Papers, Box 3, Miscellaneous—Political, American Conservative Union Mailing n.d., pp. 1–2.

65. This argument was first set forth in Joan Hoff, *Nixon Reconsidered* (New York: Basic Books, 1994).

66. Bruce Schulman, *The Seventies: The Great Shift in American Culture, Society, and Politics* (Cambridge, MA: Da Capo Press, 2001), 34.

67. Kornbluh, "'Who Shot FAP?'" 127. For an in-depth discussion of the congressional debate over FAP, with special focus on the role played by liberals in its defeat, see Dominic Sandbrook, *Eugene McCarthy: The Rise and Fall of Postwar American Liberalism* (New York: Alfred A. Knopf, 2004), 233–38.

68. George McGovern: "Address Accepting the Presidential Nomination at the Democratic National Convention in Miami Beach, Florida," July 14, 1972, archived by Gerhard Peters and John T. Woolley, *The American Presidency Project,* http://www.presidency.ucsb.edu/ws/?pid=25967; NWHM Part 2, 72-8-13, Charles Colson, Memorandum for the President's File, August 14, 1972, p. 1; Election of 1972, in Peters and Woolley, *The American Presidency Project,* http://www.presidency.ucsb.edu/showelection.php?year=1972.

69. Jones, "Black Political Empowerment in Atlanta," 102.

70. "Mayor in Gutter," *Baltimore Afro-American,* October 16–20, 1973, p. 5.

71. Maynard Jackson Interview, Eyes on the Prize II, October 24, 1988, Washington University Digital Gateway Texts, http://digital.wustl.edu/e/eii/eiiweb/jac5427.0710.075maynardjackson.html.

72. Ronald Bayor, "African American Mayors and Governance in Atlanta," in *African-American Mayors: Race, Politics, and the American City,* ed. David Colburn and Jeffery Adler (Urbana: University of Illinois Press, 2001), 180.

73. Thompson, "Rethinking the Collapse of Postwar Liberalism," 224–25.

74. Booker Griffin, "Bradley's Victory Ends Plantation Years," *Los Angeles Sentinel,* June 7, 1973, A7. The remaining four parts of Griffin's election analysis special report appeared in the *Los Angeles Sentinel* editions dated June 14 and 19 and July 12 and 19, 1973.

75. Maynard Jackson Interview, Eyes on the Prize II, October 24, 1988.

76. Godfrey Hodgson, *The World Turned Right Side Up: A History of the Conservative Ascendancy in America* (New York: Houghton Mifflin, 1996), 188–90.

77. Sides, *LA City Limits,* 180–81.

78. AFL-CIO Civil Rights Department, Southern Office Papers, 1964–1979, Series II, Subseries B, Box 1596, Folder 67, Davey Gibson to Al Kehrer, February 4, 1976, p. 1; Sides, *LA City Limits,* 184.

79. Urban League of Northeastern New York Papers, Series 3, Box 1, National Urban League 1975 Annual Conference Materials, p. 4; ibid., Vernon Jordan Speech, National Urban League Conference, July 27, 1975, p. 6.

80. Urban League of Northeastern New York Papers, Series 3, Box 1, Vernon Jordan Speech, National Urban League Conference, July 27, 1975, pp. 2, 8–10; Sean Wilentz, *The Age of Reagan: A History, 1974–2008* (New York: HarperCollins, 2008), 35–41, 78–85.

81. Thompson, *Double Trouble,* 11, 14.

82. David Harvey, *A Brief History of Neoliberalism* (New York: Oxford University Press, 2005), 45–48, 3.

83. Thompson, *Double Trouble,* 40–41.

84. Tom Bradley Papers, Box 597, Folder 1, "Tom Bradley First Term Record," January 19, 1977, p. 2.

85. Ibid., 5; The Impossible Dream: Tom Bradley (Oral History), April 13, 1979, pp. 274–75, 270–71; Parker, "Tom Bradley and the Politics of Race," 160, 164.

86. Sonenshein, *Politics in Black and White,* 163.

87. Tom Bradley Papers, Box 597, Folder 1, "Issue Paper on Economic Development" (1977), 1.

88. Thompson, *Double Trouble,* 17.

89. Sides, *LA City Limits,* 194. As Sides notes, although Bradley did succeed in getting the LAPD to stop using its controversial "choke hold" on suspects, the number of shootings that occurred barely changed at all over the course of his administration. On Bradley's pro-business policies and approach, see Sonenshein, *Politics in Black and White,* esp. 163–75.

90. California Democratic Council Records, Box 20, Folder 1, State of California, "California Voter's Pamphlet: Primary Election," June 6, 1978, pp. 56–58; Sides, *LA City Limits,* 195; Marable, *Race, Reform, and Rebellion,* 193.

91. Stone, "Partnership New South Style," 101–2, 105.

92. Harold Andrews, "Tax Proposal Challenges Well-to-Do Atlantans," *Atlanta Voice,* December 21, 1974, p. 1.

93. Bayor, "African American Mayors and Governance in Atlanta," 182.

94. Jones, "Black Political Empowerment in Atlanta," 109, 116.

95. Huey P. Newton Foundation Records, Series 2, Box 57, Folder 7, Georgia State Black Panther Party Press Release, May 2, 1973, p. 1. For a detailed discussion of the Inman sacking, see Hornsby, *Black Power in Dixie,* 143–47.

96. Stone, "Partnership New South Style," 102–3.

97. Maynard Jackson Interview, Eyes on the Prize II, October 24, 1988.

98. Bayor, "African American Mayors and Governance in Atlanta," 185.

99. Jones, "Black Political Empowerment in Atlanta," 110, 113, 111.

100. Maynard Jackson Interview, Eyes on the Prize II, October 24, 1988.

101. Thompson, *Double Trouble,* 41.

102. Bayor, "African American Mayors and Governance in Atlanta," 185–86; Maynard Jackson Interview, Eyes on the Prize II, October 24, 1988.

103. Voices of Labor Oral History Project, Dorothy Bolden Interview, August 31, 1995, p. 39.

104. Parker, "Tom Bradley and the Politics of Race," 168–70; Jones, "Black Political Empowerment in Atlanta," 115.

105. Marable, *Race, Reform, and Rebellion,* 134–35.

106. For the most recent in-depth analysis of affirmative action's roots, see Antony Chen, *The Fifth Freedom: Jobs, Politics, and Civil Rights in the United States* (Princeton: Princeton University Press, 2009). On the development of affirmative action under the Kennedy and Johnson administrations, see Terry H. Anderson, *The Pursuit of Fairness: A History of Affirmative Action* (New York: Oxford University Press, 2004), 49–108.

107. MacLean, *Freedom Is Not Enough,* 105–8. For a discussion of Latinos' and women's responses to affirmative action legislation, see ibid., 117–84. For an exploration of how affirmative action inspired minority rights activism, see John David Skrentny, *The Minority Rights Revolution* (Cambridge, MA: Harvard University Press, 2002).

108. Kotlowski, *Nixon's Civil Rights,* 97; Anderson, *The Pursuit of Fairness,* 117, 94. As Anderson explains, while the principle of proportional representation was loosely accepted by the Nixon administration in its endorsement of goals and timetables, it had been rejected by the Johnson administration on the basis that the generally lower levels of educational attainment among African Americans would likely ensure that qualifications would be trumped by racial preference in hiring.

109. Kotlowski, *Nixon's Civil Rights,* 9, 97–155; Fergus, *Black Power, Soft Power,* 153–62.

110. See Anderson, *The Pursuit of Fairness,* 161–216; MacLean, *Freedom Is Not Enough,* 207–11. The philosophical debate over the merits of affirmative action that unfolded at the time is well captured in Steven M. Cahn, ed., *The Affirmative Action Debate* (New York: Routledge, 1995).

111. Anderson, *The Pursuit of Fairness,* 134–36; Bayor, "African American Mayors and Governance in Atlanta," 182.

112. Tom Bradley Papers, Box 4727, Folder 16, Press Release, November 25, 1971.

113. The Impossible Dream: Tom Bradley (Oral History), April 13, 1979, pp. 261, 265; Parker, "Tom Bradley and the Politics of Race," 161–63.

114. Bayor, "African American Mayors and Governance in Atlanta," 181.

115. The Impossible Dream: Tom Bradley (Oral History), April 13, 1979, pp. 263–64.

116. Maynard Jackson Interview, Eyes on the Prize II, October 24, 1988.

117. Thomas D. Boston, *Affirmative Action and Black Entrepreneurship* (New York: Routledge, 1999), 11; Kotlowski, *Nixon's Civil Rights,* 141, 144–45.

118. "Black Business: The Need for a Giant Step," *Los Angeles Sentinel,* July 12, 1973, A9.

119. Tom Bradley Papers, Box 597, Folder 1, "Tom Bradley First Term Record," January 19, 1977, p. 6.

120. Maynard Jackson Interview, Eyes on the Prize II, October 24, 1988; Boston, *Affirmative Action and Black Entrepreneurship,* 13.

121. Boston, *Affirmative Action and Black Entrepreneurship*, 12–14. For an in-depth discussion of the airport project, see Hornsby, *Black Power in Dixie*, 159–63.

122. Boston, *Affirmative Action and Black Entrepreneurship*, 12–14, 11; Marable, *Race, Reform, and Rebellion*, 183–86.

123. Twentieth Century Organizational Files, 1912–1980, Box 7, Folder 22, Mervyn Dymally, "The Face of Justice in California," June 25, 1971, pp. 1–2.

124. Sides, *LA City Limits*, 202–3, 201. For discussion of the 1992 LA riots, see, for example, Lynell George, *No Crystal Stair: African Americans in the City of Angels* (New York: Anchor Books, 1994); Mark Baldassare, ed., *The Los Angeles Riots: Lessons for the Urban Future* (Boulder, CO: Westview Press, 1994).

125. Parker, "Tom Bradley and the Politics of Race," 164–70; Thompson, *Double Trouble*, 47.

126. Thompson, *Double Trouble*, pp. 59–61; Bayor, "African American Mayors and Governance in Atlanta," 188–96; Reed, *Stirrings in the Jug*, 117–62.

127. Grady-Willis, *Challenging U.S. Apartheid*, 210, 206–7.

128. "Atlanta Contractors Host 'Thank You' Banquet for Ex-mayor Jackson," *Jet*, November 25, 1985, p. 27.

129. Emma Darnell Interview, Eyes on the Prize II, October 27, 1988, http://digital.wustl.edu/e/eii/eiiweb/dar5427.0325.035marc_record_interviewee_process.html.

CONCLUSION

1. Clayborne Carson, *In Struggle: SNCC and the Black Awakening of the 1960s* (Cambridge, MA: Harvard University Press, 1995), 215. As Carson explains, the vision of Black Power that SNCC and Carmichael articulated reflected the organization's increasingly critical analysis of mainstream American society and politics.

2. Lerone Bennett Jr., "Stokely Carmichael: Architect of Black Power," *Ebony*, September 1966, pp. 26–27.

3. Stokely Carmichael and Charles Hamilton, *Black Power: The Politics of Liberation in America* (New York: Vintage Books, 1967), 40–41.

4. For a list of works that have revealed, in particular, the impact of America's antipoverty battle on and the struggles of minority communities for racial and economic justice and political empowerment in cities and communities nationwide, see note 11 of the introduction.

5. On Kennedy's CDC program, see Schmitt, *President of the Other America*, 123–28. For a discussion of Nixon's black capitalist initiatives, see Fergus, *Liberalism, Black Power, and the Making of American Politics*, 196–231; Fergus, "Black Power, Soft Power," 148–92; Kotlowski, *Nixon's Civil Rights*, 125–56; Weems and Randolph, "The National Response to Richard M. Nixon's Black Capitalism Initiative."

6. For a perspective on this devotion to the "American Dream" in the postwar period, see Andrew Weise, "'The House I Live In': Race, Class, and African American Suburban Dreams in the Postwar United States," in *African American Urban*

History since World War II, ed. Kevin Kusmer and Joe Trotter (Chicago: University of Chicago Press, 2009), 160–78.

7. Dorothy Lee Bolden Papers, Series IV, Box 1633, Folder 181, John Lewis Jr., "4 Widows Cited by Caucus, 3,000 Hear Mayor Jackson," *Baltimore Afro-American,* October 5, 1974, p. 1.

8. Black Power historiography has changed a great deal over the past decade and a half and has undermined the shallow and largely negative stereotypes popularly associated with the movement. For some of the best of this scholarship, see the works cited in notes 14 and 20 of the introduction. Despite these recent advances, the relationship between mainstream white politicians and institutions and Black Power remains relatively neglected within the field of study (see note 4, introduction).

9. Conservative Party of New York State Records, 1962–2004, Series 7, Box 3, Folder 87, Leanita McClain, "The Middle-Class Black's Burden," *Newsweek,* n.d. (October 1980). For more on the literary career of Leanita McClain, see Richard Guzman, *Black Writing from Chicago: In the World, Not of It?* (Carbondale: University of Southern Illinois Press, 2006), 250–59; Leanita McClain and Clarence Page, *A Foot in Each World: Essay and Articles* (Evanston, IL: Northwestern University Press, 1986).

EPILOGUE

1. See WLCAC: Watts Labor Community Action Committee, www.wlcac.org.

2. For some of the most recent work on American race relations in the early twenty-first century, see Keeanga-Yamahtta Taylor, *From #Black Lives Matter to Black Liberation* (New York: Haymarket Books, 2016); Marc Lamont Hill, *Nobody: Casualties of America's War on the Vulnerable, from Ferguson to Flint and Beyond* (New York: Atria Books, 2016); Ta-Nehisi Coates, *Between the World and Me* (New York: Spiegel & Grau, 2015); Jesmyn Ward, ed., *The Fire This Time: A New Generation Speaks about Race* (New York: Simon & Schuster, 2016); Angela Y. Davis, *Freedom Is a Constant Struggle: Ferguson, Palestine, and the Foundations of a Movement* (New York: Haymarket Books, 2016); Eddie Glaude Jr., *Democracy in Black: How Race Still Enslaves the American Soul* (New York: Crown, 2016).

3. In 2014, the federal government's poverty threshold was an income of $19,055 or less for a family consisting of two adults and one child. Henry J. Kaiser Family Foundation, "Poverty Rate by Race/Ethnicity: 2014," http://kff.org/other/state-indicator/poverty-rate-by-raceethnicity/; Thomas J. Sugrue, *Not Even Past: Barack Obama and the Burden of Race* (Princeton: Princeton University Press, 2010), 104; "Residential Segregation—Black/White," County Health Rankings and Road-maps, http://www.countyhealthrankings.org/measure/residential-segregation-blackwhite; Algernon Austin, "The Unfinished March: An Overview," Economic Policy Institute, June 18, 2013, pp. 2–7, http://www.epi.org/files/2013/EPI-The-Unfinished-March-An-Overview.pdf; Glaude, *Democracy in Black,* 31.

4. See "King's Dream Remains an Elusive Goal; Many Americans See Racial Disparities," Pew Research Center, Social and Demographic Trends Project, August

22, 2013, p. 25, http://www.pewsocialtrends.org/2013/08/22/kings-dream-remains-an-elusive-goal-many-americans-see-racial-disparities/; National Center for Education Statistics, Digest of Education Statistics, Table 302.20., http://nces.ed.gov/programs/digest/d15/tables/dt15_302.20.asp?current=yes.

5. U.S. Department of Commerce, Minority Business Development Agency, "Fact Sheet: U.S. Minority-Owned Firms," January 2016, http://www.mbda.gov/sites/default/files/2012SBO_MBEFactSheet020216.pdf.

6. In 2012, the top two metropolitan areas for black business ownership nationally were New York (250,890) and Atlanta (176,245). Los Angeles was home to 81,536 black-owned businesses. See U.S. Census Bureau, "Los Angeles County, a Microcosm of Nation's Diverse Collection of Business Owners, Census Bureau Reports" (news release), December 15, 2015, https://www.census.gov/newsroom/press-releases/2015/cb15-209.html.

7. Henry Louis Gates, "Black America and the Class Divide," *New York Times,* February 7, 2016, ED2.

8. See America's Congressional Black Caucus, Members, https://cbc-butterfield.house.gov/members.

9. See Jens Manuel Krogstad, "114th Congress Is Most Diverse Ever," Pew Research Center, Factank: News in the Numbers, January 12, 2015, http://www.pewresearch.org/fact-tank/2015/01/12/114th-congress-is-most-diverse-ever/.

10. In Atlanta, power at the city level has remained in black hands, with only African American mayors having been elected since Maynard Jackson's election in 1973. The current Atlanta City Council also has an eleven-to-four black majority. See Council Members, Atlanta City Council, http://citycouncil.atlantaga.gov/#. Blacks make up 20 percent of the membership of the Los Angeles City Council, though African Americans are only 10 percent of the local population. See Council Directory: Elected Officials, City of Los Angeles, https://www.lacity.org/your-government/elected-officials/city-council/council-directory. In New York, the state assembly recently appointed its first African American Speaker, Bronx Democrat Carl E. Heastie, and African Americans continue to be well represented both in state government and on the New York City Council. See About the Council, New York City Council, http://council.nyc.gov/html/about/bla.shtml; Assembly Members, New York State Assembly, http://nyassembly.gov/mem/

11. See William Darity, "Closing the Racial Wealth Gap in the U.S.," *RSF Blog,* Russell Sage Foundation, March 25, 2016, http://www.russellsage.org/blog/closing-racial-wealth-gap-us.

12. Minority Business Development Agency "Fact Sheet: U.S. Minority-Owned Firms."

13. Glaude, *Democracy in Black,* 13–26.

14. Rakesh Kochhar and Ricard Fry, "Wealth Inequality Has Widened along Racial, Ethnic Lines since the Great Recession," Pew Research Center, Factank: News in the Numbers, December 12, 2014, http://www.pewresearch.org/fact-tank/2014/12/12/racial-wealth-gaps-great-recession/.

15. Austin, "The Unfinished March," 2–7.

16. Richard V. Reeves and Edward Rodrigue, "Five Bleak Facts on Black Opportunity," Brookings Institution, Social Mobility Memos, January 15, 2015, http://www.brookings.edu/blogs/social-mobility-memos/posts/2015/01/15-mlk-black-opportunity-reeves.

17. Melanie De La Cruz–Viesca, Zhenxiang Chen, Paul Ong, Darrick Hamilton, and William Darity, *The Color of Wealth in Los Angeles* (Duke University Research Network on Racial and Ethnic Inequality; The Milano School of International Affairs, Management, and Urban Policy at The New School; and UCLA Asian American Studies Center, March 2016), p. 5, http://www.aasc.ucla.edu/besol/Color_of_Wealth_Report.pdf; Glaude, *Democracy in Black,* 15, 25; "State of New Yorkers," Furman Center for Real Estate and Urban Policy, New York University, August 28, 2013, http://furmancenter.org/files/sotc/SOC2012_StateofNewYorkers.pdf.

18. This is a point made especially clearly by African American sociologist William Julius Wilson during the late 1970s and 1980s. See, for example, Wilson, *The Declining Significance of Race: Blacks and Changing American Institutions* (Chicago: University of Chicago Press, 1978), 99–111; and Wilson, *The Truly Disadvantaged: The Inner City, the Underclass, and Public Policy* (Chicago: University of Chicago Press, 1987), 138–64.

19. Jules Lichtenstein, "Demographic Characteristics of Business Owners," Issue Brief No. 2, Small Business Administration, Office of Advocacy, January 16, 2014, p. 2, https://www.sba.gov/sites/default/files/Issue%20Brief%202,%20Business%20Owner%20Demographics.pdf.

20. Minority Business Development Agency, "Fact Sheet: U.S. Minority-Owned Firms."

21. For a discussion of color-blind conservative ideology, see, for example, David R. Roediger, *How Race Survived U.S. History: From Settlement and Slavery to the Obama Phenomenon* (New York: Verso, 2008), 169–211; and MacLean, *Freedom Is Not Enough,* 225–64.

22. J. Wesley Leckrone, Michelle Atherton, Nicole Crossey, Andrea Stickley, and Meghan E. Rubado, "'Does Anyone Care about the Poor?' The Role of Redistribution in Mayoral Policy Agendas," *State and Local Government Review,* Vol. 47, No. 4 (2015), 240–54.

23. See MacLean, *Freedom Is Not Enough,* 265–332.

24. This trend has been especially clear at the city level, characterizing the political approach of many black mayors since the 1970s. For a discussion of the development of this black political tradition, see Thompson, *Double Trouble,* 39–153; and Fredrick C. Harris, *The Price of a Ticket: Barack Obama and the Rise and Decline of Black Politics* (New York: Oxford University Press, 2012), 137–69.

25. Dawson, *Not in Our Lifetimes,* 93. For discussion of Thomas Sowell and Clarence Thomas, see MacLean, *Freedom Is Not Enough,* 240–41; and Marable, *Beyond Black and White,* 93–109, 169, 210.

26. Dawson, *Not in Our Lifetimes,* 93.

27. Michael Eric Dyson, *Is Bill Cosby Right? (Or Has the Black Middle Class Lost Its Mind?)* (New York: BasicCivitas Books, 2005), xiii–xiv.

28. Fredrick C. Harris, "The Rise of Respectability Politics," *Dissent,* Vol. 61, No. 1 (Winter 2014), 33.

29. William Julius Wilson, "Obama Heads Right Way on Poverty, Jobs," *The Root,* January 9, 2013, p. 1, http://www.theroot.com/articles/politics/2013/01/obama_poverty_policy_heads_right_way_in_2013/.

30. See Jane Mayer, *Dark Money: The Hidden History of Billionaires behind the Rise of the Radical Right* (New York: Doubleday, 2016); Godfrey Hodgson, *More Equal Than Others: America from Nixon to the New Century* (Princeton: Princeton University Press, 2006).

31. For a discussion of Obama's political ideology, image, and record, see Michael Eric Dyson, *The Black Presidency: Barack Obama and the Politics of Race in America* (Boston: Houghton Mifflin, 2016); Harris, *The Price of a Ticket,* 170–92; James T. Kloppenberg, *Reading Obama: Dreams, Hope, and the American Political Tradition* (Princeton: Princeton University Press, 2011); Sugrue, *Not Even Past.*

32. Derek T. Dingle, "Obama's Big Plan for Small Business," *Black Enterprise,* August 3, 2012, http://www.blackenterprise.com/mag/president-obamas-big-plan-for-small-business/.

33. Adolph Reed, "Obama No," *The Progressive,* April 28, 2008, http://www.progressive.org/mag_reed0508. For example, leading black public figures such as Cornel West, Tavis Smiley, and Harry Belafonte, among others, have all spoken out on various aspects of Obama's political style and policies.

34. Glaude, *Democracy in Black,* 90

35. Clarence Lang, "Race, Class, and Obama," *Chronicle of Higher Education,* August 28, 2011, http://chronicle.com/article/Race-ClassObama/128787/; Rahiel Tesfamariam, "Why Jay-Z Has No Desire to Be Our Generation's Harry Belafonte," *Washington Post,* July 25, 2013, https://www.washingtonpost.com/blogs/local/wp/2013/07/25/why-jay-z-has-no-desire-to-be-our-generations-harry-belafonte/.

36. Jelani Cobb, "The Matter of Black Lives," *New Yorker,* March 14, 2016, http://www.newyorker.com/magazine/2016/03/14/where-is-black-lives-matter-headed.

37. Taylor, *From #Black Lives Matter to Black Liberation,* 153–90. For a discussion of the relationship between BLM and the black church, see Emma Green, "Black Activism, Unchurched," *Atlantic,* March 22, 2016, http://www.theatlantic.com/politics/archive/2016/03/black-activism-baltimore-black-church/474822/.

38. Taylor, *From #Black Lives Matter to Black Liberation,* 177–79.

39. Julie Hirschfield Davis and Michael D. Shear, "Unrest over Race Is Testing Obama's Legacy," *New York Times,* December 9, 2014, A1, http://www.nytimes.com/2014/12/09/us/politics/unrest-over-race-is-testing-obamas-legacy-.html.

40. Jamiles Lartey, "Obama on Black Lives Matter: They Are "much better organizers than I was,'" *The Guardian,* February 19, 2016, https://www.theguardian.com/us-news/2016/feb/18/black-lives-matter-meet-president-obama-white-house-justice-system.

41. Cobb, "The Matter of Black Lives."

42. Sandhya Somashekhar, "Challenge for Protesters in Wake of Police Killings: Turning Anger, Grief into Action," *Washington Post,* December 8, 2014, https://www.washingtonpost.com/politics/challenge-for-protesters-in-wake-of-police-killings-turning-anger-grief-into-action/2014/12/08/36c72366–7f3b-11e4–9f38–95a187e4c1f7_story.html.

43. Michael D. Shear and Liam Stack, "Obama Urges Activists to Do More Than 'Yelling,'" *New York Times,* April 23, 2016, A14, http://www.nytimes.com/2016/04/24/us/obama-says-movements-like-black-lives-matter-cant-just-keep-on-yelling.html?_r=0.

BIBLIOGRAPHY

ARCHIVAL SOURCES (BY COUNTRY, STATE, CITY, ARCHIVE)

United States

Berkeley, California
Bancroft Library, University of California
  Eldridge Cleaver Papers, 1963–1988
  NAACP Western Regional Office Records

Los Angeles, California
Charles E. Young Research Library, University of California
  Augustus F. Hawkins Papers, 1935–1990
  California Democratic Council Records
  California Republican Assembly Records
  The Impossible Dream: Tom Bradley (Oral History)
  State Government Oral History Program: Mervyn Dymally Interviews,
    Vols. I–III
  Tom Bradley Papers

Los Angeles City Archives
  Councilman Tom Bradley Records
  Sam Yorty Papers

Southern California Library for Social Studies and Research
  Black Panther Party Collections
  Twentieth Century Organizational Files, 1912–1980

Palo Alto, California
Green Library, Stanford University
  Huey P. Newton Foundation Records

Sacramento, California
California State Archives
 California State Office of Economic Opportunity Records
 Yvonne Braithwaite Burke Papers

San Marino, California
Huntington Library
 Kenneth Hahn Collection

New Haven, Connecticut
Sterling Memorial Library, Yale University
 John V. Lindsay Papers

Atlanta, Georgia
Auburn Avenue Research Library on African American Culture
 Andrew J. Young Papers
 Dorothy Lee Bolden Papers
 Ella Mae Wade Brayboy Papers, 1934–1994
 Southern Regional Council Collection, 1944–1977

Kenan Research Center, Atlanta History Center
 Muriel Lokey Papers
 Sam Massell Jr. Papers

Manuscript, Archives, and Rare Book Library, Emory University
 Community Council of the Atlanta Area Records, 1960–1974
 Eliza K. Paschall Papers, 1932–1988
 Richard L. Stevens Papers, 1964–1969

Robert W. Woodruff Library, Archives and Special Collections, Atlanta
University Center
 Atlanta Urban League Papers
 Frankie V. Adams Collection

Special Collections and Archives Library, Georgia State University
 AFL-CIO Civil Rights Department, Southern Office Records, 1964–1979
 Georgia Government Documentation Project
 Voices of Labor Oral History Project, Dorothy Bolden Interview

Boston, Massachusetts
John F. Kennedy Presidential Library
 Ford Foundation Papers: Inventory of the Bedford Stuyvesant Restoration
  Corporation
 Thomas M. C. Johnston Papers, 1936–2008

Robert F. Kennedy Oral History Collection
Robert F. Kennedy Senate Papers, 1964–1968

Albany, New York
M. E. Grenander Department of Special Collections and Archives, State
University of New York
    Conservative Party of New York State Records, 1962–2004
    New York State Republican Committee Records, 1881–2001
    Urban League of Northeastern New York Papers

New York, New York
Municipal Archives, City Hall
    Mayor John V. Lindsay Papers, 1966–1973
    Timothy Costello Papers

Schomburg Center for Research in Black Culture; Manuscripts, Archives and
Rare Books Division; New York Public Library
    Black Panther Party Harlem Branch File, 1969–1970
    Community News Service Records, 1969–1976
    Congress on Racial Equality Papers
    East Harlem Triangle Plan
    George Metcalf Papers
    Student Nonviolent Coordinating Committee Papers
    Twenty-First Century Foundation Papers

Rare Book and Manuscript Library, Columbia University
    Howard Samuels Gubernatorial Papers

Germany

Berlin
The John F. Kennedy Institute for North American Studies, Freie Universität
    Nixon White House microfiche: Part 2, President's Meeting File, 1969–1974
    Nixon White House microfiche: Part 6, President's Office Files, 1969–1974
    The War on Poverty, 1964–1968 [microfilm]. Mark I. Gefland, ed.

INTERVIEWS WITH THE AUTHOR

Carl McCall, February 13, 2012
Major Owens, November 8, 2010

NEWSPAPERS AND PERIODICALS

Atlanta Daily World
Atlanta Inquirer
Atlanta Journal
Atlanta Voice
Atlantic
Baltimore Afro-American
Black Enterprise
Chronicle of Higher Education
Ebony
Equity and Excellence in Education
Fortune
Great Speckled Bird
Jet
Los Angeles Sentinel
Los Angeles Times
The Nation
New York Amsterdam Times
New York Herald Tribune
New York Times
New Yorker
Newsweek
The Progressive
The Root
Southern Changes
Time
Village Voice
Wall Street Journal
Washington Post

PUBLISHED PRIMARY SOURCES, MEMOIRS, AND AUTOBIOGRAPHIES

Allen, Robert. *Black Awakening in Capitalist America: An Analytic History* (New York: Doubleday, 1969).

Cahn, Steven M., ed. *The Affirmative Action Debate* (New York: Routledge, 1995).

Carmichael, Stokely, and Hamilton, Charles. *Black Power: The Politics of Liberation in America* (New York: Vintage Books, 1967).

Chisholm, Shirley. *The Good Fight* (New York: Harper & Row, 1973).

Edelman, Marian Wright. *Lanterns: A Memoir of Mentors* (Boston: Beacon Press, 1999).

Enck-Wanzer, Darrel, et al., eds. *The Young Lords: A Reader* (New York: New York University Press, 2010).

Foner, Philip S., ed. *The Black Panthers Speak* (New York: Da Capo Press, 1995).

Forman, James. *The Making of Black Revolutionaries* (Seattle: University of Washington Press, 1995).

Galbraith, John Kenneth. *The Affluent Society* (Boston: Houghton Mifflin, 1958).

Harrington, Michael. *The Other America: Poverty in the United States* (New York: Macmillan, 1962).

Hilliard, David, and Lewis Cole. *This Side of Glory: The Autobiography of David Hilliard and the Story of the Black Panther Party* (Chicago: Lawrence Hill Books, 2001).

Hilliard, David, and Don Weise, eds. *The Huey P. Newton Reader* (New York: Seven Stories Press, 2002).

Humphrey, Hubert. *War on Poverty* (New York: McGraw-Hill, 1964).

King, Martin Luther, Jr. *Where Do We Go from Here: Chaos or Community?* (Boston: Beacon Press, 1967).

Lester, Julius. *Revolutionary Notes* (New York: Richard W. Baron, 1969).

Lindsay, John V. *The City* (New York: W. W. Norton, 1970).

Malcolm X. *Malcolm X Speaks: Selected Speeches and Statements.* Edited by George Breitman (New York: Grove Press, 1994).

McClain, Leanita, and Clarence Page. *A Foot in Each World: Essay and Articles* (Evanston, IL: Northwestern University Press, 1986).

Moynihan, Daniel. *Maximum Feasible Misunderstanding: Community Action in the War on Poverty* (New York: Free Press, 1969).

Newton, Huey P. *Revolutionary Suicide* (New York: Writing and Readers Publishing Inc., 1973).

Phillips, Kevin. *The Emerging Republican Majority* (New Rochelle, NY: Arlington House, 1969).

Seale, Bobby. *Seize the Time: The Story of the Black Panther Party and Huey P. Newton* (London: Hutchinson, 1970).

Sellars, Cleveland, and Robert Terrell. *The River of No Return: The Autobiography of a Black Militant and the Life and Death of SNCC* (Jackson; University Press of Mississippi, 1990).

Teodori, Massimo, ed. *The New Left: A Documentary History* (New York: Bobbs-Merrill, 1969).

U.S. Senate. *Supplementary Detailed Staff Reports on Intelligence Activities and the Rights of Americans, Book III: Final Report of the Senate Select Committee to Study Governmental Operations with Respect to Intelligence Activities* (Washington, DC: U.S. Government Printing Office, 1976).

Van Deburg, William L., ed. *Modern Black Nationalism: From Marcus Garvey to Louis Farrakhan* (New York: New York University Press, 1997).

Ward, Jesmyn, ed. *The Fire This Time: A New Generation Speaks about Race* (New York: Simon & Schuster, 2016).

Young, Andrew. *An Easy Burden: The Civil Rights Movement and the Transformation of America* (New York: HarperCollins, 1996).

Adler, Jeffrey. "Introduction." In *African-American Mayors: Race, Politics, and the American City*, 1–22. Edited by Jeffrey Adler and David Colburn (Urbana: University of Illinois Press, 2001).

Allitt, Patrick. "American Catholics and the New Conservatism of the 1950s." *U.S. Catholic Historian*, Vol. 7, No. 1 (Winter 1988), 15–37.

Anderson, Alan B. *Confronting the Color Line: The Broken Promise of the Civil Rights Movement in Chicago* (Athens: University of Georgia Press, 1986).

Anderson, Terry H. *The Pursuit of Fairness: A History of Affirmative Action* (New York: Oxford University Press, 2004).

Ashmore, Susan Youngblood. *Carry It On: The War on Poverty and the Civil Rights Movement in Alabama, 1964–1972* (Athens: University of Georgia Press, 2008).

Austin, Curtis J. *Up against the Wall: Violence in the Making and Unmaking of the Black Panther Party* (Fayetteville: University of Arkansas Press, 2006).

Back, Adina. "'Parent Power': Evelina Lopez Antonetty, the United Bronx Parents, and the War on Poverty." In *The War on Poverty: A New Grassroots History, 1964–1980*, 184–208. Edited by Annelise Orleck and Lisa Gayle Hazirjian (Athens: University of Georgia Press, 2011).

Badger, Anthony. *The New Deal: The Depression Years, 1933–1939* (Chicago: Ivan R. Dee, 2002).

Baldassare, Mark, ed. *The Los Angeles Riots: Lessons for the Urban Future* (Boulder, CO: Westview Press, 1994).

Bauman, Robert. *Race and the War on Poverty: From Watts to East L.A.* (Norman: University of Oklahoma Press, 2008).

Bayor, Ronald. "African American Mayors and Governance in Atlanta." In *African-American Mayors: Race, Politics, and the American City*, 178–99. Edited by David Colburn and Jeffery Adler (Urbana: University of Illinois Press, 2001).

———. *Race and the Shaping of Twentieth Century Atlanta* (Chapel Hill: University of North Carolina Press, 1996).

Bean, Jonathan J. "'Burn, Baby, Burn': Small Business in the Urban Riots of the 1960s." *Independent Review*, Vol. 5, No. 2 (Fall 2000), 165–87.

Berg, Manfred. *The Ticket to Freedom: The NAACP and the Struggle for Black Political Integration* (Gainesville: University Press of Florida, 2005).

Biondi, Martha. *The Black Revolution on Campus* (Berkeley: University of California Press, 2012).

———. *To Stand and Fight: The Struggle for Civil Rights in Postwar New York City* (Cambridge, MA: Harvard University Press, 2003).

Biles, Roger. "Mayor David Dinkins and the Politics of Race in New York City." In *African American Mayors: Race, Politics, and the American City*, 130–52. Edited by Jeffrey Adler and David Coburn (Urbana: University of Illinois Press, 2001).

Bloom, Joshua, and Waldo E. Martin. *Black against Empire: The History and Politics of the Black Panther Party* (Berkeley: University of California Press, 2012).

Boston, Thomas D. *Affirmative Action and Black Entrepreneurship* (New York: Routledge, 1999).

Brilliant, Mark. *The Color of America Has Changed: How Racial Diversity Shaped Civil Rights Reform in California, 1941–1978* (New York: Oxford University Press, 2010).

Brinkley, Alan. *Liberalism and Its Discontents* (Cambridge, MA: Harvard University Press, 2000).

———. "The Problem of American Conservatism." *American Historical Review,* Vol. 99, No. 2 (April 1994), 409–29.

Brown, Scot. *Fighting for US: Maulana Karenga, the US Organization, and Black Cultural Nationalism* (New York: New York University Press, 2003).

Brown-Nagin, Tomiko. *Courage to Dissent: Atlanta and the Long History of the Civil Rights Movement* (New York: Oxford University Press, 2011).

Bush, Rod. *We Are Not What We Seem: Black Nationalism and Class Struggle in the American Century* (New York: New York University Press, 2000).

Bynum, Cornelius L., *A. Philip Randolph and the Struggle for Civil Rights* (Urbana: University of Illinois Press, 2010).

Cannato, Vincent. *The Ungovernable City: John Lindsay and His Struggle to Save New York* (New York: BasicBooks, 2001).

Caro, Robert A. *Master of the Senate.* Volume 3 of *The Years of Lyndon Johnson* (New York: Alfred A. Knopf, 2002).

Carson, Clayborne. *In Struggle: SNCC and the Black Awakening of the 1960s* (Cambridge, MA: Harvard University Press, 1995).

———. "Rethinking African American Political Thought in the Post-Revolutionary Era." In *The Making of Martin Luther King and the Civil Rights Movement,* 115–27. Edited by Brian Ward and Tony Badger (New York: New York University Press, 1996)/

———. "Two Cheers for *Brown v. Board of Education.*" *Journal of American History,* Vol. 91, No. 1 (June 2004), 26–31.

Carter, Dan T. *The Politics of Rage: George Wallace, the Origins of the New Conservatism, and the Transformation of American Politics* (Baton Rouge: Louisiana State University Press, 2000).

Carter, David C. *The Music Has Gone out of the Movement: Civil Rights and the Johnson Administration, 1965–1968* (Chapel Hill: University of North Carolina Press, 2014).

Cazenave, Noel A. *Impossible Democracy: The Unlikely Success of the War on Poverty Community Action Programs* (Albany: State University of New York Press, 2007).

Chafe, William H. *Civilities and Civil Rights: Greensboro, North Carolina, and the Black Struggle for Freedom* (New York: Oxford University Press, 1980).

———. *Never Stop Running: Allard Lowenstein and the Struggle to Save American Liberalism* (Princeton: Princeton University Press, 1998).

Chappell, Marisa. *The War on Welfare: Family, Poverty, and Politics in Modern America* (Philadelphia: University of Pennsylvania Press, 2010).

Chen, Antony. *The Fifth Freedom: Jobs, Politics, and Civil Rights in the United States* (Princeton: Princeton University Press, 2009).

Clayson, William S. "'The Barrios and the Ghettos have Organized!': Community Action, Political Acrimony, and the War on Poverty in San Antonio." *Journal of Urban History,* Vol. 28, No. 2 (January 2002), 158–83.

———. *Freedom Is Not Enough: The War on Poverty and the Civil Rights Movement in Texas* (Austin: University of Texas Press, 2010).

Coates, Ta-Nehisi. *Between the World and Me* (New York: Spiegel & Grau, 2015).

Cohen, Lizabeth. *A Consumers' Republic: The Politics of Mass Consumption in Postwar America* (New York: Random House, 2003).

Collier-Thomas, Bettye, and V. P. Franklin, eds. *Sisters in the Struggle: African American Women in the Civil Rights–Black Power Movement* (New York: New York University Press, 2001).

Countryman, Matthew. *Up South: Civil Rights and Black Power in Philadelphia* (Philadelphia: University of Pennsylvania Press, 2006).

Davies, Gareth. *From Opportunity to Entitlement: The Transformation and Decline of Great Society Liberalism* (Lawrence: University of Kansas Press, 1996).

Davis, Angela Y. *Freedom Is a Constant Struggle: Ferguson, Palestine, and the Foundations of a Movement* (New York: Haymarket Books, 2016).

———. *Women, Race, and Class* (New York: Vintage Books, 1983).

Dawson, Michael C. *Not in Our Lifetimes: The Future of Black Politics* (Chicago: University of Chicago Press, 2011).

Delmont, Matthew F. *Why Busing Failed: Race, Media, and the National Resistance to School Desegregation* (Oakland: University of California Press, 2016).

Denton, Gina. "'Neither guns nor bombs—neither the state nor God—will stop us from fighting for our children': Motherhood and Protest in 1960s and 1970s America." *The Sixties,* Vol. 5, No. 2 (2012), 205–28.

Dillard, Angela. "Malcolm X and African American Conservatism." In *The Cambridge Companion to Malcolm X,* 90–100. Edited by Robert Terrell (New York: Cambridge University Press, 2010).

Dittmer, John. *Local People: The Struggle for Civil Rights in Mississippi* (Urbana: University of Illinois Press, 1994).

Dowd Hall, Jacquelyn. "The Long Civil Rights Movement and the Political Uses of the Past." *Journal of American History,* Vol. 91, No. 4 (March 2005), 1233–63.

Dyson, Michael Eric. *The Black Presidency: Barack Obama and the Politics of Race in America* (Boston: Houghton Mifflin, 2016).

———. *Is Bill Cosby Right? (Or Has the Black Middle Class Lost Its Mind?)* (New York: BasicCivitas Books, 2005).

Edelman, Peter, "The War on Poverty and Subsequent Federal Programs: What Worked, What Didn't Work, and Why? Lessons for Future Programs." *Clearinghouse REVIEW Journal of Poverty Law and Policy* (May–June 2006), 7–18.

Ellis, William Russell. *People Making Places: Episodes in Participation, 1964–1984* (Berkeley: University of California, 1987).

Estes, Steve. *I Am a Man! Race, Manhood, and the Civil Rights Movement* (Chapel Hill: University of North Carolina Press, 2005).

Fairclough, Adam. "Race and Red-Baiting." In *The Civil Rights Movement: Rethinking History,* 90–102. Edited by Jack E. Davis (Oxford: Blackwell, 2001).

———. *A Class of Their Own: Black Teachers in the Segregated South* (Cambridge, MA: Belknap Press of Harvard University Press, 2007).

Fergus, Devin. *Liberalism, Black Power, and the Making of American Politics, 1965–1980* (Athens: University of Georgia Press, 2009).

———. "Black Power, Soft Power: Floyd McKissick, Soul City, and the Death of Moderate Black Republicanism." *Journal of Policy History,* Vol. 22 (2010), 148–92.

Ferguson, Karen. *Top Down: The Ford Foundation, Black Power, and the Reinvention of Racial Liberalism* (Philadelphia: University of Pennsylvania Press, 2013).

Flamm, Michael W. "The Politics of 'Law and Order.'" In *The Conservative Sixties,* 142–52. Edited by David Farber and Jeff Roche (New York: Peter Lang, 2003).

Fogelson, Robert M. *Violence as Protest: A Study of Riots and Ghettos* (New York: Anchor Books, 1971).

Fortner, Michael Javen. *Black Silent Majority: The Rockefeller Drug Laws and the Politics of Punishment* (Cambridge, MA: Harvard University Press, 2015).

Frazier, Nishani. "A McDonalds That Reflects the Soul of a People: Hough Area Development Corporation and Community Development in Cleveland." In *The Business of Black Power: Community Development, Capitalism, and Corporate Responsibility in Postwar America,* 68–92. Edited by Laura Warren Hill and Julia Rabig (Rochester, NY: University of Rochester Press, 2012).

Freund, David M. P. *Colored Property: State Policy and White Racial Politics in Suburban America* (Chicago: University of Chicago Press, 2007).

George, Lynell. *No Crystal Stair: African Americans in the City of Angels* (London: Verso, 1992; reprinted, New York: Anchor Books, 1994).

Gill, Andrea. "'Gilding the Ghetto' and Debates over Chicago's Gatreaux Program." In *The Business of Black Power: Community Development, Capitalism, and Corporate Responsibility in Postwar America,* pp. 184–214. Edited by Laura Warren Hill and Julia Rabig (Rochester, NY: University of Rochester Press, 2012).

Gilmore, Glenda Elizabeth. *Defying Dixie: The Radical Roots of Civil Rights, 1919–1950* (New York: W. W. Norton, 2008).

Glaude, Eddie, Jr. *Democracy in Black: How Race Still Enslaves the American Soul* (New York: Crown, 2016).

Gore, Dayo F., et al., eds. *Want to Start a Revolution? Radical Women in the Black Freedom Struggle* (New York: New York University Press, 2009).

Grady-Willis, Winston A. *Challenging U.S. Apartheid: Atlanta and Black Struggles for Human Rights, 1960–1977* (Durham, NC: Duke University Press, 2006).

Guzman, Richard. *Black Writing from Chicago: In the World, Not of It?* (Carbondale: University of Southern Illinois Press, 2006).

Hall, Simon. "The NAACP, Black Power, and the African American Freedom Struggle, 1966–1969." *The Historian,* Vol. 69, No. 1 (March 2007), 49–82.

Hamilton, Charles V. *The Bench and the Ballot: Southern Federal Judges and Black Voters* (New York: Oxford University Press, 1973).

Harris, Fredrick C. *The Price of a Ticket: Barack Obama and the Rise and Decline of Black Politics* (New York: Oxford University Press, 2012).

———. "The Rise of Respectability Politics." *Dissent,* Vol. 61, No. 1 (Winter 2014), 33–37.

Harvey, David. *A Brief History of Neoliberalism* (New York: Oxford University Press, 2005).

Hazirjian, Lisa Gayle. "Combating NEED: Urban Conflict and the Transformations of the War on Poverty and the African American Freedom Struggle in Rocky Mount, North Carolina." *Journal of Urban History,* Vol. 34, No. 4 (May 2008), 639–64.

Heyman, C. David. *RFK: A Candid Biography* (London: Heinemann, 1998).

Hill, Marc Lamont. *Nobody: Casualties of America's War on the Vulnerable, from Ferguson to Flint and Beyond* (New York: Atria Books, 2016).

Hill, Laura Warren. "FIGHTing for the Soul of Black Capitalism: Struggles for Black Economic Development in Postrebellion Rochester." In *The Business of Black Power: Community Development, Capitalism, and Corporate Responsibility in Postwar America,* 42–67. Edited by Laura Warren Hill and Julia Rabig (Rochester, NY: University of Rochester Press, 2012).

Hill, Laura Warren, and Julia Rabig. "Introduction." In *The Business of Black Power,* 1–14. Edited by Laura Warren Hill and Julia Rabig (Rochester, NY: University of Rochester Press, 2012).

———. "Toward a History of the Business of Black Power." In *The Business of Black Power: Community Development, Capitalism, and Corporate Responsibility in Postwar America,* 15–42. Edited by Laura Warren Hill and Julia Rabig (Rochester, NY: University of Rochester Press, 2012).

Hine, Darlene Clark. "Black Professionals and Race Consciousness: The Origins of the Civil Rights Movement, 189–1950." *Journal of American History,* Vol. 89, No. 4 (March 2003), 1279–94.

Hodgson, Godfrey. *More Equal Than Others: America from Nixon to the New Century* (Princeton: Princeton University Press, 2006).

———. *The World Turned Right Side Up: A History of the Conservative Ascendancy in America* (New York: Houghton Mifflin, 1996).

Hoff, Joan. *Nixon Reconsidered* (New York: BasicBooks, 1994).

Horne, Gerald. *The Fire This Time: The Watts Uprising and the 1960s* (Charlottesville: University Press of Virginia, 1995).

Hornsby, Alton. *Black Power in Dixie: A Political History of African Americans in Atlanta* (Gainesville: University Press of Florida, 2009).

Isserman, Maurice, and Michael Kazin. *America Divided: The Civil War of the 1960s* (New York: Oxford University Press, 1999).

Jacobson, Matthew Frye. *Roots Too: White Ethnic Revival in Post–Civil Rights America* (Cambridge, MA: Harvard University Press, 2006).

Jackson, Kenneth T. *Crabgrass Frontier: The Suburbanization of the United States* (New York: University of Oxford Press, 1985).

Jackson, Thomas F. *From Civil Rights to Economic Rights: Martin Luther King Jr. and the Struggle for Economic Justice* (Philadelphia: University of Pennsylvania Press, 2007).

Jefferies, Hasan Kwame. *Bloody Lowndes: Civil Rights and Black Power in Alabama's Black Belt* (New York: New York University Press, 2009).

Jeffries, Judson, ed. *On the Ground: The Black Panther Party in Communities across America* (Jackson: University of Mississippi Press, 2010).

Johnson, Cedric. *Revolutionaries to Race Leaders: Black Power and the Making of African American Politics* (Minneapolis: University of Minnesota Press, 2007).

Johnson, Kimberley. "Community Development Corporations, Participation, and Accountability: The Harlem Urban Development Corporation and the Bedford-Stuyvesant Restoration Corporation." *Annals of the American Academy of Political and Social Science,* Vol. 594 (July 2004), 109–24.

Jolly, Kenneth S., *Black Liberation in the Midwest: The Struggle in St. Louis, Missouri, 1964–1970* (New York: Routledge, 2006).

Jones, Charles E., ed. *The Black Panther Party Reconsidered* (Baltimore: Black Classic Press, 1998).

Jones, Mack. "Black Political Empowerment in Atlanta: Myth and Reality." *Annals of the American Academy of Political and Social Science,* Vol. 439 (September 1978), 90–117.

Jones, Patrick. "'Not a Color but an Attitude': Father James Groppi and Black Power Politics in Milwaukee." In *Groundwork: Local Black Freedom Movements in America,* 259–81. Edited by Jeanne Theoharis and Komozi Woodard (New York: New York University, 2005).

———. *The Selma of the North: Civil Rights Insurgency in Milwaukee* (Cambridge, MA: Harvard University Press, 2009).

Joseph, Peniel E. "The Black Power Movement: A State of the Field." *Journal of American History,* Vol. 96, No. 3 (December 2009), 1–25.

———. *Waiting 'til the Midnight Hour: A Narrative History of Black Power in America* (New York: Henry Holt, 2007).

———. *Dark Days, Bright Nights: From Black Power to Barack Obama* (New York: BasicCivitas Books, 2010).

Karenga, Maulana. "Black Studies: A Critical Reassessment." In *Dispatches from the Ebony Tower: Intellectuals Confront the African American Experience,* 162–70. Edited by Manning Marable (New York: Columbia University Press; 2001).

Katznelson, Ira. *City Trenches: Urban Politics and the Patterning of Class in the United States* (New York: Pantheon Books, 1981).

Kessler-Harris, Alice. *In Pursuit of Equity: Women, Men, and the Quest for Economic Citizenship in 20th Century America* (New York: Oxford University Press, 2001).

Kiffmeyer, Thomas. *Reformers to Radicals the Appalachian Volunteers and the War on Poverty* (Lexington: University Press of Kentucky, 2008).

Klarman, Michael J. "How *Brown* Changed Race Relations: The Backlash Thesis." *Journal of American History,* Vol. 81, No. 1 (June 1994), 81–118.

Kloppenberg, James T. *Reading Obama: Dreams, Hope, and the American Political Tradition* (Princeton: Princeton University Press, 2011).

K'Meyer, Tracy E. *Civil Rights in the Gateway to the South: Louisville, Kentucky, 1945–80* (Lexington: University of Kentucky Press, 2009).

Kornbluh, Felicia Ann. *The Battle for Welfare Right: Politics and Poverty in Modern America* (Philadelphia: University of Pennsylvania Press, 2007).

———. "'Who Shot FAP?' The Nixon Welfare Plan and the Transformation of American Politics." *The Sixties,* Vol. 1, No. 2 (December 2008), 125–50.

Kotlowski, Dean J. *Nixon's Civil Rights: Politics, Principle, and Policy* (Cambridge, MA: Harvard University Press, 2001).

Kruse, Kevin. *White Flight: Atlanta and the Making of Modern Conservatism* (Princeton: Princeton University Press, 2006).

Lane, James B. "Black Political Power and Its Limits: Gary Mayor Richard G. Hatcher's Administration, 1968–1987." In *African-American Mayors: Race, Politics, and the American City,* 57–79. Edited by Jeffrey Adler and David Colburn (Urbana: University of Illinois Press, 2001).

Lang, Clarence. *Grassroots at the Gateway: Class Politics and Black Freedom Struggle in St. Louis, 1936–75* (Ann Arbor: University of Michigan Press, 2009).

Lazerow, Jama, and Yohuru Williams, eds. *In Search of the Black Panther Party: New Perspectives on a Revolutionary Movement* (Durham, NC: Duke University Press, 2006).

Leckrone, J. Wesley, Michelle Atherton, Nicole Crossey, Andrea Stickley, and Meghan E. Rubado. "Does Anyone Care about the Poor? The Role of Redistribution in Mayoral Policy Agendas." *State and Local Government Review,* Vol. 47, No. 4 (2015), 240–54.

MacLean, Nancy. *Freedom Is Not Enough: The Opening of the American Work Place* (New York: Russell Sage Foundation; Cambridge, MA: Harvard University Press, 2006).

Mantler, Gordon K. *Power to the Poor: Black-Brown Coalition and the Fight for Economic Justice, 1960–1974* (Chapel Hill: University of North Carolina Press, 2013).

Marable, Manning. *Beyond Black and White: Transforming African American Politics* (New York: Verso, 1995).

———. *Black Leadership* (New York: Columbia University Press, 1998).

———. *Race, Reform, and Rebellion: The Second Reconstruction and Beyond in Black America, 1945–1982* (Jackson: University of Mississippi Press, 1983).

Martin, Harold H. *Atlanta and Environs: A Chronicle of Its People and Events.* Volume 3: *Years of Change and Challenge, 1940s–1970s* (1987; reprinted, Atlanta: Atlanta Historical Society; Athens: University of Georgia Press, 2011).

Marwell, Nicole P. *Bargaining for Brooklyn: Community Organizations in the Entrepreneurial City* (Chicago: University of Chicago Press, 2007).

Matusow, Allen. *The Unraveling of America: A History of Liberalism in the 1960s* (New York: Harper & Row, 1984).

Matlin, Daniel. *On the Corner: African American Intellectuals and the Urban Crisis* (Cambridge, MA: Harvard University Press, 2013).

Mayer, Jane. *Dark Money: The Hidden History of Billionaires behind the Rise of the Radical Right* (New York: Doubleday, 2016).

McGirr, Lisa. *Suburban Warriors: The Origins of the New American Right* (Princeton: Princeton University Press, 2001).

McKee, Guian A. *The Problem of Jobs: Liberalism, Race, and Deindustrialization in Philadelphia* (Chicago: University of Chicago Press, 2008).

———. "'This Government Is with Us': Lyndon B. Johnson and the Grass-roots War on Poverty." In *The War on Poverty: A New Grassroots History, 1964–1980*, 31–62. Edited by Annelise Orleck and Lisa Gayle Hazirjian (Athens: University of Georgia Press, 2011).

McKnight, Gerald. *The Last Crusade: Martin Luther King, Jr., the FBI, and the Poor People's Campaign* (Boulder, CO: Westview Press, 1998).

Minchin, Timothy J. *From Rights to Economics: The Ongoing Struggle for Black Equality in the U.S. South* (Gainesville: University Press of Florida, 2007).

Moore, Leonard N. *Carl B. Stokes and the Rise of Black Political Power* (Urbana: University of Illinois Press, 2002).

Murch, Donna. *Living for the City: Migration, Education, and the Rise of the Black Panther Party in Oakland, California* (Chapel Hill: University of North Carolina Press, 2010).

Nadasen, Premilla. *Welfare Warriors: The Welfare Rights Movement in the United States* (New York: Routledge, 2005).

Novick, Peter. *That Noble Dream: The "Objectivity Question" and the American Historical Profession* (New York: Cambridge University Press, 1988).

O'Connor, Alice. "Community Action, Urban Reform, and the Fight against Poverty: The Ford Foundation's Gray Areas Programs." *Journal of Urban History*, Vol. 22, No. 5 (July 1996), 586–625.

———. *Poverty Knowledge: Social Science, Social Policy, and the Poor in Twentieth-Century U.S. History* (Princeton: Princeton University Press, 2001).

Ogbar, Jeffrey O. G. *Black Power: Radical Politics and African American Identity* (Baltimore: Johns Hopkins University Press, 2004).

O'Neill, William L. *Coming Apart: An Informal History of America in the 1960's* (1971; repr., Chicago: Ivan R. Dee, 2005).

Orleck, Annelise. "Introduction: The War on Poverty from the Grass Roots Up." In *The War on Poverty: A New Grassroots History, 1964–1980*, 1–28. Edited by Annelise Orleck and Lisa Gayle Hazirjian (Athens: University of Georgia Press, 2011).

———. *Storming Caesars Palace: How Black Mothers Fought Their Own War on Poverty* (Boston: Beacon Press, 2005).

———. "The War on Poverty and Politics since the 1960s." In *The War on Poverty: A New Grassroots History, 1964–1980*, 437–61. Edited by Annelise Orleck and Lisa Gayle Hazirjian (Athens: University of Georgia Press, 2011).

Orleck, Annelise, and Lisa Gayle Hazirjian, eds. *The War on Poverty: A New Grass-roots History, 1964–1980* (Athens: University of Georgia Press, 2011).

Palermo, Joseph. *In His Own Right: The Political Odyssey of Senator Robert F. Kennedy* (New York: Columbia University Press, 2001).

Parker, Heather. "Tom Bradley and the Politics of Race." In *African-American Mayors: Race, Politics, and the American City,* 153–77. Edited by David Colburn and Jeffery Adler (Urbana: University of Illinois Press, 2001).

Patterson, James T. *Freedom Is Not Enough: The Moynihan Report and America's Struggle over Black Family Life, from LBJ to Obama* (New York: BasicBooks, 2010).

Payne, Charles M. *I've Got the Light of Freedom: The Organizing Tradition and the Mississippi Freedom Struggle* (Berkeley: University of California Press, 1995).

Payne, Charles M., et al., eds. *Groundwork: Local Black Freedom Movements in America* (New York: New York University, 2005).

Pecorella, Robert F. *Community Power in a Postreform City: Politics in New York City* (Armonk, NY: M. E. Sharpe, 1994).

Perlstein, Daniel. *Justice, Justice: School Politics and the Eclipse of Liberalism* (New York: Peter Lang, 2004).

Perlstein, Rick. *Nixonland: The Rise of a President and the Fracturing of America* (New York: Scribner, 2008).

Podair, Jerald. *The Strike That Changed New York: Blacks, Whites, and the Ocean Hill–Brownsville Crisis* (New Haven: Yale University Press, 2002).

Pulido, Laura. *Black, Brown, Yellow, and Left: Radical Activism in Los Angeles* (Berkeley: University of California Press, 2006).

Rabig, Julia. "'A Fight and a Question': Community Development Corporations, Machine Politics, and Corporate Philanthropy in the Long Urban Crisis." In *The Business of Black Power: Community Development, Capitalism, and Corporate Responsibility in Postwar America,* 245–72. Edited by Laura Warren Hill and Julia Rabig (Rochester, NY: University of Rochester Press, 2012).

Ransby, Barbara. *Ella Baker and the Black Freedom Movement: A Radical Democratic Vision* (Chapel Hill: University of North Carolina Press, 2003).

Ravitch, Diane. *The Great School Wars: A History of the New York City Public Schools* (Baltimore: Johns Hopkins University Press, 2000).

Reed, Adolph, Jr. *Stirrings in the Jug: Black Politics in the Post-segregation Era* (Minneapolis: University of Minnesota Press, 1999).

Rhea, Joseph Tilden. *Race Pride and American Identity* (Cambridge, MA: Harvard University Press, 1997).

Rhodes, Jane. *Framing the Black Panthers: The Spectacular Rise of a Black Power Icon* (New York: W. W. Norton, 2007).

Rickford, Russell. *We Are an African People: Independent Schools, Black Power, and the Radical Imagination* (New York: Oxford University Press, 2016).

Rieder, Jonathan. *Canarsie: The Jews and Italians of Brooklyn against Liberalism* (Cambridge, MA: Harvard University Press, 1985).

Roderick, Tom. *A School of Our Own: Parents, Power, and Community at the East Harlem Block Schools* (New York: Teachers College Press, 2001).

Roediger, David R. *How Race Survived U.S. History: From Settlement and Slavery to the Obama Phenomenon* (New York: Verso, 2008).

Rogers, Ibram H. *The Black Campus Movement: Black Students and the Racial Reconstitution of Higher Education, 1965–1972* (New York: Palgrave Macmillan, 2012).

Rojas, Fabio. *From Black Power to Black Studies: How a Radical Social Movement Became an Academic Discipline* (Baltimore: Johns Hopkins University Press, 2007).

Sandbrook, Dominic. *Eugene McCarthy: The Rise and Fall of Postwar American Liberalism* (New York: Alfred A. Knopf, 2004).

Schafer, Byron E., and Johnson, Richard. *The End of Southern Exceptionalism: Class, Race, and Partisan Change in the Postwar South* (Cambridge, MA: Harvard University Press, 2006).

Schlesinger, Arthur. *Robert F. Kennedy and His Times* (London: Heinemann, 1978).

Schmitt, Edward R. *President of the Other America: Robert Kennedy and the Politics of Poverty* (Amherst: University of Massachusetts Press, 2010).

Schulman, Bruce. *The Seventies: The Great Shift in American Culture, Society, and Politics* (Cambridge, MA: Da Capo Press, 2001).

Self, Robert O. *All in the Family: The Realignment of American Democracy since the 1960s* (New York: Hill & Wang, 2012).

———. *American Babylon: Race and the Struggle for Post-war Oakland* (Princeton: Princeton University Press, 2003).

Sides, Josh. *LA City Limits: African American Los Angeles from the Great Depression to the Present* (Berkeley: University of California Press, 2004).

Skrentny, John David. *The Minority Rights Revolution* (Cambridge, MA: Harvard University Press, 2002).

Smith, Robert C. *We Have No Leaders: African Americans in the Post–Civil Rights Era* (Albany: State University of New York Press, 1996).

Sonenshein, Raphael. *Politics in Black and White: Race and Power in Los Angeles* (Princeton: Princeton University Press, 1993).

Southern, David W. *Gunnar Myrdal and Black-White Relations: The Use and Abuse of* An American Dilemma, *1944–1969* (Baton Rouge: Louisiana State University Press, 1987).

Stone, Clarence. "Partnership New South Style: Central Atlanta Progress." *Proceedings of the Academy of Political Science,* Vol. 36, No. 2 (1986), 100–110.

Sugrue, Thomas J. "Affirmative Action from Below: Civil Rights, the Building Trades, and the Politics of Racial Equality in the Urban North, 1945–1969." *Journal of American History,* Vol. 91, No. 1 (June 2004), 145–73.

———. *Not Even Past: Barack Obama and the Burden of Race* (Princeton: Princeton University Press, 2010).

———. *The Origins of the Urban Crisis: Race and Inequality in Postwar Detroit* (Princeton: Princeton University Press, 1996).

———. *Sweet Land of Liberty: The Forgotten Struggle for Civil Rights in the North* (New York: Random House, 2008).

Taylor, Clarence. *Knocking at Our Own Door: Milton A. Galamison and the Struggle for School Integration in New York City Schools* (New York: Columbia University Press, 1998).

———. "Robert Wagner, Milton Galamison, and the Challenge to New York Liberalism." *Afro-Americans in New York Life and History: An Interdisciplinary Journal,* Vol. 31, No. 2 (July 2007).

Taylor, Keeanga-Yamahtta. *From #Black Lives Matter to Black Liberation* (New York: Haymarket Books, 2016).

Theoharis, Jeanne. "Black Freedom Studies: Re-imaging and Redefining the Fundamentals." *History Compass,* Vol. 4, No. 2 (March 2006), 348–67.

———. "W-A-L-K-O-U-T!: High School Students and the Development of Black Power in L.A." In *Neighborhood Rebels: Black Power at the Local Level,* 107–32. Edited by Peniel Joseph (New York: Palgrave Macmillan, 2010).

Theoharis, Jeanne, and Komozi Woodard, eds. *Freedom North: Black Freedom Struggles outside the South, 1940–1980* (New York: Palgrave Macmillan, 2003).

Thompson, Heather Ann. "All across the Nation: Urban Black Activism, North and South, 1965–1975." In *African American Urban History since World War II,* 181–202. Edited by Kevin Kusmer and Joe Trotter (Chicago: University of Chicago Press, 2009).

———. "Rethinking the Collapse of Postwar Liberalism: The Rise of Mayor Coleman Young and the Politics of Race in Detroit." In *African-American Mayors: Race, Politics, and the American City,* 223–48. Edited by David Colburn and Jeffery Adler (Urbana: University of Illinois Press, 2001).

Thompson, J. Phillip, III. *Double Trouble: Black Mayors, Black Communities, and the Call for Deep Democracy* (New York: Oxford University Press, 2006).

Tuck, Stephen G. N. *Beyond Atlanta: The Struggle for Racial Equality in Georgia, 1940–1980* (Athens: University of Georgia Press, 2001).

Tyler, Bruce M. "The Rise and Decline of the Watts Summer Festival, 1965–1986." *American Studies,* Vol. 31, No. 2 (Fall 1990), 61–81.

Tyson, Tim. "Robert F. Williams, 'Black Power,' and the Roots of the African American Freedom Struggle." *Journal of American History,* Vol. 85, No. 2 (Sept. 1998), 540–70.

Unger, Irwin. *The Best of Intentions: The Triumphs and Failures of the Great Society under Kennedy, Johnson, and Nixon* (New York: Doubleday, 1996).

Van Deburg, William. *New Day in Babylon: The Black Power Movement and American Culture, 1965–1975* (Chicago: University of Chicago Press, 1992).

Weems, Robert E., Jr. *Desegregating the Dollar: African American Consumerism in the Twentieth Century* (New York: New York University Press, 1998).

———. "The Revolution Will Be Marketed: American Corporations and Black Consumers during the 1960s." *Radical History Review,* Vol. 54 (Spring 1994), 94–107.

Weems, Robert E., Jr., and Lewis Randolph. "The National Response to Richard M. Nixon's Black Capitalism Initiative: The Success of Domestic Détente." *Journal of Black Studies,* Vol. 32, No. 1 (September 2001), 66–83.

Weems, Robert E., Jr., with Lewis Randolph. *Business in Black and White: American Presidents and Black Entrepreneurs in the Twentieth Century* (New York: New York University Press, 2009).

Weise, Andrew. "'The House I Live In': Race, Class, and African American Suburban Dreams in the Postwar United States." In *African American Urban History since World War II*, 160–78. Edited. Kevin Kusmer and Joe Trotter (Chicago: University of Chicago Press, 2009).

Widener, Daniel. *Black Arts West: Culture and Struggle in Postwar Los Angeles* (Durham, NC: Duke University Press, 2009).

Wilder, Craig Steven. *A Covenant with Color: Race and Social Power in Brooklyn* (New York: Columbia University Press, 2000).

Wilentz, Sean. *The Age of Reagan: A History, 1974–2008* (New York: HarperCollins, 2008).

Williams, Rhonda Y. *Concrete Demands: The Search for Black Power in the Twentieth Century* (New York: Routledge, 2015).

———. *The Politics of Public Housing: Black Women's Struggles against Urban Inequality* (New York: Oxford University Press, 2004).

Williams, Yohuru. *Black Politics/Whitepower: Civil Rights, Black Power, and the Black Panthers in New Haven* (St. James, NY: Brandywine Press, 2000).

Wilson, William Julius. *The Declining Significance of Race: Blacks and Changing American Institutions* (Chicago: University of Chicago Press, 1978).

———. *The Truly Disadvantaged: The Inner City, the Underclass, and Public Policy* (Chicago: University of Chicago Press, 1987).

Wohlstetter, Priscilla, and Karen McCurdy. "The Link between School Decentralization and School Politics." *Urban Education*, Vol. 25, No. 4 (January 1991), 391–414.

Wolters, Raymond. *Race and Education, 1954–2007* (Columbia: University of Missouri Press, 2008).

Woodard, Komozi. "Amiri Baraka, the Congress of African People, and Black Power Politics from the 1961 United Nations Protest to the 1972 Gary Convention." In *The Black Power Movement: Rethinking the Civil Rights–Black Power Era*, 55–78. Edited by Peniel Joseph (London: Routledge, 2006).

———. *A Nation within a Nation: Amiri Baraka (LeRoi Jones) and Black Power Politics* (Chapel Hill: University of North Carolina Press, 1999).

Zeitz, Joshua M. *White Ethnic New York: Jews, Catholics, and the Shaping of Postwar Politics* (Chapel Hill: University of North Carolina Press, 2007).

ELECTRONIC RESOURCES

Austin, Algernon. "The Unfinished March: An Overview." Economic Policy Institute, June 18, 2013. http://www.epi.org/files/2013/EPI-The-Unfinished-March-An-Overview.pdf.

County Health Rankings 2016 Annual Report. http://www.countyhealthrankings.org/measure/residential-segregation-blackwhite.

De La Cruz-Viesca, Melanie, Zhenxiang Chen, Paul Ong, Darrick Hamilton, and William Darity. "The Color of Wealth in Los Angeles." March 2016. http://www.aasc.ucla.edu/besol/Color_of_Wealth_Report.pdf

Henry J. Kaiser Family Foundation. "Poverty Rate by Race: 2014." http://kff.org/other/state-indicator/poverty-rate-by-raceethnicity/.

Johnson, Lyndon B. State of the Union Address, 1964. Public Broadcasting Service. http://www.pbs.org/wgbh/americanexperience/features/primary-resources/lbj-union64/.

Lichtenstein, Jules. "Demographic Characteristics of Business Owners," Issue Brief No. 2. Small Business Administration, Office of Advocacy. January 16, 2014. https://www.sba.gov/sites/default/files/Issue%20Brief%202,%20Business%20Owner%20Demographics.pdf.

National Center for Education Statistics. Digest of Education Statistics, Table 302.20. http://nces.ed.gov/programs/digest/d15/tables/dt15_302.20.asp?current=yes.

Pew Research Center Social and Demographic Trends Project. http://www.pewsocialtrends.org/2013/08/22/kings-dream-remains-an-elusive-goal-many-americans-see-racial-disparities/.

Roosevelt, Franklin D. Annual Message to the Congress on the State of the Union, January 11, 1944. Franklin D. Roosevelt Presidential Library and Museum. http://www.fdrlibrary.marist.edu/archives/address_text.html.

"State of New Yorkers." Furman Center for Real Estate and Urban Policy, New York University. August 28, 2013. http://furmancenter.org/files/sotc/SOC2012_State-ofNewYorkers.pdf.

U.S. Census by Race, 1790–1990, Table 1, http://www.census.gov/population/www/documentation/twps0056/tab01.pdf.

U.S. Department of Commerce, Minority Business Development Agency. "Fact Sheet: U.S. Minority-Owned Firms." January 2016. http://www.mbda.gov/sites/default/files/2012SBO_MBEFactSheet020216.pdf.

U.S. Census Bureau. "Los Angeles County a Microcosm of Nation's Diverse Collection of Business Owners, Census Bureau Reports." December 15, 2015. https://www.census.gov/newsroom/press-releases/2015/cb15-209.html.

The American Presidency Project

Election of 1972 (statistics). http://www.presidency.ucsb.edu/showelection.php?year=1972.

McGovern, George: "Address Accepting the Presidential Nomination at the Democratic National Convention in Miami Beach, Florida." July 14, 1972. http://www.presidency.ucsb.edu/ws/?pid=25967.

Civil Rights Digital Library, Digital Library of Georgia, Walter J. Brown Media Collection

WSB-TV newsfilm clip of African Americans reacting to a speech by Mayor Sam Massell, Atlanta, Georgia, October 6, 1971. http://crdl.usg.edu/cgi/crdl?action= retrieve;rset=002;recno=5;format=_video.

WSB-TV newsfilm clip of African Americans reacting negatively to Mayor Sam Massell's speech on politics and government, Atlanta, Georgia, October 6, 1971. http://crdl.usg.edu/cgi/crdl?format=_video&query=id%3Augabma_ wsbn_64296&_cc=1.

Eyes on the Prize II Interviews, Washington University Digital Gateway Texts

Campbell, Les. Interview, November 3, 1988. http://digital.wustl.edu/e/eii/eiiweb /cam5427.0642.028marc_record_interviewee_process.html.

Darnell, Emma. Interview, October 27, 1988. http://digital.wustl.edu/e/eii/eiiweb /dar5427.0325.035marc_record_interviewee_process.html.

Jackson, Maynard. Interview, October 24, 1988. http://digital.wustl.edu/e/eii /eiiweb/jac5427.0710.075maynardjackson.html.

Peoplestown Project Oral Histories

Bodell, Sister Marie. Interview, July 23, 2009. http://thepeoplestownproject.com /2011/mimi-sister-marie-bodell-2/.

Britt, Silvia Griggs. Interview, August 16, 2009. http://thepeoplestownproject.com /2011/silva-griggs-britt/.

Erdmanczyk, Tom. Interview, August 31, 2009. http://thepeoplestownproject.com /2011/emmaus-house-oral-history/.

Ford, Father Austin. Interview March 6, 2009. http://thepeoplestownproject.com /2011/austin-ford/.

Goldstein, Dennis. Interview, July 31, 2009. http://thepeoplestownproject.com /2011/dennis-goldstein/.

Griggs, Margret. Interview, August 31, 2009. http://thepeoplestownproject.com /2011/margaret-griggs/.

Morath, David. Interview August 10, 2009. http://thepeoplestownproject.com /2011/david-morath/.

UNPUBLISHED SECONDARY SOURCES

Cloud, Ralph Martin. "The Management of an Antipoverty Program: A Case of Economic Opportunity Atlanta, Incorporated." Unpublished thesis, University of Georgia, Athens, 1967.

Harrison, Christy Garrison. "They Led and a Community Followed: The Community Activism of Ella Mae Brayboy and Dorothy Bolden in Atlanta, Georgia, 1964–1994." Unpublished thesis, Clark Atlanta University, 2007.

Podair, Jerald. "The Ocean Hill–Brownsville Crisis: New York's *Antigone*." Conference paper presented at the Conference on New York City History. City University of New York, New York, October 6, 2001. Archived at https://www.researchgate .net/publication/237650298_The_Ocean_Hill-Brownsville_Crisis_New_ York%27s_Antigone.

INDEX

black capitalism *(continued)*
  affirmative action; Nixon, Richard;
  Office of Minority Business Enterprise
  (OMBE)
black city politicians: and black capitalism
  and affirmative action policies, 204–
  213; constraints faced by, 169–171
  195–199, 204; and 'rainbow' coalitions,
  194–195. *See also* black political power
black community activism: and public
  education, 116–118, 166; and self-
  determination politics, 7; and the War
  on Poverty, 7, 29–43, 46–50. *See also*
  Black Power; civil rights movement;
  community control; community
  development corporations (CDCs);
  Emmaus House; welfare rights activism
Black Congress, 134–135, 142
Black Enterprise, 100, 232
black freedom struggle. *See* black
  community activism; Black Power
  movement; civil rights movement
Black Lives Matter (BLM), 233–235
black middle class and elite: in Atlanta,
  39–43, 126–128, 162–164, 168–169;
  political views of, 8–9, 228, 230–231;
  support for black elected officials, 205,
  233; success of, 3–4, 8–9. *See also* black
  city politicians; black political power
Black Nationalism, 7, 82–83. *See also* Black
  Power; Black Power movement;
  economic nationalism
black-owned businesses: development of,
  82–83, 103, 216; policy preference for,
  211–214; state of, 80, 214, 226–227. *See
  also* affirmative action; black capitalism;
  Office of Minority Business Enterprise
  (OMBE)
Black Panther Party for Self-Defense
  (BPP): in Atlanta, 159–160, 202; and
  black community activism, 134, 137,
  147, 159–160; historiographical
  representation of, 86; in Los Angeles,
  104, 134, 150, 184, 185; in New York, 86,
  147; political worldview of, 6, 73,
  85–86, 158, 186–187; scholarship on,
  238n10; state-sponsored repression of,
  183–184

black political power: class bias in, 195–196,
  199–200, 203–205, 209–216, 230–231;
  growth and development of, 172–181,
  226–227. *See also* black city politicians
Black Power: as a concept, 1–2, 4–6; and
  grassroots community activism, 3, 5,
  135–141, 146–150, 166; impact on black
  progress, 8–9, 240n18; and mainstream
  white politicians and institutions, 1–7,
  59, 63, 109, 113, 141–146, 186–187, 220–
  224; as radical leftist ideology, 1, 6, 86,
  183–186; scholarship on, 240n20; and
  the War on Poverty, 34, 38–39. *See also*
  Black Nationalism; Black Power
  movement
Black Power movement: in Atlanta, 159–
  160, 202; and education, 139–140;
  surveillance and repression of, 183–184.
  See also black community activism;
  Black Nationalism; Black Panther
  Party for Self-Defense (BPP); Black
  Power; Malcolm X
Black Studies, 103, 139–140, 154, 240n20
Board of Education: in Atlanta 122–123,
  124, 126, 153–154, 162–164; in Los
  Angeles, 121–122, 138, 145; in New
  York, 120–121, 128, 130, 131, 144. See
  also *Brown v. Board of Education*;
  school segregation
Bolden, Dorothy, 204
Boone, Joseph, 164
Boone, Richard, 26, 32, 49
Borders, William Holmes, 153–154
Bradley, Tom, 11, 186*fig*; and affirmative
  action, 209, 210; and black capitalism,
  187, 213; black middle class support for,
  205, 233; on Black Power, 187;
  campaigns for mayor, 183, 184–187,
  194–195; criticism of, 184–186, 204, 215;
  early life of, 181–182; legacies of, 195, 196,
  200, 215, 230; policies and governance
  of, 171–172, 199–200, 204–205, 209,
  210, 215, 273n89; political philosophy of,
  181, 182–183, 186, 194, 221–222;
  scholarship on, 267n4
Brown Berets, 150
Brown v. Board of Education, 115–116, 118,
  120, 123, 124, 126, 151, 231

Brown, Elaine, 186
Brown, H. Rap, 180
Bundy, McGeorge, 72, 131
busing: anti-busing politics, 124, 152, 179,
    181; in Atlanta, 11, 117, 154–158, 161–165,
    167; in Los Angeles, 145, 151–152. *See
    also* school segregation

Calhoun, John, 39–40, 126, 163
Calhoun v. Latimer, 122–123, 126, 155–156,
    162–164, 166
Campbell, Les, 140–141
Carmichael, Stokely, 85–86, 137, 175, 218,
    220, 269n1
Carson, Sonny, 76–78, 96–97
Carter, Jimmy, 197, 214
Carter, Leonard, 38
Central Atlanta Progress (CAtP), 201,
    202–203
Central Brooklyn Coordinating Council
    (CBCC), 31, 58, 75–79, 93
City University of New York (CUNY), 95
Civil Rights Act (1964), 19, 208
civil rights movement: and Black Power, 1,
    175–176, 239n14; and domestic
    anticommunism, 22–24; image of, 56;
    impact and legacies of, 9, 23, 138, 146,
    208; and mainstream politics, 5, 20. *See
    also* black community activism; Black
    Power movement
Clark, Kenneth B., 120
Cleaver, Eldridge, 85
Cloward, Richard, 24–25, 26, 30, 31, 51
Cold War liberalism: and black protest, 5;
    domestic policy making of, 22–24,
    26–28, 63–64. *See also* Great Society;
    New Deal; welfare state liberalism
"color-blind" conservatism, 229–231
Community Action Agency (CAA). *See*
    Community Action Program, the
    (CAP)
Community Action Program (CAP): and
    black community activism, 45, 99,
    135–136; controversy over, 30–34,
    43–46; development of, 24–26;
    legislative attack on, 48–49, 245n75;
    rationale of, 29–30, 45. *See also* War on
    Poverty

Community Alert Patrol (CATPL), 13–14,
    114
Community Antipoverty Committee
    (CAPC), 33
Community Association of the East
    Harlem Triangle (CAEHT), 98–99,
    101, 104, 111, 219
community control: in Atlanta, 153, 165–
    167; and Black Power, 117, 137–139,
    146–150, 179, 219; black teachers'
    support for, 140, 141; activism in Los
    Angeles, 117, 134–135, 136, 138–140,
    142–143, 145, 146, 151; as multiracial
    enterprise, 117, 148–150; activism in
    New York, 117, 132–133, 140–141,
    143–144, 146–149, 150–151, 152; origins
    of, 121, 128–135; theory of, 10–11, 116,
    132–133, 137–141; and the War on
    Poverty, 69–71, 116, 135–137, 219; white
    opposition to, 124, 135, 141–146, 151–
    152. *See also* school segregation
community development block grant
    (CDBG), 200, 201, 203
community development corporations
    (CDCs): and black business and
    economic development, 59, 61, 63–66,
    69–71, 206; and the black middle class,
    59, 71–72; and black radicalism, 2–3, 6,
    59, 71, 72–74; and community control,
    135–136, 152; decline in political
    support for, 110–111; gender and class
    bias within, 72–73; philanthropic
    support for, 59–61, 81, 102, 105, 253n47;
    policy initiative, rationale and
    development of, 2–3, 10, 59–61, 63–66,
    69–74, 81, 87–88; scholarship on,
    62–63; and the War on Poverty, 63–64,
    69–71; work done by, 62–63, 90–95,
    97–113. *See also* black capitalism
Congress of Racial Equality (CORE), 19,
    66, 84, 99, 174
Congressional Black Caucus (CBC),
    178, 180–181, 197, 221, 226–227,
    270n33
conservatism: and affirmative action, 208,
    230; political resurgence of, 8–9, 53–54,
    55–57, 81–82, 190–192, 195, 197–198,
    232; and pro-black business

conservatism *(continued)*
development policies, 7, 83–88, 220, 222; and the War on Poverty, 14–15, 16, 18, 27, 48–49. *See also* "color-blind" conservatism; Nixon, Richard; Reagan, Ronald; "Silent Majority"
Crawford v. Board of Education of Los Angeles, 122, 151
Crowther, Jack, 142

Darnell, Emma, 216
deindustrialization, 65, 119, 196
Democratic Party: and African Americans, 20, 30, 174, 176, 177, 180, 208–209; declining support for, 16, 48, 53, 192. *See also* Cold War liberalism; Great Society; New Deal; welfare state liberalism
Diggs, Charles, 178
Doar, John, 89, 96
Donovan, Bernard, 133

East Harlem Block Schools (EHBS), 130–131
Economic and Youth Opportunities Agency of Greater Los Angeles (EYOA), 33–34, 36–38
Economic nationalism: among African Americans, 82–84, 103–106, 109, 211–217; masculinist vision of, 82–83, 212–213. *See also* black capitalism
economic citizenship, 17–23, 28–29
"Economic Bill of Rights", 21–22, 23
Economic Opportunity Act (EOA), 26, 71, 80
Economic Opportunity Atlanta, Incorporated (EOA Inc.), 39–42, 49
Emmaus House: and Black Power, 158–161, 165; founding of, 156; programs of, 156–157, 158–160, 161–165; and local grassroots activism, 156–157, 165
Equal Employment Opportunity Act (EEOA), 208–209

Fair Employment Practices Commission (FEPC), 21
Family Assistance Plan (FAP), 52, 191–192

Farmer, James, 19, 85–86, 122
FBI (Federal Bureau of Investigation), 62, 184
Ferguson, Gene, 159–160, 161*fig*
Ford, Father Austin, 156, 157–158, 159. *See also* Emmaus House
Ford, Gerald, 110, 197
Ford Foundation: and early antipoverty policymaking initiatives, 24–26; funding activities and strategy of, 12, 102, 133, 150, 234; and Restoration, 72, 75, 76, 78, 91, 92; support for CDCs and black business development, 59–61, 81, 105
Fox Piven, Frances, 51

Galamison, Rev. Milton, 120–121, 131, 141, 148
Gary Agenda. *See* National Black Political Agenda
Gary convention. *See* National Black Political Convention
GI Bill, 28
Gitelson, Judge Alfred, 145, 151–152
grassroots black activism. *See* black community activism. *See also* community control; community development corporations (CDCs); welfare rights activism
Great Recession, 227, 228
Great Society: aims of, 26, 27–29; and 'breadwinner liberalism', 28–29; impact of, 15, 48–49; opposition to, 8–9, 27, 191; and the Vietnam War, 47, 70. *See also* Johnson, Lyndon; War on Poverty
Greater Watts Development Corporation (GWDC), 102–103

Hackett, David, 26, 32
Hall, Robert, 100, 103, 108, 140
Hames, Margie Pitts, 162–163
Harlem Commonwealth Council (HCC), 99, 101, 103–104, 109, 111, 136
Harlem Intermediate School 201 (IS 201), 129–130, 131–133, 137, 148
Harlem Parents Association, 129
HARYOU-ACT, 31, 67–68, 136, 251n26

political hostility to, 44, 48–49, 54–55. *See also* Community Action Program (CAP); War on Poverty

Office of Minority Business Enterprise (OMBE), 61, 80–81, 211, 226. *See also* black capitalism

Ohlin, Lloyd, 24–26, 30

Oliver, Rev. C. Herbert, 133, 147

Operation Bootstrap (OB), 111, 134, 138, 140; founding of, 100; programs of, 100–101, 103, 106–109, 136

Packnett, Brittany, 235

Paley, William, 95

Parents And Taxpayers (PAT), 124, 129

People's Board of Education, 131–132, 148

Peoplestown. *See* Emmaus House

Philadelphia Plan, 206

Poor People's Campaign (PPC), 61–62

Powell, Adam Clayton, 31

pro-growth urban policy, 198–199, 215, 229–230

Proposition 13, 200

Proposition 14, 125–126

Pulley, Ainslin, 234–235

racial inequality, 3–4, 18–19, 47, 196–197, 226–229; in Atlanta, 66, 127, 215–216; and civil rights activism, 22–23; in Los Angeles, 121–122, 200; in New York, 74, 120–121, 129; in public education, 115, 118–120

Reagan, Ronald: as gubernatorial candidate and governor of California, 13–14, 81, 101, 143, 150–151, 152, 191; political program and impact as president, 110, 172, 198, 200, 214, 222, 229

Reddin, Thomas, 13, 55

redlining, 64–66

Republican Party, 110, 191. *See also* conservatism; Nixon, Richard; Reagan, Ronald; "Silent Majority"

Restoration. *See* Bedford-Stuyvesant Restoration Corporation

Richardson, Elsie, 58, 76, 79, 253n56

Robinson, Edward "Abie", 143

Robinson Jr., Isaiah, 99, 129, 136, 144

Rockefeller Foundation, 102, 253n47

Rockefeller, Nelson, 31, 239n17

Roosevelt, Franklin, 21–22, 23. *See also* New Deal

Rose, Lucille, 76, 79, 253n56

school segregation: in Atlanta, 123, 124, 154–155; black support for, 126–128; development of, 118–120; in Los Angeles, 119, 121–122; in New York, 120–121; white support for, 123–126. See also *Brown v. Board of Education*; community control

Screvane, Paul, 30–31

Shanker, Albert, 129, 141, 143–144, 150

Shindana Toys, 103, 108–109

Shriver, Sargent, 44, 47, 51, 55

"Silent Majority": African American equivalent of, 7, 239n17; concept of, 53; political views of, 53–54, 81–82, 207. *See also* conservatism; Nixon, Richard

Small Business Administration (SBA), 80, 81, 253n58

Smith, Lou, 100, 103, 108–109, 138

social science, 24–26, 66

Soul City, 84, 254n72

Southern Christian Leadership Conference (SCLC), 61–62, 164, 212

Southern Conference of Black Mayors (SCBM), 172–173

Southern Manifesto, 124

Special Impact Program (SIP), 71, 99

Spencer, David, 133

student activism, 117, 121, 124–125, 138–140; in Los Angeles, 134–135, 138–139, 142–143, 145–146, 149–150

Student Nonviolent Coordinating Committee (SNCC), 148, 174–175, 180, 246n94, 269n15, 275n1

Swann v. Charlotte-Mecklenburg Board of Education, 155, 161–162

Sweat, Dan, 39–40

Tate, Horace, 154, 155

Tea Party, 232

tenant rights, 66, 69, 93–94, 157–158

Tenants United For Fairness (TUFF), 157

Thomas, Franklin, 78, 88–89, 90